PENGUIN BOOKS

FRIENDS IN HIGH PLACES

'[A] highly readable excursion . . . In it [Jeremy Paxman] considers various branches of "The Establishment" . . . He does so with an engagingly jaundiced eye, fortified by solid research: a quintessential *Newsnight* performance, no less . . . By the end of this book you are left knowing what constitutes the old Establishment a lot better – as well as gleaning some useful insights into what approximates the new' – Charles Kennedy in *Punch*

'Paxman is, in fact, a sharp observer with a vivid pen. Most of his vignettes, particularly of the people he has interviewed, are both lively and perceptive . . . A provocative and timely book' – Anthony Howard in the *Sunday Times*

'He conveys two complementary messages in his new book. The first is that the existence of the Establishment was a fatal inhibition to Britain's advance in the second half of the twentieth century; the second, that the mortal sickness of the Establishment and especially the erosion of its values, will accelerate Britain's decline. The outcome is a gloomy but exceedingly enjoyable book' – Mary Warnock in the *Observer*

'As a snapshot of the changing nature and composition of the élites who "run Britain" behind the façade of electoral politics, *Friends in High Places* is thoroughly convincing . . . Unclouded by partisan concerns, Paxman has – with enviable panache – poured illumination into the labyrinthine "corridors of power"' – Matt Seaton in the *Literary Review*

About the author:

Jeremy Paxman was born in Yorkshire and educated at Cambridge. He is an award-winning journalist who spent ten years reporting from overseas, notably for *Panorama*, and is currently anchorman on *Newsnight*. His last book was *Through the Volcanoes: A Central American Journey* (1975). He lives in London.

FRIENDS IN HIGH PLACES

WHO RUNS BRITAIN?

JEREMY PAXMAN

PENGUIN BOOKS

For my mother and father

PENGUIN BOOKS

Published by the Penguin Group
Penguin Books Ltd, 27 Wrights Lane, London W8 5TZ, England
Viking Penguin, a division of Penguin Books USA Inc.
375 Hudson Street, New York, New York 10014, USA
Penguin Books Australia Ltd, Ringwood, Victoria, Australia
Penguin Books Canada Ltd, 2801 John Street, Markham, Ontario, Canada L3R 1B4
Penguin Books (NZ) Ltd, 182–190 Wairau Road, Auckland 10, New Zealand

Penguin Books Ltd, Registered Offices: Harmondsworth, Middlesex, England

First published in Great Britain by Michael Joseph 1990
Published in Penguin Books 1991
1 3 5 7 9 10 8 6 4 2

The author and publishers would like to thank the following for
permission to reprint extracts from copyright material:

Hodder & Stoughton Ltd for *The Changing Anatomy of Britain* by Anthony Sampson
(p. 17); *The Independent* (p. 18); The Noël Coward Estate for *Operette* by Noël Coward
(pp. 19, 159); Chatto & Windus Ltd for *Ancestral Voices* and *Caves of Ice* by James
Lees-Milne (pp. 19 and 21); Constable Publishers for *The Young Melbourne* by David
Cecil (pp. 21–2); Peters Fraser & Dunlop Group Ltd for 'Epitaph on the Politician
Himself' (p. 73) and 'The Modern Traveller' (p. 221) by Hilaire Belloc from *Complete
Verse*; A. P. Watt Ltd on behalf of The Executors of the Estate of Lady Herbert for
'Sad Fate of a Royal Commission' from *Mild and Bitter* by A. P. Herbert (p. 103);
Warner Chappell Music Ltd for 'Ideology' by Billy Bragg © Chappell Music Limited
(p. 130); the estate of the late Sonia Brownell Orwell and Secker & Warburg for *Boys'
Weeklies* by George Orwell (p. 161); Scolar Press for 'Thoughts on rereading Belloc's
famous lines on dons' by A. N. L. Munby (p. 173); Macmillan Ltd for *All Souls and
Appeasement* by A. L. Rowse (p. 178); Curtis Brown Group Ltd for *The City* by Paul
Ferris © 1960, 65 (p. 274); Faber & Faber Ltd for *The Culture Club*
by Bryan Appleyard (p. 293).

Printed in England by Clays Ltd, St Ives plc

Contents

Contents

Preface

This book started life with a simple question.

During the late seventies and early eighties I had spent a good deal of time reporting from foreign countries, notably in the Third World. I came to realize that the questions I asked myself freshly on arrival at another airport were always much the same. They started off at the level of childhood geography exams, 'What makes this place tick?' 'How does the economy work?' and 'Who runs this country?'

The answers to this last question were usually simple enough. In much of Africa it was one man. In most of the Middle East it was one family or the army (with the exception of Lebanon, where it was several families and several armies). In Guatemala it had been the United Fruit Company and was now the army.

I had never asked the same questions about my own country. It might seem perverse, early in a decade which will see the fiftieth anniversary of the creation of the Welfare State in Britain, to do so. Could anyone doubt that the experience of the previous decade meant that the only serious answer to the question 'Where does power reside in Britain?' was 'Inside 10 Downing Street'? Exaggerated though her influence might be, the hand of Britain's first female prime minister was seen behind everything from the management of industry to the appointment of professors.

The frequently repeated suggestion that Margaret Thatcher's tenure of office in Downing Street marked the beginning of a presidential style of government, along the lines of the American system, masked another conflict, about the limits of popular power. The shift of political power away from the aristocracy began over a century and a half ago. To outward appearances – a few dotty old boys in the House of Lords apart – the British nobility has been stripped of its influence. None of the last four occupants of Downing Street was born to a wealthy family. The education system is open to all.

Yet the clear thrust of many Conservative government policies through the eighties and into the nineties indicated that in their hearts they were scarcely sure that the values of the carriage trade had been eroded. Implicit in the new politics which characterized the Thatcher phenomenon was an acceptance of the thesis advanced by one historian after another that the decline of Britain was the consequence of a social system in which the overwhelming ambition of wealth creators was to become gentlemen. The alchemy by which this was achieved – the public schools, Oxford and Cambridge, the professions – extracted from the British élite any desire to get their hands dirty in trade or industry, and so produced a slow sclerosis of those organs which had created the national prosperity in the first place.

The new-style Conservative government therefore set out to create another élite. Not only did all the rhetoric about 'rewarding wealth creators' create a new monied class, a neoteric caste of patrons was being built, who would be asked to do anything from sorting out the Sir Humphreys in Whitehall to recreating the roles of the Victorian philanthropists. There was a conscious attempt to bring the disciplines of business to the bureaucracy, the universities, even to the arts. In inserting these figures into the upper echelons of British society, Downing Street was endeavouring to come to grips with what has become known as 'the Establishment'.

It is a harlot of a word, convenient, pliant, available for a thousand meaningless applications. One week, I made a note of the number of times I came across it in newspapers, television or conversation but gave up on the fourth day, when the total was standing at forty-two.

But the idea of the Establishment appeals because it appears to capture the sodality that lies behind the Jermyn Street sheen of the British ruling class. If it exists in any meaningful sense, it makes nonsense of the boast that Britain has broken free from the chains of the class system. The Establishment (assuming it exists) has changed form time and again, accommodating itself to both reforming liberal and radical socialist governments and finding a comfortable home among the succession of consensus administrations which ruled Britain for thirty years after the war.

Friends in High Places is about the Establishment in the 1990s. In trying to answer the question Who runs Britain? I am not concerned primarily with the actions of government, although they are important. The book is about the network of institutions and individuals who between them make up the framework through which power and influence are exercised.

No book or journalism is ever entirely free of bias, and truly dispassionate reporting, like a railway timetable, is useful but desiccated stuff. Since all opinions are the product of a multiplicity of influences, not all of them even recognized, you are entitled to know a little about the background from which I approach this subject.

Some of the institutions examined here, I have personal experience of. I was sent away to cold showers and homesickness at prep school at the age of nine or so, in the belief that the earlier one started that sort of education, the better one's chances in later life. Our teachers were the usual collection of eccentrics, drunks and no-hopers. Latin masters whose threadbare jackets rattled with matchboxes filled with pinched-out fag-ends, their cigarette fingers stained the colour of mahogany, and the occasional young teacher whose enthusiasm carried him through it all regardless. One retired colonel who taught French was fired in front of the school over breakfast for failing to pass the marmalade to the headmaster's wife. He was robbed even of a decorous departure when he loaded his one battered suitcase into his bubble car and tried to roar off in a cloud of contempt, only to discover we had jacked it up by putting bricks under the axles. He sat inside his perspex bowl chewing the tips of his clipped moustache, vainly clinging to the remnants of his dignity.

The school was shut down a few years after I left, as were other similarly ramshackle places. The wonder is that they had survived so long so unchallenged. The interruptions to our education from changes of staff or other interludes – on one occasion, the headmaster armed us all with hatchets, machetes, pickaxe handles and air rifles even, I think, a shot-gun, and sent us off in our shorts to hunt down the gangs of youths he believed were about to invade the school – are much more memorable than the grind through uninspiring rote-learning of maths or Latin. Science lessons consisted merely of copying down from the blackboard the results of experiments we ought to have conducted with Bunsen burners and test tubes because the class had none. None the less, I was able to progress to public school at Malvern, a decent second-division school which had improved hugely from the hearty, bloodthirsty bear-pit described by C. S. Lewis.

The great lesson of public-school life I learned early when, at age thirteen, I refused to get into bed after being ordered to do so by a short, fair-haired and very stupid prefect. It led to the first of several experiences of the elaborate ritual attached to beatings. The most recently-appointed prefect would be sent to the dormitory after lights-out, arriving with the words 'put on your dressing gown and come with me.' Down below in their common room, the prefects would be seated in a circle, boot-faced young men with the casual confidence of an ascendancy subaltern.

'Why didn't you obey orders to get into bed?' asked the Head of House, a rugby-playing thug who later became a country solicitor.

'Because' I replied, 'I don't respect him.'

'The *purpose* of a public-school education, Paxman, is to teach you to respect people you don't respect,' he continued, reaching for the ceremonial shoe with which beatings were administered. 'Take off your dressing gown and bend over.'

I never forgot this explanation of the purpose of an expensive education.

I imagine that my generation were probably the last to experience such a rigorously Victorian view of the function of the public school. The system of fagging, which obliged younger boys to spend two years cleaning the studies, spit-and-polishing the shoes and warming the outside lavatory seats for prefects, was abolished at Malvern shortly before I left in the late sixties. I hated the place, stood as a communist in the school elections, wrote dutiful weekly letters home and was saved from expulsion twice only by the intercession of a kind and thoughtful housemaster.

At Cambridge, it was the age of protest, against the Vietnam War, Apartheid, or the regulations which required the college gates to be locked at midnight. Life was a succession of demonstrations and sit-ins of one kind or another, most of them led by the same all-purpose cast of bell-bottom ideologues with a slogan for every problem. There was an orthodoxy to the dissent every bit as unappealing as the conformity against which protest was directed.

The highlight of the protest business came in my second term, in February 1970. The Greek Tourist Board took the curious decision to choose Cambridge as the place in which to promote their country as a holiday destination. At the time Greece was ruled by a military junta which preferred toenail pliers to ballot boxes. Protests began with the burning of travel brochures on the pavement, and ended in a full-scale riot at the Garden House Hotel, where local worthies were being entertained at a dinner to celebrate the end of Greek Week. By the standards of Paris or Berkeley it was a pretty tame affair, with a few broken windows, two injured proctors, but a lot of genuinely frightened guests. Six students were subsequently packed off to gaol for up to eighteen months by Mr Justice Melford Stevenson, with the warning that the sentences would have been heavier if he had not believed that they had been subject to the 'evil influence' of various lecturers.

This struck me then, as it strikes me now, as yet another example of the remoteness of many British judges. There were, it was true, a few radical dons (they could be counted on the fingers of one hand), but they were comfortably outnumbered by the hundreds of others whose understanding of politics extended no further than the latest factional squabbling in faculty boards. Like many of my generation, university life passed in a bizarre combination of protest marches and drinks parties, a thoroughly privileged and enjoyable time, for which, like most who underwent it, I was insufficiently grateful.

Several of my contemporaries have subsequently translated their student political careers into lives as MPs of various parties. For me, exposure to the beliefs I heard them expound with such certainty at such a youthful age merely confirmed a profound scepticism of all political organizations, right or left. Having read H. L. Mencken's opinion that the correct relationship of a journalist to a politician was that of a dog to a lamppost, there was really only one career open to me, and it is a trade I have pursued since the mid-seventies, in one form or another. It was something of a shock to discover that many of the eminent people I interviewed in research for this book believed that, because of the power of the mass media, one had become part of 'the Establishment' oneself. I hope not.

London
June 1990

Acknowledgements

In the course of research for *Friends in High Places* I interviewed over 150 prominent figures in British society. Many are named in the text or footnotes. Others would only see me with the promise of confidentiality, and I am happy to respect their wishes. I am grateful to all for their time, patience and wisdom. I owe particular thanks to the following:

Maj.-Gen. Sir Christopher Airy, Dr Eric Anderson, Col. John Anderson, Lord Annan, Lord Armstrong of Ilminster, Tom Arnold MP, Gen. Sir Hugh Beach, the Very Reverend Canon Trevor Beeson, Marshal of the RAF Sir Michael Beetham, Tim Bell, Lord Benson, Sir Kenneth Berrill, Baroness Blackstone, Lord Bonham-Carter, Lord Bradford, Melvyn Bragg, Lord Bramall, Tim Brighouse, Harold Brooks-Baker, Lord Bullock, Dr David Butler, Lord Callaghan, Lord Camoys, Sir Peter Carey, Lord Carrington, Lord Carver, Lord Charteris of Amisfield, William Clarke, Sir Frank Cooper, Gen. Simon Cooper, Dr Byron Criddle, Prof. Sir Ralf Dahrendorf, Lord Dainton, Dr Grace Davie, Dr Graeme Davies, Ian Hay Davison, Michael De-la-Noy, the Duke of Devonshire, Gen. Roy Dixon, Sir James Eberle, Richard Eyre, Lord Fanshawe, Lord Ferrers, Christopher Fildes, Prof. Sammy Finer, Mark Fisher MP, Lord Flowers, Sir Angus Fraser, Lord Fraser of Kilmorack, Lord Garmoyle, Andrew Gifford, Sir Ian Gilmour MP, Gen. Sir James Glover, Sir Nicholas Goodison, Lord Goodman, Peter Grant, Sir Peter Hall, J. Dundas Hamilton, Brian Hanson, Alison Harding, David Hare, Lord Harewood, Robin Harper, Robert Harris, Max Hastings, P. D. G. Hayter, Denis Healey MP, Geoffrey Helliwell, Peter Hennessy, Sir Reg Hibbert, Prof. A. M. Honoré, Sir John Hoskyns, Anthony Howard, Robin Hutton, Jeremy Isaacs, Michael Ivens, Robert Jackson MP, Lord Jay, Peter Jay, Caroline Kay, Sir Anthony Kershaw, Lord King, Prof. Anthony King, Bill Kirkman, Sir Hector Laing, Gavin Laird, Angela Lambert, Robin Leigh-Pemberton, Lord Lewin, Donald Lindsay, John Lloyd, Clifford Longley, Lord March, Prof. David Marquand, Peter Maugham, Robert McCrum, John Miles, Sir Derek Mitchell, Bob and Jill Montgomerie, Hugh Montgomery-Massingberd, D. G. Morrell, Col. Trevor Morris, Sir Jeremy Morse, Sir Claus Moser, Sir Patrick Nairne, Julia Neuberger, Sir John Nott, Sir Richard O'Brien, Stephen O'Brien, Cranley Onslow MP, David Owen MP, Sir Peter Parker, Sir Geoffrey Pattie MP, Derek Pattinson, Enoch Powell, Lord Pym, Dr John Rae, Lord Rayne, John Redwood MP, Lord Rees-Mogg, the late Bishop of Rochester, Kenneth Rose, Jacob Rothschild, A. L. Rowse, Anthony Sampson, Commander Michael Saunders Watson, Sir David Scholey, Nick Serota, Sir Roy Shaw, Lord Shawcross, Michael Shea, Lord

Shelburne, Allen Sheppard, Lord Sherfield, Sir Maurice Shock, Nick Sigler, Christopher Sinclair-Stevenson, Tom Snow, Sir Nicholas Somerville, Prof. Sir Richard Southwood, the Bishop of Stepney, the Reverend Henry Thorold, Tony Travers, Sir Ian Trethowan, Dennis Trevelyan, the Reverend Canon Timothy Tyndall, Ed Victor, John Ward, Brian Wenham, the Duke of Westminster, Sam Whitbread, David Whitehead, Andreas Whittam Smith, Charles Wilson, Chris Wrigley, Stanislas Yassukovich, the Archbishop of York.

A handful of self-important figures declined to talk to me. But overall, whatever the British tendency to unnecessary secrecy, the willingness of busy people to spare time for a journalist was encouraging.

I was helped with much of the basic research by Richard Good, an enthusiastic and enterprising fellow digger. The staffs of the London Library, the British Library and the Pembridge Square Library rooted out obscure references. My editor, Susan Watt, remained enthusiastic when I felt overwhelmed by the scale of the undertaking: her guidance was invaluable. Alexander Stilwell proved an inspired text editor.

Introduction

The halls of life are always full,
The doors are always ajar,
And some get in by the door marked push
And some by the door marked pull.

‒ ANON.

EARLY IN 1988 Alan Bennett presented the National Theatre with the manuscripts of two plays about the greatest scandal to undermine the postwar British ruling class. One of them concerned the life in exile of Guy Burgess, the homosexual Old Etonian who had betrayed his country's secrets to the Russians. The other, *A Question of Attribution*, dealt with Anthony Blunt. Bennett thought the affair – which, more than any other, revealed the decay that had rotted the heart of a section of the governing class – had comical overtones. The drunken, lecherous Burgess he found amusing, while the effete, languorous Blunt 'seems to be condemned as much out of pique and because he fooled the Establishment as for anything he did.'[1] This is the voice of the 1960s speaking, contempt and fascination mingled. Few words are more redolent of that era, when talented young people like Bennett exuberantly cast aside the dull grey conformity of the fifties, than his summoning up of the idea of 'the Establishment'. The word had passed into common currency in the dying years of that dreary decade, and conjures up instantly the small, clubby world of the governing types of the time. For Alan Bennett, a bright grammar-school boy from Leeds, and his contemporaries it encapsulated everything that was wrong with Britain.

Bennett's second play included as its centrepiece a remarkably funny portrayal of a meeting between Anthony Blunt and the Queen. Blunt, the master of legerdemain, had returned from a wartime spent betraying his country to become Surveyor of the Queen's Pictures, and had even been made a Knight Commander of the Royal Victorian Order, an honour in the personal gift of the monarch. The intriguing question of what the Court did or did not know about his wartime treason has never been satisfactorily answered. Bennett dealt with the matter by way of allegory. *A Question of Attribution* was concerned with whether or not a Titian portrait was genuine. As Blunt held forth, the Queen responded with the same blank look of interested lack of interest she is obliged to display on a thousand royal visits to open municipal swimming pools. It was a not unaffectionate portrait, but she did come across as a bit dowdy and slow.

A Question of Attribution was scheduled to have its first performance at the National Theatre late in 1988. Richard Eyre, the National's artistic director, thought it was one of the wittiest plays he had read for years and had put it into rehearsal without extensive consultation with the theatre's Board. Six weeks before the play was due to open, Eyre received a telephone call from the life peer and property tycoon, Lord (Max) Rayne, the theatre's chairman, summoning him to his office. Rayne, a modest and diplomatic man who had begun life as the son of a poor East End tailor, had presided over the Theatre for nearly seventeen years. He was popular with the artistic staff because he tended to support them when they came under periodic attack for the occasional radical production. But this was something else.

Eyre was dumbfounded by what he heard. 'I must ask you to take this play off,' said Rayne. 'I've heard about what's in it, and you must realize it will bring the National Theatre into discredit. I appeal to your sense of decency.' Only a few months previously Lord Rayne had submitted an application to Buckingham Palace for the company to be renamed the *Royal* National Theatre, believing it would, among other things, make it easier to raise money. Senior staff had been hostile to the idea (one had described it to the *Guardian* as 'an attempt to draw the National into the Establishment's embrace'), fearing that it would lead to a form of creeping paralysis. They were to be proved right surprisingly quickly.

Eyre, a director with a long history of challenging drama, was stunned by Lord Rayne's request: the National Theatre, after all, existed as a showcase for the best of British drama, and in his judgement the manuscript was 'simply superb'. He refused to concede, but privately spoke of resignation. Several days later he was summoned to a meeting in the tatty administrative offices at the back of the National's concrete auditorium on the South Bank.

It was, in the words of one of those present, 'the most venomous occasion I have ever experienced'. Apart from Eyre and Rayne, those present included the National's business manager, David Aukin, and two other members of the board, Sir Derek Mitchell, a former senior civil servant, and the Labour peer, Lord (Victor) Mishcon. This time, the assault came not from Lord Rayne, but from Mishcon. Although he too had risen from a modest background – his father was an East End rabbi – Mishcon was a powerful figure, an expensive solicitor on first-name terms with half the House of Lords.

Mishcon said there were serious difficulties about representing living people in the theatre. There were particularly serious problems about representing the monarch on stage.[2] And there were acute difficulties about portraying a living monarch on the boards of the *Royal* National Theatre. Eyre, unimpressed and still convinced of the play's worth, stood his ground: the play was a fine piece of drama, and the National existed as a showcase for the best contemporary writing.

Finally Mishcon leaned across and asked him, 'Do you agree that there is such a thing as the Establishment in this country?'

Eyre thought he did; it was almost an accepted item of faith among his generation, who had been through university in the early sixties.

'And do you agree', asked Mishcon, increasingly exasperated, 'that there is such a thing as respect for the Establishment and respect for the monarchy, and that those things are synonymous?'

'As it happens,' Eyre replied quietly, 'I don't agree.'

Mishcon spluttered, then explained again the unique responsibilities of the National Theatre. Eyre knew he had to remain impassive. Surrender meant resignation. An irresistible force met an immovable object.

Finally, the retired Whitehall mandarin Sir Derek Mitchell weighed in. He had had a great deal of experience of the Establishment, he said. It had weathered many a storm before. It would not be buffeted by a single play in the theatre. Then he introduced the argument which won the day. On the balance of disadvantage, to cancel the play at this stage would generate more bad publicity than allowing it to go ahead and risking any controversy. 'And suddenly,' one of the participants recalls, 'it was as if the sun had come out. Everybody was smiling, and Mishcon trotted off to the Opera.'

What was this sensitive thing, the Establishment, that Lord Mishcon was so keen to protect from insult?

It is one of those ideas, an abstraction, which like imagination's vision of God, has potency because of its vagueness. The vision keeps regenerating itself by adjusting to new orthodoxies and extending its embrace to those who might threaten it. Lords Mishcon and Rayne, after all, were never born Establishment stock. And, while it was constantly changing at the periphery, the Establishment remained fixed at the centre, easier to define by saying who was definitely not part of it than by a roll-call of those who might be members. Virtually no-one admits to membership of the thing.

It is not enough to talk of an ascendancy. Of course an ascendancy is ascendant. And the Establishment is more than another way of talking about the perennial British preoccupation with class. Throughout the fifties, sixties and seventies, parts of it used to break cover periodically, as one government or another thrashed around in the throes of scandal, embarrassment or muddle; from deep below Whitehall a column of worthies would emerge blinking into the daylight, to make up one royal commission or committee of inquiry after another. These sound and comfortable men – one writer calls them 'the auxiliary fire service of the ruling class'[3] – would take evidence on the matter in question, ruminate, and ages later produce a report, by which time the fire had been well and truly smothered. But the register of the Great and Good, from which these reliable chaps were drawn, included only a small part of the Establishment.

The Establishment had its battalions secured behind the battlements of dozens of institutions, few of them obviously part of the business of politics. They could be found throughout the professions, that humanistic priesthood Coleridge once termed the 'clerisy' of the nation – the professors, physicians, judges, scientists, generals, even artists, 'all the so-called liberal arts and sciences, the possession and application of which constitute the civilization of a country.'[4] The fact that they were self-governing, proud and independent gave these professions a certain grandeur, which invested the independent institutions too. The Foreign Office, the very grandest of the departments of state, had this self-assurance in abundance: governments might come and go, but British interests went on forever. The armed forces, sworn to serve Queen and country, had a similar loyalty to something deeper than mere government. The BBC, nourished by tales (often, in fact, myths) of impartiality, similarly believed itself to be serving some higher purpose than the mere dictates of political parties. In the City, loyalty to a code of honour summed up in 'my word is my bond', elevated the humdrum business of making money into something altogether more respectable.

These deeper loyalties seem to me to be one of the reasons for

Britain's fabled stability. But the danger is that they allow things to go rotten from within. At Lloyd's of London, the most distinguished of the gentlemen's clubs upon which rested the reputation of the City of London, one syndicate after another abused the privileges of self-regulation in the seventies and early eighties. For a time, parts of M.I.5 had allegedly succumbed to a similar arrogance, believing that some higher authority entitled them, in Peter Wright's words, to 'bug and burgle their way across London'. And although the armed forces have resisted similar temptations, some of the same impulse lay behind the mad-cap schemes of the early seventies dreamed up by retired officers like Colonel David Stirling and General Sir Walter Walker with their plans to save the nation from itself.[5]

When, at 4.30 on the afternoon of Wednesday 8 May 1968, Lord Mountbatten opened the door of his Knightsbridge flat to admit Cecil King, boss of the *Mirror* group of newspapers, he might have allowed a part of the monarchy to become involved in similar folly. King, gauche, wealthy and obsessed by the thought that civilization in Britain was on the verge of collapse, with civil war even a distinct possibility, wanted Mountbatten – 'Uncle Dickie' to the rest of the royal family – to consider leading an emergency government to save the nation. While there was, by all accounts, no actual talk of a *coup d'état* it came perilously close, as Lord (then Sir Solly) Zuckerman, Mountbatten's other guest, recognized at once. Zuckerman, recently invited to join the Order of Merit for his academic brilliance and his service in the ranks of the Great and Good, listened to King's proposals, then got to his feet, declaring 'this is rank treachery'. Opening the door to leave he added, 'All this talk of machine guns at street corners is appalling. I am a public servant and will have nothing to do with it. Nor should you, Dickie.'[6] Mountbatten took the advice, jotting in his diary that night the two words 'Dangerous Nonsense!', although Zuckerman wondered afterwards to Hugh Cudlipp, the fourth person at the meeting, 'what Dickie would have said if I hadn't been there.'

All of these incidents together add up to no more than a few straws in the wind, and the fact that nothing ever came of them rather points up the strength of the political system. Lord Zuckerman's robust rejection of any idea of interference with democratically elected government might serve as a model for all public servants. Yet the notion persists in the minds of conspiracist sandal-wearers and spikey-haired anarchists that beneath the surface British public life is a fraud, operating like the Freemasons or some secretive religious cult. Nor is this suspicion the exclusive preserve of the left.

'I fear, young man, that you are hunting the snark,' said Enoch Powell, the perennial heretic of British politics. In his narrow house in Chelsea, beneath shelves groaning with Plato, Herodotus and the Victorian poets, he spent an hour and a half trying to define the idea of the Establishment.

'Bagehot wrote that the British like to defer to those in power. Command and obedience, Establishment and deference, they're two sides of the same coin. The Establishment is unacknowledged power.' The watery grey eyes were fixed on some point in the middle distance. 'It is', he paused for a moment, '*the power that need not speak its name*.' As a description of the phenomenon it will serve as well as any.

In its loosest sense, almost every country in the world, every area of human endeavour, has its establishment. They are the people who get things done. In a nation it is used as shorthand for those who have power. In a banana republic it may comprise a few dozen families. In the Soviet Union it runs into thousands. In each case, the local establishment tends to have a common background and shared beliefs.

The distinctive thing about authority in British society is the class system. In the eighteenth century it was possible to talk of a genuine governing class in Britain: it supplied the bishops, the parliamentarians, the army officers and the courtiers. But by the time that 'the Establishment' (in its purest, original, sense, the expression actually meant the unique position of the Anglican Church in Britain) received its current coinage, in the 1950s, the phenomenon was long gone. For the idea to have any meaning its members must have certain things in common, notably, a shared view of how they want society to be. Furthermore, they must be able to recognize one another, and, critically, be powerful enough to be able to put their beliefs into effect. A person may be upper class and have no influence, he may not be upper class and yet wield considerable power. The heart of the 1950s Establishment tended to be made up of those who had both breeding and, if not power, then certainly influence.

Yet the last prime minister who could be said to have belonged to this circle, the fourteenth Earl of Home, held office for only one year nearly three decades ago. None of the prime ministers since – Wilson, Heath, Callaghan or Thatcher – has been anything other than middle or lower-middle class. The fact that she was a woman, a non-conformist and a scientist to boot meant that Margaret Thatcher arrived at power much less influenced by the forces which had knocked the corners off her predecessors. She was never a member of anything which could be called the Establishment before she gained power, and managed to remain outside it even after more than a decade in Downing Street.

Outside politics, the changes in the last thirty years have been just as profound. The royal family, which, as Lord Mishcon observed, was at the heart of the Establishment, was more and more exposed to public gaze, and although public relations consultants have worked hard to give them a common touch, the gawking eyes of a thousand cameras rather accentuate how unlike the rest of Britain they are. The honours system, through which the benefits of 'good blood' were supposed to be passed down through society to humbler folk, no longer has much to do with honour, and a great deal to do with commercial flair and the right political allegiances.

The City of London, once run by the commercial wing of the Establishment, has burst its cork like shaken champagne, and is physically scattered, deregulated and professionally confused. As individuals, even teams, move between different companies, chasing the latest fat salary cheque, loyalty has become the most unfashionable of virtues.

The universities, which were once the preserve of the small number of young people produced by the fee-paying schools, have been opened to all, regardless of the depth of parental pocket. The number of universities has doubled since the end of the Second World War, reducing the exclusivity of Oxford and Cambridge, while the gurus of the eighties were men like Friedrich von Hayek (Vienna and the University of Chicago), rather than John Maynard Keynes (Eton, Cambridge and Bloomsbury).

The higher professions, from the law to medicine, have undergone the most radical changes visited upon them for a generation, while the poor old Church of England, guardian of the values of the Establishment, is just ignored.

Yet still the idea persists. References to it occur in the newspapers, on television and in conversation every week, often prefaced by an expletive, as in 'of course, he ran foul of the bloody Establishment', an excuse for failure of one kind or another because of the supposedly dead hand of a coterie who somehow manage to continue to control our national life. The most uninformed definitions seem to think it has something to do with inclusion in *Who's Who*. This casts the net very wide indeed, since the fat red book automatically mentions all under secretaries and above in the civil service, all judges and QCs, all MPs, generals, bishops, archdeacons and deans, the chairmen and chief executives of the 250 biggest British companies, all foreign ambassadors and High Commissioners ever posted to London, even the chief police, fire and education officers of the larger counties. Of course, the more interesting names are those chosen by the anonymous committee of consultants on grounds of genuine merit. But, with 28,000 names, it is far too large to represent any sort of coherent group, and since no-one gets dropped once they've been included, a sizeable proportion have anyway been harmlessly pottering about in the gardens of their retirement homes in Wiltshire for years. During interviews for this book I heard dozens of different definitions. As a rough generalization, those who had been born outside what one might consider the Establishment and made their way into it believed that such a thing existed. Those who had been born within the Establishment and rejected it had the same view. It was only those who had been born, brought up in, and still exercised power or influence within it who denied its existence outright.

Looking for the Establishment is like taking apart one of those Russian dolls with layer after layer inside. By the time you reach its heart, you have already missed the pattern of beliefs and ideas which hold it together and give it form. There is little unchangeable about these patterns: the Establishment has an infinite capacity to absorb people and ideas, is endlessly adaptable. Although the monarchy is central to the whole idea, even the court can somehow consider itself apart from it. Lord (Martin) Charteris, at the time assistant private secretary to the Queen, recalls that when the term passed into common usage in the fifties, they would sit around in the Palace and, as conversation passed to one individual or another, say, 'Oh, gosh, he's definitely a member of the Establishment.' What they meant was that they thought the individual belonged to some inner circle, a social and political freemasonry, whence networks of contacts radiated out like the tentacles of an octopus. It would be hard to think of anyone closer to the heart of this network than a figure like Lord Charteris of Amisfield, whose alphabet soup list of decorations – GCB, CB, GCVO, QSO, OBE, PC – reflect a lifetime of proximity to the throne, who progressed from the royal household to the boards of British multinationals like Rio Tinto Zinc, who held grand public posts like the trusteeships of the British Museum and the National

Heritage Memorial Fund, and who finally became provost of Eton, presiding over the most influential network of alumni in the land.

It is characteristic of many of those closest to the centre of this presumed network of power that they doubt its potency. But even those who deny that the Establishment exists any longer have to concede that it is a potent fiction which has a reality for that enormous group who believe in it. It has proved one of the most enduring political ideas of the postwar period.

Like many a good journalistic idea, the term had been plagiarized. 'The Establishment' is generally thought of as the creation of Henry Fairlie in the *Spectator* in September 1955. But two years earlier, the historian A.J.P. Taylor had used the term in an article on the early nineteenth-century radical William Cobbett for the *New Statesman*.[7] Cobbett had talked about 'the Thing'. Taylor refashioned the idea for the 1950s; he had seen the British ruling class at work, and felt simultaneously fascinated and repelled:

> Trotsky tells how, when he first visited England, Lenin took him round London, and, pointing out the sights, exclaimed: 'That's *their* Westminster Abbey! That's *their* Houses of Parliament!' Lenin was making a class, not a national emphasis. By *them* he meant not the English, but the governing classes, the Establishment. And indeed in no other European country is the Establishment so clearly defined and so completely secure. The Victorians spoke of the classes and the masses; and we still understand exactly what they meant. The Establishment talks with its own branded accents; eats different meals at different times; has its privileged system of education; its own religion, even, to a large extent, its own form of football. Nowhere else in Europe can you discover a man's social position by exchanging a few words or breaking bread with him. The Establishment is enlightened, tolerant, even well-meaning. It has never been exclusive, rather drawing in recruits from outside, as soon as they are ready to conform to its standards and become respectable. There is nothing more agreeable in life than to make peace with the Establishment – and nothing more corrupting.[8]

This was painting the canvas with a pretty broad brush, equating the Establishment with almost the entire upper and upper-middle class. Taylor was in no doubt about its pernicious influence; 'the Thing' was a paralysing virus:

> If we did not have to carry the incubus of the gentry, the clubs and bishops, *The Times* – Cobbett's 'bloody old *Times*' – and the public

schools, we should be nearly as prosperous as Cobbett wanted us to be. Unfortunately, if you knock one Thing down, another bobs up.[9]

It was the defection of Burgess and Maclean which provided the occasion for a more precise definition of what the Establishment was. The discovery that Guy Francis de Moncy Burgess and Donald Duart Maclean, one the son of a former cabinet minister, the other an Old Etonian, had been supplying the Russians with entire briefcases full of secret documents had the sort of undermining effect on the British ruling class that an unanticipated outbreak of hereditary insanity might have in the sole heir of an ancient dynasty. The full extent of the protection the two had enjoyed while committing their treachery is staggering even at four decades' distance. Even after they had fled the country, Maclean's wife Melinda was allowed to follow him unhindered because although both the secret service and the newspapers believed she might lead them to the two, they apparently considered pursuit would have been harassment.

In his column in the *Spectator* in September 1955, soon after Burgess and Maclean surfaced publicly in Moscow, the magazine's young political correspondent, Henry Fairlie, wondered how it was that two men who had inflicted such damage could have enjoyed such protection:

> No-one whose job it was to be interested in the Burgess–Maclean affair from the very beginning will forget the subtle but powerful pressures which were brought to bear by those who belonged to the same stratum as the two missing men. From those who were expecting Maclean to dinner on the very night on which he disappeared, to those who just happened to have been charmed by his very remarkable father, the representatives of the 'Establishment' moved in.

The affair was just one example of the unique way in which influence was wielded in Britain:

> I have several times suggested that what I call the 'Establishment' in this country is today more powerful than ever before. By the 'Establishment' I do not mean only the centres of official power – though they are certainly part of it – but rather the whole matrix of official and social relations within which power is exercised. The exercise of power in Britain (more specifically in England) cannot be understood unless it is recognized that it is exercised socially. Anyone who has at any point been close to the exercise of power will know what I mean when I say that the 'Establishment' can be seen at work in the activities of, not only the Prime Minister, the Archbishop of Canterbury and the Earl Marshal, but of such lesser mortals as the chairman of the Arts Council, the Director-General of the

BBC, and even the editor of *The Times Literary Supplement*, not to mention divinities like Lady Violet Bonham Carter.[10]

The implication is that most of these figures are members of the Establishment *ex-officio*, but a word of explanation is necessary about Lady Violet. Certainly it would be hard to name anyone in contemporary Britain who even approximates to her status. Her father, Herbert Henry Asquith, had become prime minister in April 1908, when she was twenty-one, and remained in Downing Street for almost nine years, a record exceeded this century only by Margaret Thatcher. Her son, Lord (Mark) Bonham-Carter, who himself entered the world of the Great and Good by becoming the first chairman of the Race Relations Board, vice chairman of the BBC and a director of the Royal Opera House, believes that while the Establishment was, as Fairlie indicated, male-dominated, much of her influence had been acquired precisely because of her sex:

> If you are a reasonably attractive woman, and are born into a position where your father has power, you become familiar with power and power-brokers for a much longer time than any man. It's partly because men like talking to young women. My mother therefore knew almost everyone who held office from 1908 until she died sixty years later. No man would get into that position until he was forty or more.[11]

Underlying the whole of Fairlie's attack were the frustrations born of the fact that the country had endured a World War in which almost every citizen had been a combatant. The war had acted as a solvent, dissolving the glue which had held much of the pre-war edifice of power in place. It had been followed by a socialist government, determined to create a new order. 'We are the masters at the moment, and not only at the moment, but for a very long time to come,' the Labour Attorney General, Sir Hartley Shawcross had boasted.[12] But somehow, like ice above a roaring river, the old élite had refrozen itself. The Labour party had failed to create a counter-Establishment, indeed had seemed only too willing to collaborate with the old order. The new Lord Chief Justice, Rayner Goddard, was a well-known right-winger, and to succeed William Temple as Archbishop of Canterbury Attlee had chosen Geoffrey Fisher, a public school headmaster. The Conservative party, meanwhile, although less frivolous than before the war, was none the less still stuffy, clubby and the back-benches dominated by the knights from the shires. To some extent, then, the electoral process seemed almost an irrelevance, because beneath the surface the same people ran the country. A decade after the end of the war the old masters were back in charge, the same comfortable network of the right people who had been to the right schools, with the right accents, the right beliefs, and a conviction in their divine right to rule. The Establishment was almost the last *ancien régime* to survive in Europe.

Fairlie's article had poked a stick into a wasps' nest, and for weeks afterwards the correspondence columns of the *Spectator* were filled with stinging attacks from outraged members of the social network he had described. Lady Violet (she had sat on the selection board which chose Maclean for the Foreign Office), claimed she had been traduced: her sole objective had been to try to protect the Maclean family from harassment by journalists. The editor of the *Observer*, the Hon. David Astor, accused Fairlie of a smear: 'his suggestion amounts to saying that the higher echelons of our public life are a racket'. Sir Robert Boothby, who described himself as having bumped into the Establishment periodically for thirty years 'and seldom emerged unscathed' (slightly less than frank – he had been bumping into Macmillan's wife, Dorothy, for years and always getting away with it), listed its members:

> It was never confined, as is commonly supposed, to what used to be known as the 'Upper Ten'. Nor did it embrace all the Cabinet ministers of the day. It always included the reigning Archbishop of Canterbury, Editor of *The Times*, Governor of the Bank of England and Secretary to the Cabinet.

The most telling counter-argument came from the senior common room at Christ Church, Oxford, where Hugh Trevor-Roper, recently married to Field Marshal Haig's eldest daughter, remarked that

> it is hardly novel to observe that there is here and now, as everywhere and at all times, a governing class. Since this is a necessary condition of social existence, the best we can hope for is that this 'establishment' should not be (as in some countries) so held together by conscious or institutional solidarity that it escapes competition and criticism. Fortunately . . . the British 'establishment' is loose, heterogeneous and fissile.

Much of the debate concentrated too closely on what Enoch Powell described in our conversation thirty years later as 'the copper wire rather than the electricity'. Fairlie, who claimed that the existence of an Establishment was 'desirable' because it kept out unspecified worse influences, conceded that membership was not closed. But the central feature of the Establishment, ignored by many then and now, is not who's in or out. Its essence was not individuals, it was shared opinion, a way of viewing the world, a consensus, agreement on the right way of doing things. Fairlie observed:

> the members of the Establishment do nothing which it is not their right or duty to do. But when they combine, when the whole process is set moving, as it was throughout the Munich period,* as it was on the issue of commercial television,† as I believe it was in the Burgess–Maclean affair, its power is formidable, and as a student of politics I think its existence is the most important fact about the exercise of power in this country.

On Thursday 5 October 1961, a new nightclub opened in Soho, lair of London's lowlife. Named the Establishment to put up two fingers to the people Fairlie had identified as wielding social power in Britain, it opened as a club to evade what Jonathan Miller called 'the bloodshot gaze'[13] of the Lord Chamberlain, who had powers to censor performances in theatres. 'The Establishment represents a research station in which we might see developed the weapons necessary for the final overthrow of the Neo-Gothic stronghold of Victorian good taste,' he grandly announced.[14]

The audience turned up expecting to be shocked, and they were not disappointed. The shadow of the Lord Chamberlain was openly mocked, the performers swore profusely and their material was more explicitly political than anything yet seen on the London stage. The young satirists appeared on a tiny platform in a long, smoky room. Their victims on the first night included the Prime Minister, Harold Macmillan, his Foreign Secretary, the Earl of Home, the Home Secretary, R.A. Butler as well as Jomo Kenyatta, then leading his country towards independence. The performers were having the time of their lives. Peter Cook told *The Times*, 'the Prime Minister was sent an invitation, but his reply must have got lost in the post. But we have many Establishment members, including a bishop who has sworn me to secrecy.'[15] Uninhibited by any false modesty, John Wells reflected their exuberant belief in the power of their own raillery. 'We really began to believe that we were in some sense the underminers and detonators of politicians . . . that thanks to us Macmillan had collapsed.'[16]

---

* Appeasement is one of the greatest sins laid at the door of the Establishment. All Souls College, Oxford, a much more influential place then than now, was one of the institutions where the policy took root most tenaciously.

† Lady Violet Bonham Carter (what a prodigiously active woman she must have been!) was prominent in the National Television Council, with Lords Waverley (former public servant, wartime home secretary and Chancellor of the Exchequer), Halifax (former foreign secretary and viceroy of india) and Brand (banker and public servant). They prophesied an unstoppable torrent of debasing vulgarity if commercial television was introduced.

But his friend Peter Cook was closer to reality. The members of the Establishment whom they set out to pillory either ignored them or loved them to death. A cartoon in the *Spectator* at the time of the Conservative party conference showed the doorman at the club assuring customers of a seat, as most of the regulars were away in Brighton. Two years later the place was bankrupt and converted into a gambling den. In the opinion of long-time Soho habitué Jeffrey Bernard the acts had got as bad as the food, which was pretty dire.

By now the word 'Establishment' had become a convenient grab-bag for everything student protest rebelled against. The expression had crossed the Atlantic, in the process becoming a mythical monster the sex and drugs generation were determined to slay. When Charles Manson and his deranged disciples broke into the mansion on Cielo Drive, Hollywood, to commit their gothic butchery it was, said one of them at their trial, 'to instill fear into the Establishment.'[17]

Fairlie was already infuriated by the way the word had been appropriated by all sides to describe powerful enemies. 'There is much to be said for the view that it (the idea) should have been left to ferment in the more obscure vats of A. J. P. Taylor's writings,' he observed.[18] It was, he thought, sloppy or wrong-headed to impute political characteristics to the Establishment. It was not a power élite, and neither was it an existing political party. Indeed, its distinguishing characteristic was that its members had no roots in any one class or interest. They had an almost spectral quality:

> They move in a world which is utterly separated from reality, governed only by its own mystique. Deprived of real experience, impelled by no real interest, avoiding any real conflict, it is to this, the exalted representation of nothing, that they would like to reduce the social and political life of Britain.[19]

Whatever else may be said of the last fifteen or so years in British political life, they cannot be described as 'the exalted representation of nothing'. The greatest realignment for a generation has taken place. If, as Fairlie has claimed,[20] his real enemy at the time he coined the phrase was consensus, then the battle against the Establishment has been won. For a decade of radical Toryism, the foundations upon which the Establishment rested came under assault.

David Marquand, once a bright young Labour MP, now a professor of contemporary history, told me:

> Fifteen years ago the commanding heights of British society were occupied by a group of institutions which, while governments came and went,

seemed to go on forever: the civil service, the universities, the Church of England, the BBC. It was understood by politicians that governments had to accommodate themselves to these institutions: they were proud, independent and owed their life to something beyond mere politics. One by one they have been besieged, and one by one they have crumbled. One has a strong suspicion that deep in their souls they were unsure any longer what they were for.[21]

This is gloomy talk, and there is every chance that in another fifteen years' time the institutions he thinks have so lost their way may have recovered their self-confidence.

But it is a curiosity of recent history that the Establishment, so reviled by high priests of radical socialism, should have suffered its greatest reverses at the hands of a Conservative government: in institutional terms, Mrs Thatcher sent seismic shocks through many of the pillars of society which Socialists from Ramsay MacDonald to Jim Callaghan had not dared to touch. Under Margaret Thatcher the outsiders, according to the fashionable view, became insiders, and it was their beliefs – in materialism, competition and the wisdom of the marketplace – which provided the framework not only for political affairs but for the entire range of British public life. The Lady Violet Bonham Carter of the 1990s, they argued, will be a self-made businesswoman.

Common beliefs which had held sway since the end of the Second World War either survived as sad, attenuated things or were discarded. With the possible exception of Northern Ireland, where a feeling of hopelessness is common to both major parties, cross-party collaboration was reduced to a minimum. The sort of co-operation between the Conservative R. A. Butler and his Labour under-secretary, James Chuter-Ede, which produced the 1944 Education Act – the framework of state schooling for thirty years – was now almost unimaginable. There was no longer even agreement on which of the tools of the state, from the public utilities to railways and telecommunications, truly belonged in common ownership.

The 1980s were the first decade in which the commanding heights of society began to be scaled by men and women who had not been through the shared hardships of wartime. In their predecessors, the experiences of the Depression and Total War had produced the Welfare State. Not only did the New Right believe that the postwar consensus crippled enterprise, they had allies in the generation below them. The social revolution of the sixties wore the clothing of compassion, but it also made self-indulgence respectable. The most indulged members of the counter-culture were privileged Oxbridge-types anyway, and although its alumni affected to dislike capitalism, particularly multinational capitalism, many ended up translating their taste for individual gratification into a form of entrepreneurship.

A survey of the changes during the Thatcher years was conducted by John Lloyd, former editor of the *New Statesman*, in an influential series of articles in the *Financial Times* in the summer of 1988. He was unambiguous. 'Britain is no longer run by an Establishment. In its place is a Disestablishment comprising men and women whose values, assumptions and habits are those of outsiders.'[22] Lloyd thought he detected wholesale changes throughout most of the great institutions, with the notable exception of the Church of England. The values of the new entrepreneurs, many of them Jews or Nonconformists, had permeated everything from the upper levels of the civil service to the finance houses in the City and the editorial conferences of the BBC. *The Times*, which in 1957 had proudly talked about itself in internal memoranda as 'the organ of the governing class', was in the hands of the Australian-born buccaneer Rupert Murdoch and running a form of bingo each day. Now, the Top People had usually started at the bottom.

Between 1980 and 1986, the number of millionaires in Britain doubled, from nine thousand to eighteen thousand. Wealth became a thing to be admired in itself. The new arrivals in the House of Windsor were happy to be caught by the *paparazzi* sharing a drink or a dance with minor showbiz figures, and showed much less suspicion of new money than their parents' generation.

Previously, industrialists had had their work cut out to make it into the old Establishment. Now, the wisdom of the marketplace became the wisdom of the hour. As the Thatcher advance rolled on, the saboteurs of the old edifice were selected businessmen, periodically parachuted into government departments to knock them about and make them efficient. The most celebrated of these was the property developer David Young (later made a peer by a grateful Prime Minister), who was infiltrated first into the Manpower Services Commission, then made a special adviser at the Department of Industry, before ending up as a member of the cabinet without ever having contested an election.

So what has become of the amorphous being that Henry Fairlie and the rest of them thought they had discovered thirty or more years

earlier? Anthony Sampson, whose masterly survey of British institutions, *The Anatomy of Britain*, was published in July 1962, had spent
eighteen months in search of the Establishment, and concluded that
an overarching association of individuals gathering in country house
drawing rooms and leather armchairs in St James's was a 'mirage':

> The rulers are not at all close-knit or united. They are not so much in the
> centre of a solar system, as in a cluster of interlocking circles, each one
> largely preoccupied with its own professionalism, and touching others only
> at one edge ... they are not a single Establishment but a ring of
> Establishments, with slender connections. The frictions and balances
> between the different circles are the supreme safeguard of democracy. No
> one man can stand in the centre, for there is no centre.[23]

You could say much the same today. But this analysis tends to make
light of the very things which the rulers had in common. The great
institutions were run by people who had been to the same schools,
spoke with the same accents, and shared the same values. The
philosophy of the gentleman amateur defined the boundaries of
change. On the positive side, they were relatively immune to financial
corruption. But they were too ready to assist in what the head of the
home civil service, Sir William Armstrong, once frankly called 'the
orderly management of decline'.[24]

All of this was anathema to the Conservative government which
came to power under Margaret Thatcher in 1979, convinced of the
need to save Britain not merely from external pressures but from
herself. The new style of the times is different. But talk of a ruling
'Disestablishment' misses the point. The old Establishment not only
had shared values, but they were able to act in concert to enforce
them. The new men – and they were still almost all men – believed in
the virtues of enterprise, self-help and pulling yourself up by your
bootstraps. They were individualists and as individualists cannot be
members of an establishment.

But before we dance on the Establishment's grave, we should
examine some other areas of public life. Look at the bishops sitting in
their white surplices in the House of Lords, the judges processing to
the opening of a new legal term, any officers' mess in the Household
Division, or the weekly gathering of permanent secretaries in Whitehall. The only thing more uncommon than a woman's face is a black
or Asian one. The majority of these white middle-aged males still tend
to have the same education, to dress similarly, to come from the same
backgrounds. When, in October 1989, the British legal system set free

four Irish people who had spent fourteen years wrongfully imprisoned for allegedly bombing pubs in Guildford and Woolwich, it was succumbing less to the justice of their cause than to the eminence of those who had taken it up. *The Independent* described the lobbying of the Home Secretary, Douglas Hurd, by Cardinal Basil Hume on behalf of the prisoners thus:

> A scholar of Eton, and also of Trinity College, Cambridge, received discreet representations from a cleric educated at Ampleforth and St Benet's Hall, Oxford. It was reported that the cleric had five influential supporters. Three of these had been to Oxford, one to Cambridge, and one to the London School of Economics ... The scandal of the Guildford Four suggests that to beat the Establishment, you need other members of it on your side.[25]

It reads as if nothing much has changed in Britain, that the death knell of the Establishment has a hollow ring and that those in a position to make things happen are much the same as they've always been for the last forty years, speaking in the same accents, dressing in the same style, succumbing to popular pressure only when to do otherwise would just make life too difficult.

The individual elements of this association – the Conservative party, the bureaucracy, the upper reaches of the Church, the public schools – will be examined in later chapters. But this Establishment was itself a successor to an earlier one, when the country was run almost as a collection of family businesses. It is as well to start by looking at what became of it.

CHAPTER ONE

Lords, Squires and Pipsqueaks

> The stately homes of England,
> How beautiful they stand,
> To prove the upper classes
> Have still the upper hand;
> Though the fact they have to be rebuilt,
> And frequently mortgaged to the hilt
> Is inclined to the take the gilt
> Off the gingerbread.
>
> – NOËL COWARD

This afternoon I took the tube to Richmond, and thence a bus to Petersham. I walked down the long drive to Ham House. The grounds are indescribably overgrown and unkempt. I passed long ranges of semi-derelict greenhouses. The garden is pitted with bomb craters around the house, from which a few windows have been blown out and the busts from the niches torn away. I walked round the house, which appeared thoroughly deserted, searching for an entrance. The garden and front doors looked as though they had not been used for decades. So I returned to the back door and pulled a bell. Several seconds later a feeble rusty tinkling echoed from distant subterranean regions. While waiting I recalled the grand ball given for Nefertiti Bethell which I had attended in this house some ten years or more ago. The door was roughly jerked open, the bottom grating against the stone floor. The noise was accompanied by heavy breathing from within. An elderly man of sixty stood before me. He had red hair and a red face, carrot and port wine. He wore a tail coat and a starched shirt front which had come adrift from the waistcoat. 'The old alcoholic family butler,' I said to myself. He was not affable at first. Without asking my name, or business, he said, 'Follow me.' Slowly he led me down a dark passage. His legs must be webbed, for he moved in painful jerks. At last he stopped outside a door, and knocked nervously. An ancient voice cried 'Come in!' The seedy butler then said to me, 'Daddy is expecting you,' and left me. I realized then that he was the bachelor son of Sir Lyonel Tollemache, aged eighty-nine. As I entered the ancient voice said, 'You can leave us alone, boy!' For a moment I did not understand that he was addressing his already departed son.[1]

HERE IS THE authentic picture of the post-war British aristocracy, half-mad, drunken, degenerate and broke, the ruling class on its uppers. For this description comes not from a parody by Evelyn Waugh or Tom Sharpe, but from the diaries of James Lees-Milne. He had been commissioned to travel the country in the 1940s, deciding which stately homes were to benefit from takeover by the National Trust, then functioning as a sort of outdoor relief for the landed aristocracy. The picture he drew of the decaying house, trees growing from the roof, eyeless windows, overgrown terraces, the family desperate to decamp to a suburban villa, is a persistent theme of British fiction since the First World War, to the point where it has become a modern myth. Convenient as this myth may be in fending off criticism of the aristocracy – why kick a man when he's down? – it is just not true any longer.

The influence of the British aristocracy has been declining ever since the industrial revolution ensured that most people made their living from the local mill-owner rather than the local squire. Universal adult suffrage might have been expected to terminate their political power once and for all, yet still about 785 hereditary peers have the right to sit in the House of Lords and amend legislation passed by the House of Commons. Titled families are estimated to own almost one third of the country. And many are still fabulously rich. A list of the two hundred richest people in Britain, published by the *Sunday Times* in 1990, and omitting several of the wealthiest families, discovered that over half were what might be called 'Old Money', including fifty-four aristocrats, a majority of whom had been at school at Eton. It is a remarkable survival. Landholdings give only part of the measure, and as money is not a subject talked about in polite society, there is no corresponding league table from the 1890s with which to make a comparison. But with the fortunes being made from Victorian trade and industry, it is unlikely that the proportions of old and new money would have been any different. Where, then, did this myth of the aristocracy's current powerless penury originate?

James Lees-Milne had spent his childhood at Eton, Oxford and Miss Blakeney's Stenography School for Young Ladies in Chelsea. It was while he was a dinner-guest at the great Jacobean mansion of Rousham, near Oxford, that the event occurred which gave him his mission to save Britain's country houses. His host for the evening, the 'capricious alcoholic . . . rich, clever, and slightly mad' Maurice Hastings, amused himself after the port first by horsewhipping the Kneller and Reynolds family portraits, and then by shooting at the private parts of the eighteenth-century statues in the classical gardens. Lees-Milne, less drunk than the other dinner-guests, was outraged. When, in 1936, the National Trust decided that it would launch a scheme to save some of the great houses whose owners could no longer afford their upkeep, Vita Sackville-West recommended Lees-Milne for the post of secretary.

Lees-Milne's marvellously entertaining diaries of the war and post-war years are suffused with the aroma of decline. What was passing with the decay of the great houses and ancient families was not merely a way of life but a tradition of government. It was, it seemed, the end of the Ruling Class. As they struggled through the privations of wartime, with only the occasional bottle of Château Haut-Brion 1920 for sustenance, and plovers' eggs well-nigh unobtainable, there was a feeling that the game was finally over. Lees-Milne was a crashing snob, and guessed – rightly – that the decline of the great houses would be accompanied by a diminution in the influence of their owners. It was the end of an era. In June 1947 he was in Worcestershire:

> I walked down to Lower Brockhampton just before dark, the trees dead quiet, not even whispering, and the undergrowth steaming. Two enormous black and white bulls gave me a fright by noiselessly poking their great faces over a gate and peering at me in a meditative manner. This evening the whole tragedy of England impressed itself upon me. This small, not very important seat in the heart of our secluded country, is now deprived of its last squire. A whole social system has broken down. What will replace it beyond government by the masses, uncultivated, rancorous, savage, philistine, the enemies of all things beautiful? How I detest democracy. More and more I believe in benevolent autocracy.[2]

A few years later, in 1961, Lees-Milne was in Gloucestershire, where he visited a country churchyard. On the wall inside the church he read a memorial plaque, erected by a son to his father. 'The last of the squires,'[3] it read: the young inheritor had decided he certainly wasn't going to take on his father's role.

The aristocracy *was* the Establishment. It provided the politicians who framed the laws, the officers who defended the nation's shores, and the priests who defined her morals. It possessed a common background, had a common education, and, above all, generally shared a common set of values. Political power and social power were one and the same. David Cecil captures the world perfectly:

> It was, before all things, a governing class. The Whig lord was as often as not a minister, his eldest son an MP, his second attached to a foreign embassy. So that their houses were alive with the effort and hurry of

politics. Red Foreign Office boxes strewed the library tables; at any time of the day or night a courier might come galloping up with critical news, and the minister must post off to London to attend a Cabinet meeting. He had his work in the country too. He was a landlord and magistrate, often a lord lieutenant.[4]

For much of the eighteenth century British public life was dominated by a couple of hundred families, and the aristocracy's grip upon political power proved remarkably tenacious. In the 1833 Parliament, 217 MPs were either the sons of peers or themselves baronets. The comparable figure in 1880 was 170.[5]

This was not the rule of money, it was the rule of land: mere money was a vulgar, impotent thing. To enter the ruling class you had to have estates. The fifteenth Lord Derby, who owned 69,000 acres of British soil, enumerated the benefits of land-ownership succinctly:

> The objects which men aim at when they become possessed of land may be enumerated as follows: 1) political influence; 2) social importance, founded on territorial possession, the most visible and unmistakable form of wealth; 3) power exercised over tenantry; the pleasure of managing, directing and improving the estate itself; 4) residential enjoyment, including what is called sport; 5) the money return – the rent.[6]

It is a revealing ordering of priorities, and again accentuates the connection between political and social power and the soil.

The last comprehensive examination of land-ownership in Britain took place over a century ago. Bateman's *New Domesday Survey*, amplified in 1883 by his *Great Landowners of Great Britain and Ireland*, proved a spectacular 'own goal' for Lord Derby, who had urged Parliament to sponsor and publish the investigation to disprove 'wildest and reckless exaggerations' suggesting that most of the country was owned by relatively few people. To his considerable embarrassment, the survey confirmed the exaggerations: three quarters of Britain was owned by seven thousand people. One quarter of England and Wales was in the hands of a mere 710 citizens.[7] The concentration of ownership was most pronounced in Scotland, where no less than half the Highlands belonged to just fifteen owners. Admittedly, Scottish land was worth much less than prime estates in England, but still the Duke of Sutherland's 1.25 *million* acres, or the 460,000 acres, many of them in England, belonging to the Duke of Buccleuch, were massive holdings by any standards. A further couple of dozen peers had landholdings of over 100,000 acres. Below the great estates held by a small number of families the ownership pyramid broadened, to include what Bateman called one thousand or so 'greater gentry', owning between three thousand and ten thousand acres. Beneath them were two thousand squires, or 'minor gentry', with landholdings of between one thousand and three thousand acres.

Bateman carried out his survey at the height of aristocratic land-ownership, and within a few years, huge tracts of Britain were going under the auctioneer's hammer. To qualify for inclusion in the original *Burke's Landed Gentry* landowners had to have at least two thousand acres, and between 1833 and 1906 the number of families listed grew from four hundred to five thousand. But by 1914, half of those families which had appeared in the 1863 edition had vanished from the book's pages, and by the end of the First World War so many families had lost so much land that the property qualification was removed: the idea of 'landed gentry' merely meant people who had once had some connection with a family seat.[8] The reasons for the flight of the aristocracy from the land have been well chronicled – the introduction of estate duty, legislation establishing tenants' rights, Lloyd George's 1909 budget, the agricultural depression, and so on – although by the turn of the century, the power of the landowners was withering for other reasons.

As the thundering industries in the cities swallowed up droves of new workers, the population on the land shrank and the influence of the local landowners counted for less. In the 1870s, the agricultural depression caused the value of land to plummet and meant that estates could not generate enough income to support themselves. Local government, which had been the responsiblity of the gentry and the clergy (themselves often the younger sons of the gentry) under statutes and commissions dating as far back as Edward III, was transferred to newly-created county councils. The 1882 Militia Act took away military responsibilities and the peerage itself was being diluted by the creation of new grandees. Even Disraeli, hardly the picture of a country gent, had become respectable when he acquired several hundred acres around Beaconsfield, while Gladstone presided over seven thousand acres in Cheshire. But a growing number of peers came from 'trade' and industry. The leaders of smart London society continued to be drawn from the old landed families, but of the two hundred new peers created between 1886 and 1914, one third represented the wealth of the industrial revolution. (One other curiosity; in the same period nineteen members of the old nobility married actresses, compared to ten in the previous century.[9])

The First World War, in which the scions of so many great families perished, produced a burden of death duties under which families just sank. The pace of selling became positively frenetic. In one year a single firm of auctioneers sold an area equivalent in size to an entire county. Estimates speak of one quarter of the land area of England and Wales changing hands between 1918 and 1922, the greatest land transfer since the dissolution of the monasteries.[10] As tenants bought the fields they had previously rented, the proportion of land in the hands of owner-occupiers jumped within a decade from just over one tenth to more than a third.[11] There were many in the upper classes who felt betrayed: they had offered their sons to be cut down in the trenches, and had been rewarded by having their lands taken from them. 'With the most patriotic support to the government in the great challenge of 1914, the feudal system vanished in blood and fire, and the landed classes were consumed,' wrote one observer.[12] Shorn of their landholdings, the great houses became expensive liabilities, unviable without the income from the estates. And as their landed wealth declined, so too did the old order's claims upon government, until all that remained was the feeble bony grasp of a withered old crone. 'The old order is doomed,' the Duke of Marlborough lamented in *The Times*.[13]

The demands of the Second World War for buildings to serve as barracks, laboratories, hospitals or convalescent homes saved many houses from demolition. Even Brideshead, Evelyn Waugh remarked in that most plaintive threnody for a dying class, 'had been marked for destruction before the army came to it.'[14] D-Day was planned at Inigo Jones' Wilton, Vanbrugh's Blenheim was taken over by military intelligence and evacuated schoolboys. Many houses would never return to family occupation: the expense of refurbishment, the cost and scarcity of domestic staff and the greatly changed circumstances of the families themselves all encouraged the owners to sell or demolish their homes. All told, between 1875 and 1975, at least 1,116 country houses were demolished.[15] And for the families which hung on to the ancestral pile, the demands of postwar death duties remained a constant incentive to sell land, furniture or art collections. Once they had all gone, the only realizable asset left was the house.

Many of the ancient families recall the trauma of selling the family home as if it were yesterday (which, to some of the most long-established, it almost is). Lord Ferrers was twenty-five when he succeeded to the title, fresh from Winchester, a Cambridge degree in agriculture and the Coldstream Guards. It was October 1954: across England, estates were going under the hammer as one family after another gave up the struggle to keep the roof weatherproof, the land tilled and the bedrooms mildew-free. The twelfth Lord Ferrers called in his son and told him that Staunton Harold, the Leicestershire family home for five hundred years, complete with its magnificent Commonwealth chapel, was to be sold. The house had been occupied by the army during the war, and as the valuers moved through the rooms he told his son, 'I'm doing this because I don't want you to have the worry that I've had to go through.'[16]

But the strain of the imminent parting was too much for the old man. At 11.30 on the night before the sale, he died. At 2.30 the following afternoon the new Earl Ferrers saw Staunton Harold sold off to become a convalescent home.

Yet reports of the end of the aristocracy have been greatly exaggerated. When he came to revise his novel in 1959, even Evelyn Waugh was obliged to admit that *Brideshead Revisited* was 'a panegyric preached over an empty coffin.'[17] Certainly, over the last century the number of family seats has dropped. But remarkable numbers survive. Because of the secrecy surrounding land ownership in much of Britain (we know less now than in 1066), it is extremely hard to estimate precise figures. In 1988, Hugh Montgomery-Massingberd, a displaced person from the Lincolnshire squirearchy who has turned journalism about the landed classes into a cottage industry, calculated that about 1,600 great estates survived in England, a further five hundred in Scotland, and another 150 in Wales.[18] Two thousand two hundred and fifty family seats on the eve of the third millenium is some measure of how far the age of the common man still has to go.

The only recent survey to attempt to measure the changing fortunes of the British aristocracy, in a dissertation for a Canadian university, produced a remarkable picture. By comparing the amount of land held by a family in 1980 with the amount they were shown as owning a century earlier, it was possible to monitor how the great estates had weathered the storm. In an examination of five hundred families, Heather Clemenson discovered that 259, or fifty-two per cent, still owned some of the land they possessed at the time of the *New Domesday Survey*. Nor was the decline of the landed families uniform, for the blow had not fallen equally on both great and small. Those dukes and earls who had the biggest estates could obviously shed a few hundred, or thousand acres, and still have a substantial property left. The biggest casualties have been the minor gentry, who, unlike the landed lords, had few outside investments to cushion the blow. The sales cut a swathe through the squirearchy.

Nearly half of those families which had ten thousand or more acres still own most or all of their estates. Several owners are even able to claim that they own more land than in 1880. The Ingleborough Estate in West Yorkshire, shown in the late nineteenth century as being 1,500 acres, had grown to ten thousand acres by 1980. The Graythwaite Estate in Lancashire had expanded from 3,300 acres to 5,500.[19]

Nor is the popular image of the ruined stately home entirely accurate. Clemenson found that 106 houses in her sample, or twenty-one per cent, had been demolished since 1880, although thirty-two of them were replaced by a new house. Another thirteen were uninhabited and ruined. Many families who had chosen to continue running their estates decided to do so without the encumbrance of the 'great house': of the five hundred houses she surveyed, 381 were either occupied or capable of being occupied, but only 210 were in private hands, the remainder being owned by institutions or the National Trust. As John Martin Robinson has pointed out,[20] while it may be true that four hundred country houses have been demolished since the war, over two hundred have been built. Again, the highest survival rate was among the largest landowners.

Chief among these survivors have been the British dukes, who sat at the commanding heights of the old ruling class. They remain an exclusive band, only two dozen of them, leaving out the Duke of Edinburgh and other royalty. In 1943, Lord Kinross had written of them as

> Men who cannot rise, only descend in the social scale. Men condemned to eternal publicity, whose private lives are seldom their own. Men who may live only where their grandfathers have chosen, and where the public expects. Men hamstrung by an inherited amateur status, to whom barely a profession is open. Men born limited by the responsibilities of too large an income. Men born into a world where there is one law for the duke and another for the poor, perpetually victim of their own class government.[21]

Because of their perceived limitations, there is a tendency to regard the dukes as walk-on characters from some comic opera. In some cases, they earn the role effortlessly. The twelfth Duke of St Albans, descendant of Charles II and Nell Gwyn (Charles II's mistresses spawned four of the dukedoms), used to tell the porter at Brooks's

Club to 'wind up my watch for me, there's a good fellow', and threatened to turn up for the 1953 coronation with a live hawk on his arm in his role as Hereditary Grand Falconer of England: when told he could only bring a stuffed bird he decided not to go at all. His successor, a former salesman and jobbing journalist, went to live in the south of France after being sued for unpaid income tax and accused of improper behaviour in his business dealings.[22] The fourteenth Duke is a chartered accountant.

Yet, although they do not flaunt it, some of the dukes remain staggeringly wealthy. Chief among them is the Duke of Westminster, estimated while still under forty to be the richest man in Britain. The family's luckiest break was the marriage of the Duke's ancestor, the minor Cheshire gentleman Sir Thomas Grosvenor to Mary Davies, the daughter of a rich Middlesex farmer: the dowry included pasture which subsequently became the heart of Mayfair. The Duke's current estates, which stretch from properties in Hawaii to 100,000 acres of Scotland, are valued at well over £3,000 million. The Duke of Buccleuch, once a Conservative MP, has over a quarter of a million acres, and works of art which are too valuable to insure, and therefore travel with him when he moves between his several stately homes. The Duke of Atholl, customarily described as 'a confirmed bachelor', and the last man in Britain allowed to maintain his own private army, is reckoned to be worth between £150 and £200 million. The Duke of Northumberland, thirty-seven, is the largest landowner in England, with eighty thousand acres: his father, who died in 1988, was known as 'the King of Northumberland'. The Duke of Beaufort, an art dealer and landowner, is thought to be worth between £100 and £140 million. The Dukes of Rutland, Wellington and Grafton are reckoned to be worth £50 million apiece.

Although no duke has become prime minister since Wellington in 1834, others have come close, notably the eighth Duke of Devonshire, who spent forty years in political life, and declined the office three times. This Duke is the one renowned for making the most stupendously boring speeches, once yawning in the middle of one of them, and excusing himself because he was 'so damned dull'. (As he grew older he dropped off increasingly frequently; on one occasion, 'I had a horrid nightmare. I dreamed I was making a speech in the House of Lords and I woke up and found I was actually doing so.'[23]) The ninth Duke became Secretary for the Colonies and Governor General of Canada. The eleventh Duke of Devonshire was the last Duke to hold political office in Britain. 'I cannot think of a single cause, except perhaps the environment, that would not be harmed by my support,' he said when we met.

Andrew Robert Buxton Cavendish, eleventh Duke of Devonshire, is a vague, irascible, vulnerable yet sprightly old man. Our appointment is set for 2.30 in the afternoon, at Chatsworth, the magnificent ochre pile in 105 acres of gardens on the banks of the Derbyshire Derwent. I arrive ten minutes early in my best suit and tie, slightly apprehensive that he might decide at the last moment he is too busy to see me. (Busy at what? I wondered later.) Why should a duke be any more daunting to meet than a cabinet minister or a president, both of which I had interviewed with some frequency in the past? Evidence, I suppose, of the curious power of faded glory.

The gateman, in a smart grey suit, hands me over to the Duke's crisp young secretary, in impeccable black dress. In the hall, the Duchess, 'Debo' of the Mitford clan, is sitting on a table chatting on the telephone. She smiles a greeting. Following the clipping heels across the stone floor, it is hard to imagine that the other 174 rooms at Chatsworth have an equally lived-in feeling. In the duke's study the walls are lined with books from floor to ceiling, but the only open one is the latest edition of the Racing Calendar on his desk. A red Amaryllis from the estate hot-houses stands on a side table.

The Duke appears in his study a few minutes later, in shiny cavalry twill trousers and suede slippers. An old green tweed jacket is tightly buttoned across a blue sweatshirt emblazoned with some embarrassing fairground message ('a family joke' he won't divulge), a red labourer's handkerchief is knotted at his throat. He is carrying a decanter of port, and seats himself in a battered leather chair in front of his desk. He is wearing yellow socks.

The eleventh Duke of Devonshire stood for Parliament as Conservative candidate twice, and was soundly defeated both times. He got government office through nepotism: Harold Macmillan had married his aunt Dorothy. When Macmillan became MP for Stockton-on-Tees in 1924, one estimate speaks of his having sixteen relatives in Parliament. His government was almost the last in which the upper classes still held sway, as the Duke admits. 'It was the old boy net. The power of the aristocracy had long since gone, but the upper classes still had very considerable influence.'[24]

The Duke of Devonshire's career as a junior minister for Commonwealth and Colonial affairs (in those days Britain not only had politically active dukes, she had overseas possessions too) was undistinguished. The most significant piece of legislation with which he had a minor involvement was the act enabling Commonwealth citizens to settle in Britain. The only specific achievement the Duke now recalls was his success in persuading the government of Tanzania to accept a smaller aid package than they either needed or the British government could have afforded. The 1964 election ended his taste of ministerial briefs.

The dukes' loss of political power came about both because the Conservative party changed and because there was a very obvious limit to their usefulness. The election of first Edward Heath and then Margaret Thatcher as Conservative leader marked the triumph of the middle classes. After the 1964 election defeat the Duke of Devonshire enjoyed a brief and undistinguished period as transport spokesman in the House of Lords, a post he was better perhaps suited to than most, since he did not drive. But, he felt, his wealth was an obstacle to further advancement. 'If you have a title like mine, then you aren't taken seriously,' he recalls . 'How could I have been given a post talking about unemployment or health or social services, when everyone knows I've got all my millions here at Chatsworth? If you are as privileged as I am, and you have the material good fortune that you see all around you,' he gestured across the Capability Brown parkland rolling away outside the windows, 'then you must realize that the price you pay for that is that you cannot have influence.'

But those who have clung to their estates do still exercise considerable power in their local communities, as employers if nothing else. Chatsworth alone runs to 26,000 acres, supporting a community of employees, families and dependants of over seven hundred. Unlike the Kensington earls, the landed aristocracy are people of substance, and in the shires local people still believe they wield influence. Sometimes they run for elected office, like the Duke of Rutland, who, owning eighteen thousand acres of the place, for a while became chairman of Leicestershire County Council.

The Duke of Westminster, the boyish master of Eaton Hall, the ghastly stately home in Cheshire built for the last duke in the 1960s, is the most active of them. The house he inherited, looking like the library block from some sixties polytechnic, is the centre of a massive estate, and the Duke's liberal Whig policies there prompted Prince Charles to invite him to lead an initiative against rural poverty. It is not a subject of which he has great personal experience – he gave his

first press interview at the age of seven, when he inherited £10 million
from his grandfather and the Inland Revenue maintains a separate
department just to deal with the family businesses. What he lacks in
experience he makes up in good intentions.

A slight, bland-looking man, straight hair falling across his forehead,
he chains his way through a pack of Marlboroughs as he talks about
the iniquity of poverty. In the early eighties he visited a drug
rehabilitation centre in Liverpool and was demonstrably moved by the
experience. 'They had a look in their eyes which I had only ever seen
in the poorest areas of India and Pakistan,' says the smooth, perfectly
rounded voice. 'A hopelessness I thought I'd never see in this
country.'

The Duke's estate provides employment for more people now than
in Victorian times, in a plethora of small businesses, fishing fleets,
farms, garden centres and so on. An appeal from Prince Charles on
behalf of Business in the Community, an organization the Duke had
originally dismissed as 'just a knee-jerk response to some City banker's
conscience',[25] led to his being asked to take on a similar role elsewhere.
If it has not been a conspicuous success, he can hardly be criticized for
trying.

Patron of about 150 charities, the Duke of Westminster is proof
that, if they choose to, the aristocracy can still find a socially useful
role. The concept of 'duty' means something to him. 'I've lived my
life as an "ought to",' he told me. 'I recognize I'm bloody lucky. I
now have to put back something.' When I called on him he was in the
midst of a battle with Westminster Council, a model of the new
Toryism, trying to prevent them selling council houses. He was
particularly proud of his role in raising money for the London
Hospital in Whitechapel:

> The hospital asked me to become a trustee. The children's unit was a
> disgrace, and they'd been kicking unsuccessfully against the local health
> authority for years. But I leaped over the authority's heads. I went to see
> the Health Secretary myself. I told him the situation, said 'this is what we
> need,' told him that the local people had already raised nearly a million,
> and we needed another million. And he gave it to me. We got the money
> within three months.

The capacity of the Duke of Westminster to raise money for deserving
causes, his first name terms with the Archbishop of Canterbury, his
ready access to the Prime Minister, all demonstrate the enduring
strength of the grander aristocrats. But mostly their influence is less

obvious. Every day the Duke of Devonshire, for example, receives letters asking him to become involved in one activity or another from people who have a more elevated view of his own role than he does himself.

'It tends to be opening bazaars nowadays,' he says.

But why do they invite you?

> Why indeed? It's a curious thing: the British don't like privilege, but they do like a Duke to open their bazaar. People are immensely conservative. There've been Dukes of Devonshire here for a great many years, and they think I'll turn up, and it won't offend anybody if I do it. But there's no power in that. I cannot stress too strongly I've no power, except for here on the estate. I had a letter this morning from some people worried because there are plans to make changes to a park in Manchester. I wrote back and told them that I'd love to come to their assistance, but if I, as a terrible old anachronism, were to get involved, the local council would just think this was intolerable interference in their affairs. And it would do a great deal more harm than good.

There is, one senses, a rather corrosive uncertainty about the trappings of aristocracy, the succession of invitations to become patron of this or president of that just because you happened to inherit a title. They are names loaned out to a hundred good causes. The achievement of which the Duke of Devonshire is most proud is his twenty years as chancellor of Manchester University. 'I feel that it's something I achieved on my own merits and I didn't inherit,' he said cheerfully. Then he paused, as he recalled that the eighth Duke had been the original chancellor, and added, slightly deflated, 'So OK, if I hadn't been Duke of Devonshire, I probably wouldn't have got that. But at least there wasn't any nepotism about it.'

The only explanation for the success of the land-owning nobility in preserving their acres is that they care more about keeping them than others do about taking them away. It is their single greatest preoccupation. It helps if you have deep pockets, of course. Convinced that an association of permanent secretaries, High Court judges, and jealous aristocrats ('the Establishment' in his words) were conspiring against him, the Duke of Westminster spent fifteen years fighting a case through every court in the land to prove he wasn't liable for death duties on the estate of his uncle, the fourth Duke. He won.

'Stewardship' is the word which falls most often from their lips in this context, and to be able to hand the estate on to the next generation either intact or extended is their life's work. The carefully nurtured picture of a nation's aristocracy in irresistible decay, selling off first their art treasures, then their land, and finally the great house and its possessions is just no longer true. The image is based upon a few celebrated cases, like Mentmore or Warwick Castle. But the distinctive charactersitic of both those cases was that the house had become separated from the land, and a house without land is 'like a torch without a battery or a mill without a wheel', as Lord Saye and Sele remarked.[26]

For the first decade of membership of the European Community, the relationship between the great landowners and the Brussels bureaucracy was that of some dim remittance-man to the family at home, as European taxpayers paid them to produce more food than the Community could eat. Those dynasties which held their nerve and clung on to the family seat through the bad years have emerged from the valley of the shadow of death, and look out on a society which is more interested in amassing the money to join them than trying to rehouse them in council houses. Nobody did better out of the reduction in top levels of taxation brought in during the eighties: where once they surrendered ninety-eight pence in the pound they now gave only forty pence. Penalties on unearned income were slashed. Rocketing property and land prices hugely increased their worth, while those with portfolios of stocks and shares saw their value more than double in real terms.

The fact that people are able to amass, and keep, large sums of money, has also greatly extended the inheriting class. Some families, like the Clive-Ponsonby-Fanes in Somerset, have actually bought back their eighty-room family seat at Brympton D'Evercy from the school which had taken it over. Inheritance Tax allows the family home to be handed on from one generation to another, free of liability, while other dynastic seats have been transferred to charitable trusts, enabling the family to continue living there. By the end of the 1980s, aristocrats who had once spent sleepless nights worrying about how they would mend the roof had used the income from the estate to restore the decorations, repair the drive and the tennis courts, and were now experiencing the 'greenhouse effect', replacing the outbuildings. The servant shortage has been overcome by better kitchens, heating and plumbing and a retreat to smaller habitable corners of the big houses. Many are happy to play host to foreign tourists and native companies, and those who own grouse moors can rent them out for £1,000 or more per gun per day.

The spiralling prices paid for works of art have given them the chance to fund repairs or extend their lands by the sale of one or two paintings. Often, they can sell their works of art and still retain the pleasure of them, as when, in 1988, Lord Courtenay sold two twelve-foot tall bookcases for £455,000 to the Victoria and Albert, using public money from the National Heritage Memorial Fund. The bookcases are displayed to tourists in his lordship's library at Powderham Castle, Devon.

Shyness and hopelessness about money used to be one of the endearing eccentricities of the aristocracy. It has long gone. Now, they are as aware of the value of their assets as any dealer in a City trading room. They track currency and stock market fluctuations as avidly as any broker, and receive print-outs showing the value of their possessions every two or three weeks. They discuss their 'business plans' with no embarrassment.

They have also been beneficiaries of one of the main growth industries of recent years, the 'heritage' trade. As mile after mile of Britain succumbed to the advancing sprawl of suburbia, the big estates provided some defence against the ruination of the countryside. But during the eighties alone, one quarter of the labouring workforce left the land, and their cottages, the barns they stacked, the churches in which they worshipped, were snapped up as dormitory homes or weekend cottages by urban adventurers. In some villages there now might be two places where a mother could get her legs waxed and nowhere she could buy a pint of milk. Often the only places where genuine village life survived, where you could see on a weekday a young mother pushing a pram or a farmworker on a bicycle, were the estate villages still owned by the gentry.

But the demands of the industrial masses for recreation in the country also created an opportunity. The National Trust proved the public interest in visiting stately homes. The first private-enterprise stately home to be opened to the public on a large scale was Longleat, owned by the sixth Marquess of Bath, in April 1949. It was, without doubt, a vulgar idea, but it was undeniably successful (it attracted 135,000 visitors in its first year), and nothing overcomes scruples of taste like the prospect of money. In 1955, the Duke of Bedford recognized that the demotic forces which were stripping away his inheritance could be made to work to his benefit. The family fortune had been in decline throughout the twentieth century, but catastrophe struck after the Second World War, when both the eleventh and twelfth Dukes died within thirteen years. The succeeding Duke, the product of a cold, bloodless family, had been brought up by paid staff. He didn't even see Woburn, with its twenty-two sitting rooms, twelve dining rooms and endless corridors, until he was sixteen. 'Having been brought up by servants, I have a servant's mind,' he said,[27] and set out to turn himself into a tourist attraction, using his title, his house and his estates in shameless commercial enterprise. (At one stage he even became a member of Equity, so sedulously did he play the role of Duke.)

By the mid-eighties, over eight hundred English country houses were open to the public, and more people were visiting historic houses than attended all live arts performances in Britain.[28] This huge expansion will turn the whole of Britain into a giant museum-cum-theme-park sometime next century.[29] At the same time as the old landowners advanced behind the banner of history and heritage, so large numbers of the public have turned to them as reassuring relics of the one thing Britain seems to have in abundance. 'Lordolatry is part of our creed, and our children are brought up to respect the *Peerage* as the Englishman's second bible,' Thackeray had remarked in his *Book of Snobs* almost a century earlier.[30] By the 1990s it was clear this devotion was no passing Victorian fancy: as much as their churches, the British looked to their stately homes to give them a fix by which they can navigate into an uncertain future. A casual visitor to Britain at the start of the nineties might well wonder how many of the 450,000 'listed' monuments are actually the living remnants of some feudal dynasty.

On the fifth floor of a drab conference centre in west London, the delegates from Britain's most well-bred trade association gather for their annual conference. They are, by and large, an unexceptional-looking lot. Here is a young man in wing-collar and frock coat, there is a middle aged woman in the scruffy uniform of the English landed classes, baggy tweed skirt and sweater out at the elbows. But the rest of them you might meet anywhere. The pin-stripe suits of the menfolk are perhaps slightly better cut than most, and the expensive subfusc of the women is set off by strings of undoubtedly real pearls. The plastic name-tags with which they have been supplied at the door look totally out of place and are anyway unnecessary: many of them are related through the rambling tracery of British squirearchal marriages.

'Arabella well?' asks a cut-glass voice.

'Frightfully good form,' comes the reply. But here the conversation, far from wandering off into formal or friendly enquiries about the health of various family members, turns to business. For it is trade that has brought them together.

'We've cut the advertising budget and got into conferences in a big way this year.'

'We turned over another twenty thousand last year.'

'We did an extra ten thousand visitors.'

'Marvellous.'

In the lobby outside the conference hall, exhibitors vie for the delegates' attention. Auctioneers, much less busy now than in the days when the contents of great houses were coming up for sale every month, offer to value furniture or paintings. There are stands promoting burglar alarms, security systems, audio guides, restoration services, dehumidifiers, personalized plastic bags, confectionery, fine-art insurance for the grander homes, and ersatz 'medieval armour' for the less grand.

A few delegates' names point up the pedigree of this gathering – the Earl and Countess of Annandale and Hartfell, the Earl and Countess Bathurst, the Lord and Lady Carnarvon, the Earl of Dalkeith, Mr and Mrs J.W. Chandos-Pole, the Viscount Windsor, a handful of marquesses and a brace of baronets. The address list is spattered with well-known castles, halls and great houses.

It is the annual general meeting of the Historic Houses Association, founded to campaign against the introduction of a wealth tax in the early 1970s, when the owners of the nation's stately piles considered themselves an endangered species. The association has brought off one of the most accomplished lobbying operations in recent political history, so effective that many of those who twenty years ago were shivering away beneath a leaking roof and mildewed walls now look forward to passing on to their children a stately home which functions as a worthwhile business. The squirearchy are back.

Inside the conference hall the outgoing president of the association, Commander Michael Saunders Watson RN, owner of Rockingham Castle in Northamptonshire, reflects upon his period of leadership. A tall, breezy figure, brisk and friendly, several MPs consider him one of the most effective lobbyists the House of Commons has ever experienced. In the early days of his involvement the new Labour government had promised to squeeze the rich 'until the pips squeak'. No-one is squeaking now.

The members of the association have chipped in to make a small presentation to Commander Saunders Watson and his wife as a token of their appreciation – a specially commissioned 160-piece china service, a gold and diamond brooch, and the leftovers, a cheque for a further £2,000.

Commander Saunders Watson's family have lived in Rockingham Castle, high on a hill in Northamptonshire, since 1584. Nestling beneath the hill is the village, like some idealized re-creation from a 1920s picture postcard. A line of thatched cottages, primroses and daffodils in the front garden, aubretia tumbling over the warm orange stone. A woman is leaning over the garden gate, smiling at two children with a small dog. There is no litter, no petrol station, no advertising hoardings – the scene might come from any time in the last hundred years. Yet this is not miles from anywhere, hidden away in rural Cornwall, but on the edge of industrial Corby and Kettering. There is one clue to the timelessness of the scene. All the gates and doors are painted the same shade of green, the sure sign that this is an estate village.

There are probably hundreds of similar villages scattered across rural Britain, the property of the local landowner. In the late 1980s, over a dozen big estates were actually buying back villages they had sold in the previous decade. In Northamptonshire, the countryside is so liberally spattered with ancient landed families, many of which go back uninterrupted to the sixteenth century and several earlier, that it is known as the 'land of spires and squires'.

Charles Dickens was a regular guest of Commander Saunders Watson's great-great-grandparents at Rockingham Castle, and the house became the model upon which he based Chesney Wold in *Bleak House*. The place has changed since Dickens wrote:

> Now the moon is high and the great house, needing habitation more than ever, is like a body without life. Now it is even awful, stealing through it, to think of the live people who have slept in the solitary bedrooms; to say nothing of the dead.

'It's all going rather well at the moment,' says the Commander, fit and sprightly in cavalry twills and tweed jacket, spaniels at his heels as he strides across the gravel. 'The estate's in good order, the village you've already seen. We had nearly forty thousand visitors last year. We're carrying out major repairs, we've got all sorts of conservation programmes going on with the fabric of the house, the books, the Long Gallery.'[31]

Back at the Historic Houses annual general meeting, expectation is rising. Such is the influence of the lobby these days that they have persuaded the incumbent Environment Secretary, Nicholas Ridley, to leave Westminster on the most glittering day in the parliamentary calendar to talk to them. While they wait for his arrival the members discuss internal matters. A Jorrocks-like member from Dorset complains that contributors to the journal *Historic House* are prejudiced in favour of shooting parties. They should show more understanding for foxhunters. 'We're like the army in Northern Ireland,' he blusters, 'we're in the front line these days.' A lady member rises to suggest a campaign for tax-relief on the employment of gardeners. Loud rumbles of 'hear, hear'.

Before more worries can be aired, Ridley arrives. While his cabinet colleagues stand in the House of Lords to hear the Queen at the State Opening of Parliament outline the legislation planned for the coming session, Ridley lays out his policy on the stately homes of England. It is a confident performance. The country houses were under threat for years, but now there's a new prosperity. Tax rates have been slashed. 'Millionaires abound.' The government wants to see the country houses survive, he adds, lived in by real families, not preserved as a museum. It is music to their ears.

Then he lobs a firecracker into the audience:

> But we cannot provide a permanent guarantee to a particular family. Many families who pride themselves on having always lived in a house in fact married into it, bought it or stole it at some point in their murky history, when they were robber barons, property speculators, or simply won the pools.[32]

This goes down about as well as a fraternal address by Robespierre. A double-breasted suit within earshot harrumphs that his family damn well *built* their home four hundred years ago, and have lived there ever since.

But the message is unambiguous: if you can't afford to keep up your home, then sell it. Someone else can. 'There have to be opportunities for today's *nouveaux riches*: so I am not impressed by the case of the *anciens pauvres*.' There are mutterings that this is the sort of talk you'd expect from someone like Ridley: he is, after all, a younger son. The Viscountcy went to his elder brother, subsequently appointed Lord Lieutenant of Northumberland.

That Ridley is right on the buoyancy of the market in great estates is borne out every month. The Australian entrepreneur Alan Bond

flew in from Sydney, bought the Glympton Park Estate in Oxfordshire
for £11 million, and, when he got into financial difficulties eighteen
months later, easily found another buyer at the same price. Asil Nadir,
the tycoon behind the Polly Peck empire, bought Baggrave Manor and
seven hundred acres of Leicestershire. The 1,000 acre Daylesford
estate in Gloucestershire was sold to the engineering heir, Anthony
Bamford. Wentworth Woodhouse, Britain's largest classical stately
home, with a reputed 365 rooms, was sold to an unmarried businessman with plans to turn the house back into a home after decades of
service as a teacher-training college.

These are all considered parvenu figures by the blue-blooded
members of the Historic Houses Association. They are happy to see
the energizing effect that new money has on the value of their
properties, but that is as far as it goes. There is a world of difference
between the successful entrepreneur who buys his country pile to
demonstrate to the world that he has arrived, and the old families who
have been there for years. They see themselves, with the family
portraits of long dead local MPs, justices of the peace, commanders of
the militia and parsons, as rooted in the local community, its ancient
establishment. The stately homes lobby has persuaded government
and public opinion that their houses are an essential part of the
nation's history. They have been agreeably surprised to discover that
their family treasures have now been translated into 'treasures of the
nation'. The houses have been rescued by the heritage industry. At
the same time, the families have been saved too.

The turning point came in 1975. The nimbler landowners had
escaped some of the worst effects of taxation by 'gifting' property to
their heirs long before they died. The introduction of Capital Transfer
Tax, which made tax payable at the time land was transferred rather
than at death, blocked that loophole. Quick to issue a characteristic
jeremiad, one commentator predicted that the tax would mean 'the
break-up of a land pattern which has existed for a thousand years.'[33]
But there was worse to come. The Labour Government was committed
to the introduction of a 'wealth tax', which would penalize the richest
one per cent of the population by imposing an annual tax on the value
of their possessions, from houses to works of art. Country house
owners immediately began an intensive lobbying campaign. One by
one, the crucial officials at the Treasury and the Inland Revenue and
influential MPs were invited to Rockingham and other stately homes
for lunch, dinner or the weekend.

Owners of historic houses requested visitors to put their names to a petition: by the end of the season, they had well over one million signatures against the tax. An exhibition at the Victoria and Albert museum called *The Destruction of the Country House 1875-1975*, with hundreds of sad photographs of ruined, vandalized and decaying country houses, suggested that large parts of the nation's history were being wantonly destroyed by the ravages of taxation, insurance, security precautions and so on. A campaign mounted by the lobby group, Heritage in Danger, enjoyed the support not only of country house owners, but supposedly apolitical national institutions like the National Gallery and the British Tourist Authority. Sir Roy Strong, the Director of the V&A, proclaimed, 'country house owners are the hereditary custodians of what was one of the most vital forces of cultural creation in history. They deserve consideration and justice as much as any other group within our society as they struggle to preserve and share with us the creative richness of our heritage.'[34] The campaign was extraordinarily effective. The parliamentary select committee examining the implications of the proposed wealth tax was thrown into such confusion that it produced five competing draft reports. The country house lobby had won the day. As the art critic Robert Hewison observed, the Capital Transfer Tax Act of 1975, which gave exemptions to owners who opened their houses to the public for sixty days, and allowed the creation of private charitable trusts, actually improved their position.[35]

The national obsession with heritage has enabled the country house lobby to convince politicians of all parties that the survival of the families and their homes is somehow essential to the well-being of Britain. But it does not mean that the public have automatic rights over these great houses: in fact, only one quarter of the homes represented in the Historic Houses Association are even open to the public.

This antipathy to having hordes of tourists tramp around the ancestral pile is nothing new. In the late fifties, annoyed by her remarks about the vigour of the aristocracy, Evelyn Waugh wrote a peppery counterblast to Nancy Mitford denying that they enjoyed opening their homes to the public:

> The English, you should remember, have a way of making jokes about
> their disasters, but you would find, if you lived here, that the loudest jokes
> about opening Stately Homes are made by the wives who have recent and
> perhaps direful associations with them, rather than their husbands. Half of

Bowood, you should know, is being demolished because its owner prefers privacy.[36]

One can only speculate about what Evelyn Waugh would make of Bowood House today. The building demolished in 1955, the 'Big House', had been taken over as an RAF barracks during the war. What was left can be visited by anyone who chooses to follow the brown tourist signs on the M4 near Swindon.

Charles Maurice Petty-Fitzmaurice, Earl of Shelburne and heir to the eighth Marquess of Lansdowne, appears indistinguishable from any other businessman, still smelling of his after-lunch cigar as he talks on the telephone in his top-of-the-range BMW. But his accent marks him instantly as something else, the slightly nasal pronunciation of the letter 'O', that languorous self-confidence that comes from a childhood as Page of Honour to the Queen and at Eton. He is also distinguished by the merchandise in which he deals. Lord Shelburne is selling his home, his family and himself.

It is an interesting enough commodity. It was a Shelburne who negotiated the peace which ended the American War of Independence. The third Marquess became Chancellor of the Exchequer at the age of twenty-five and held office under eight prime ministers, twice declining the post for himself. The fifth Marquess became foreign secretary, secretary for war, governor general of Canada and viceroy of India. The family art gallery holds Gainsboroughs, Reynoldses, Ciprianis, the skeleton of a collection once much grander, which included statues by Michelangelo and Raphael and paintings by Rubens, Tintoretto and Turner.

By the time the present Earl inherited the estate, in 1972, it had been in decline for the best part of a century. In the closing years of the nineteenth century the income from the estates was insufficient to support the family in grand enough style (one of the reasons for the fifth Marquess choosing to live as the Queen's representative in Canada). In the struggle for Irish independence, tenants first refused to pay their rents on the family lands there, and then burned down the family house, Derreen. The London property, Lansdowne House in Berkeley Square, was sold in the twenties. In the thirties, the heir to the sixth Marquess died three years before his father, and in the forties, the seventh Marquess and his brother were both killed in action. The accumulated pressures of death duties made the sale or destruction of the great house at Bowood more or less inevitable.

But penury is a relative notion, and 'Charlie' Shelburne is reckoned to be worth £30 million or so. The family art collection is no longer in decline, as new oils and watercolours are added. The rectangular remnants of Bowood, including the family chapel, an orangery designed by Adam and five thousand acres of Wiltshire provide a country house far grander than that of many an industrial magnate aspiring to the squirearchy. The Earl's success was based upon a simple business calculation: the number of historic houses in Britain had been declining for years, while the population had access to increasing amounts of money and leisure. Properly marketed, he thought, the laws of supply and demand would preordain viability. Bowood was to become less of a family seat, and more of a leisure complex. From a single ice-cream kiosk in the early seventies, the house has spawned a restaurant, museum, gift-shop, appalling wax-works, adventure playground, garden centre and pick-your-own fruit farm. 'Please wear your shirt in the house', the brown and white notices request. There are plans to build a hotel and golf-course, as the Duke of Richmond and Gordon has done at Goodwood. The accounts show twenty-seven different 'profit centres', but the key to the estate's prosperity is tourism. Between 1976 and 1987 the number of visitors increased ten-fold, from eighteen thousand to 180,000. And these are not the middle-class couples who trail around National Trust mansions, drunk on the vicarious thrill of baronial splendour, but families from working-class housing estates in Bristol, Cardiff or London. Their affection for the place may be judged by the fact that Bowood suffers less vandalism at the hands of nearly 200,000 tourists than when a private house.

In the nineteenth century, Lord Derby once denounced a departing guest with the words 'Fellow admired my chairs – damned cheek!' and the nakedly commercial approach of parts of the aristocracy to their family history would have their precedessors spinning in their graves. They appear in smiling groups on the brochures welcoming the tourists to their homes, aware that part of the attraction for visitors is the sense that they are in somebody else's home. Richard Thomas Orlando Bridgeman, the bearded seventh Earl of Bradford has solved the problem of £8 million death duties by giving works of art to the Treasury and turning his home, Weston Park on the Shropshire/Staffordshire border, into a conference centre ('The Midlands' finest venue'). It is available for hire for anything from country house weekends to casino evenings. The Earl is also a director of 'Unicorn Heritage', the company behind 'Royal Britain', which offers tourists 'an unforgettable walk through a thousand years of living history', inside the bleak concrete of the Barbican Centre, London. He is conservatively estimated to be worth £55 million. Today, much of the aristocracy farms visitors in the way it once farmed sheep.

The tenth Duke of Richmond moved into Goodwood House on the Sussex Downs in 1969 and had the decorators in for six years. He has transformed the estate into a business turning over £6.5 million and employing 180 staff. Even those who have been severed from their family seats can find the means to regain them, as the case of Lord Camoys demonstrates.

The Camoys have been 'seated' at Stonor Park, a secluded combe in the Chiltern woodlands, since 1150. The house, in warm, variegated brick on gently sloping lawns, had passed down through the male line for eight hundred years. Edmund Campion, the Jesuit priest tortured on the rack and hanged under Elizabeth I, printed his *Decem Rationes* on a secret press at Stonor during the recusancy period, and the house remained a centre of Catholic resistance for two centuries.

Throughout the forties, fifties and sixties, Stonor appeared a classic case of aristocratic decline, as the old Lord Camoys sold off first the furniture, then the land around the house. By 1976, on the death of the old lord, the house itself was on the market. However, it was not bought by one of Nicholas Ridley's *nouveaux riches*. The bid the late lord's executors received in 1978 came from the new Lord Camoys.

He is squat, good-looking in a puggish sort of way, fifty yet still with a slightly boyish manner. After Eton and Balliol, Oxford (where he shared rooms with Lord 'Grey' Gowrie) he went into the City. A monogrammed 'C' on his striped shirt is the only thing that marks him out from a thousand other affluent middle-aged men within a hundred yards of his office above the Thames. In a decision he calls 'foolishly brave', he spent the money he had made from a share-option scheme at Rothschilds and the sale of his previous house to buy Stonor back. The explosive expansion of the City of London during the eighties created plenty of millionaires. But Lord Camoys is not one of them: he bought his family home eight years before Big Bang: what he did would be easier now.

So they flourish, the dynasties of feudal Britain. Major Sir Watkin Williams-Wynn, descendant of the legendary Sir Watkin who convinced a tourist he was mad by dozing through a train journey across Wales, and, awakened periodically by the repeated question, 'I wonder who owns this land?' would reply 'I do', before dropping off again. Seventeen thousand acres of the principality are still in the family. Sir Hereward Wake, with his two thousand acres of Northamptonshire. Edmund Brudenell, with his ten thousand acres of the same county and a family seat which has passed down the family since 1561. The Earl of Mansfield and Mansfield with 25,000 acres on the River Tay. Sir William Philip Sidney, Lord De L'Isle, with his 2,700 acres at Penshurst in Kent, the family seat since 1552.

Like the rest of the nation, they mostly live a kitchen life. All the old families have had experience somewhere in their history of predecessors who went mad, got drunk or gambled away the family fortune, and the survival instinct is bred deep in them. They are careful to take on the style of the times and to use the language of the age. Several mentioned their secret pleasure at eating a plate of fish fingers in the kitchen while a convention of local bank managers sat down to a four-course meal in the old family dining room. All are eager to explain how they manage 'without staff', although this often turns out to mean 'fewer staff'. In the case of the Duke of Richmond, for example, it means only a cook, three dailies and a chauffeur-cum-butler.

They are shielded by a cocoon of aspiration. Still the first thing the ambitious industrialist does when he makes his fortune is to try to buy a country house. Lord of the Manor titles, which confer no land, wealth or real privilege sell at auction for tens of thousands. Young couples bankrupt themselves to buy the sort of furniture which they think the nobility would have inherited. The ineffable superiority of parts of the landed classes, caught in expressions of contempt such as 'he's the sort of shit who shoots on Saturday' (i.e. he has a proper job), inspires not derision but curiosity, even envy. There are more packs of foxhounds hunting in Britain than at any other time this century: almost a million people are estimated to turn out to watch or follow them, and on Boxing Day, the Meet of the Quorn draws crowds of over five thousand.[37] The rash of 'country house hotels' across the country, although spurned by the upper class, who think good food not a sound investment, give the enriched middle class the chance briefly to ape old money.

The social influence of the landed aristocracy is more discreet now. The pettifogging conventions which decreed that no gentleman ever took soup at lunchtime, wore a brown suit in town or used a fish-knife, are almost dead letters. The recent revival of 'the Season' when again the vapid, glassy-eyed faces stare out from the pages of *Tatler* or *Harper's and Queen* every month, is a mere shadow of the real thing, which ended in 1958; a couple of hundred girls on The List, and the surrounding charity balls increasingly the preserve of the *nouveaux riches*, people damned, in the devastating judgement of one of the old families, by the fact that they have *bought their own furniture*.

Such snobbery is objectionable at any time. But it is particularly distasteful when based upon nothing. You could perhaps make a case for the privileges accorded the old nobility when they were given in exchange for service. The principle lay at the heart of the British idea of a gentleman. On other matters – sexual morality, for example – the aristocracy were delightfully tolerant. The case of the Harley family, children of the Countess of Oxford, who were known as the Harleian miscellany because of the multiplicity of fathers involved, is well-known. So commonplace was this easy-going attitude that when Lady Anne Foley wrote to her husband to announce the birth of a child she added a postscript:

> Dear Richard,
>
> I give you joy. I have just made you the father of a beautiful boy.
>
> Yours, etc.
>
> PS. This is not a circular.[38]

But whatever they got up to in, or outside, the marriage bed, the finer side of the nobility's perception of themselves was based in the ideal of chivalry and the practicalities of 'service'. It was this vision which gave the landed ruling class any moral buttress it possessed. Nor was the habit of service restricted to the grandest families. Some might serve as ministers or governors, others as naval captains or colonial district officers. By the beginning of the twentieth century, some families had produced three or more generations who had served the crown in the armed forces or colonial service.

Outside London, these were the people who ran the country, supervising the law, officering the army, and providing the housing. The decline of the influence of the British aristocracy closely parallels the decline of the British Empire. Deprived of a role overseas, and feeling themselves unwanted and penalized at home, the sheer emptiness and frivolity of much of the British upper class was apparent by the 1930s and is demonstrated time and again in the diaries of the time. But the families which survived the winnowing out were made of sterner stuff.

The last fifteen years have been kind to them. They have discovered that they can survive, even prosper, if they run their inheritance as a business in which there is little or no time for sentiment. What has disappeared is not the aristocracy but many of their better qualities. The Duke of Westminster provides an exceptional example of the responsibilities still being discharged by the nobility, but not many choose to follow him. Lord Camoys – 'I'm very busy and I'm very well-paid'[39] – has neither the time nor the inclination to take on the old duties. He lends his name to the Henley Society near his home, is a steward of the regatta, but has little interest in other work. The great Whig tradition of public service is largely gone. In the case of the Lansdownes, Lord Shelburne stood unsuccessfully as a Tory candidate in a safe Labour seat in 1979, but is now too preoccupied with running his estate as a business to find time for politics. The Duke of Devonshire potters about opening bazaars. The twinkling Duke of Richmond takes a slightly more positive attitude, and accepted invitations to become chancellor of Sussex University and deputy lieutenant of the county (admittedly, a post whose main function is to attend the funeral of other deputy lieutenants). When he calls a meeting of industrialists to discuss the local Structure Plan, they all turn up. 'I've proved there is *still* a role for people like me who live in houses like this,' he says, and adds 'if they choose to exercise it.'[40]

But most choose not to. Thirty years ago, the aristocracy were mainstays of local government. In 1960 you could find four dukes, one marquess, nine earls, four viscounts, five viscountesses, twenty-seven barons, thirty-four baronets, fifty-two knights and fifteen titled wives sitting on English county councils. Today, they have all but vanished. The wives of three peers sit on the councils in Gloucestershire and Northamptonshire, and two baronets remain, together with four knights.[41] The ranks of the aristocracy in local government were drastically cut by the abolition of the role of Alderman in the early seventies, but there has also been a conscious rejection of the responsibilities their fathers took for granted. It is as if they nowadays consider it an imposition.

The House of Lords, of course, remains a bizarre anachronism, one of the few places in the civilized world where an accident of birth confers the right to be part of the legislature. But even that power can be eschewed. Lord Harewood, a close relation of the Queen, told me he wasn't remotely interested in influence, and didn't much like people who were. 'I go to the House of Lords in order to vote against the death penalty, which I'm passionately against. The other things I'm passionately against are smoking and after dinner speaking, so that lets me off a few things,'[42] he added.

Max Hastings, a regular fishing and shooting guest, observed, 'One of the most striking characteristics of country life is its overwhelming selfishness.'[43] 'They seem to have lost their basic good manners,' comments another frequent visitor to stately homes, '. . . there is a feeling that they just don't care for anyone but themselves any more.'[44] It is not surprising that, if you have spent forty years fighting to keep your inheritance intact against the demands of the state, you may feel that the state has also removed your need to exercise paternalistic care. The fact that many of the people who might previously have been beneficiaries of aristocratic paternalism now also resent their role doesn't help. The 1980s was the decade in which greed became respectable, and the owners of the great estates did better out of it than most. But if their properties are now no more than businesses, like foundries or amusement arcades, whatever residual legitimacy the old order had has gone.

Bagehot believed that one of the great virtues of the nobility was that because the rest of society wanted to be like them, it prevented its succumbing to a more natural inclination, which was to worship money.[45] Nowadays, it seems to be the nobility who lead the procession to the altar.

CHAPTER TWO

The Fount of Honour

Our far-flung Empire imposed new rules
>And lasted a century or so
>Until, engrossed with our football pools
>We shrugged our shoulders and let it go.

But old traditions are hard to kill ·
>However knocked about they've been.
>And it's still, for some, an authentic thrill
>To go to London to see the Queen . . .

– Not Yet the Dodo NOËL COWARD

I T IS BEST hat time in the ballroom of Buckingham Palace. Seated in straight lines on the purple benches and gilt chairs, from above the guests look like a field of giant multicoloured mushrooms. In the minstrels' gallery, a string orchestra in red tunics from the Welsh Guards plays themes from film soundtracks. Gentlemen ushers in knee-length black tunics fuss about, directing last-minute guests to their seats, although most have been waiting for the best part of an hour, making stilted smalltalk to conceal their pride.

They have come up to London to see the Queen because a relative is to receive an honour. On the stroke of eleven, she bustles into the room, accompanied by the grey-haired and angular figure of the Lord Chamberlain, lugubrious as an upmarket undertaker in black tailcoat. Her outfit is aquamarine. 'I'm sure I've seen that dress before,' whispers a disappointed woman in front, but you could scarcely expect the Queen to wear a new suit for each of the fourteen investitures each year as well as all her other official functions. Two clipped young Gurkhas peel off to the side as the Queen stands before the two great thrones, flanked by a clutch of Yeomen of the Guard, pikes resting on their shoulders. And the long roll call begins.

As each name is recited by the Lord Chamberlain, the recipient steps forward, bows slightly, and kneels or inclines his head to receive the award. A tap on each shoulder, the laying on of a sash, a perfunctory smile, a few words, and it is over. Mechanical, perhaps, and, as the band plays airs from 'Raindrops Keep Falling on My Head', ordinary and faintly bathetic. Yet somehow, the whole ceremony retains an aura of mystery, the fruit of some collective dream. Soon the great awards of knighthoods give way to the decorations reserved for the civil and military services, and the shuffle of office workers is broken only by the occasional clink of a cavalryman's spur. Then come a clutch of stout ladies in flat shoes to collect their OBEs for services to different government bureaucracies, and pallid men honoured for 'services to ice skating', 'to the South Eastern Electricity Board', 'to London Regional Transport'. This last recipient had obviously not used London Transport to get to the Palace or he'd have missed the ceremony 'due to mechanical failure on the Circle Line'.

One hundred and thirty men and women are honoured, the majority of them late middle aged, middle class and obviously very proud. In this convocation of the worthy there is only one black face, a tall, handsome young man, Victor John-Charles, given an OBE for services to karate. There is something curious, too, about the gradation of honours, so that a Ministry of Agriculture clerk is called before the young sergeant from the Royal Ulster Constabulary who chanced his life in some undisclosed anti-terrorist operation. And then it is over, the royal entourage sweeps out, the orchestra strikes up a medley from *The Mikado*, and beneath the six great chandeliers the room starts to buzz with congratulations.

The British royal family remains the one truly regal family in Europe. Where other kings and queens have adjusted to the spirit of the age, installed in some suburban villa, pedalling a bicycle around town, the House of Windsor retains palaces, massive estates and considerable influence. Most importantly, it retains mystery. The machine helps. The Queen will arrive at 11.33, and at 11.33 she is there. She will meet Mrs Jones who has spent twenty years running a shelter for battered cats, and Mrs Jones is there. She will lunch with selected guests in the new council offices, and an hour beforehand they are all turned out in their best suits and dresses fidgeting in anticipation.

While the younger members of the family are treated by the British press and public as stock characters in some soap opera, when one of them speaks, on architecture, AIDS or literacy, the news media none the less report their comments seriously. This ambivalence is the consequence of the techniques adopted by the court to 'sell' the royal family, and the product of two distinct styles of royal behaviour. The

Queen remains a remote figure, glacial and impenetrable except when caught by the press cameras watching one of her horses winning at the races. Prince Charles, on the other hand, has developed an apparently informal style, easy, genuinely popular, with a nice line in self-deprecating jokes. Between them, they have solved the problem of finding a role for an institution which a few decades ago looked to be under siege.

In the autumn of 1955, while the pages of the *Spectator* continued to be filled with angry reaction to Henry Fairlie's remarks about the Establishment, its radical counterpart, the *New Statesman* tackled the family which lay at the Establishment's heart. Malcolm Muggeridge asked whether it wasn't time for the monarchy to engage professional public relations consultants, 'in place of the rather ludicrous courtiers who now function as such.' The royal family had to make a decision:

> do they want to be part of the mystique of the century of the common man or to be an institutional monarchy; to ride, as it were, in a glass coach or on bicycles; to provide the tabloids with a running serial or to live simply and unaffectedly among their subjects like the Dutch and Scandinavian royal families. What they cannot do is to have it both ways.[1]

Much of this could be as plausibly argued today as thirty or more years ago: the extraordinary achievement of the public relations advisers who replaced the 'ludicrous courtiers' has been to ensure that the royal family do still have it both ways. Muggeridge had been percipient in recognizing that the monarchy would increasingly have to live in a goldfish bowl and that would provide a new challenge for the image-makers.

The underlying problem was, perhaps, that too much had been expected of the Queen. She came to the throne after a decade of war and rationing. The new Elizabethan age was to drive out the age of austerity. It was a great deal to hope of anyone, particularly since the political and intellectual principles of the Welfare State were so utterly at odds with the privileged hierarchical structure which had the monarchy at its head.

John Osborne turned his invective on the Palace in 1957 in an article in *Encounter*:

> My objection to the royal symbol is that it is dead; it is the gold filling in a mouthful of decay. While the cross symbol represented *values*, the crown simply represents a *substitute* for values. When the Roman crowds gather outside St Peter's, they are taking part in a moral *system*, however detestable it may be. When the mobs rush forward in the Mall they are

taking part in the last circus of a civilization that has lost faith in itself, and sold itself for a splendid triviality.[2]

This was the wholesome outrage you might expect from any conscientiously angry young man, and could be safely ignored as the sort of bubbling over occasionally to be expected in intellectual cauldrons like *Encounter*. But the comments which most hit home were those of the young Lord Altrincham, in his *English and National Review*, a magazine of scarcely greater significance, but which had the good fortune to publish its August 1957 edition on a newsless Bank Holiday. It was a godsend to news editors. His target was the Court rather than the Queen herself: 'the Queen's entourage,' he wrote, 'are almost without exception the "tweedy" sort.' They had failed to change with the times, so the speeches they wrote for the Queen did her no favours. 'The personality conveyed by the utterances which are put into her mouth is that of a priggish schoolgirl, captain of the hockey team, a prefect and a recent candidate for confirmation.'[3]

Altrincham was writing not so much out of malice as out of a wish to save the monarchy if not from itself, then from the court. He had acutely put his finger upon the fact that the new tools of mass culture, television and radio, exposed the old ways of the royal household to a merciless stare from which they did not emerge well. The article unleashed a storm about his head, the more so because of his peerage, which he renounced six years later. 'Lord Altrincham is a bounder,' thundered the Earl of Strathmore, 'he should be shot.'[4] Two thousand letters arrived on Altrincham's doormat, many of them venting the British class obsession. 'What right have you, you pompous pimp of a Peer, to criticize Her Majesty?' asked one. 'I am a commoner, and know it; you are damnably common and do not know it,' wrote another. 'They say you are a known homosexual; we believe it,' added a third.[5] Shortly after appearing on an independent television programme to discuss his views (no BBC programme invited him on), Altrincham was hit in the face by a furious official of the League of Empire Loyalists.

Apart from demonstrating one of the unwavering laws of British journalism, that nothing sells newspapers like royalty, and nothing makes a better editorial column than declamations of simple patriotism, the curious thing about these assaults is how much they belong to a period. The position of the royal family is simply no longer part of political debate. Three or four pamphlets and books have attacked 'the pernicious myth of monarchy',[6] but serious discussion of the usefulness or otherwise of the royal family has been driven out by simpering nonsense from a pack of tabloid reporters who devote their not inconsiderable imaginations to dreaming up new twists to a comic-strip family drama with a cast-list now augmented by half-a-dozen non-royal spouses and their families. The main criticisms levelled by the 1950s critics – the inadequacy of their public relations and the remoteness of the court – have been tackled, more effectively than anyone could have predicted.

The links between most of the aristocracy and the Crown have grown ever weaker, as the royal family progressively became the *only* special family in Britain. The court circular announced within three months of the Altrincham criticisms that the business of debutantes' presentation at court would be ended. The whole process had become discredited once various members of the indigent upper classes had taken to hiring themselves out as proxy mothers to daughters of self-made industrialists, in order that they might contract a marriage with a desperate aristo. (The Countess of Clancarty, rumoured to have been the Earl's cook once upon a time, charged £2,000 for the service, and Lady St John of Bletso, whose provincial protégées were known as 'the Blets', the same amount.[7])

A new style of official entertaining came in at the Palace and still survives. Invitations to royal garden parties are despatched each year to worthies across the land who have spent their lives raising money for charity or supervising the work of the council sewers and drains committee. Attendance at these affairs, which involves queueing for the sandwiches, queueing for a glimpse of the Queen, queueing for the lavatories, queueing to leave, is potent evidence of the continuing talismanic influence of the monarchy. So wide does the Palace cast its net when it comes to official entertaining that some of the invitees can find their fellow-guests a real let-down. One recent visitor told me:

> I was invited to lunch one day. I was thrilled. Can you imagine my disappointment when I saw the sort of riff-raff that had also been invited – a distinctly dubious businessman, a scruffy rabbi who I think makes his living as a stand-up comic, a second-rate academic? Frankly, a lot of them I wouldn't have allowed in my own home, let alone the Palace.

But by appearing to separate the royal family from most of the rest of the aristocracy, the Queen's advisers have ensured the Windsors' survival in a mature democratic society. It is, however, more a matter of style than substance. The idea has been carefully propagated that they lead a 'middle-class' way of life. It is nothing of the sort: however often houseguests at Balmoral may find themselves entrapped into games of charades after dinner, they retire to bed secure in the knowledge that a staff of 120 is plenty large enough to provide each couple with their personal footman and maid. The friends of the Queen belong to a small coterie of aristocrats, the children are educated exclusively (one of the reasons Gordonstoun seemed a good bet was because, unlike metropolitan Eton, it was miles away in rural Scotland), and all are limited to a narrow circle of suitable acquaintances. It hardly amounts to ordinariness.

If 'the Court' is an expression scarcely ever heard in everyday conversation, it is not because it has ceased to exist but because it no longer wields overt influence. Despite her love of the Commonwealth, and Prince Charles' concern for the inner cities, there is not a single black or Asian face to be seen in the inner circle, and scarcely any white ones drawn from outside a very small pool. Leaving aside positions like the Earl Marshal, which is largely concerned with organizing coronations and state funerals, and has been in the Duke of Norfolk's family since 1672, the court is knitted together by blood and marriage. The Lord Chamberlain, who acts as head of the royal household, is the Earl of Airlie, an Old Etonian banker whose wife, Virginia, is a longstanding Lady of the Bedchamber and whose younger brother, the Hon. Angus Ogilvy, is married to the Queen's cousin, Princess Alexandra. His father, the twelfth Earl, spent almost three decades as Lord Chamberlain to the mother of the present Queen. His grandmother, the Countess of Airlie, was such a close friend of the Queen's grandmother, Queen Mary, that she spent fifty years as a lady-in-waiting. The Lord Steward, Viscount Ridley, another Etonian, is married to the daughter of the Earl of Scarborough, who served as the young Queen's first Lord Chamberlain. His sister-in-law, Lady Grimthorpe, is Lady of the Bedchamber to the Queen Mother. The present Lord Scarborough is married to the daughter of the Earl of Dalhousie, the Queen Mother's Lord Chamberlain.

The tightness of the circle extends to professional staff at the Palace too, all of whom are appointed on personal recommendation. Inevitably, the process produces an unimaginative, safe shortlist, made up of products of established court families. At times, it looks like little more than nepotism: The Prince of Wales' last private secretary, Edward Adeane had been a page-of-honour to the Queen in his teens; his father, Lord Adeane, had been the Queen's private secretary for nearly twenty years, and his great-grandfather, Lord Stamfordham had been private secretary to George V. George VI's private secretary, Sir Alan Lascelles, was a cousin of the sixth Lord Harewood, husband of Princess Mary. Sir Martin (later Lord) Charteris, who became the Queen's private secretary in the seventies, had gone to work for the then Princess Elizabeth because his family were friends of the Lascelles. The man appointed the Queen's private secretary in the autumn of 1990, Sir Robert Fellowes, is married to the sister of the Princess of Wales. His father was the royal agent at Sandringham.

His predecessor, Sir William Heseltine, had at least been fresh blood. Stung by the Altrincham criticisms, instead of plunging into the British middle classes, the royal household turned to dependable outsiders in the white Commonwealth. A Canadian was appointed to the Press Office, followed in 1960 by Heseltine, a career civil servant from Western Australia, who had spent the previous four years as private secretary to Robert Menzies. Heseltine, a stocky man who has lost his Australian accent but retained an attractive Australian directness, is one of the principal architects of the new style of monarchy.

His passport carries the word 'courtier' in the space set aside for occupation – a joke he came to regret when arriving at Darwin airport to be faced by a massive, bronzed Australian immigration official who looked down and told him 'that's not the way you spell courier, mate.'

Heseltine has the status of a permanent secretary in one of the big departments of state. What his office lacks in staff by comparison – he has a mere twenty or so – it makes up for in influence. He is the doorway to the Queen, deciding who will or will not be granted access. He is her link not only with the British government, but with all monarchical Commonwealth governments. He is the Queen's impresario, influencing where she goes and what she does. The Queen's press secretary works under him. He sees the Queen every day. When the prime minister arrives at the Palace for the weekly audience, the private secretary acts as host and spends a few minutes beforehand in conversation. Afterwards, he will offer less bustling prime ministers a whisky-and-soda. He speaks to his counterparts in the offices of the Prime Minister, the Foreign Secretary, the Cabinet Office, Home Office and Privy Council office several times every week, often every day. He does so not only on the Queen's express instructions, he knows the Queen's mind.

It has been Bill Heseltine more than anyone else who brought the royal family into the age of the photo-opportunity. Little could be done to counteract the John Osborne criticisms, for they abominated the very idea of monarchy. But the style of the court could be changed, and the public relations could be sorted out. In the event, some of the consequences of the solution have proved as irksome as the problem, but they have done the trick. The decisions made in 1968 and 1969 by Heseltine, then just appointed press secretary, and the equerry to Prince Charles, Squadron Leader David Checketts, opened a door which could not afterwards be closed. In collaboration with Nigel Neilson, a colourful former SAS officer who had set up his own public relations company, they decided to 'sell' the royal family. The investiture of Prince Charles as Prince of Wales could be turned into a perfect television event, and they recommended in addition that he be made available for radio and television interviews. The documentary director, Richard Cawston, was invited behind the gates of the royal palaces, to film the royals at home. The resulting film, *Royal Family* (or 'Corgi and Beth' as it was nicknamed), in which, among other things, the Queen was shown cooking the steaks at a barbecue, was revolutionary in its revelations, and considered inside the Palace to have been a public relations triumph. 'Richard Cawston's film could not have had a better critical reception if it had been the combined work of Eisenstein, Hitchcock and Fellini,' wrote the critic in the *Evening Standard*.

In one of his celebrated aphorisms about the monarchy, Bagehot remarked that 'Its mystery is its life. We must not let in daylight upon magic.' True, there was something unbearably starchy about much of the supposed 'informality' in the film, but it appeared to have cast a full tungsten glare over a few of the secrets of the magicians. They could never again claim the right to be above the scrutiny of the media. And the mundane could not be reconstituted as the unknown.

Having opened the door to invite public inspection, the Palace found it impossible to close again. All manner of gatecrashers followed for the next twenty years. Once the royal family had been shown as human beings it was impossible to stop the media treating them as such. The process of demystifying the monarchy, necessary if it was to survive the second half of the twentieth century, turned it instead into a grand soap-opera, in which some minor members of the family seemed only too happy to play a demeaning part, one of the more absurd examples occurring when several of the Queen's children took part in the television party-game show *It's A Knockout!* Royalty dressed as stage-royalty.

One of the difficulties is the sheer size of the family. Attempts to refloat the monarchy after the 1936 abdication of Edward VIII were made easier by the fact that the royal family included a king with a stammer and two princesses. By the 1990s the royal family spanned four generations, and the two princesses had acquired a husband each (one marriage ended in divorce), six children, three children-in-law and half-a-dozen grandchildren. As the cast list expanded through royal marriages and the creation of a brood of 'nearly royals' – frivolous young men and women staking a claim to attention in the gossip columns simply because another member of the family had a genuine connection with the Windsors – the roles could be constantly juggled to satisfy an appetite which had been primed by the Palace itself.

The change from mythic beings to human beings, while it demeaned individual younger members of the royal family ('How big is Fergie's bottom?'), did make their personal lives easier in one respect. In 1953, Princess Margaret had been obliged to call off her relationship with the divorced Group Captain Peter Townsend on the advice of the prime minister and the Queen's private secretary. When, in 1989, Princess Anne and her husband, Mark Phillips, separated, they did so with scarcely a murmur, two people whose marital problems were half understood by millions. It is a mark of the success of the policy that although they are often regarded as real people, they are rarely treated as such.

Public relations is the most vital business of the royal household, the expression of an instinct for self-preservation which has grown steadily more sophisticated as the years have rolled by and the appetite of the media has grown more voracious. It is a task which some of the more well-bred staff in the royal household find frankly distasteful – the private secretary to the Prince of Wales, Sir John Riddell, reputedly once told a producer from Thames Television, working on a fortieth birthday tribute to the Prince, that 'dealing with you people is like having one's private parts slowly nibbled by rats' – but they go along with it because the deferential attitude of most of the media is the means of engaging popular support for the institution of monarchy.

It has proved remarkably effective. Republicanism has failed to become a serious issue in twentieth-century politics. The sort of outright hostility which was felt towards the dissolute Hanoverians is unheard of and the inheritors of the nineteenth-century radicals are a disconsolate bunch of Sunday afternoon ranters at Speaker's Corner. The Labour party has consistently taken the view that the monarchy is simply an irrelevance. 'The king fraud will disappear when the exploiting of the people draws to a close,' claimed Keir Hardie,[8] and even those on the radical wing of the party usually decide the game is scarcely worth the candle. Consider the change in Neil Kinnock. During the February 1975 House of Commons debate on plans by the Wilson Government to increase the civil list allowances to the royal family, Kinnock, then an MP of five years standing, launched into a characteristically blustering attack on 'the senior executives of what I may call "the Crown Limited"', who were 'outrageously overpaid'. 'I seriously consider it is time we undertook a job inspection of Her Majesty as an employer,' he added.[9] By the time that Kinnock was party leader such rhetoric had become an embarrassing youthful memory. The royal family, he told a television interviewer eight years later, was safe with him.[10]

There are no votes in plans to pension off the Queen, and the House of Windsor has achieved a stability which would have surprised some previous royal households. Edward VII thought it possible that his son might be the last British king, and during the reign of George V, Harold Nicolson reckoned that five emperors, eight kings and eighteen minor dynasties had come to an end. In Britain, by contrast, affection for the monarchy appears undiminished, most devotional when directed towards those, like the Queen Mother, who have least apparent power or influence. The notion that the price they have paid for their popularity is to live their lives under an insufferable glare of publicity is one of the great fictions of the middle class. 'Poor things, no life of their own,' they say, simultaneously thrilled and appalled as they pore over the latest 'revelations' in the *Mail* or *Express*. But the information the public is tossed about royalty are crumbs from the table.

Today the Court has acquired a spectral sort of quality, as if the 447 appointments divided among the offices of the Lord Chamberlain (sixty-seven), the Queen's household (fifty-two), the Privy Purse and Treasurer's office (twenty-eight), the Ecclesiastical household (fifty-six), the Medical household (fifteen), the household in Scotland (forty-eight), the Central Chancery of the Orders of Knighthood (forty-six), the Royal Company of Archers (thirty-two), the households of Prince Philip (ten), of the Queen Mother (twenty-five), of the Prince and Princess of Wales (sixteen), and all the households of other members of the family (a further fifty-two) did not exist. The life of the royal family is divided into statutory relationships with deserving institutions like the Queen's position as Colonel-in-Chief to a regiment, slightly more informal but none the less prescribed relations with deserving causes as in the patronage of charities, and informal relations between the royals and their friends (in the case of some of the younger royals, a decidely untweedy group of property developers, showbiz celebrities, and Gstaad nightclubbers).

The formal powers of the royal family have diminished as the yardage about them in the newspapers has grown. The Queen's speech at the opening of parliament is of course written for her by the government of the day. Theoretically, she can dissolve Parliament without advice, but the right has been in abeyance for years. Technically she might also refuse a request for a dissolution, although it is hard to imagine her ever doing so. She retains the power to appoint the prime minister, although this is usually pretty straightforward, involving an invitation to the leader of the largest party. (But in 1923, George V chose Stanley Baldwin to become prime minister over the more experienced Lord Curzon, and in 1957 the Queen passed over R.A. Butler in favour of Harold Macmillan.) The last occasion on which the monarch was required to make a real choice occurred when the Queen was obliged to dance attendance on a sick Harold Macmillan in October 1963.[11] Since then, the Conservatives' system for electing a leader has effectively removed this power from the monarch, and providing each election produces an outright winning party, her actions are pretty well preordained. If no single party were to win an overall majority, then the Queen might have real power to choose a government. It has not happened since the end of the Second World War, but before the 1987 election, when some commentators were predicting a hung parliment, much thought was given to what the Queen would do about forming a government if they turned out to be right. Meetings between the Queen's private secretary, the cabinet secretary and the prime minister's private seretary concluded that it was unlikely the party leaders would be unable to come to an agreement among themselves. If they failed to reach agreement, the Queen would summon them and simply say that it was their business to ensure that the Queen's government was carried on. In the event, the formula was never put to the test, but it provides an idea of the way the Palace would expect to pass the buck.

The remainder of the formal powers of the monarchy are strictly limited. The royal prerogative was surrendered at the Glorious Revolution and gives governments the power to make war, treaties and appointments without consulting parliament. Amid all the excitement and turbulence of the days after an election, newly appointed cabinet ministers must find a moment to learn how to kneel and kiss the hand of the Queen, in order that they may become members of the Queen's Privy Council, together with opposition leaders, selected Commonwealth statesmen, churchmen like the Archbishop of Canterbury and senior civil servants. The Council's thirteenth-century oath, 'You will in all things to be moved, treated and debated in Council, faithfully declare your Mind and Opinion, according to your Heart and Conscience; and will keep secret all Matters committed and revealed unto you,'[12] lies at the heart of the British culture of official secrecy, and the enigma of monarchy remains the secret from which all other secrets flow.

So, while formal powers are limited, the influence of the royal family is still considerable. There is not a good cause in the land which does not seek the imprimatur of royal patronage, and the number of official engagements carried out by members of the family doubled during the eighties. During 1989, both the Queen and the Duke of Edinburgh carried out over 550 official engagements, the Prince of Wales over 450. Most industrious of all was the Princess Royal, who appeared at 737 functions on official business.[13] Two hundred letters a day arrive at Buckingham Palace addressed to the Queen. The speeches of Prince Philip on the preservation of wildlife, of Prince Charles on modern architecture or inner city deprivation, gain entry to the newspapers and television news bulletins automatically, although the sentiments they express are unexceptional, the ideas unoriginal and their delivery undramatic. Although they usually no more than reflect back ideas which are already common currency, they get immediate attention because they are delivered by royalty.

A mere list of statutory rights and public duties ignores the question of experience. Simply, the Queen has spent far more of her life at the heart of politics than any of the party leaders. Twice a day for the best part of four decades a box has been arriving at the Palace containing the reports from British ambassadors overseas. Every week the memoranda which have been written by ministers for discussion in cabinet are delivered to the Palace, followed by the minutes of the ensuing cabinet meeting. The weekly reports by the Joint Intelligence Committee, seen by only the five senior politicians in the land are delivered to Buckingham Palace unexpurgated. The Queen has been talking to prime ministers every week since the early fifties: when it comes to practical experience, she is better placed to give advice than her own advisers. Once Queen Victoria had been established on the throne for a few decades, she acquired a natural authority when dealing with her prime ministers. Queen Elizabeth is already the longest-serving monarch of the twentieth century, and may possibly be on the throne even longer than Victoria.

The perspective is bound to encourage a consensus attitude. 'I cannot forget that I was crowned head of the United Kingdom', said the Queen in her Silver Jubilee speech in May 1977. It was seen as an unveiled hint of royal displeasure at Scots separatists (the elaborate investiture of Prince Charles as Prince of Wales, at a time when Welsh nationalism was acquiring an increasingly strident tone, had been intended to have a similar impact) but it might also serve as a text for all the concerns of the monarchy. The royal family persistently talks in the 'common good' language of the fifties so unfashionable among those who held power throughout the eighties. Certain themes run through pronouncements by all members of the family – interest in national unity; worries about the environment, from Prince Charles's confrontations with modern architects to Prince Philip's affection for the giant panda; concern about family life, at home in the Inner Cities or overseas through the Save the Children Fund.

The visit had been known about for weeks. A grey, litter-strewn north London wilderness, high in unemployment, crime, drug abuse, homelessness and all the other signs of high-rise putrefacton. A meeting had been called at one of the local schools, another in a series of as yet fruitless attempts to persuade businesses not to abandon the area to inner-city rot. Prince Charles, in his capacity as president of the charity Business in the Community, was to be the guest speaker.

But the moment he got to his feet to begin his speech, the windows began to rattle with the din from outside. Conch-shells, drums and trumpets almost drowned the sound of his voice. He persevered to the end, inaudible at times, incomprehensible at others. Finally one of his hosts explained the source of the racket, a hut in the yard outside.

The moment he left the hall, the Prince strode away from his escort, opened the door of the hut, and stepped inside. He was faced by about forty young black people, several very aggressive. Many had clearly spent the afternoon smoking ganga. 'He just stood there in a cloud of smoke,' recalls one of the people first through the door after him, 'while they effed and blinded at him and told him what they thought of what had been going on in the hall. He just stood there and listened.

'Then, to my amazement, he said, "You know, I think I agree with you. Let's see what we can do."'

The incident is a more extreme example of a common enough practice in the development of a new popular style for royalty. Where Elizabeth failed to find a way of reinventing the monarchy, Charles, a child of the television age, succeeded. The most remarkable thing is the way in which someone from the most privileged home in the land should strike a chord with those from the most deprived backgrounds. But watch the Prince working a crowd and compare him with a politician in the same situation. Where one comes to talk to people, the other comes to listen. And there is something more profound. It is more than mere style, something beyond the old 'something must be done' concern. Stephen O'Brien, Director of Business in the Community, who has accompanied the Prince on numerous visits to inner city slums, has seen what happens when he arrives:

> He seems to be above, or able to cut through, all the normal suspicions that alienated young people have of the 'Establishment' in a quite remarkable way. They want to talk to him. Not just because of who he is, but because they think that he understands and cares, and may be able to intercede.

The genuine popularity of the Prince, his self-evident concern and compassion, and events like his fortieth birthday party (held in a Birmingham tram shed) are drawing on new sources of support for the institution of monarchy beyond the recesses of middle-class dreaming. A somewhat lonely figure, often mocked for his retreats to the Kalahari or the Hebrides, he has managed to tap popular concern about the environment, education, and racial disadvantage. His interest in, and knowledge of, inner-city problems is more profound and personally felt than that of most government ministers and civil servants, according to those who have spent time with him. 'I think he'd take the view that the government needs to be educated,' says one. 'He believes intensely in localness and smallness instead of centralness and bureaucracy.'

'Something as curious as the monarchy won't survive unless you take account of people's attitudes,' the Prince told an interviewer in 1982, in a remark which gives some clue to the task he set himself. 'I think it can be made a kind of elective institution. After all, if people don't want it, they won't have it.'[14]

His popularity, and the seriousness with which his views are treated is a measure of his achievement. Not all the causes he took up were quite the product of personal initiative that they later came to seem. Casting around for a task for the Crown Prince, Palace advisers had considered putting him to work leading a development campaign within the Commonwealth, before the inner-city initiative seized his imagination.

The skill with which the royal family have identified not merely the good causes which will garner public sympathy, but some of the issues which tap the popular pulse has enabled them to weather any potential challenge from republicans. It is their good fortune to have the luxury of comment without the responsibility of action that enables them to appear more in tune with public feeling than the ideologists of either side of the political spectrum. The House of Windsor has become highly adept at the business of its own survival. That there is no popular opposition is testimony not only to how successful they have been, but also to the fact that there appears to be simply no desirable alternative: the British just do not like their politicians enough to want them made head of state.

Relations between the Queen and Mrs Thatcher are, by all accounts, cool to the point of frosty formality, although probably not as uncomfortable as dealings between Queen Victoria and Gladstone at their worst. What takes place at their weekly meetings is unknown. The prime minister is met at the door of the Palace at 6.30 on Tuesday evenings by the Queen's private secretary, and ushered into the royal drawing room by a footman. On the words, 'The Prime Minister, Your Majesty,' the Queen invites the prime minister to sit down, and the two are left alone. No minutes are taken of their conservation, no record of any kind exists, beyond what either may record in their diary, although the private secretaries, who hold a parallel meeting below stairs, have some idea of the topics under discussion. James Callaghan, when prime minister, would have the subjects he planned to raise on a piece of card, but often didn't bother to raise them, as they gossiped about politics or took a stroll around the gardens on summer evenings. In the last few minutes he would fumble in a inside pocket, and the Queen in her handbag, and they would quickly run through the formal subjects for discussion.

The relationship with Callaghan, who freely confesses he found the Queen's advice highly supportive,[15] was easier not only because his policies were less socially divisive, but also because, taken to its philosophical conclusion, the Thatcherite dream of a dynamic, enterprise-based meritocracy had no place for a family which reigned simply by blood-right. The monarchy is the keystone which holds the arching class system in place. It promotes the idea that advancement is by acceptance rather than enterprise or originality. If Britain's performance since the war has been worse than that of many of her competitors, then the Crown must take part of the blame.

Yet patriotism is the easiest of declamatory prejudices. Since the monarchy is in so many respects the visible representation of the nation, the merest whiff of criticism draws the fire of every tub-thumping little Englander with access to a microphone. George Bernard Shaw claimed that 'Kings are not born, they are made by universal hallucination'. The common assumption is that the survival of the monarchy is proof of the enduring British attachment to its hallucination. But it is also the consequence of effective management and skilful public relations by a unique family and their advisers. Neither Socialist nor right-wing governments have come remotely close to threatening the monarchy, demonstrating the relative institutional strengths of the political world and the privileged, quasi-magical world of the Court. The benefits of this curious survival – stability, 'one nation'-ism and the rest, are well enough chronicled. But we should recognize the disadvantges too.

Should a nuclear bomb ever fall on Norfolk, the handful of bureaucrats, policemen and soldiers scrambling into the underground bunker will be joined by a mustard manufacturer. Timothy James Colman, a director of Reckitt and Colman, is married to a lady-in-waiting to Princess Alexandra. He has been Lord Lieutenant of Norfolk since 1978, and lord lieutenants are guaranteed a seat in the emergency underground seats of government.

Precisely what they would do to justify their share of the precious filtered air in the bunker is unclear, although only marginally less so than the process by which they were chosen for the job in the first place. They represent one of the last truly feudal institutions in Britain. Although procedurally they are selected by the appointments secretary at Downing Street, in practice the Queen is asked for her informal approval before a nomination is made: the prime minister's private secretary writes to the Queen's private secretary saying 'the Prime Minister has it in mind to recommend to Your Majesty the appointment of Fotherington-Smythe to be Lord Lieutenant of Borsetshire.' As the lord lieutenant acts as the monarch's personal representative in the county in question, whom the Queen selects for the post gives an interesting insight into the sort of people with whom the royal family identifies.

No formal list of qualifications for the job exists. The little blue handbook given to newly-appointed lieutenants explains that their prime responsibility is to 'uphold the dignity of the Crown'. They are further charged with promoting the industrial and social life of the county and encouraging good works. Ordinary people who have been awarded 'less important' decorations like the British Empire Medal may well find it pinned on their chest not by the Queen but a lord lieutenant in the form of a retired colonel or minor baronet. At the Annual General Meeting of the Lord Lieutenants' Association – surely Britain's most exclusive trade union – there is much discussion of such knotty questions as whether the pushy chairman of the local district council has, as he insists he has, the right to be presented to the Queen before the laid-back leader of the county council.

These may seem somewhat recondite fripperies, but the activities of the lord lieutenants ensure that the fine gradations of class distinction filter out from the Court across the land. And contact with royalty gives the lord lieutenants real influence. Because everyone knows they have a direct channel of communication to the Palace, their ear is sought. They can recommend individuals for honours or awards – often the district postmistress who has spent fifty years behind the counter and then receives an unexpected OBE will have been suggested by the local lord lieutenant. The socially ambitious know it is the lord lieutenant who arranges who gets to meet the Queen, so the embossed invitations to his receptions are rarely refused. His phone calls do not go unanswered, and because few councillors or officials will decline to speak to him he has a disproportionately influential voice on questions like the route of a planned by-pass. More than one lord lieutenant told me almost apologetically of the number of supplicants who sought his intervention with the democratically-chosen authorities.

The lord lieutenancy was originally devised by the Tudors as a means of internal security. The first true holder of the post, Lord Russell, had been ordered by the privy council to raise his troops to put down a West Country revolt against the prayer book. Under Mary, the Crown set up a sliding scale of military liability, so that poorer members of the community were obliged to supply a suit of armour, spear and bow and arrow, while those worth a thousand pounds or more were expected to provide sixteen horses, sixty suits of armour, fifty helmets, forty pikes, thirty long-bows, twenty bills, and twenty arquebuses. At the peak of this hierarchy, Elizabeth I set a personal commander in each county, who was to have charge of the local militia; the lord lieutenant thus became the monarch's personal representative. The responsibilities of the lord lieutenant for raising the militia only disappeared in 1921.[16]

The other duty of the lord lieutenant under Elizabeth was the appointment of justices of the peace. He was thus at the head of the rule of the squires. They still often continue, in the capacity of *Custos Rotulorum*, to be the senior magistrate in the county and usually sit as chairman of the committee which recommends the names of new justices of the peace to the Lord Chancellor, a partial explanation for the dull, middle-class nature of the magistracy.

The justification for reserving this not uninfluential role to a small number of wealthy, landed families was that since they had to act as the Queen's hosts when she visited the county, they needed a house big enough to accommodate her and her entourage. Nowadays, if staying overnight far away from any of the royal residences, she tends to use the royal train, but lord lieutenants continue to be drawn from the same big houses. In practice, most of them have previously been deputy lieutenants. As deputy lieutenants are chosen not by the Queen or the Downing Street appointments secretary, but by the existing lord lieutenant, 'subject to the non-disapproval of the Queen', most of the lieutenancy is a self-electing little clique.

They are a distinguished-looking bunch, particularly when arrayed in all their blue, gold and scarlet finery for some official function. Not surprisingly, a significant number have a military background. They are almost all rich old men, since most are appointed when in their fifties and don't retire until they reach seventy-five: Lord Leverhulme was appointed Lord Lieutenant of Cheshire in 1949 and served for forty years. In 1990 there were two women among them, Mrs Susan Williams, a keen race-goer who represents the Queen in South Glamorgan, and Lavinia, Duchess of Norfolk, in West Sussex. The rest were viscounts, earls, baronets and scions of 'county' families with names Ike Bowes-Lyon, Ponsonby and Smith-Ryland. Many had fathers who were lord lieutenants before them. In Scotland they are particularly weighted towards ancient titles and service ranks – only two unadorned names jostle among the thirty-one earls, baronets and colonels. They also tend to be substantial landowners. The Earl of Yarborough, a mere deputy Lord Lieutenant in Lincolnshire, has twenty-eight thousand acres, over which the family's pack, the Brockleby Hounds range freely. Robin Leigh-Pemberton, who has a full-time job as Governor of the Bank of England in addition to being Lord Lieutenant of Kent, sits on an estate of 2,400 acres. Lord Leverhulme has eight thousand acres in Lancashire and another twenty-seven thousand acres in Sutherland.

There are a number of counties – Berkshire, Norfolk, Aberdeenshire, and now Gloucestershire – in which, because they contain royal residences, the Queen takes a particularly close personal interest. It is revealing, therefore, to see what sort of people are thought to fit the bill in these places. In Berkshire she chose Colonel Gordon Palmer, an Old Etonian heir to the biscuit empire of Huntley and Palmer. In Norfolk she picked Timothy Colman; in Aberdeenshire, Captain Colin Farquharson, formerly of the Brigade of Guards and subsequently a land agent; and in Gloucestershire, Colonel Martin Gibbs, another military Old Etonian. All told, of the forty-six male English lord lieutenants in 1990, no less than thirty had been at Eton.

There are occasional signs of attempts by Downing Street to infiltrate a new type of person into the ranks of the lieutenancy. When the need arose to find a new lord lieutenant for East Sussex in succession to the Queen's horseracing chum, the Marquess of Abergavenny, the name which emerged from Downing Street was not that of another grand county family but Admiral Sir Lindsay Bryson, a retired naval engineering officer whose address, 74, Dyke Road, Brighton, hardly hinted at rolling acres. Admiral Bryson, an expert on guided weapons, was not of conventional lord lieutenant stock. Apart from anything else, his family came from Glasgow (unlike twenty-five of the thirty-one Scottish lord lieutenants, Admiral Bryson had also been educated in Scotland), as several of the big Sussex landowners who had been hoping for the job quickly pointed out. The Queen had taken little or no interest in the appointment when the informal suggestion of Admiral Bryson came from Downing Street in 1989. When she heard the grumbles of the county landowners after the announcement, she may have wished she had done.

Their apparent wealth notwithstanding, there are rumblings of unease within parts of the lieutenancy about the cost of it all. Except for an entitlement to a police car and driver when attending official functions, they receive no formal allowances. Most expect to meet the out-of-pocket expenses of the job themselves, but some feel the whole business is getting too costly. To begin with, there is the expense of the uniform, which London military tailors run up for about £2,000. Most lord lieutenants are scarcely in jobs where they have employers breathing down their necks about time off, but there can be substantial day-to-day expenses. In corners of rural Scotland the lord lieutenant may only be required to turn out four or five times a year, but in densely populated industrial areas like the West Midlands, Charles Ian Finch-Knightley, the eleventh Earl of Aylesford, may be performing several times a month. In Kent, the rate runs at an average of one official engagement a week. The lord lieutenants have used their association to act like any trade union, and lobbied for a government grant. They were more successful than most trade unions confronting the government in the 1980s: a hugely discreet slush fund now exists under which their lordships can be reimbursed by the taxpayer. Payments are made through the Home Office in England, and the Welsh, Scottish and Northern Ireland Offices elsewhere. In the year 1990–91, £250,000 was made available by the Home Office to the lord lieutenants. Precisely what the taxpayer got in return is less easily quantified.

There are few more impressively glittering sights in Britain than the summer afternoon at the start of Ascot week when the members of perhaps the most prestigious order of chivalry in Christendom process through the grounds of Windsor Castle. Preceded by the quaintly named Fitzalan Pursuivant Extraordinary, Rouge Croix Pursuivant, Portcullis Pursuivant and the ten other equally lexicographically obscure officers of the College of Arms, each in crested and quartered gold tunics, the two dozen knights of the Order of the Garter shuffle slowly into St George's Chapel beneath a cloudless sky.

They walk ponderously in their crimson velvet hoods and black caps, ostrich plumes nodding on their old men's heads. Two or three look so pale and frail, you wonder whether the heat and the heavy robes will all be too much. What is the protocol for removing a collapsed Knight of the Garter? Inside the chapel the Honourable Company of Gentlemen at Arms, swords drawn and helmets catching the rays of sun through the windows, guard the Quire. A fanfare sounds. There are perhaps two or three hundred uniforms on display, scarlet, blue, gold and white. It all appears perfectly timeless but, like so much British pageantry, it is a relatively modern creation. The honour itself, however, dark velvet and buckled just below the knee on the left leg, is genuinely ancient, for the Garter is the second oldest decoration, founded by Edward III in about 1348. Apart from its royal members, the number of Knights of the Garter is limited to twenty-four, and this restriction, coupled with the fact that since 1946 it has been once more in the personal gift of the monarch, makes its membership peculiarly exclusive.

They are all old men she has chosen, men in the cloudy twilight of past glories. For generations it was customary that the heads of certain households became members, so that 'Garter families' developed: at least twenty-five out of thirty-eight Beauforts, Marlboroughs, Northumberlands and Salisburys have been admitted as members.[17] But as they processed into the Quire of the royal chapel in June 1988 the ancient families were in a minority. Taking their seats beneath their personal banners were the former socialist prime ministers Lords Callaghan and Wilson, the past Conservative cabinet ministers Lords Carrington and Hailsham, two departed governors of the Bank of England, a representative from the retired top brass of each of the services, two White Commonwealth knights, the explorers Lords Hunt and Shackleton. The Dukes of Norfolk, Northumberland and Grafton were there, Lords Leverhulme and Waldegrave and Sir Cennydd Traherne to represent county life. Viscount De L'Isle VC and Lord Longford were rewarded for military and moral valour. Of the twenty non-royal knights who processed into the chapel, all except for the two former Labour prime ministers had been at public schools. Three had taken military training, and the remaining fifteen had attended either Oxford or Cambridge. From the terrace beside the chapel you look down on the playing fields of Eton. I wondered how many of them glanced down as they processed in their finery into the castle for tea with the Queen. Their lives had been a circular journey: no less than nine of them had spent their schooldays there.

The frequently mistranslated motto of the Garter, *Honi soit qui mal y pense*, derives from an incident at the ball to celebrate the capture of Calais when the Countess of Salisbury, either accidentally or otherwise, dropped a garter. King Edward bent to pick it up amid suggestive laughter, declaring 'shame on him who thinks evil of it', and prophesying that he would make it the most sought-after badge of honour in Britain. They are not words which spring immediately to mind when considering the honours system in general. Apart from the Garter, the Order of the Thistle, the Order of Merit, and the Royal Victorian

Order, other decorations come not from the fount of honour but from the desk of a Whitehall functionary or the nudge of a political friend. Many of the most apparently distinguished honours are a reward for little more than longevity or political servitude.

The class hierarchy is alive and well in the gradations through the 250 different decorations which the Crown awards. The system ensures that those who might seem most deserving receive perhaps an Order of the British Empire (OBE) – or a British Empire Medal (BEM) for those 'who do not qualify by rank for the higher awards' – while a bureaucrat who has successfully worked his way to the top of the civil service without putting a foot wrong will get a knighthood in the Order of the Bath. The civil division of the Order of the Bath is the jealously guarded preserve of the home civil service, so that every six months a new crop of bureaucrats begin making their way from Companion of the Bath to Knight Commander or Dame Commander to Knight Grand Cross. The principle is the good old British device of Buggins' Turn. The ambitious soldier can expect a similar progression, from Commander of the Bath when he becomes brigadier, to KCB when he reaches lieutenant-general and GCB when he eventually storms the summit of military life. Foreign Office worthies look forward to a parallel rise through the ranks of the Order of St Michael and St George, from CMG (Call Me God), to KCMG (Kindly Call Me God) to GCMG (God Calls Me God), on the theory that gullible foreigners will be more impressed by the ambassador of a second-division power if he's called Sir Cuthbert Smith instead of plain Mr Smith. Melbourne remarked of the Order of the Garter that 'there's no damned merit in it'. The same could be said of most of these awards, which are simply a perk of the post, along with the £60,000 or £70,000 salary, retirement at sixty, and an index-linked pension thereafter.

The fiction is maintained that these lists of the worthy, the deserving and the hitherto unrecognized are supervised, if not by the Queen herself, then at least by her staff. In reality, the list has taken shape in the Cabinet Office. Senior civil servants somehow find time from the burdens of office to sit around deliberating over who really deserves what. Not only do they agonize over which of their colleagues deserve which piece of ribbon, they are unafraid to set themselves in judgement upon those whose candidacy for an honour is based upon genuine distinction, perhaps in the arts or by voluntary work. The moment one list has been published, the various subcommittees begin drawing up the next. Only about one fifth of names submitted make it through to the final roll-call of the main Honours Committee. There are exquisite gradations of worth to be decided upon: what does Colonel Bristlebrow deserve for his services to Scouting, an MBE or an OBE? Doubtless their minds are uncluttered by the thought that in the fullness of time they themselves will appear on the list. But they are not renowned for their adventurousness and the final product has an arbitrary dullness about it that suggests the product of a predictable corporate culture. It is the cast of mind which decrees that Henry Cotton, the most successful British golfer of the last fifty years should get an MBE rather than a knighthood, the same level of honour as a shorthand note-taker in the House of Commons or the draftsman of regulations governing haddock quotas.

The intellectual life of Britain is, not surprisingly, under-represented. One honour, the Order of Merit, restricted to a couple of dozen members, is designed to reflect intellectual eminence, and is in the personal gift of the Queen. Cultural standards in the court have risen since George III remarked to Edward Gibbon, when the latter had just finished his *Decline and Fall of the Roman Empire*, 'Another big fat book! Scribble, scribble, scribble, eh, Mr Gibbon?' and this century the Order has been awarded to Thomas Hardy, Ralph Vaughan Williams and Bertrand Russell. Their successors include Graham Greene, Sir Yehudi Menuhin, Lord Zuckerman, Dame Veronica Wedgwood, Sir Sidney Nolan, Sir Isaiah Berlin and Professor Dorothy Hodgkin. A perk of the office is to be invited to lunch with the Queen every few years. Some of them are also Companions of Honour, an order additionally used as a way of rewarding prime ministers' political friends, so that Norman Tebbitt and Lord Whitelaw, neither known as retiring aesthetes, rub shoulders with Anthony Powell, Lucien Freud and Dame Ninette de Valois.

The honours system provides governments with a means of distributing favours at no cost. Macmillan showered political honours on his backbenchers like confetti, and during the thirteen years of Conservative government which ended in 1964 over two hundred MPs, one third of all those who sat on the Tory benches, were rewarded with some sort of gong.[18] In the next Conservative government, Edward Heath was so lukewarm about the idea that between 1970 and 1973 only nine political knighthoods were awarded, provoking complaints of knight starvation. From Julian Critchley, destined for a lifetime on the backbenches, came the anguished question:

Is then an MP, who must keep the hours of a street-walker; who is understood to be – if the public is to be believed – either impotent or corrupt; who spends the best years of his life listening to Ministers' speeches, and to the complaints of his constituents; is he to receive as his only reward after twenty years of service a signed photograph of Jim Prior? Surely not.[19]

Mrs Thatcher was cute enough to see the need to cultivate the backbenchers who made up her lobby fodder and the knighthood became once again the reward for wrecked marriages and broken health caused by sitting up all night to vote as the whips instructed. Her first honours list contained fifty awards for Conservative party politicians and supporters. By the end of the decade, 100 MPs had become knights or lords.

Not all of the recipients of honours were backbenchers, and over the following years journalists, industrialists and bankers sympathetic to the cause were handed decorations of one kind or another. Businessmen who served as political advisers, like Jeffrey Sterling, Derek Rayner and John Hoskyns were given knighthoods. Political friends like the former Labour MP Woodrow Wyatt were rewarded with peerages, and other loyal supporters in the press also benefited. Sir Larry Lamb of the *Sun*, Sir John Junor of the *Sunday Express*, Sir David English of the *Daily Mail*, Lord Matthews of Express Newspapers and Lord Stevens of United Newspapers, all owe their handles to political loyalty.

Although nothing like as corrupt as the practices of Lloyd George and his broker Maundy Gregory, when a visitor to his office at 38 Parliament Street could buy a knighthood, baronetcy or peerage, depending upon whether he wished to spend £10,000 or £100,000, there are plenty of signs of a correspondence between political donations and the receipt of honours. In the first six years of the Thatcher premiership eleven private sector industrialists were given peerages. Subsequent analysis by the Labour Research Department revealed that they all directed companies which had given donations totalling £1.9 million to Conservative party funds.[20] Sir Nicholas Cayzer, whose baronetcy had been given to his father by Lloyd George, was raised to the peerage by Margaret Thatcher in 1982. That year his company had given £95,810 to party funds. Sir James Hanson's Hanson Trust gave £82,000 to the cause the year he became a Lord. Alistair McAlpine became Lord McAlpine of West Green in the year that his firm donated £43,000. Lords Forte, Taylor (of the construction giant Taylor

Woodrow), Weinstock, King, Edwin McAlpine, Matthews, Vinson and Sieff had also coincidentally been associated with companies which had given money to the Conservative cause.

There is no suggestion that these honours were 'bought', nor that the recipients were anything other than entirely worthy and deserving. But it is quite a coincidence.

Political honours have to pass the scrutiny of a committee made up of Lords Shackleton, Pym and Grimond, a team scrupulously chosen to represent the three main strands of opinion in parliament, and each of them himself the recipient of a life peerage at an earlier date.

Harold Wilson's resignation honours list was the one which has caused the committee most anxiety in recent years. Its honours for impresarios and maverick businessmen – what The Times called examples of 'unrepentant Darwinism, of the business survival of the fittest and of nature red in tooth and claw'[21] – so appalled them and the Palace that it took several weeks for approval to be obtained. Two of the recipients, Joseph Kagan, a mackintosh manufacturer subsequently convicted of theft, and the property developer Eric Miller, who shot himself during a fraud investigation some eighteen months later, proved the justice of the concern. It subsequently emerged that part of the list had been drawn up by Wilson's private secretary, Lady Falkender (plain Marcia Williams until ennobled in another honours spree), on a sheet of lavender writing paper. When the list reached Buckingham Palace the Queen found herself almost as impotent as George V fifty years earlier. The name of a sports promoter disappeared from the list, and another candidate was downgraded from a peerage to a knighthood. For the rest, the Queen's private secretary merely asked whether Sir Harold was serious. He was. The Queen acceded.

George V had found Lloyd George's scattering of honours 'disagreeable and distasteful', according to his private secretary, Lord Stamfordham,[22] and while no subsequent prime minister has abused the system to anything like the same degree, they cannot kick the habit. The Crown, in whose name the whole thing is being enacted, can only accept a *fait accompli*.

The honours system developed in medieval Britain as a means of maintaining the strict hierarchy necessary for monarchical rule: a place for everyone and everyone in their place. It is too strong to say that it has been corrupted – after all, James I dished out so many knighthoods (2,600) that the Venetian ambassador to London thought the knights 'no longer distinguishable from common people' – but at best it is dull. The majority of higher honours are dished out to people who have done nothing more than their job, for which they are already well rewarded. The civil and foreign services treat the whole thing as if a gong is just another perk of the job. Those who are nominated from outside the government service are a predictable mixture of retired headmistresses, regional general managers and council clerks. Political honours are either an almost contemptuous gesture towards those who have kept silent when their consciences might have told them to vote against a government bill, or a reward for money or advice. And there is something bizarre and distasteful about the juxtapositions the system can create. In the same list of honours in which one of the firemen who broke his ribs fighting the disastrous fire at Bradford football stadium received the lowly BEM, Gordon Reece, an advertising executive who helped run Margaret Thatcher's election campaign, was given a knighthood.

The essence of royalty is its exclusivity. Bagehot's magic depends upon the fact that the common man or woman remains just that; he or she cannot, except by the most exceptional marriage, become part of the royal family. Yet the purpose of the honours system is to confer a form of proxy, subsidiary, membership of this family. It is a contradiction which thousands happily go along with because they are keen to advance up the social ladder.

The British – even those who claim to be attached to the virtues of the enterprise culture – are too addicted to the class system and the honours baubles to give them up. Of all the letters sent out each year inquiring, disingenuously, whether 'this mark of the Queen's favour' would be acceptable, only about a dozen get a negative reaction. If we are to keep the whole pantomime, the grounds for the awarding of honours need re-examining, and some thought given to how to make the business more representative of a broader spectrum of achievement. And the time is long past when the question of who deserves what was taken out of the hands of politicians and time-serving bureaucrats and given to a genuinely independent and truly meritorious body which might set about trying to put honour back into the honours system.

CHAPTER THREE

Etonians and Estonians

Here richly, with ridiculous display,
The Politician's corpse was laid away.
While all of his acquaintance sneered and slanged
I wept: for I had longed to see him hanged.

– 'Epitaph on the Politician Himself' HILAIRE BELLOC

'I T USED TO BE an honour to have the local MP to dine,' a big Yorkshire landowner told me. 'Now you count the spoons after they've gone.'

This handing over of the Conservative party, in Denis Healey's phrase, 'from the estate owners to the estate agents', has been a process upper class Tories have watched with distaste. Like a vile-tasting patent medicine, they appreciate the need for treatment, but find it hard to swallow. They distrust the people who have replaced them. The caricature Tory MP of thirty years ago was a knight of the shires; his contemporary counterpart might more accurately be called Morden Man. His most striking characteristic is his suburbanity. The knights of the shires have disappeared as the shires themselves have succumbed to an urban sprawl in which the Sunday place of worship is no longer the village church but the DIY superstore. (So much so that when, at the 1989 party conference, a delegate got up to speak in defence of Sunday as a day of worship, he was met with a chorus of boos from shopkeepers on the floor.) The dominant interest represented on the Conservative backbenches is that of the dormitory town and the metropolitan county. Even Sir John Stokes, the bristle-brushed old gent for whom 'the twentieth century has been a mistake', sat in the Commons representing the Birmingham dormitories of Halesowen and Stourbridge, where the closest most of his supporters had come to a foxhunt was a roadside cocktail lounge called the Whip and Saddle.

The parliamentary party has taken on a new style, in which the old alliance of interests to which Henry Fairlie alluded has fractured. Mention the Archbishop of Canterbury or the Director-General of the

BBC to many of the new Tories, and there is an instantaneous, Pavlovian, hostility. Although prepared to get into the occasional lather over the destruction of 'heritage', many have little time for old money, and profess their heroes to be self-made men who have succeeded by their own efforts. Where the old Tory MP had joined the party to keep the country the way it was, the present Conservative joined to change it.

It was all so different in 1959, when Julian Critchley, the party's resident music-hall artiste, rumbled into Westminster in his Ford Popular as a new MP:

> You could tell a Tory just by looking at him. He was well suited. The party still retained something of its pre-war sleekness; elderly gentlemen in Trumper's haircuts, wearing cream silk shirts and Brigade or Old Etonian ties. Everyone seemed related to everyone else. I was forever being accosted, when sitting quietly in the Smoking Room (the far corner of which was occasionally occupied by the grander Labour MP such as Hugh Gaitskell or Richard Crossman), by nice old buffers who claimed to have known my father. Many had had a 'good war', and one cure for contempt was to discover, while sitting in the Library during all night sittings, a slim volume such as *How I Rowed Across The North Sea Singlehanded*, by Sir Hugh Munro Lucas-Tooth.
>
> Within my first week or so in the House, I was sitting in the Smoking Room reading a book. Charles Hill, who had spoken for me at Chatham Town Hall during the election, came up to me. 'Young man, it does not do to appear clever: advancement in the party is due entirely to alcoholic stupidity.' I have taken care never to open a book since . . .
>
> I sat uneasily in this assembly of bumblebees. Shrewsbury, the Sorbonne and Pembroke College, Oxford, enabled me, or so I thought, to pass for white, although of my grandfathers one had been a railwayman on the London and Northwestern and the other a clerk in Bristol Gas Works. I gave up the stiff white collars that I had worn at the advertising agency and was careful to wear plain ties; but my suits were Burton's at £10 a time. One evening I was in the 'No' lobby waiting to file past the clerks to record my vote on a three-line whip. Out of a crowd of more than three hundred I noticed Sir Jocelyn Lucas, with whom I had never exchanged a word, making his way determinedly in my direction, and I watched him breast the wave like Captain Webb, twisting and turning. Could he be about to invite me to dinner? Or to congratulate me on my maiden speech? He took my elbow in the palm of his hand. 'You're wearin' suede shoes,' he said, and promptly vanished. Today we are all wearing suede shoes. [1]

Critchley's party-piece has the rounded phrasing, the well-turned punchline of frequent rehearsal (it's claimed that some of his fans can recite it back to him), but it captures the tone of the Tories in those

days perfectly. The party of that generation was dominated by amateurs. They went into politics because it was one of the things that a
certain type of person in a certain station did. It has been romanticized
as a tradition of public service when much of it was about the
protection of vested interests. But in the end, politics for many of
them was a sideline, a diversion, a supplement. Something happened
to political life in Britain when it became the preserve of professionals.
It was not a sudden transformation, but by the late eighties there were
precious few figures prominent in political life who were anything
other than careerists. 'Career politicians are almost the only politicians
left in the upper echelons of British politics and government,' observed
Professor Anthony King, the loquacious professor of government at
Essex University in the early eighties.[2]

The breed of Tories who passed through the Commons 'on their
way from the Brigade of Guards to the House of Lords', is no more.
After the 1987 election, the parliamentary party had only eleven MPs
who had served in the Guards, and a further eight who had been
cavalry officers. Most new MPs enter the Commons in their thirties
and forties; there are fewer very young politicians, and – despite all
the blather about the 'party of enterprise' – fewer going into politics
in their fifties, after a successful career elsewhere. The party expects
its young hopefuls to fight at least one unwinnable seat in a rotting
inner city or municipal wilderness before letting them have a crack at
a seat in the safe suburbs. So, they spend more and more time in the
business of politics and less and less in the business of business.

And the proposition that the Conservative benches are now occupied
by men and women whose ambitions have been forged in industry is
greatly exaggerated. The proportion of Tory MPs in the 1951 parliament with a background in business was thirty-five per cent. By the
1987 parliament it had risen only to thirty-seven per cent.[3] This is not
a party dominated by technocrats who have fearlessly built great
industries, but 'Increasingly politicians without a great deal of first-
hand experience of the world outside politics are running the country,
including the economy, in conjunction with civil servants who similarly
lack first-hand experience of the world outside politics,' Anthony
King noted as long ago as 1981.[4] The new Conservatives not only
wear off-the-peg suits, they adopt off-the-peg philosophies: they have
something their predecessors would have sneered at. They have ideolo-
gies.

Lord Home, the last Etonian prime minister, disliked politics because it interfered with his sport. He kept a set of bags packed inside the door of Downing Street, so he could escape at the earliest opportunity to the grouse moors or trout streams. By contrast, the 1987 intake included a mere nineteen MPs who were farmers or landowners, and only twenty-four who listed any kind of field sports as a recreation, a far cry from the party of thirty years earlier. As political life became dominated by people who were in it as a career, the shires felt betrayed. The *Field* complained:

> We are represented by men hungry for high political office who will therefore not rock the party boat; men whose loyalty is to their political careers, not necessarily their constituents; men who know nothing of rural life, for why should they, nurtured as they were in towns or suburbs? What do such men or women know (or care) about agriculture, forestry, field sports, immigration (for they are immigrants themselves)?[5]

Many of the new breed were people for whom, in Andrew Roth's words 'capitalism doesn't have an unacceptable face'.[6] It was most noticeable at the annual conferences, held in windswept seaside resorts in early October. Old-fashioned MPs, unlike the new generation who happily turn up at the annual conference, went out of their way to dream up family illnesses, unavoidable business meetings or urgent missions to Kurdistan to avoid these gatherings. The annual demands to bring back the rope, the murmurings about repatriating immigrants, the calls to purge the nation of social welfare scroungers, were for them a sojourn in purgatory. Those who could not escape put in a token appearance, showing themselves before the delegates from their local constituency association and then scuttling off on the first train back to civilization. There was more than a touch of class disdain in their attitude, but it also signified a political distance, an understanding that the parliamentary representatives had softer views and a broader idea of their responsibilities than the mere enactment of their supporters' prejudices.

There aren't many nobs left in the Commons. The last representative of the four-hundred-year-old Cecil family political tradition left at the 1987 election. Lord Cranborne, son of the sixth Marquess of Salisbury, had sat for the family constituency of south Dorset for eight years: his grandfather, 'Bobbety' the fifth Marquess, had served eleven and a half years as an MP before joining the peerage and becoming one of the most influential party men in the fifties. The grandest MP to remain in the Commons today is Lord James Douglas-Hamilton, brother of the Duke of Hamilton, a former Oxford boxer and author. One other MP sitting on the government benches under an apparently plebeian name, Richard Needham, is in reality the sixth Earl of Kilmorey, an Irish title. The chain-smoking Nicholas Ridley is the younger son of the third Viscount Ridley, and has had ancestors on the Tory benches for two hundred years. William Waldegrave's father, the twelfth Earl Waldegrave, was a junior agriculture minister under Macmillan, and his sister, Lady Susan Hussey, is a lady-in-waiting to the Queen. Archie Hamilton, son of the third Baron Hamilton, who served as Parliamentary private secretary to Margaret Thatcher, is another example of the old tradition accommodating itself to the new spirit in the party.

There are a handful of representatives of well-known political families, like Nicholas Soames and the present Winston of the Churchills, the Douglases Hogg and Hurd, who are both the sons and grandsons of MPs, while the father of Sir Charles and Peter Morrison ('Pinky and Perky') was Lord Margadale, who had been chairman of the backbench 1922 Committee in the fifties and sixties. The journalist Hugh Montgomery-Massingberd, continuing his indefatigable quest for the *ancien régime*, identified a clutch of MPs who owned country houses, including Paul Channon and Mark Lennox-Boyd of the Guinness dynasty (the story goes that when Channon was selected for his seat in Southend, which had been represented by the family since 1912, local advertising hoardings were proclaiming 'Have Another Guinness!'). Alan Clark, son of the distinguished art historian, lives at Saltwood Castle, and William Benyon, the MP for Milton Keynes, owns the Englefield estate, fourteen thousand acres of agricultural land in the home counties.

The 1990s are likely to see the last days of the political baronets. Sir Anthony Meyer's self-destructive challenge to the leadership of Margaret Thatcher cost him the support of his constituency party early in 1990, but, like Sir Ian Gilmour, he was merely symptomatic of a cast of mind common to many of the baronetcy. They are a declining band. 'That is not to say that the squirearchy is extinct, rather that the squires that survive would not touch politics with a pitchfork.' 'Oh my Bromley-Davenport and Anstruther-Gray of long ago,' lamented Montgomery-Massingberd. 'The inevitable conclusion is that the Tory party in the Thatcher age has become irredeemably middle-class.'[7]

Or so goes the conventional wisdom. It is instructive to see what has become of the role in the party of Britain's most exclusive school.

All but one of the seventeen MPs mentioned in the preceding three paragraphs had attended Eton, but the proportion of Etonians on the Conservative benches has been dropping steadily ever since the end of the Second World War. After the 1945 election more than a quarter of the Conservative parliamentary party had been at Eton. By 1959, the proportion had dropped to one fifth. After the 1987 election, scarcely more than a tenth (eleven per cent) of MPs had been at the school. This is still a remarkable proportion for one school to produce, but it is a shadow of Eton's former prominence.

'The Tory party is run by about five people,' Oliver Poole had said in 1961, 'who all treat their followers with disdain. They're mostly Etonians, and Eton is good for disdain.'[8] Iain Macleod, the former Chairman of the Party, thought the group slightly bigger, a 'magic circle', in which 'eight out of the nine mentioned . . . went to Eton.'[9] The occasion of Macleod's fury was the process by which Lord Home had come to be chosen as Leader of the party and thereby Prime Minister in succession to Harold Macmillan. The party's idea of internal democracy was, to say the least, idiosyncratic. When Anthony Eden resigned the premiership in broken health in January 1957, the two obvious contenders had been R.A. Butler and Harold Macmillan. Before going to the Palace to advise the Queen on whom she should summon, 'Bobbety' Salisbury called the Cabinet to his office, and simply asked, in his thin, piercing voice, 'Well, which is it to be, Wab or Hawold?'[10] In choosing Macmillan over Butler they were choosing Eton over Marlborough.

Although hailed by Randolph Churchill as being 'Tory democracy in action', the 1963 process was no more open. 'The customary processes of consultation' would be gone through, Macmillan had written to the Conservative party conference in Blackpool from his hospital bed in London, racked with the pain of an inflamed prostate gland. He instructed the Chief Whip to sound out MPs and the Lord Chancellor to gauge the mood in the Cabinet. But in private he had already told Lord Home that he should prepare to succeed him, and the 'customary processes' duly resulted in Home being chosen.

The fourteenth Earl of Home had been marked for prominence since childhood. Cyril Connolly had been a contemporary at Eton, and painted the most celebrated pen-portrait of the Prime Minister-to-be in 1938. He recalled that Home had been

the kind of graceful, tolerant, sleepy boy who is showered with favours and crowned with all the laurels, who is liked by the masters and admired by the boys without any apparent exertion on his part, without experiencing the ill-effects of success himself or arousing the pangs of envy in others. In the eighteenth century he would have become prime minister before he was thirty; as it was he appeared honourably ineligible for the struggle of life.[11]

Connolly's observation is often taken to confirm him as a better judge of literature than of politics, but in many ways he was remarkably prescient: Home was indeed 'honourably ineligible' for the new age which was dawning in the Tory party. His selection, the last spasm of the grouse-moor class, provoked feelings of extraordinary vehemence both among the growing band of young meritocrats within the party and many outside, among them Sammy Finer, then a professor of politics at Keele University. 'How could they choose this nothing man simply by a bit of finagling and jiggery-pokery behind the scenes. I said to myself I will not vote for the Conservative party again.'[12]

Once exposed, the Magic Circle succumbed to the relentless advance of the new middle-class Conservatives like Macleod, Reginald Maudling, Enoch Powell and Edward Heath. When Sir Alec lost the 1964 election their hour arrived, and all but Macleod stood for the leadership under a new system of open elections within the party. With the choice of Heath, the era of the bright grammar-school boys had arrived.

'We've failed a number of Etonians recently,' Tom Arnold, the party vice-chairman in charge of candidates in 1990, told me. 'They were the sort of people who twenty-five years ago would have been deferred to because they were gents. It won't wash any longer.'[13] Arnold, the genial, unassuming son of an impresario (and godson of Ivor Novello), cheerfully admits that the people likeliest to succeed in getting adopted as Tory candidates are those with the strongest suburban credentials.

So it is the middle class and upper middle class to whom the parliamentary party now belongs. Between 1945 and 1974, according to research analysing the backgrounds of Tory MPs,[14] the back benches remained dominated by the public schools and Oxford and Cambridge. Since then, however, the complexion has begun to alter significantly. The much publicized working-class Conservative has yet to take command of the green leather benches. True, increasing numbers are past pupils of day schools, notably the former 'direct grant' schools. To take two able junior ministers at random, no-one could claim that Peter Lilley, the son of a personnel officer, or John

Redwood, whose father was an accounts clerk, belonged in the patrician old Tory party.

By the 1990s the change to the meritocrats had begun to affect the highest levels of the party. Apart from herself and John Biffen, all nineteen members of Mrs Thatcher's first cabinet were public school men. Sixteen had been at Oxford or Cambridge, as had the Prime Minister. Three others had gone straight from public school into the services. Five had served in the Guards, two in the Cavalry. Six were Etonians, three were peers, and another three were knights or baronets. By 1990, only Sir Geoffrey Howe survived from the first cabinet. The number of Etonians had been cut by half (Douglas Hurd, Lord Belstead and Nicholas Ridley were the alumni remaining), and the great majority (sixteen of twenty-two) were still graduates of Oxford or Cambridge. Some of the new generation of cabinet ministers were products of city grammar schools like Nottingham (Kenneth Clarke), Lancaster (Cecil Parkinson) or Llanelli (Michael Howard). But in the main the Cabinet was the preserve of the second division public schools like Charterhouse (John Wakehan), Rugby (Tom King), or Sedbergh (David Waddington). The figures are inevitably distorted by the fact that several of the great old grammar schools opted to join the private sector after the Labour governments' reform of secondary education in the 1970s, but of the twenty-two schools attended by Cabinet ministers, eighteen belonged to the 1990 Headmasters' Conference. Not quite the supremacy of the self-made man that the party liked to pretend, but a distinct shift none the less.

The great change has been the disappearance of the landowners from the Tory benches. The distinctive tone of the old Conservative party was set by the land: even those who did not belong to great landed families still believed in some romantic notion of the spiritual strength of England's green and pleasant land. The creed had such a powerful hold upon the party that even Quintin Hogg, who later chose the life-peerage title Lord Hailsham of St Marylebone – you can hardly get more urban than that – was opining in 1947 that 'the Conservative believes that farming is more than a business; it is a way of life, essential to the community in war and peace.' The following year, R. A. Butler told the party conference:

> In saving agriculture, we are saving more than our own economy. We are saving a way of life in which the features are kindliness, freedom and above all, wisdom. These are the qualities of the countryman and the

countrywoman. They are instinctive with Conservative policy, they are
vital to our existence.[15]

This rosy view of rural life – no mention of manual toil, poor housing,
low wages – was easily developed into an outright contempt for
business and industry. 'We are not the party of unbridled, brutal
capitalism,' Eden confidently declaimed at the 1947 conference, adding
'and never have been.'

The old-fashioned shire Tories had instincts where others might
have policies, and there was an inevitable tension within the party
between paternalism and the spirit of free enterprise. The achievement
of Macmillan (who before the war once declared that 'Toryism has
always been a form of paternal socialism') was to adopt the more
liberal ideas of men like Butler to render the rest of the meal
palatable. Edward Heath's attempts to commit the party to something
more dynamic, outward-looking and enterprise-based, after the meeting at Selsdon Park in 1970, collapsed in the face of a corporate
culture which had become used to having things its own way under a
succession of both Conservative and Labour governments. In the end,
the radical change of direction which the country took under Mrs
Thatcher was the result not merely of the party donning a new suit of
clothes but of the electorate despairing at the failure of thirty years of
consensus politics to do anything to arrest the inexorable process of
national decline. Old-fashioned Tories were an inevitable focus for
animosity.

One of her wealthy former Cabinet ministers told me:

Margaret looks down on people like me. Because she and the others like
her rose by their own merits, they dislike those born above them. But they
also dislike those who were born into the same station in life, or further
down, and who haven't risen as far as they have. It doesn't leave many
people to like.

She thinks that we have absolutely no understanding of anybody because
we were born with a silver spoon in our mouths. I know she's wrong. I
spent the war years living alongside these chaps, living, eating and sleeping
with them a lot of the time. She got out of her background – which
incidentally was comfortable and middle class. I spent the war with chaps
who'd come into the army straight from the dole queues.[16]

The importance of the Second World War to this generation cannot
be overstated. In the first place the experience knitted these men
together, both to one another and to others who subsequently made

up 'the Establishment'. William Whitelaw's brother officers in the
Scots Guards included, for example, a future Archbishop of Canterbury, a future Lord Chamberlain, the man who would become Moder-
ator of the Church of Scotland, the future chairman of United
Biscuits and five lord lieutenants as well as the Home Secretary: not
bad for a single officers' mess. Not only did these men share the
hardships of combat, their very survival imbued many with a pre-
disposition to paternalism. Still deeply marked by the folk-memory of
the Depression, they looked kindly upon Keynesianism and would do
almost anything to avoid the dangers of mass unemployment. The
horrors of war made them want to prevent conflict. And the paternalistic traditions of the great landowners could be married relatively easily
to the responsibilities of a Welfare State, because in many ways they
were not really that different.

When Margaret Thatcher became leader the party was still dominated by these men who had been through the war together. Her
campaign for the leadership was run by Airey Neave, a war hero who
had escaped from Colditz and prosecuted Nazi war criminals after the
war was over. She had been only nineteen when the Second World
War ended, and by the start of the nineties was the elder statesman in
a cabinet which included several who had still been in nappies in 1945.
In the 1990 House of Commons there were only twenty-three Conservative MPs who had fought in the army during the war. It cannot
be mere coincidence that the abandonment of paternalism came about
when the party was on the cusp of a new generation of leaders.

The 1922 Committee of backbench MPs is led by Cranley Onslow,
stocky, ginger-haired and looking unaccountably like a surveyor who
has just arrived to advise on suspected dry rot in the roof. He belongs
to the slightly grand sector of the party, related to the Earls of Onslow
and married to the daughter of a fourteenth Earl. He rejects the
suggestion that they are no longer united by a common experience.
'We may not all have been through the war together,' he told me, 'but
we're all Conservative MPs and want to stay that way.'[17]

It is a revealing remark. Unity of ambition is a poor substitute for
unity of vision. It had all begun to unravel with Sir Keith Joseph's
Damascus Road conversion in September 1974, announced during his
seminal speech in Preston. It was the most important disavowal of
consensus politics in recent history. Sir Keith had been a member of
the Heath cabinet throughout the disastrous Tory administration of
the early seventies. Now he proclaimed that inflation was a much

more serious threat to national wellbeing than unemployment, which anyway was a greatly overestimated danger, and that what was needed was a much tighter control of the money supply and the budget deficit. By implication, the whole thrust of post-war economic policy had been misguided, dominated by a totally unrealistic fear of a return to the 1930s. 'We talked ourselves into believing that those gaunt, tight-lipped men in caps and mufflers were round the corner and tailored our policy to match these imaginary conditions.'[18] He had dared to slaughter a sacred cow.

The Centre for Policy Studies was only one of a series of institutions which now began to churn out papers, briefings, and a stream of serious young advisers in dark suits who saw it as their role to steer the party away from the errors of its past ways. Unlike the Labour party, where policy is made after debate at the annual conference, power over Conservative policy rests entirely with the headquarters in Central Office, the Cabinet or Shadow Cabinet, subject to the influence of MPs. The think tanks therefore had a much greater influence than they might have achieved with any other party. With the arrival of Mrs Thatcher in Downing Street, the new Toryism, something which was quite distinct from traditional Conservative policy, gained the upper hand.

Some of the advisers brought into government by Mrs Thatcher disliked the old-style Conservatism almost as much as they detested socialism. John Hoskyns, who was later knighted by a grateful Prime Minister for his work in running her Policy Unit, talked of the Churchill/Eden/Macmillan/Home period as 'the thirteen wasted years', a phrase borrowed from a Labour campaign slogan. In a fit of gloom at the failure of consensus, Hoskyns had sold his company in the seventies. Deciding to become involved in politics, he first sought out Lord Plowden, one of the grandest figures of the Great and Good, who had spent the thirty years since the war as one of Whitehall's most distinguished gofers. Hoskyns called on the great man in his chairman's office at Tube Investments. 'We began to talk,' Hoskyns recalled, 'and suddenly he stopped everything, and just asked "Who are you?" What he really meant was "I've looked you up in *Who's Who* and you're not there. And I don't know who you are."'[19] The meeting broke up a short time after, a bewildered Hoskyns leaving more convinced than ever that change would have to be wholesale. He detested the old-style Conservatives. 'The whole squirearchy, old school tie, old boy network was a recipe for disaster. A narrow social grouping just doesn't produce a rich enough mixture of ability and talent to regenerate a country. Even geneticists would agree with that.'[20]

'Out go the Etonians. In come the Estonians,' Harold Macmillan is said to have remarked after one of Margaret Thatcher's early cabinet reshuffles, and the men to whom the Prime Minister turned were certainly outside this small genetic pool. She owed a notable debt to Jews. It was Sir Keith Joseph who opened her eyes to what was subsequently dubbed 'Thatcherism'. He came from a comparatively well established family – the baronetcy he had inherited after Harrow and Oxford had been created in 1943. Others she favoured included Nigel Lawson, her Chancellor of the Exchequer, the grandson of a refugee from Latvia, and David Young, to whom she gave a peerage and a seat in the cabinet – his father had come from Lithuania. Leon Brittan, Trade Secretary until the Westland scandal, and Malcolm Rifkind, her Scottish Secretary, were also Jewish. Other kindred spirits were self-made gentiles, like Norman Tebbit, Cecil Parkinson or John Major, whose capacity to drag themselves up by their bootstraps appealed to her Methodist conscience.

The Whips' office is as good a place as any to examine the new complexion of the party. Since its task is to hold the vote together, by threat, bribe or flattery it is purposely chosen to give a political, social and geographical spread. Despite official denials that a blackball system exists, it has all the characteristics of a club, or as one member boasted, 'the Mafia'. At their regular dinners together, a former whip recalls, 'the atmosphere is very much like that at a second-rate public school or a duff regiment.' For a party supposedly in the hands of a new breed of Tories, the Commons whips were, in 1990, a pretty predictable bunch. For a start, there were no women. The fourteen men included two Etonians, and those who might be described as having a business background were outnumbered by bankers and professionals. No less than eleven of them were the products of public schools. The fabled working-class Tory MPs, such as they are, appear to continue sitting on the back benches, awaiting the orders of the officer-class.

Where once Tory MPs were made at Eton, now they are graduates of home counties motels. One sunny weekend at the end of April 1990, there are forty-six would-be members of Parliament milling around in the lobby of a formless overnight stopover near Heathrow Airport. It is not an immediately obvious choice for a dirty weekend, but the only other guests are those taking advantage of 'celebrate romance' special deals to keep the place ticking over while the weekday corporate businessmen are away. 'We will cosset you with fluffy towelling bathrobes, fresh flowers, a glossy magazine and a chilled bottle of champagne with breakfast,' promises the brochure.

In the old days, would-be MPs were spared all this embarrassment. You could pick up a seat by knowing the right people, having gone to the right school or being thought to be worth a few thousand – almost the first question put to the prospective MP for Richmond, Sir George Harvie-Watt, when he went up before the local selection committee in 1937 was whether he would subscribe £700 to the local association. Sir Neill Cooper-Key, Lord Rothermere's son-in-law, procured the safe Conservative seat of Hastings because, as a young army officer in 1945 he happened to be drinking in the bar of the Berkeley Hotel. The chairman of the Hastings Conservative association, a stolid chap with a serious need to find an MP fast, was staying at the hotel while he visited Central Office to collect a list of suitable candidates. None of them he knew personally, and most were completing their war service. Seeing a young officer in the bar, the chairman bought Cooper-Key a drink and asked him to give the list a quick once-over. Was he familiar with any of the names?

'Yes, I know him,' Cooper-Key would say, 'first-class chap. Pity about that business with the little boys in Cairo.' Or, 'should be recovered enough from the shell-shock by polling day.' Or, 'think he's fine now he's dried out.' Aghast at the roll-call of drunks, adulterers and pederasts that Central Office had fobbed off upon him, the baffled chairman turned to Cooper-Key and asked 'I don't suppose by any chance you'd consider it yourself would you?'

'Well,' Cooper-Key paused for a judicious few seconds, 'if you insist.' And so began a happy parliamentary career lasting until 1970.

It was a system which not merely connived at nepotism, it depended upon it. Those who got selected either for constituencies, or for the Central Office list when it was established in the 1950s, tended to be those whom old buffers in the party already had a pretty good idea about, because they knew their fathers, their regiments or their schools. It was the main reason the party stayed so long the creature of the Magic Circle and the explanation for the exclusion, time and again, of otherwise talented party-members who didn't happen to have the right pedigree. The selection procedure the forty-six week-enders were undergoing was devised in 1980 to recognize talent, wherever it came from. It may prove to be Margaret Thatcher's most lasting contribution to her party, for it is changing it irrevocably.

The system was invented by Brigadier Sir Nicholas Somerville, a former director of army recruiting, to a brief set by Sir Anthony Royle, then the party vice-chairman in charge of candidates. Somerville's procedure subjects would-be MPs to argument, interview, drafting tests and debate, and has some similarities with the selection tests for the Foreign Office or civil service: where the Foreign Office once had a country house, the Conservative party has a motel. The other difference is that the vast majority of successful candidates would undoubtedly fail the exams for entry to the higher levels of the bureaucracy.

The Conservative selection board was designed to bring the candidates' list into the latter half of the twentieth century by including more industrialists, more women, more representatives of ethnic minorities, and reducing the number of barristers looking for a congenial second career. Among the aspirant politicians milling around in the lobby are fourteen people from the world of business, a handful of barristers, a couple of teachers, two farmers, two academics, a journalist or two, a couple of housewives and a taxi-driver. Less than ten are women and only one – a fifty-eight-year-old Indian doctor making his fourth attempt – is from an ethnic minority.

Divided into groups of eight, each watched over by a party official, an MP and an industrialist, they begin with a series of discussions about current affairs. Most have spent all their sentient life as paid-up devotees, and the glib phrases soon roll off the tongue. In one room, a discussion about law and order soon gives a Yorkshire solicitor the chance to ask rhetorically, 'And do you know the age of the average criminal?' They all do, of course, since law and order is the one subject on which every single one has instinctive, visceral, views. He plunges on, before anyone can interject 'Yes, fifteen!'

Next door, the same discussion draws forth from a youth who looks about fifteen himself, 'We teach them the three Rs. Well let's add two more – right and wrong.' The slogan is so grey-haired that even at party conferences it wouldn't get a ripple of applause. He looks around for a moment, pleased as punch, then realizes that his fellow group members have all heard it a dozen times before.

'We are the party that has put the police back on the beat,' says the Indian doctor. 'The streets are safe. It is a real pleasure to see these young lady constables and to pass the time of day with them.' Other members of the group shift awkwardly at this picture of Arcadia in Southall, until an economist announces coldly that 'it is axiomatic that anything the state does it does worse than the private sector.'

There is a code to all of this. 'Professors' are ivory tower wastrels. 'Teachers' are marxist theologians. 'Councillor' – when applied to the opposition – means prodigal hooligan. Most appear economically illiterate. With opinion polls showing support for the party at its lowest mid-term level for decades, the common belief is not that the Government is out-of-touch or seen as tired and uncaring, but that it hasn't gone far enough. Those who have spent time on the big metropolitan councils seem to feel it most acutely. The bitterness of repeated daily confrontation with left-wing majorities has given them a steeliness entirely absent from the old-fashioned candidates.

It is most apparent in people like the councillor from Middles-brough, a big, feisty woman with close-cropped red hair and a voice like a Teeside fishwife. In the second exercise, in which groups are required to come up with ideas about how to improve education, force of personality ensures that she is elected as chairman, in which capacity she proposes new local authorities to supervise the schools, 'from which councillors would be banned.' This idiosyncratic view of local democracy does not prevent her finishing the board with a pass, and the recommendation to Central Office that she 'would make the perfect candidate for a safe Labour seat in the Northeast.'

By now, the candidates are being called out individually for inter-views with the backbench MPs. Do they want to become MPs for the money (some, it seems hard to credit, apparently are dim enough to think so), for the glamour (one glance at the crumpled dandruff-laden figure putting the question should disabuse them of that idea), for the influence? Then, as the planes roar down the flightpath to Heathrow, the one designed to prevent the ultimate nightmare of exposure in a Sunday tabloid. 'Is there, ahem, anything in your personal life which would embarrass the party if it became public?'

Most who would fail on this count have already been weeded out in preliminary interviews with the party vice-chairman and local area officials, but it can still stop a potential career in its tracks.

Drinks before dinner are spent in bizarre oscillation between an Essex taxi-driver advancing his theories on the need for a return of the 'glasshouse' for young offenders, and a syrupy smooth young Etonian on the Turnbull and Asser wing of the party who in previous times might have glided effortlessly into a constituency. (He failed on this occasion.)

By the following morning's exercises – discussion of how to set about winning a Labour seat when the other candidate won't share a public platform with you, a mock television interview and a debate, several of the candidates who appeared strongest – including a chairman of the party's Bow Group – seem to have given up the fight. The television performances range from the tedious (insuring antiques) to the hilarious (a Colonel defending foxhunting to an urban Tory. 'How many people hunt in your county? And who are they?') The debate has the style of a Westminster confrontation, and you get the strong impression that even the complete no-hopers must sneak off at home to lie in the bath to practise cries of 'shame', 'hear, hear' and other parliamentary harrumphing.

By lunchtime on the second day, they are finished. The officials, the MPs and the industrialists get together over sandwiches to mark each candidate for their intellectual capacity, the ability to speak, write and organize, and personal qualities like their influence on others, their sense of responsibility or determination. It turns out to be a surprisingly exact science, in which ten or fifteen minutes are spent deliberating over whether someone deserves to be graded 'adequate' or 'limited' for their motivation or their ability to organize. It struck me as an intelligent and fair system which had the merit of being open and above-board and easily comprehensible. Only the most objectionable individual could manage simultaneously to antagonize all three assessors.

About three quarters of the contestants at each board are graded as suitable for the candidates' list, some of them with recommended restrictions (the Indian doctor was reckoned 'suitable for consideration for an ethnic seat'). Others, like the councillor from Diss who are rejected, are given warm words about their unsung voluntary work for the party, and invited to continue ('Bliss in Diss,' said the chairman).

In the group to which I paid closest attention my surprise was more at the unremarkable calibre of several who did get through than at any apparently unfairly rejected. Can it really be that five 'O' levels, no original ideas and a pretty indifferent speaking ability is 'adequate' for an MP? The assessors explain that they are not looking for the best; 'that'd be hopeless. We'd end up with 350 MPs who all wanted to be prime minister. So we're looking for the good, the average, and the unexceptional as well.'

Those who passed out successfully had as broad a range of social backgrounds as the original list of applicants – certainly more broadly based than the parliamentary party. Both the taxi driver and the privatizer of the police force failed to get a place on the candidates' list, and the small number of women did proportionately better than the men.

'No constituency will select her, of course,' one of the MPs remarked after a female candidate had been passed for the list, reflecting a certain realism about the whole process. Despite often being dominated by women, the local associations, to whom those on the list must make application if the sitting MP falls under a bus, are frequently biased against them. They usually resent any guidance from Central Office, and sometimes deliberately pick as their candidate someone reckoned by headquarters to be a dead loss.

So most of the 750 or so who have emerged victorious from their motel weekend over the last decade are condemned, like the Ancient Mariner, to spend their lives trailing around the country, telling their tale to uninterested local Conservative worthies in the hope they'll be offered the honour of fighting the seat. For most, just getting on to the list will be the end of the road. Because of the kudos it can bring at the golf club, once there they are hard to dislodge. (One even refused to stand down although he would have been seventy-six at the time of the next election.)

The motel weekends are slowly changing the basic bloodstock of the parliamentary party. Those who succeed are much more in the image of representatives at the party conference than members of the old 'Establishment'. The gulf between the party organization and the MPs is narrowing all the time. The suburban southern venue for the selection board is more than just convenient (a sortie into Lancashire was abandoned after the second session), it is a metaphor for the new style of the party.

Almost the first MP to pass through the selection process and win a seat in the Commons was Nicholas Soames. As Mr Soames was the grandson of Winston Churchill, it might look as though the end-products were much the same as before. They are not. Although broader in the range of their social backgrounds, they are somehow homogenized to a degree previously unthinkable.

The selection process is not unlike that for a giant multinational corporation, and those who win through have some similarities to corporate executives. They are people to whom the Conservative party is meat and drink and there are few enough eccentrics among them. With parliamentary life now dominated by machines rather than individuals, the back benches are packed with men and women whose only hope is to be offered a job in the Whips' Office or a junior ministerial brief. Even those who have long since abandoned hope of winning Downing Street's favour have increasingly won their places after passing through a selection process which prevents the eccentric and the too-individualistic getting a look-in. Small wonder the back benches look so dull.

Because MPs enjoy such low status, because the work is so poorly paid, because the upper classes have largely abandoned ideas of 'service', and because the selection process has killed off the old boy network, there is less and less interest in politics in the Conservatives' traditional reservoir of support. But, despite the much-publicized flirtations of a few aristocrats with the centre parties, the Tories are still the natural home for the landed gentry. It is impossible to imagine their ever retaking control, but at a philosophical level the estrangement of the party from some of the old landed values still seems more a separation than a divorce. And the House of Lords provides them with the only forum in the western world in which an accident of birth assures them legislative power. Take the case of the thirteenth Earl Ferrers, a man to whom all drinking folk have reason to be grateful.

Six foot five, bright-eyed, unmistakably English with his clipped grey military moustache, pepper and salt tie and well-cut black pinstripe, Lord Ferrers singlehandedly changed the licensing laws of England. In English pubs the time between two and three on a Sunday afternoon should perhaps be named 'The Ferrers Hour'.

'I altered the law of the country,' he says brightly. 'One man did it, on his own.' Then he pauses, before adding, 'By mistake.'

In early 1988 the government had decided to liberalize the anti-quated English licensing laws, to enable pubs to stay open longer on weekdays. But, in deference to religious pressure groups, the Sunday hours were to remain unchanged. The Earl, summoned from his Suffolk estates to become deputy leader of the solid phalanx of Conservative peers in the House of Lords, was in charge of steering the bill to a successful conclusion. To his mild surprise he found himself confronted by rows of peers determined to fight on behalf of the brewing industry, a fearsomely effective lobby. They tried to force an amendment, to extend the Sunday closing time from two to three p.m. A similar amendment had been introduced in the Commons and quickly voted down by the government. Earl Ferrers, whose closest friends would not call him an intellectual, was unfamiliar with the arcane procedure of the House.

When the question was put, the Earl shouted 'not content', and lay back on the buttonback red benches to await the division.

But, because his was the only voice to shout 'not content', the amendment was put again. This time, he was silent. To his amazement, he suddenly heard the words 'the contents have it'. The government was defeated.

'I looked up, the thing had gone. There was the most fearful flapdoodle afterwards. I'd bogged it.'

The following morning a photograph of a dejected-looking Lord Ferrers appeared in *The Times*, brows furrowed, mouth glum as a basset hound. Three days later, he received a letter. 'Don't be depressed,' wrote a reader of *The Times*, 'every Sunday at two o'clock, people in pubs across the land will raise their glasses and toast your health. You'll be remembered long after the occupants of Number 10 have come and gone.'

The Ferrers family pedigree is woven into a silk pennant thirty feet long, a complicated lineage because the first Earl had twenty-seven legitimate children and a reputed thirty bastards. It is not a particularly political family, although the fourth Earl did attend the House of Lords in 1760 to be tried for shooting his steward. He attempted to plead insanity, but did it so effectively that they concluded he must be sane. Sentenced to be hung by the peer's privilege of a silken rope, for his transportation to Tyburn he dressed in his wedding suit, on the grounds that his marriage was the only occasion in his life to have caused him as much distress as his execution. Although the family seat was sold off in the fifties, the thirteenth Earl finds himself in a very similar sort of house, and the comparison is instructive. Ditchingham Hall, sitting on two thousand acres landscaped by Capability Brown, previously belonged to Lord Ferrers's father-in-law, a retired brigadier. The brigadier ran from room to room swathed in overcoats: now the house is centrally heated by a straw-burning boiler. The Earl has benefited from government grants, by the boom in agriculture and, more profoundly, by a change in public attitude. I asked whether he thought he had the same difficulties as his father:

My problems are precisely the same as my father's, but the climate's different now: in those days, people who had large houses were thought to be plutocrats who ran society, the Establishment if you like. And people thought that it all had to be changed. So many houses went then, that nowadays people say, 'Good heavens, look at this marvellous heritage! We must preserve it.' It's totally different now.[21]

The revival has given aristocrats like Lord Ferrers the opportunity to play an active role in politics again. He gives a passable imitation of a man at the wrong end of a coconut shy.

'It's hellish hard work. You're confined to this place,' he waves his gangly arm around his tiny office in the Lords one Wednesday afternoon, 'stuff flies at you from left, right and centre,' he snorts, as his forehead furrows. 'You just have to try to keep your head above water. And as for those bloody red boxes,' he says pointing to the battered containers which deliver official papers to Ditchingham Hall every weekend, 'hate 'em.'

Lord Ferrers and his like continue to provide the Conservatives with a steady supply of workhorses because, whatever its move away from traditional Toryism in the eighties, the party remains the only natural home of the aristocracy. Apologists for the House of Lords argue that it ceased to be the exclusive preserve of the upper classes with the creation of Life Peerages in 1958. But the hereditary peers provide a ballast which distorts any pretence at representativeness. Over three quarters of the House of Lords attended fee-paying schools of one sort or another. Of the 766 hereditary peers listed in *Dod's Parliamentary Companion* in 1987, almost all had been educated at public school, no less than 371 of them – almost half – at Eton. Adding life peers to the calculation inevitably reduces the Etonian proportion, but Eton still accounted for four hundred out of a total 1,156, over one quarter of the entire chamber.

And a sort of title inflation continues. In the time of Henry VIII there were reckoned to be fifteen lords for each million of the population. By 1990, the figure was one peer for every 48,000 people. The granting of peerages to former politicians, chiefs of the defence staff and so on has the effect of enhancing the status of those whose only achievement in life is having been engendered by a privileged set of loins. Furthermore, the institution is inherently politically biased. Not only do the hereditary peers entitled to sit in the House of Lords outnumber life peers by over two to one, but the hereditary principle ensures a constant supply of new blood, while during the eighties the Labour benches became thinner and thinner, as their life peers grew older and more infirm. The independence of the cross-benchers provided little balance: calculations in 1988 showed that they voted two-one in favour of the government.[22]

It is tempting to ask whether this unrepresentativeness really matters. During the seventies, Lord Hailsham dismissed the place as 'arguably less persuasive than a powerful leading article in *The Times*, or even a good edition of *Panorama*.'[23] During the eighties, however, the Lords recovered their self-confidence. Faced with a massive majority in the House of Commons and racked by their own internal problems, for much of the decade the opposition parties had a distinctly toothless appearance. The House of Lords, however, inflicted a series of amendments on government legislation. Articles with titles like 'The New Opposition' and 'Power Returns to the Lords' began appearing in the newspapers. They seemed a force for change. So swollen did the self-confidence of the House of Lords become that in June 1990 it rejected a measure (the War Crimes Bill) already decisively passed by the House of Commons on a free vote, the first such confrontation since 1949.

But the independence of the Lords was of a studiously limited kind. Lord 'Bertie' Denham, the bluff and genial Chief Whip who floated between the Lords, White's and Pratt's proffering a glass of whisky to any peer tempted to vote against a government bill, likes to maintain that there is no inbuilt Conservative majority in the Lords, and during the first two Thatcher terms the government did indeed lose 111 votes. But this was really the freedom of a lord of misrule, and generally any serious damage was undone back in the Commons. On important matters, Lord Denham still had a vast hereditary army of Etonians to call upon, Chesterton's 'great democratic protest against the eternal insolence of the aristocracy of talents.'[24]

One of the most dramatic demonstrations of the continued existence and potential power of the Lords occurred in May 1988. The Duke of Westminster, the richest man in Britain, was typical of several aristocrats with a residual sense of paternalistic decency who found government proposals to reform local government finance by replacing a graduated rating system with a flat-rate 'community charge' or poll tax deeply offensive. Calling it 'one of the worst taxes ever created in the history of man', the Duke appeared to speak for the old Conservative tradition. 'It is thoroughly and unutterably embarrassing that a stalker, a ghillie or a farmworker should be paying the same tax as me. It's just unfair.'[25] Other peers in the paternalist tradition, led by the former knight of the shires, Lord Chelwood (the much-

parodied Sir Tufton Beamish), planned an amendment which would
have required the tax to be related to ability to pay. The poll tax
proposal had already been passed by the government's overwhelming
majority in the Commons. Bertie Denham went to work to turn out
the vote.

Lord Denham is a cunning man. What was said in the phone calls
to ivy-clad stately homes across the land is unknown. Certainly to
some he made the point that a government defeat would raise potential
constitutional problems – the Lords could not lightly defy the will of
a democratically elected House of Commons. But there were other
considerations, too, of which self-interest was only one.

He produced the second highest attendance in 150 years. Across the
nation aristocratic backwoodsmen, a tribe previously thought to be on
the verge of extinction, tottered off to the nearest railway station to
obey the summons. Five hundred peers turned up to vote, giving the
government a majority of 317 votes to 183. The total number attending
was only nine less than on the question of membership of the
European Community seventeen years earlier, and forty more than
had voted on the Government of Ireland bill in 1893. As they poured
into Westminster from remote corners of the Scottish highlands and
seats in the English shires (fifty-nine of the government supporters
had attended less than one tenth of the sittings of the house in that
session[26]), it was clear that those who had championed the House of
Lords as a place where party discipline took second place to wisdom
had an altogether too rosy view of things. Among the peers identified
by the parliamentary writer Andrew Roth as voting in favour of a
measure which would oblige a labourer to pay the same amount of tax
as a millionaire were the Duke of Buccleuch, the biggest landowner in
Europe, the beef magnate Lord Vestey, another of the richest men in
Britain, and the eighty-three-year-old Marquis of Bath, of the Longleat
Estate.

The men who obey their party's call in the House of Lords do so
for the highest of motives. Expressions like 'don't want to let the side
down', and 'it's better to be a giver than a taker', fall unselfconsciously
from the lips of men like Lord Ferrers. The Viscount Massereene and
Ferrard wrote in 1973:

> At a time when the clarion call is for intensified training, higher education
> and greater specialization, it is a contradiction in terms to attempt to
> eradicate one of the best educated specialized sectors of the community, a
> sector that has taken hundreds of years to be created and which has the

rare advantage of combining its specialized knowledge with a practical technique inherited over centuries.[27]

The author of these words, John Clotworthy Talbot Foster Whyte-Melville Skeffington, the thirteenth Viscount Massereene and sixth Viscount Ferrard, became one of the great institutions of the House of Lords, an inveterate campaigner for field sports. He introduced the Deer Act and spoke seventy-seven times during the Wildlife and Countryside Bill ('I cannot understand why anyone should want to shoot a curlew. They are filthy to eat ...'[28]). He once began a memorable contribution to a debate on the 1981 riots in Brixton with the words, 'My Lords, I think I am the only member who has spoken today who has had agricultural estates in Jamaica.'[29]

Even hereditary peers who have served with distinction in the House of Lords, like Lord Carrington, are inclined to wonder about the legitimacy of the place when they hear speeches like that. His personal preference is for an elected second chamber. In the seventies a report from Lord Home recommended replacing the House of Lords with a new body, two thirds of whose members would be elected. But when the Conservatives gained power they did nothing to implement the scheme. In the eighties, a secret cabinet committee under William Whitelaw considered further ideas for reform, including joint Lords/Commons committees, and dividing the Lords into voting and non-voting peers, but again they ducked out of taking any action.

The Labour party first committed itself to abolition of the House of Lords in 1910, yet it has done less to diminish the power of hereditary peers than either the Liberals or Conservatives. In 1968 the Wilson government's attempts to reform the House of Lords, taking voting rights away from hereditary peers and creating a nominated group of voting life-peers, fell victim to sabotage from both Left and Right. Enoch Powell derided the bill as an absurdity: you couldn't just invent a second chamber. 'You don't ask what an oak tree is for, it's a silly question,' he once said. 'There are oak trees, they came that way. And you don't ask that question about institutions of society.'[30] From the other flank, Michael Foot thought plans for reform gave too great a power of patronage to the prime minister and mocked the very idea of a representative democracy. The two filibustered spectacularly. On one day in March 1969, four and a half hours were spent on points of order and discussing the confidentiality of attendance records. Ten days were needed on the first few clauses alone. In April Harold Wilson admitted what everyone else already knew: the Bill was a dead duck. Twenty years later, after including a pledge to abolish the Lords in the 1983 manifesto and dropping it from the 1987 manifesto, the Labour party again committed itself to reform of the Lords: now they planned to replace it with an elected chamber designed more to reflect the diversity of the nation and the regions, but with less legislative power. It will be a brave prime minister who decides that the game is worth the candle.

The House of Lords' survival hangs upon its very idiosyncrasy. No-one would have planned a system like it, but, the argument goes, its powers to examine and revise legislation are scarcely great enough to make it worth the bother of finding something to replace it. If it were less an absurdity, the House of Commons would have to take it seriously. The House of Lords would certainly not have survived had it not been reformed by Harold Macmillan's Life Peerages Act of 1958. Lord Carrington had entered the House thirteen years earlier and recalls a relaxed, convivial place with an overwhelming political bias:

> It was totally unbalanced – there were ten or so Labour people, and about four hundred Conservatives – it sat for about three hours every day, and there were a great number like Halifax, Salisbury, Beaverbrook who had been prominent in political life. Then there were what you might call the 'county magnates', who were important in their counties. They had a common feeling: not that they were necessarily agreeing with one another, because often they weren't. It was more that it was genuinely in those days a club.

This common feeling, shared by the knights from the shires scattered along the Conservative back benches in the Commons, was more than mere aristocratic disdain, although if you were already seated in a large country estate it cast a different light upon the tiresome business of dealing with the Whitehall bureaucracy. Carrington describes the prevailing outlook as

> a more detached view of what was the right thing or the wrong thing to do, a tradition of what national life was like, and what it ought to continue to be like. That there were certain standards of conduct by which public life was conducted.[31]

This cast of mind is easily recognizable as the outlook of the traditional ruling class.

They did not give up their privileges easily. The second Lord Redesdale once stood up in the House of Lords to argue that 'denial of the hereditary principle is a direct blow at the Crown. Such a denial is, indeed, a blow at the very foundation of the Christian faith.' He explained this extraordinary assertion to his family by saying that the aristocratic rule of primogeniture was the same as that by which Jesus Christ had inherited the kingdom of heaven (at which his daughter, Nancy, remarked, 'Oh, I thought you meant it would be a blow at the faith because the Lord's son would lose the right to choose the clergyman.'[32]). When the proposal to create life peers – and peeresses – came before the full House of Lords, it was Lord Glasgow who formulated the classic argument. It would put intolerable pressure on the limited number of parliamentary lavatories.

On a winter's day the Lords has the dozy ambience of a modernized and centrally-heated Victorian stately home. An electric imitation coal fire glows in the fireplace, the walls are dark panelled, the wallpaper plush, the ceilings arched and gothic. There is only the occasional indication of the dangerous realities of life outside: behind the wooden revolving door from the peers' car-park (the best free car-park in London) is a rolled-up stretcher and a notice warning of bomb alerts. Old men shuffle across the tiles to be greeted with 'Good afternoon, milord', by tailcoated attendants.

In the tea room, beneath the yellow fleur-de-lys wallpaper, several dozen elderly men munch their way through buttered toast and crumpets. Many of the faces are vaguely familiar from faded newspaper photographs of dark suits coming and going in Downing Street. There is a genteel buzz in the room, like four o'clock in a spa-town hotel.

Suddenly, the division bells ring and the room empties, milords making their way to vote in a debate of which they may have heard not a word. They move towards the sound of gunfire, a slow wave of grey flannel, chattering amiably among themselves, with no urgency, no uncertainty on this or many other matters, old folk in the kindest of retirement homes.

Although it is the hereditary peers who give the House of Lords its *raison d'être*, it is the life peers who give the place its intellectual distinction and who produce the most impressive arguments in examining the details of legislation. Although their creation had the disadvantage of prolonging the existence of the House of Lords long beyond its natural term, it has had one beneficial effect in broadening the representation of women in parliament. In this most male of chambers, by 1989 there were sixty-six women members. Surprisingly, perhaps, it is pretty free of sexual discrimination. Baroness Seear, a leader of the Liberal peers for several years, remarks that 'I can honestly say that I have never been in a place that treats you better on male-female equality. And that includes the London School of Economics, where I've lectured for years.'[33]

Despite the fact that it can seem at times as if half the figures on the red benches are comatose – a chastened Lady (Barbara) Wootton concluded after eight years in the place that at any one time about ten per cent of the participants in a debate were fast asleep – the quality of argument can be incomparably higher than in the House of Commons, and the pool of expertise available from the ennobled professors, judges, generals and bureaucrats makes for more informed contributions. Undoubtedly the House of Lords performs a useful role in revising legislation and moderating extremes. But its independence is exaggerated. Under a Conservative government it has the licence of the troublesome relative, indulged because in the end they're family.

But nothing gainsays the basic objection to the Lords, that there is no inherent justice in it. No plausible argument can be advanced to defend the place. Certainly, no-one devising a system of government for a late twentieth-century industrial democracy would give the right to alter legislation to a group of people whose only qualification is the fact that at some time in the dim and distant past a grateful monarch rewarded the loyalty, bravery, intrigue, obsequiousness or blackmail of an ancestor with the grant of a title and the profits of plunder. The only excuse for the House of Lords is that it exists.

It has survived so long because abolishing it would have been more trouble than it was worth, but that does not make it any better in itself. What would you replace it with? the argument goes. One wonders how much longer this reasoning will hold water, as a steadily growing proportion of British legislation begins life in Brussels or Strasbourg. The House of Lords can only look more and more an anachronism. If every other advanced democratic country can cope with the challenge of fully democratically elected parliaments, it is hard to see why it should present insuperable problems in Britain.

CHAPTER FOUR

Let Us Now Praise Famous Men

And apologetic statesmen of a compromising kind,
Such as – What d'ye call him – Thing'em-bob, and likewise – Never-mind,
And 'St-'st-'st – and What's-his-name, and also You-know-who –
The task of filling up the blanks I'd rather leave to *you*.
But it really doesn't matter whom you put upon the list,
For they'd none of 'em be missed – they'd none of 'em be missed!

– *The Mikado* W.S. GILBERT

I F YOU SPOTTED P. D. James, the crime novelist, in a street
anywhere from Canton to Buenos Aires, you could guess her
nationality at once. From her sensible shoes to her practical
haircut, her appearance proclaims her membership of that generation
of British women who survived the privations of wartime and went on
to spend their lives in ungrumbling toil creating the now tarnished
Jerusalem of the Welfare State.

After thirty years as an administrator in the National Health
Service and an adviser on policing, Miss James was enlisted for
service in the corps of commissionaires of British public life. Her
distinctive combination of qualities – literary talent and experience of
public service – combined with the fact that she was a woman, made
her a natural. By the time of her seventieth birthday she had served
on the Board of Governors of the BBC, the Corporation's General
Advisory Council, the Arts Council and the British Council and their
respective literary committees, to say nothing of her work with such
organizations as the Royal Society of Literature. Such was the number
of committees that writing itself had to be suspended.

When she returned from one of the innumerable meetings and one
of her daughters asked who had been present, her usual reply would
be, 'Oh, the Great and the Good. And me.'

It is characteristic that the more modest members of these august
committees fail to recognize themselves as belonging to the Great and
Good, a tribe which lives in the great *terra incognita* of Quangoland.
Most of them are well-meaning, public-spirited souls with little desire

for glory, committee people prepared to serve their lives huddled over blotters in council chambers from the broadcasting authorities to the Sea Fish Authority, successor to the legendary White Fish Authority. As you might expect, the great are much outnumbered by the good.

The list from which they are selected is held on a small computer on the second floor of the drab grey Cabinet Office building in Whitehall. The names on its files provide a gazetteer to the map of much of this Unknown Land. The list itself is secret, although it is a fair bet that it contains only a few genuinely brilliant minds, and fewer still who are likely to rock the boat. Although broader than the days when Lord Rothschild described it as populated entirely by men who 'are aged fifty-three, live in the South East, have the right accent and belong to the Reform Club',[1] it is hardly representative of the population as a whole.

For the twenty-three years after 1950, the list was run by Miss Mary Bruce, a caricature white-haired Whitehall spinster more interested in horses than in people and who scared the pants off all who worked with her. Miss Bruce's distaste for innovation made itself manifest in the dreary proposals served up to the Conservative and Labour governments in the seventies – whenever a request for names for public duties arrived in her in-tray, the same roll-call of has-beens fell out of her out-tray. The new Public Appointments Unit set up in 1975 to revivify the List was run by Jonathan Charkham, a well-heeled nomad who had begun his career as a barrister, went into industry, and by the late eighties was working for the Bank of England. Charkham enjoyed his job, coining the phrase that 'patronage is second only to the act of love in conferring pleasure on all parties concerned.'[2] In an attempt to get away from Lord Rothschild's stereotype, he trawled the country for new names, although it was not until 1980 that people were able to write in to nominate themselves. Under the present director, Geoffrey Morgan, a soft-spoken Welshman whose main outside interest is silkworms, the list of names has moved away from the Reform Club and further out into Middle England, although it is still a very long way short of representing a cross-section of the population. In January 1990 it included 5,953 names, of whom 4,141 were men. The thirty per cent who were women represented a doubling within a decade, but the great majority were still well into middle age – only 344 (eighty-five men and 259 women) were aged forty or less. Half lived in the South East of

England.[3] This is still only about one eighth of the number of people required to fill public appointments of one kind or another.[4]

The plum tasks for which the Great and Good might be chosen are Royal Commissions or Committees of Inquiry, the device by which governments buy the days when faced with demands for change, political embarrassment, or questions too deep for quick political answers. Because of the sensitivity of the subjects under consideration, the highest recommendation in considering who might be suitable to sit on these investigations is the fact that they have a safe pair of hands. Mavericks need not apply. The impulse to put safety first is understandable enough, but it is hardly a formula either for dynamism or for originality.

Once someone has established themselves as being the right sort of chap, then their name crops up time and again. In a career which lasted over sixty years Lord Benson, Britain's most distinguished accountant, served on over twenty different governmental or quasi-governmental committees or inquiries. In 1943 he was seconded from the army to advise on how to reorganize the munitions factories. Exactly forty years later, at the age of seventy-four, he was still in post as adviser to the governor of the Bank of England. He attributes his succession of government jobs to 'a sort of grapevine'. 'If you do one job adequately, then your name gets passed on. And then, of course, you can become fashionable, like doctors or dentists.'[5]

Lord Shawcross, who at one time or another was chairman of the Bar Council, the Press Council, the Medical Research Council, the Takeover Panel, and assorted royal commissions and tribunals of inquiry, claimed when questioned that the consideration uppermost in the minds of such figures was 'the national interest'. It was, he admitted, hard to define precisely what this was:

> It's a matter of background and philosophy, which one can't really explain or analyse. But a person going about it seriously has to discount his own personal opinion, which may be that all coloured people should – um – be expelled from the country, and decide what is in the best interests of the country as a whole, given that there is a large – er – ethnic problem. And to do that he has to draw on whatever sources of knowledge he has, and try to arrive at an honest, unbiased conclusion. It depends upon his personal honesty and intellectual competence.[6]

In the case of immigration, a rare insight into the selection of the Great and Good occurred in January 1986, when, under the thirty year rule, government documents of the mid-fifties were declassified.

Alarmed by inner-city tensions in reaction to mass immigration from the Commonwealth, in June 1955 the Home Secretary asked Sir Anthony Eden to set up a committee of inquiry, to drum up support for immigration controls. He listed the composition of such a body. Ideally, it would be chaired by the law lord, Lord Radcliffe. There would be an MP from each of the three parties, a token Welsh and Scottish member, an employers' representative and one from the trade unions, an economist, a social worker ('preferably a woman'), a local authority representative and two members nominated by the Commonwealth and colonial secretaries.[7] It is hardly an inspired cast-list – it is characteristic that it includes no representatives from the community under investigation – but in its apparent breadth it is typical of an attitude of mind.

Members of the Great and Good appointed to these bodies not only had similar backgrounds and education, but acceptance of the job, with its admission to a distinguished club, involved adopting if not identical views, at least a similar perspective. Lord Shawcross thought that

> they of course tended to believe in the country. They wanted to see it happy and successful and as far as possible united. They did not want to provoke conflict between different sections of society. They wanted to give everyone an equal opportunity at the beginning of their lives, in health and in education. It was Butskellite, I suppose.[8]

Here is a key to the post-war Establishment so distrusted by Henry Fairlie and the others. They were consensus men. The idea proved remarkably durable. Professor Sir Richard Southwood, who became vice-chancellor of Oxford in the autumn of 1989, entered the world of the Great and Good thirty years after Lord Shawcross and found things largely unchanged. A down-to-earth ecologist with a taste for mutton-chop sideboards and a cloth cap, Southwood was part of a stream of distinguished biologists in post-war public life, including Lords Rothschild, Zuckerman, and Swann. By the early eighties he had held half-a-dozen public appointments, including the chairmanships of the Royal Commission on Pollution and of the Trustees of the Natural HistoryMuseum:

> There were all sorts of different views of the future, but everyone had the same ideas about what was worth preserving. The principle that education was to be open to all, irrespective of means; public galleries and museums should be open to all, the National Health Service likewise. There was also a view that there was an unacceptable face of capitalism. We were drawn

from both sides of the political fence, but the key idea was consensus. Even if you had different views, you felt you should not impose those views on a significant minority. We always strove to get a solution that was acceptable all round.[9]

In the context of the times, this approach had practical as well as philosophical attractions. In the twenty years between 1960 and 1980, the tenancy of Downing Street changed between Labour and Conservative four times, an average occupancy of only five years: the Great and Good were trying to produce policies which would be durable enough to survive the swings. Their loyalty was therefore to some profounder vision of Britain than that expressed in mere party politics.

And there were inevitable structural constraints built in. Lord Annan, who led the Committee on the Future of Broadcasting in the 1970s, noticed them:

Firstly, the idea of balance is written into the very idea of a Royal Commission. Then you take evidence from everyone who might have anything to say on the subject. And then the next question is, what you do with all this mass of material you've collected?[10]

Established to tackle thorny problems, it was hardly surprising that, in the words of Lord Shawcross, 'if you couldn't find a solution which commanded general support, then at least you'd find a way which would enable the whole matter to be put on the back shelf.'[11]

There is more than a grain of truth in the observation by A. P. Herbert that royal commissions were usually appointed 'not so much for digging up the truth, as for digging it in.' Herbert also penned the verses which have come to sum up the general fate of such investigations:

> I saw an old man in the Park;
> I asked the old man why
> He watched the couples after dark;
> He made this strange reply:
>
> I am the Royal Commission on Kissing
> Appointed by Gladstone in '74;
> The rest of my colleagues are buried or missing;
> Our minutes were lost in the last Great War.
> But I'm still a Royal Commission.
> My task I intend to see through,
> Though I know, as an old politician,
> Not a thing will be done if I do.[12]

A capacity for burying problems made royal commissions and the like instantly attractive to politicians besieged by one knotty issue or another. In the four decades after the war, there were 589 such inquiries, an average of almost fifteen each year. Only thirty-seven were full-scale royal commissions, although Harold Wilson splashed out on them so liberally that even the Great and Good began to complain that the currency had been devalued. Many of the post-war inquiries were into big, difficult subjects, like the investigation carried out by Sir Edmund Compton into allegations of security force brutality in Northern Ireland, or the inquiry by Sir John Wolfenden into homosexual offences and prostitution, which led to changes in the law. But at other times they seem like sledgehammers to crack nuts. Were Sir Charles Wilson's frequent trips to inquire into the future of the Dundee Institute of Art and Technology really necessary? And what was the Duke of Northumberland doing for two years investigating recruitment into the veterinary profession? Or the eminent Welsh barrister, Roderic Bowen QC, wrestling with the problems of bilingual roadsigns?

Since the war, the three most distinguished figures in this band of auxiliaries – the greatest of the Great and Good – in the opinion of the percipient Whitehall commentator, Peter Hennessy, were Lords Waverley, Radcliffe and Franks. Lord Waverley (John Anderson) occupied the post of grandest grandee until 1952. Lord (Cyril) Radcliffe, a brilliant barrister who had come to attention by his achievements in the wartime civil service, succeeded Waverley that year, and lasted until 1977. On his death, the mantle fell upon Lord (Oliver) Franks, who, on returning to Britain in 1952 after serving as ambassador in Washington, turned down the editorship of *The Times*, the director-generalship of the BBC and the eventual headship of the civil service.

Margaret Thatcher's distaste for royal commissions is well known, but when her government faced the most serious foreign policy misjudgement of recent years – the failure to predict and forestall the Argentine invasion of the Falkland Islands – it was time to send for Oliver Franks again. The five privy counsellors chosen to assist – the former Conservative Chancellor of the Exchequer, Lord (Anthony) Barber; the one-time Labour Cabinet minister, Lord (Harold) Lever; Sir Patrick Nairne, the delightful former permanent secretary and master of St Catherine's Oxford; James Callaghan's home secretary, Merlyn Rees; and the industrialist and Conservative politician, Lord

(Harold) Watkinson were unlikely to come to radical conclusions. But that is one of the points of such enquiries. None the less, their investigation appears to have been scrupulously thorough, painting what Callaghan called 'a splendid picture', and pointing out political, diplomatic and military deficiencies by the British government. But then, in the last paragraph, they concluded that 'we would not be justified in attaching any criticism or blame to the present Government for the Argentine Junta's decision to commit its act of unprovoked aggression in the invasion of the Falkland Islands.'[13] It was as if, said Callaghan, they had got bored with the subject, and suddenly 'chucked a bucket of whitewash over it.'[14] The Great and Good still had their uses.

There will always be subjects which can only be handled by referring them to apparently independent adjudicators outside government. The Thatcher administration felt the behaviour of the tabloid press in invading people's privacy was one such matter – although their behaviour outraged all civilized standards, the worst offending newspapers were owned by political sympathizers like Rupert Murdoch. In the spring of 1989 David Calcutt, Master of Magdalene College, Cambridge, was asked to lead an inquiry, and, sure enough, fifteen months later came up with proposals which appeared to satisfy both government and proprietors, even if it left victims distinctly underwhelmed. Calcutt, the son of a Home Counties chemist who won a Cambridge scholarship after a minor public school scholarship and then held down a successful practice at the Bar, has a common Great and Good pedigree. In being trusted with one delicate mission after another (the Diplomatic Service Appeals Board, compensation for the wrongfully imprisoned Guildford Four, the grievances of the former M.I.5 officer, Colin Wallace) Calcutt was bidding fair to become the chief of this tribe in the nineties.

What lay behind the beliefs of the Great and Good was a sense of custodianship. It was rooted in a cast of mind raised to an ethic in the professions. In an age when politicians, journalists, estate agents and even advertising executives claim to be 'professionals', it is easy to forget that the description once carried with it a certain cachet. Once the reforms of the late nineteenth century had taken hold, it would be the self-governing professions, an aristocracy of merit, that would take over much of the social responsibilities of the hereditary peerage. Even Adam Smith acknowledged their special status:

> We trust our health to the physicians, our fortune and sometimes our life and reputation to the lawyer and attorney. Such confidence cannot safely be reposed in people of very mean or low condition. Their reward must be such as may give them that rank in society which so important a trust requires.[15]

George Bernard Shaw was altogether more worldly-wise, observing that 'all professions are conspiracies against the laity,' and while they affected contempt for the medieval craft guilds, with their closed shops, the professions were in reality based upon very similar principles. Lawyers and doctors had their own institutions dating back to Tudor times, but the great expansion of the professions occurred in the Victorian age. A vast new respectable society arose round the professions, dignified by the belief that what they were doing (although it might be exorbitantly expensive) was in pursuit of some higher calling. 'Medicine is a profession, dentistry is largely a business,' sniffed the British Medical Journal in 1878,[16] but the professional tag was so sought after that the rush to respectabilize was unstoppable. By the end of the century, architects, accountants and engineers had all created their own professional institutions.

By the 1920s, in the twilight of the aristocracy, instead of respect switching to industrialists, deference was accorded to the professions. They appeared to attach chivalric values to the business of private gain. 'The meaning of a profession', wrote that great Christian socialist R. H. Tawney, 'is that it makes the traitors the exception, not, as they tend to be in industry, the rule.'[17] The dignifying characteristic of the professions was that they had their own codes of ethics. Because of the professional's specialized area of knowledge, the layman was unlikely to know what was best for himself. He depended on the integrity of the professional. Codes of practice were supposed to protect the customer, by dangling the threat of expulsion and consequent loss of income over the practitioners. The professions therefore became midwife to the 'we know best' philosophy on which later the Establishment was to rest.

By the 1930s not only had admission to a profession become the goal of every middle-class family in the land, but they had come to seem bulwarks of society. In a positively eulogistic survey in 1933, one author proclaimed them as a saving glory of European society as against newer cultures like the United States where 'crude forces' threatened the social structure. In Britain, by contrast, 'the family, the church, the universities, certain associations of intellectuals, and above all the great professions, stand like rocks against which the waves raised by these forces beat in vain.'[18] Which goes some way towards explaining the relative stagnation of the British economy.

While it was not axiomatic that the professional institutions were politically conservative, they were almost always culturally so. The Royal Academy of Arts, for example, maintained a slavish loyalty to portraiture, landscapes and the inspiration of literature, while just across the English Channel the art world was alive with one 'ism' after another – Impressionism, Fauvism, Cubism, Surrealism. 'You did not speak about the Royal Academy if you pretended to be interested in modern art,' said one young critic.[19] Confined to the fine arts, this clinging to the safe and known was just a brake upon innovation and exuberance. But in professions concerned with providing a service, where resistance to new ideas was allied to undisguised self-interest, it was a big obstacle to entrepreneurial dynamism.

Aneurin Bevan was only able to defeat the opposition of doctors to the National Health Service in 1944 by buckling together a compromise with Lord Moran, president of the Royal College of Physicians, 'stuffing their mouths with silver', and promising to respect their independent practice. Similarly, the 1989 plans to loosen barristers' stranglehold on appearance in court ran into such heavy opposition even from radicals – or what passes for radicalism in such a deeply orthodox business – that the plans of an elected government were tempered by vested interest.

In the legal world, the most archaic of the lay professions, the idea of status was closely linked to the notion of the grandeur of the law itself: if the population had no respect for judges and barristers, they would soon have no respect for the law of the land. The importance attached to 'character' was, therefore, considerable and even after the introduction of competitive examinations in the 1870s, the social composition of the bar scarcely changed. A century later, the Royal Commission on Legal Services discovered that the profession of barrister was still largely the preserve of the upper and middle classes.[20] Not only did the cost of supporting themselves during their training and pupilage deter would-be barristers from poorer backgrounds, but the anachronistic requirement that they then find a place in 'chambers' from which existing advocates were working inevitably favoured those with the right contacts or family connections.

In the 1990s the Bar likes to proclaim that all that has changed, that it is no longer dominated by men who have been to public schools followed by Oxford or Cambridge. Certainly there are many more women barristers to be seen around beneath the horsehair wigs, and the occasional black or Asian face. But it is a deeply conservative trade which has resolutely resisted most attempts to bring it into the twentieth century, to make it more efficient, or to make access to the law more available to the ordinary citizen. And while the spread of backgrounds may be wider now than it was, it scarcely shows in the appearance and mannerisms of the lawyers. The aloofly anachronistic style of the bar, the stentorian joshing, the minor public-school humour remain the common coin, and even those who started life as the children of railway porters soon assume the mannerisms of the people whose bags their fathers carried.

The curious nature of the Bar would matter less were it not for the fact that it supplies the vast majority of judges. In continental European countries, where lawyers can choose to become judges soon after qualifying, the judiciary looks very different to Britain, with, for example, near parity in numbers between men and women in countries like France and the Netherlands. In Britain, it is almost entirely made up of upper-middle class, late-middle aged, white men. In early 1990 there were no female law lords, only one woman (the redoubtable Dame Elizabeth Butler-Sloss) among the thirty lord justices of appeal, one female judge out of eighty in the High Court, and only eighteen women among the 422 circuit judges in England and Wales. Black and Asian people were even more notable by their absence; there was one black judge among the circuit judges and, at the lower level of the judiciary, five among the 703 recorders. This is not the multi-racial, equal opportunity society in which the rest of Britain is living.

Successive Lord Chancellors have gone on record stating their keenness to create a judiciary more representative of the population as a whole. The fact that it has not happened says a great deal both about the appointments process and the legal profession. Unlike civil servants, who win their jobs by competitive examination, judges depend upon a process of consultation and soundings which reproduces the judiciary in its own image. Twenty years ago, officials admit, it was an amateurish, informal process. Now, aspiring judges are called to a room at the western end of the Palace of Westminster overlooking the Thames, and, seated on chairs stamped with the gilt portcullis, interviewed about their suitability for the job. After this interview, their success or failure depends upon their winning the good opinion of existing judges whose views are canvassed informally by civil servants in the Lord Chancellor's office. Once appointed, circuit judges can be sacked only for incapacity or misbehaviour (one lost his job in 1984 after involvement in a smuggling racket), while to get rid of High Court judges or their seniors demands a joint address of both Houses of Parliament to the Queen. The last time that happened was with an Irish judge in the 1830s.

It makes those who appoint judges understandably cautious. The Lord Chancellor's civil servants can, they say, only recruit judges from among advocates who have already distinguished themselves by their performance in court. Up to six or seven senior judicial figures are appointed each year, from a short list which numbers no more than a dozen. The short list is drawn up on the advice of existing judges, seeking to establish whether the candidates combine the qualities of legal skills, status within the profession and 'respectability'. Since the top judges only retire at seventy-five, the highest levels of the profession are something of a gerontocracy. One lord justice of appeal appointed in 1984, Sir David Croom-Johnson, was seventy when he took up his post, the age at which mere mortals are deemed too doddery to be trusted on jury service.

The core of the problem is simply that the judiciary is the creature of the legal profession. The translation from an ordinary barrister to the prestigious – and much more lucrative – title of Queen's Counsel, 'taking silk', is, for no good reason also administered by the Lord Chancellor's department, rather than by the profession itself, which further consolidates the relationship. The standard answer to suggestions that the judiciary is less than a representative cross-section of society is that the Lord Chancellor can only fashion judges from the timber he finds on the list of QCs. As it is a list of his own making, it is not much of an excuse.

It is instructive to look at where recent silks have come from. Close examination of the QCs appointed during the 1980s, from whom most of the judiciary will be drawn in the nineties and beyond, reveals that the old pattern has scarcely changed. Of the 450 practising QCs appointed, 406 give biographical details in *Who's Who* and other standard reference works. Of this number 262, almost two thirds, were educated at public schools, 215 of them subsequently going on to Oxford or Cambridge. Another fifty-four who had been at state schools were also Oxbridge graduates. Of the 450, a mere twenty-three, five per cent, were women. The male, public school judiciary will be with us for years to come.

Significantly, it was a Scottish Lord Chancellor, Lord Mackay of

Clashfern, the son of a Highland railwayman, who was given charge of reforming the legal profession in England and Wales. The Bar was the sort of impenetrable club with its own set of values that the Thatcher administration instinctively distrusted. But when the Central Policy Review Staff (the 'Think Tank') had suggested in the early eighties that they mount a full-scale investigation into the practices and abuses of the professions, they discovered that the influence of the lawyers upon Number 10 was so strong that the proposal was sat upon and then returned, with a suggestion they confine themselves to teachers and social workers.

At the heart of Lord Mackay's proposals years later was a suggestion that solicitors be given the right to speak, and to become judges, in any court. In the course of time, the two branches of the legal profession might be merged. The plans would seem to have the merit both of broadening the spectrum of judges and giving the consumer greater choice.

Almost to a man, barristers fought the scheme. Some of their arguments, such as that their professional standards were higher than could be maintained by law – as envisaged in the legislation – had a ring of truth to them. But there was an unmistakable whiff of vested interest about the howls of outrage. They had a considerable army of former lawyers to call upon in parliament, and the comments of the former lord chancellor, Lord Hailsham, that the Government was 'thinking with its bottom and sitting on its head'[21] caused a flurry or two. In the end, the hapless Lord Mackay's proposals were considerably watered down. And so strong is the legal culture that radical change, to make the bar and judiciary more accessible or representative, looks unlikely. The judiciary looks set to remain the preserve of elderly, slightly unworldly men whose cast of mind is rooted in the aspirations about which Tawney had been so glowing. In *The Acquisitive Society* he wrote:

> The difference between industry as it exists today and a profession is then, simple and unmistakable. The former is organized for the protection of rights, mainly rights to pecuniary gain. The latter is organized, imperfectly indeed, but nonetheless genuinely, for the performance of duties.[22]

How he could have concluded that there was anything better designed to protect 'rights to pecuniary gain' than barristers' exclusive right of audience in court is a passing curiosity. But the depiction of the motivation of the professions as being 'the performance of duties', goes to the heart of the motivation of that distinctive élite in British public life, the Great and Good. For them, 'the performance of duties' is their overriding duty.

Like the guardians in Plato's *Republic*, few achieve the ranks of the Great and Good before the age of fifty. They do not do anything that they are not entitled to do, and they usually do it reasonably conscientiously. They are put in place to represent the public, but their background, education and occupation are rarely ordinary. The 'we know best' philosophy of the professions informs their every activity. Since populism is the antithesis of everything they stand for, it is instructive to see how they have handled that most demotic of forces, television.

The birth of commercial television in the early fifties was a victory for money over breeding, of corporate power over paternalism. Among the Great and Good, scarcely a voice could be heard supporting a proposal which the BBC's founding father, Lord Reith, had said would prove as beneficial as dog-racing, smallpox or the bubonic plague. The Tory party leadership, including Churchill (who thought commercial television 'a tuppenny Punch and Judy show'), Lord Salisbury, Sir Anthony Eden and R. A. Butler, were unenthusiastic. The leaders of the Trades Union Congress, governors of the BBC, the Archbishops of York and Canterbury, to say nothing of grand figures like the former foreign secretary, Lord Halifax, the former chancellor and home secretary who gave his name to the wartime Anderson shelter, Lord Waverley, and the sainted Lady Violet Bonham Carter were all against. Henry Fairlie observed:

> The debate on commercial television remains one of the clearest examples of the Establishment in action in defence of one of its dearest illusions, namely, that it knows best what is good for other people.[23]

Yet they lost. The political allies of the Popular Television Association were initially limited to a handful of young Conservative backbenchers like John Profumo and Selwyn Lloyd, but they ran a public-relations campaign on a scale, and of a sophistication, which had not been seen before in Britain. The election of October 1951 had brought 100 new Conservative MPs into parliament all of whom received the undivided attention of the lobbyists. Many of them also nurtured hopes that a new commercial sector would offset what their flights of fancy saw as the 'bolshie' bias of the BBC. The new Tories talked of being 'on the side of the people', and when, in March 1954, the Television Bill came up for its second reading, they won the day. 'Giving the people what they want' had proved a more potent slogan than traditional Conservative paternalism. A Princeton professor who investigated the campaigns a few years later put it more bitterly: 'Cynical pseudo-egalitarianism replaced an older commitment to the maintenance of national standards.'[24]

But now the old paternalism began to reassert itself, determined that whatever shackles had been placed around the BBC should also tie down the commercial companies. An Independent Television Authority would regulate them, run by a group of people pulled out of the old drawer marked 'gentlemen amateurs'. The Postmaster General, the Earl de la Warr (Eton and Oxford), didn't think an interest in or knowledge of communications part of the job requirements. 'The qualities required in the Chairman and members were tact and sound judgement rather than energy and administrative ability,'[25] he told the Cabinet. How much of this delightfully frank list of requirements the Earl passed on to the man he approached for the job of chairman, the art historian Sir Kenneth Clark (Winchester and Oxford), is not recorded. Like most of his friends, Clark believed that independent television 'would produce a cloaca maxima of rubbish'. Later he wondered:

> Why did Buck De La Warr invite me? I can only suppose that my name had respectable associations, and he thought it might allay criticism in what might be called Athenaeum circles. In this he was mistaken. Their odium was not allayed, but was focused on me, and when, soon after my appointment was announced, I entered the dining room of the Athenaeum (as a guest) I was booed.[26]

Whitehall had no idea where to find the professionals who would stave off the imminent cultural vandalism of television. When Clark had to hire someone to become chief executive of the new regulatory authority, the Treasury gave him a list of nine admirals, seventeen generals and six air marshals and told him they'd be disappointed if he didn't find the right chap among them. Clark preferred the old boy network, and settled on an old pal from the Ministry of Information, Robert Fraser.

Clark and Fraser were trying to control a new set of television nabobs with priorities quite unlike those of the forty-year-old BBC, whose task was to 'inform, educate and entertain', in that order. 'I don't want to change people or lead them. I want to give the public what they want,' said Lew Grade. 'I know what the public wants because I am one of them.'[27] This was an entirely novel perspective: although chosen to represent the public, few of the Great and Good would have declared themselves spiritually one of them. Those members of the Independent Television Authority and its successor, the Independent Broadcasting Authority, who have been most interventionist have devoted their energies to trying to make commercial television more like the non-commercial BBC. Lew Grade and his successors put up with them, because the regulators did not prevent the companies making a profit. Time and again the IBA proved itself a sucker to serious-sounding prospectuses, awarding franchises to London Weekend Television and the new breakfast television service, TVAM, only for them to turn out complete flops which later recouped their investment by lowering standards.

It is in the field of editorial content that the Great and Good of independent television have exercised their most direct influence. Companies bidding for franchises must satisfy them that they will broadcast a sufficient proportion of 'quality' programming, a fair enough requirement perhaps, given the limitless temptations to pander to the lowest common denominator. When the Authority intervened in the decisions of individual companies, it was almost always to insist on certain BBC-type standards, whether it was the retention of *University Challenge* or the compulsory broadcasting of the Queen's Speech on Christmas Day. Twenty years later Channel Four, originally conceived as a publishing house for independent producers, succumbed to the same institutional pressures. The IBA was of course on the liberal wing of the Establishment, but it knew where to draw the line.

The consequence is that Britain has never had truly free broadcasting. When it comes to the most sensitive and important areas of journalism, like Northern Ireland or official secrecy, British broadcasters are less free to report than a camera team arriving from Perugia or Poughkeepsie.

Britain has been denied this freedom because it has never had a truly commercial broadcasting environment. There has tended to be agreement on the central question; what is broadcasting for? In other countries it was a vehicle for selling processed peas or indoctrinating the masses. But in Britain, television, like the cod-liver oil forced down the gagging throats of Welfare-State children, was supposed to be good for you. The tone had been set from the earliest days of the

BBC. 'It is occasionally indicated to us that we are apparently setting out to give the public what we think they need and not what they want – but few know what they want, and very few what they need,' Reith had pronounced.[28] This cast of mind survived for decades. In February 1965, the new Labour Postmaster General, Tony Benn, asked the chairman of the BBC, Lord Normanbrook ('a stupid man . . . at the very centre of the Establishment' Benn thought), and the Director-General, Sir Hugh Greene, why the BBC would not provide a radio service to satisfy the demand being fed by dilapidated old rust-buckets moored in the North Sea blasting rock music to the mainland day and night. 'If you had continuous music, it would be like keeping the pubs open all day,' he was told, which Benn summarized as 'a real BBC view that it is bad to give the people what they want.'[29]

As Benn's frustration indicates, the 'public good' which the BBC considered itself to be serving was not necessarily the same as that defined by government. The BBC's loyalty was to some profounder purpose. There was more than a touch of arrogance to the assumption, and clashes with governments, who could at least point to the fact that they had been elected, were inevitable. In the 1926 General Strike Winston Churchill had proposed that the BBC be commandeered. During the Suez fiasco in 1956 Eden considered an identical idea, and there were even a few voices suggesting something similar during the Falklands War in 1982. These incidents are rare not only because national emergencies are mercifully infrequent, but because for much of the time there is an instinctive understanding between the governors of the broadcasting organization and the government of the nation, as the corporation's behaviour on issues like appeasement demonstrates; Reith succumbed to the same collective delusion that had seized Chamberlain, his foreign secretary, Halifax, and most of the population.

'Of all the voices of the Establishment,' wrote Henry Fairlie in 1959, 'the British Broadcasting Corporation's is the most powerful.'[30] Not only did the BBC believe that it alone knew what was good for the audience, its pretence of impartiality was bogus and it absorbed and suffocated with banalities all differences of opinion:

> It fears, and when it does not fear, it despises, non-conformity; and if non-conformity must be allowed its say, it will gently rob it of all anger and all laughter, of all passion and all heartache, until it lacks both pith and point . . . Where the boundaries of accepted thought are being crossed, there you will not find the BBC; where there is dissidence or protest, there you will

not find the BBC; where there is irreverence or resistance to cant, there you will not find the BBC.[31]

The comment belongs very much to an era. A decade later, after the satire boom and a score of grim socially realistic documentaries, the BBC had become the *bête-noire* of a thousand Conservative social clubs. When he arrived at the BBC as deputy Director-General in 1987, John Birt even told the *Financial Times* that he found the place 'crudely, thoughtlessly anti-Establishment.'[32] This too was an exaggeration, confusing cultural licence with editorial prejudice.

The BBC is rather like a cross between the Church of England and the Post Office. On the one hand there is the lofty principle, spelled out in the inscription carved into the walls of Broadcasting House, 'that the people, inclining their ear to whatsoever things are lovely and honest, whatsoever things are of good report, may tread the path of virtue and of wisdom.' For the rest, there is the drab functionality of the place, the bureaucracy, the tatty carpets, a vast, amorphous organization given form by regulations which even prescribe the amount of money which may be claimed for riding a bicycle on official duty. Its internal organization, hierarchies, and values struck Melvyn Bragg, who joined the Corporation from Oxford in 1961, as being modelled on the public school system:

> I think the BBC has a system of promotion which is rather like the way in which people are made prefects at school. The reasons for their success are not necessarily to do with their acuteness, not necessarily to do with their originality, but everything to do with sustaining the status-quo of the institution at that time. People are seen as going up a ladder: they are trainees, they become accepted when they get to know the school rules – the ambience is that once you've survived the initiation, you're part of this club, this closed society. The club becomes the most important thing in their lives. When you talk about politics to BBC people, they immediately assume you mean BBC politics, not relations between the parties or the superpowers, but who's going to be the next DG.[33]

This distinctive corporate culture flourishes in an environment in which independence is more a matter of convention than anything else. It has no guarantee in law and the Corporation has no weapon to wield against political interference beyond an appeal to public opinion and the threat of resignations. Technically, the governors *are* the BBC. The first governors were a worthy lot. The chairman, Lord Clarendon, had been parliamentary under-secretary for the dominions;

presumably running the BBC was a similar sort of task. Reith thought him 'weak and stupid'. The others were a liberal coal-owner, an ex-comptroller of the Bank of England, and the former headmaster of Winchester (the postmaster general, who made the appointments, was a Wykehamist). The one woman, Ethel Snowden, wife of the former Chancellor of the Exchequer ('ignorant, stupid and horrid', according to Reith), was a double token, chosen to represent the interests of both the Labour party and women.

In the fifty years following there were eighty-five governors. When the historian Asa Briggs examined their backgrounds he found that fifty-six of them had been university educated, forty at Oxford or Cambridge. The three schools of Eton, Harrow and Winchester accounted for twenty governors. Among the thirty-eight who had been politically active, there were more than twice as many Conservatives as anything else – nineteen were Tories, seven Liberal and eight Labour. Their average age on taking up their post was fifty-four. Although appointed to represent a cross-section of British life – one each from Wales, Scotland and Northern Ireland; at least one academic; one trade unionist (almost always from the right-wing of the movement); one with an interest in the arts; usually a scientist; a retired diplomat to represent the Foreign Office; and in recent years one representative from the ethnic minorities – they have their amateurism in common.

Sir Alexander Cadogan, made chairman in 1952, had never seen a BBC television programme, and the ones he had seen, in the United States, he didn't much care for. Lord Tedder, vice-chairman in the early fifties, admitted that 'I know nothing at all about broadcasting, but I can learn. Specialization is one of the most dangerous tendencies. It has given us experts, not wise men.'[34] By the time that Edward Heath had to appoint a chairman twenty years later, he chose Professor Michael (later Lord) Swann, Vice-Chancellor of Edinburgh University, on the grounds that running the BBC was rather like running a university, with a ferment of ideas, plenty of eccentricity and troublesome students. Which is how the Great and Good have always seen their role.

One of the little pleasures of life in Downing Street is the opportunity it affords to dish out baubles of one kind or another. The twice yearly honours lists are the ones which attract most attention, but there is another raft of honours in the gift of Downing Street, some of which reflect professional excellence and others which confer real power and influence: jobs. For reasons best known to themselves, Downing Street declines either to list or number the posts directly in the gift of the prime minister.[35] But they include various agreeable academic posts such as the mastership of Trinity College, Cambridge, regius professorships, the boards of most of the great museums and galleries, and the deans of cathedrals (when it comes to bishops, changes introduced during the Callaghan premiership restrict the prime minister's choice to two names, submitted by a Church of England committee).

The posts may not necessarily be particularly lucrative (regius professorships are worth £100 a year, religiously paid in quarterly £25 cheques), but they are at some of the pinnacles of national life, they open doors and they command respect. Unlike other university appointments, which are made by faculty boards or governing bodies on the basis of academic achievement, there is no formal selection process, and no open competition for regius professorships. Those who wish to be appointed must somehow solicit the good opinion of the prime minister's appointments secretary. For most of the eighties this post was held by Robin Catford – of whom more later – who had the privilege of having the tenancy of the best room in Number 10. Even then, they can lose the post for the most bizarre reasons; Downing Street myth has it that Richard Cobb failed on his first attempt to get the Oxford Chair of Modern History because he wore bicycle clips throughout his interview.

Anthony Honoré, retiring Oxford Regius Professor of Civil Law, had just been canvassed by the appointments secretary when I visited him in his panelled rooms at All Souls. The search was under way for his successor, although Catford's trawl was conducted in a distinctly courtly style:

> He was both listening to suggestions and putting forward names that other people had suggested. He was interested in who the local people wanted, whether they considered that a chap would fit in with the university or college, whether he'd be acceptable to his colleagues.[36]

How particularly English that question of whether a chap will 'fit in'.

This is the dry sherry end of the appointments business. Many other jobs get handed out simply because a minister happens to know someone who might fit the bill. Sir Ian Trethowan slid comfortably out of the director-generalship of the BBC to become chairman of the Horserace Betting Levy Board because the Home Secretary, William Whitelaw, happened to know he was interested in racing. Others rise because they are politically congenial. Still others – few enough in number – advance relentlessly for reasons even they find hard to fathom.

William Rees-Mogg was the great panjandrum of the eighties. All black suede shoes and double-breasted pinstripe, he seemed central casting's idea of the ideal Establishment man. He is a genuine hate-figure for the libertarian left, who are capable of splendid outrage at the mention of his name. Anyone who takes on public duties sets himself up for attack, and in Rees-Mogg's case, the succession of posts was dizzying. Where others might have been satisfied just to become editor of *The Times*, he took on one public job after another. Some, like becoming High Sheriff of Somerset, were trouble-free baubles. But others – the chairmanship of the Arts Council, deputy chairmanship of the BBC, or leadership of the Broadcasting Standards Council – involved real work and real responsibilities.

Why did the ministerial hand hover above the name of Rees-Mogg when presented with a list of candidates for these public positions? The Broadcasting Standards Council job, as a sort of public smut-detector, demanded some acquaintance with popular taste and culture. Yet, by his own admission, 'I tuned out of pop music with Elvis Presley.'[37] He served as editor of *The Times* while unable to type, as chairman of the Arts Council while unable to drive, and was appointed to the Broadcasting Standards Council unaware that one of Britain's most popular television shows was named *Jim'll Fix It* ('Who's Jim?' he once asked).

Part of the answer lies in the unexciting fact that he is prepared to take on the jobs. He has that ingrained self-confidence most commonly attributed to the grandest old Etonians, although he failed to win a scholarship there and ended up at Charterhouse. At Oxford (at that most political of colleges, Balliol, inevitably) he ran both the Conservative Club and the Union. Even in such a nursery of ambition Rees-Mogg stood out. College contemporaries composed a new version of the song *Lloyd George Knew My Father*:

> Rees-Mogg knows the Master.
> The Master knows the Queen.
> Rees-Mogg talks to no-one
> Lower than the Dean.

His is the sort of pedigree which has produced figures who have risen to the top of public life for generations. The combination of self-assurance, ambition and an etiolated compassion is the hallmark of the great English Pooh-Bah. (Who else could write of his 'impotent guilt, on the walk from the Royal Opera House to the Savoy Hotel for supper,' on observing the homeless sleeping in doorways?[38])

Rees-Mogg's answer to the question of why his name had such appeal for Downing Street during the eighties has an undramatic plausibility about it. As he lies back in his armchair, grey hair falling across his brow and his fingertips steepled on his chest, he gives a rehearsed explanation. It's a question of contacts:

> Inevitably as a journalist you get to know a large number of people, and it's people who make appointments. If they feel reasonably safe about appointing you, you're more likely to get the job than somebody they don't know. Appointment secretaries and ministers are much more concerned with not having a disaster than with anything particular which may or may not happen. And I've never done anything really badly.[39]

It is a humdrum enough explanation which goes some way to explaining why most public appointments are so dull. It is also further evidence of the extraordinarily shallow pool from which the Great and Good are drawn. Rees-Mogg went about his business conscientiously and with a good degree of enthusiasm, and while it is hard to think of him as a representative of the common man, sheer assiduousness probably bridged the gulf between the housing estates of suburbia and the Old Rectory, Hinton Blewitt.

But the sharpest criticism of him is that while appearing to be a chip off the old block, he was in fact something else, representative of the politicization of public appointments. Certainly he never made any secret of his Conservative past, having twice stood unsuccessfully for parliament among the miners of County Durham, where his air of a slightly lost rural dean can hardly have been an asset. During his time at the BBC, when the Home Secretary, Leon Brittan, asked the Corporation not to show a documentary in the *Real Lives* series dealing with extremist politicians in Northern Ireland, it was Rees-Mogg who led the governors' demand that the management acquiesce. At the Arts Council, he accepted government wisdom about the need for alternatives to public funding. He supported attempts to suppress the *Spycatcher* memoirs of former M.I.5 man Peter Wright.

Rees-Mogg's predecessor as vice-chairman of the BBC, Lord Bonham-Carter, son of Lady Violet and grandson of Asquith, was another member of the Great and Good with a political background, having briefly been a Liberal MP. Indeed, his record was intrinsic to his being offered the job, since at the time (1975), the BBC was short of governors with political experience. I suggested to Lord Bonham-Carter that his pedigree inevitably made him a political appointee himself:

> Of course, I was a political person. But in those days things were different: appointments had to be consensual. There was balanced politicization. Now, it's an unbalanced politicization. What was unique about the BBC governors in the eighties was that you had Rees-Mogg as vice-chairman and Stuart Young as chairman – two open, committed supporters of the present Government. That had never, ever happened in the whole history of the Corporation. They had simply abandoned balance.[40]

This is a familiar refrain. Alasdair Milne, the BBC director-general sacked in 1987, also believed that the Thatcher government abandoned any attempt at bipartisan appointments, in favour of packing the BBC governors with people who would be politically sympathetic.[41] But it is a complaint that has been made before. When Harold Wilson put in Lord Hill of Luton to act as chairman of the BBC (a Conservative who, as head of the Independent Television Authority had 'made sure that their treatment of news and current affairs does not offend the Establishment', in the view of Richard Crossman[42]), he remarked, 'Charlie Hill has already cleaned up ITV and he'll do the same to the BBC now I'm appointing him chairman.'[43]

There is nothing novel in the direct involvement of the prime minister in public appointments. Under the secret rules of Cabinet procedure, the prime minister has the right to be consulted about all chairmanships and deputy chairmanships of public boards and commissions of inquiry.[44] Some politicians freely confess that they have packed supposedly 'independent' inquiries, in the hope they will produce a congenial result. In her diaries, Barbara Castle admits that when secretary for social services in 1975, she and her health minister, David Owen, deliberately appointed Alec Merrison, Vice Chancellor of Bristol University, to chair a Royal Commission on the Health Service, on the grounds that 'he was a dedicated supporter of the NHS and would have no truck with private financing and all that nonsense.'[45]

What happened in the 1980s was, say opponents, of a different order altogether. To begin with, Margaret Thatcher dispensed with royal commissions. For a government committed to radical change, they had a number of disadvantages. Firstly, as their participants confessed, they were supposed to be balanced in composition, and were inevitably predisposed towards consensus. Once established, a royal commission was out of political control. And when it had finished its inquiry, not a word of its report could be changed by government, which was also obliged to publish its findings. The Thatcher approach was to employ small teams to tackle specific problems or to issue a set of proposals, and then wait for the howls of anguish.

This was not the style of the Great and Good. Figures like Lord Bonham-Carter, appointed to his most public post, as chairman of the Race Relations Board, by the Labour Home Secretary, Roy Jenkins, and reappointed by both his Conservative successors, Robert Carr and Reginald Maudling, was committed to a more sedate, centrist approach. Like most of his ilk, he believed in the three great pillars of domestic policy: the Welfare State, full employment, and the nationalized industries. Generally, with the exception of Suez and the Common Market, there was also agreement on foreign policy. He belonged to that alliance of the professions, the remnants of old money and a smattering of intellectuals which had a romantic view of the working man and found a sympathetic ear in the leadership of more conservative trades unions.

It would be hard to overstate the contempt with which the lower-middle class were viewed. Peter Jay, who was plucked from the economic editorship of *The Times* by his father-in-law, Labour Prime Minister James Callaghan, to be made ambassador to Washington, recalls the feelings clearly:

> We felt nothing but hostility for them. We thought they were silly and selfish, with narrow, primitive, semi-educated attitudes. We grew up viewing them with contempt, and saw them as preoccupied with money so they could 'better themselves'. They made themselves ridiculous. They were contemptible, and therefore it was easy for governments to squeeze them.[46]

And squeezed they were. The petit-bourgeoisie was an easy target for governments keen to raise a little more in taxes. Their common-sense ideas about life, good housekeeping and the rest were ignored by government after government, who regarded them as an ever-productive milch-cow. There was a cultural bias against them too: much of British theatre and cinema in the fifties and sixties was peopled by heroes and anti-heroes wrestling with the small-mindedness of the lower-middle class. It was predictable, if not predicted, that one day the worm would turn.

Mrs Thatcher was a natural to lead the revolt of the petite-bourgeoisie. She was an outsider to her bones: a woman, a scientist and a non-conformist in a male, humanities and soft Anglican world. The old Establishment was masculine – the public schools, the male Oxbridge colleges, the gentlemens' clubs of St James's. Attitudes were formed as much in shared leisure as by individual endeavour. She, by contrast, seemed only happy at work. The abiding impression of eighties government is of a woman going briskly about her business, handbag over one arm, bustling off from one meeting to another, impatient at others' need for rest or reflection.

She distrusted the institutions through which they exercised influence from the moment that supreme power seemed within her grasp. Her former Special Adviser, Patrick Cosgrave, recounts how there were only two areas for which she had any respect:

> 'Do you,' a friend asked her in 1980, 'hate all institutions?' She frowned and replied, 'Not at all. I have great respect for the Monarchy and Parliament.' But for the City, the trade unions, the civil service and the Church of England she has a dislike that some would call hatred and certainly veers regularly over into contempt.[47]

Given this cast of mind, it was not surprising that during Mrs Thatcher's occupancy the Great and Good found the doors of 10 Downing Street more closed than at any time since the war. To ward off the smothering tendencies of the bishops, permanent secretaries and dons, the Prime Minister had a shifting circle of advisers to protect her, and another group who would replenish the fund of radical ideas. All prime ministers develop a small coterie of kindred spirits, but Mrs Thatcher tended to listen to individuals on individual issues, while the number of people who enjoyed sustained, continuing influence was tiny.

Industrialists, who have acquired power and influence without passing through the mollifying tunnel of public school, Oxbridge and the professions, have always represented a potential challenge to the old order. They therefore proved natural allies in her assault upon the seat of consensus in Whitehall. Some, like David Young, who had abandoned the law for a career as a property developer, she put in charge of great statutory bodies, in his case eventually raising him to the Cabinet as Lord Young of Graffham. Though much resented by

MPs who had had to go through the tiresome business of getting people to vote for them, he proved a determined and effective minister, until he decided he'd had enough of the political rough-and-tumble which went with the job.

At a second level were industrialists like Jeffrey Sterling, the chairman of the P&O shipping company, for whom she arranged a knighthood. Sterling was given an office at the Department of Trade and Industry, where he advised on industrial policy, and had a big say in plans for the future of broadcasting. Sir Roy Griffiths, Managing Director of the Sainsbury grocery chain, was put in charge of an inquiry into the National Health Service. Sir Derek Rayner was borrowed from Marks and Spencer to tackle waste in government. Sir Robin Ibbs was loaned from ICI and asked to sort out the civil service.

A small group of civil servants stayed loyal throughout the eighties, of whom the most formidable was the Prime Minister's press secretary, Bernard Ingham, the short-tempered son of a Yorkshire weaver. His bluff style, orchestration of a pliant group of lobby correspondents and capacity to communicate with the Prime Minister almost telepathically, justified the tag 'the deputy Prime Minister'. Robert Armstrong, the Cabinet Secretary, developed a genuine affection for Mrs Thatcher, which was obviously reciprocated during his term in office. Another highly influential bureaucrat, Charles Powell, was a fast-rising Foreign Office man who came to Margaret Thatcher's notice when part of the team negotiating independence for Zimbabwe. Seconded from the Foreign Office as her deputy private secretary, Powell was soon reckoned by his former colleagues to have 'gone native', and was widely resented for his continued and easy access to the Prime Minister's ear, into which he appeared to be whispering something which was definitely not the authorized FO version. All worked prodigious hours ('Charles, eez's nairver at 'ome' was the frequent complaint of Powell's sprightly Italian wife), which reinforced their remoteness from the rest of the world.

Then there were the courtiers, the greatest of whom was her husband, Denis. Others included Cecil Parkinson, whose devotion ensured his survival even after an undistinguished ministerial career and despite his former mistress presenting their illegitimate child to the press. There were also her public relations men. Tim Bell, usually described in the newspapers as 'Mrs Thatcher's favourite adman', claims the distinguishing characteristic of this group was that 'we spent time being nice to her. There's something about her which stopped other people saying "what a nice dress", or "you did well on television yesterday". They seemed to feel it was a threat to their virility.'[48] Bell is happy to cultivate the impression that he was the Svengali who transformed Thatcher's harsh, strident public persona into something softer and more voter-friendly. In fact, much of it was the work of Gordon Reece, another of her image-makers. But the acceptance of responsibility is typical of these men: modesty is not the word which springs to mind.

The office of prime minister is a lonely and uniquely stressful one, and most develop their own small circle of confidants. The Thatcher group had several characteristics which made them differ from their predecessors. Apart from the fact that most of them were self-made, the other thing they had in common is that they were all essentially 'doers', unencumbered by second thoughts. 'They are characterized by low boredom thresholds and an inability to work for other people,' thought Sir John Hoskyns. 'They're probably impossible, unattractive people. The basic premiss is that they think they know better than anyone else. They aren't team players.'[49]

The most zealous guardians of the flame were the converts. They included the former Communist, Alfred Sherman (whom she later recommended for a knighthood); Paul Johnson, one-time editor of the *New Statesman*; and her close friend the former Labour MP and *News of the World* columnist, Woodrow Wyatt. Nothing is more politically reassuring than the fact that people have abandoned their former friends to join you. Others might be suspicious of their capacity for the volte-face, but in the Thatcher Downing Street, seeing the light was the key to their fortune.

Among her policy advisers, the best-known was Sir Alan Walters, whose wraith-like presence as her adviser on the economy proved so vexatious to the Chancellor of the Exchequer, Nigel Lawson, that he resigned. Although he later affected contempt for the poor, Walters had grown up the son of a working-class Leicestershire Communist. He had been recruited by Alfred Sherman specifically to provide a counter-blast to the Treasury advisers, because Whitehall was deemed to be the source of the advice which had let the country down in the past.

Other recent prime ministers had been aware of the shortcomings of policy advice from Whitehall, but none had acquired the almost visceral distrust which characterized some of the early Thatcher advisers. The Central Policy Review Staff, or 'Think Tank', which had been run by the polymath Lord Rothschild to supply Edward Heath with independent ideas and inject new life into strategic thought, was an early casualty. Rothschild and his successors tried to take a fresh look at issues too remote, politically inconvenient or otherwise ignored, and come up with clear, concise proposals for action, if possible on a single sheet of paper. They had been on to the energy crisis, for example, years before it hit politics. Mrs Thatcher was instinctively distrustful of the group. Early on, she demanded from each member a list of the people they had consulted during the previous three months. Deciding they hadn't spent enough time talking to industrialists (Marks and Spencer was the favoured analogy), she killed it off in 1983. The first some of the Tank members knew of their fate was when they read it in *The Times*.

In place of the Think Tank the Prime Minister had the Policy Unit. The difference was vast. Members of the Policy Unit were drawn from a much broader pool and were dominated by businessmen and academics. Lest they be contaminated by too frequent contact with the fudge and mudge of Whitehall, they were entertained to frequent lunches by right-wing organizations like Aims of Industry and the Institute of Directors. Also present at these meetings in various London clubs and restaurants were representatives from employers' organizations, who recognized that to influence the Policy Unit was to influence the Prime Minister: if a minister proved unavailable, unsympathetic or intractable, they could outmanoeuvre him by enlisting Policy Unit support. Where the Think Tank tended to challenge Downing Street, the Policy Unit strengthened it.

The beliefs of this group centred on Downing Street were completely at odds with the ideas of most of the Great and Good whom, indeed, they regarded as a symptom of the problem. Tim Bell considered that Mrs Thatcher thought 'all the problems of Britain were the direct consequence of two things. One was socialism. The other was the Tory Grandees.'[50] She was fortunate in that those who had passed through their political puberty in the fifties and sixties had grown up with a hazy notion of the Establishment. Many had begun by raging against it as angry young men or women and felt terribly let down by the failure of the Wilson government to make much of a dent in it. Others, demoralized apostles of free enterprise, were appalled at the way in which the old boy network laid its palsied hand upon the business of wealth creation. By the late seventies a succession of writers, of whom Correlli Barnett and Martin Wiener were the best-known, had given this idea intellectual respectability. By the time that Mrs Thatcher entered Downing Street – after a Winter of Discontent in which rubbish was piled high in the streets and the dead lay unburied – the two ideas had been elided.

The most consistently outspoken broadsides against the old Establishment came from the Institute of Directors, a once moribund association of small businessmen and oddball intellectuals, which revived itself by taking up Thatcherism almost before the term had been coined. Even after a decade in which they had more-or-less everything their own way, they were still railing against the old enemy.

Using their favoured analogy in which the complexities of a nation-state were reduced to the simplicities of a corner shop balance sheet, the newly appointed boss of the Institute took up the cudgels again in February 1990. 'It is obvious that responsibility for 100 years of decline of UK plc must be laid at the door of the Establishment which purported to guide the affairs of the nation,' Peter Morgan told them in a speech which commanded wide attention.[51] To him, the Establishment was a liberal conspiracy. Listing the institutions which had contributed to the lamentable performance of 'UK plc', Morgan went on to lambast Oxford University ('dons caught in a timewarp'), the Church of England ('the enterprise culture is an alien concept to the established Church'), and Whitehall ('our vast body of state employees who do not have to worry where the next pay cheque is coming from').

All this went down well enough with the members of the Institute, although it conveniently ignored both the fact that large numbers of those he excoriated had been encouraged into the professions by business parents and that for an entire decade 'the Establishment' had been elbowed aside by the Thatcher appointments policy.

Margaret Thatcher understood the power of patronage early in her premiership. Her use of it was scarcely unprecedented: 'Jobs for the boys', Tory MPs had cried as Harold Wilson infiltrated another trades union general secretary or a congenial academic on to the board of one or another of the great national institutions in his gift. In Whitehall, three words came to sum up the appointments policy. The director of one of the national galleries whose trustees were appointed by Downing Street ran into them in the very early 1980s. Previously, he had merely submitted the name of the person chosen by his committee to Downing Street, where it was rubber-stamped. Now, for the first time, he was subjected to close questioning, which went beyond the usual itemizing of previous posts. 'Of course,' said the civil servant, 'the question I shall be asked when I put this name to the PM is "Is he *one of us*?"'

'One of Us' soon became the catchphrase of the Thatcher era. It did not imply membership of a social circle but an attitude of mind. The inclination was, where possible, to appoint new people, often with no experience of similar work, to jobs in Downing Street's gift. At its most blatant, posts which had once been the preserve of dons from Oxford or Cambridge were now given to businessmen. They were furious. In Oxford, the voice of the gnomic Professor Sammy Finer, a declared political agnostic, rose a full octave when I asked him about it: 'It simply isn't true any longer that merit will out. Merit *plus party* will out, but not merit on its own. You're just ignored. You might as well never have existed.'[52]

Mrs Thatcher took a much closer interest in a broader range of appointments than any other post-war prime minister. Now, when a short list of names went to Number 10, there were questions about why other names had been omitted. As often as not, they were the names of her favourite businessmen of the moment. There was nothing new in the involvement of businessmen on the boards of the great public institutions alongside the retired civil servants and august academics. But the balance began to change. The distinguished nuclear physicist Lord Flowers, a veteran of a dozen such committees, told me:

> Management is what they're good at: the old buffers are scholars. Where you want scholarship is on the inside, not on the boards. But one of the pities is that the distinguished old buffers steeped in scholarship who are a little unworldly are being eased out of things. The inevitable consequence, if that policy is practised too energetically, will be that we won't have any erudition left.[53]

However uncongenial for the old professors, the obsession with appointing businessmen to the boards of such things as the great museums and galleries undoubtedly had positive benefits in terms of efficiency and fund-raising for example. But it failed to recognize that the challenge of running an individual company was very different to that posed by a large public organization with a multiplicity of purposes whose owners weren't shareholders but taxpayers who felt entitled to demand access to those things the nation already owned. Besides which, the list of figures qualified for the job was very short. It was almost as small as the circle of names and acquaintances of the average senior civil servant, and was reduced further by the fact that once they had got on to a board, many businessmen rapidly came to resent the amount of time the job demanded.

Some of the details of this appointments policy are explored in later chapters, but it is worth noting here the way in which the philosophy of much of this new breed flew in the face of cardinal articles of faith of the Great and Good. It surfaced, for example, in the suggestion that museums and art galleries, which had previously been open to the public free of charge, should begin to charge for admission. It was not merely that such a proposition cut across yet another area of previous consensus. It was also that free admission was part of the great Victorian philanthropic tradition, part of the vision of Britain which the Establishment felt they were called to safeguard. Many of the new style trustees put in by Downing Street saw nothing wrong with the idea.

But the belief that as every post fell vacant, in marched another businessman briefed to implement the free-market orders of Downing Street soon became another myth. The Great and Good have proved more resilient than might have been expected. The new group – 'the Disestablishment' as they were christened in a series of articles in the *Financial Times*[54] – was highly fluid. Businessmen, politicians and academics came and went from it. Life was faster, demands changed more quickly, and people were included because they met a particular need at a particular time. Entry to the old Establishment was hard to achieve for outsiders, but once they were in, the successful ones, the safe pairs of hands, tended to stay in. The new group accepted and rejected with startling speed. Its central belief, in the wisdom of the marketplace, was less than immediately applicable to the running of Kew Gardens or the British Museum.

Besides which, there was a severe lack of available talent. In an attempt to find new blood to lead the science research councils, the then education secretary, Sir Keith Joseph, a great proselytizer for the new approach, hired a firm of headhunters. Unfortunately their first action was to ask those already within the system of whom they should make enquiries. Lord Dainton, one of Britain's most distinguished scientists, observed the process at first-hand:

> The really dangerous thing is the exclusivity of the ideas under discussion. It's always the same group of people. And when it comes to appointments, they just get on the blower to somebody and say 'give me your views', and it's the same circle of people they know and trust. It's not necessarily done

with bad intentions, but unless there's much greater flow in and out, then
I fear we're on a downward path.[55]

This is not the sort of complaint one would expect after years in
which Downing Street was running riot by appointing one maverick
after another. In fact, the Great and Good are not nearly as changed
as popular myth would have it.

The spectacularly political appointments of the Thatcher years, like
sending the right-wing journalist Lord Chalfont to be deputy chairman
of the Independent Broadcasting Authority, are outnumbered by the
nomination of much more traditional figures. Between 1970 and 1989,
for example, four fifths of BBC governors were men, half had been
privately educated and half were products of Oxford or Cambridge.[56]
There was a steady increase in the proportion of businessmen appointed, from two out of twenty in the 1970s to six out of nineteen in
the 1980s, but they were still outnumbered by representatives of the
professions. The man appointed chairman of the BBC by Mrs Thatcher in 1986, Marmaduke Hussey, was a businessman, it was true, but
of the most patrician style, and his wife, Lady Susan, as mentioned
before, was a lady-in-waiting to the Queen.

For all their talk about the wisdom of the marketplace, the Thatcher
government could not give up the paternalistic idea that they had to
regulate the independent television companies, with the continuation
of the Independent Broadcasting Authority in the guise of an Independent Television Commission. A Broadcasting Standards Council, to
determine what the British people may or may not watch, will be run,
under Lord Rees-Mogg, by a bishop, a headmaster, a psychologist, an
educationalist, a retired Labour MP and a former television news-
reader. None of the figures on any of the regulatory bodies was
exactly a spring chicken, and none could be called a radical. Every-
where in public life, old families, old money and titles have been in
decline, while business has advanced. But still, the great majority of
posts are held by the sort of steady chaps who have always made up
the Great and Good.

CHAPTER FIVE

The Eunuch's Consolation

God bless the civil service,
The nation's saving grace.
While we expect democracy
They're laughing in our face.

— *Ideology* BILLY BRAGG

ANGULAR, AWKWARD in a pair of threadbare jeans on a darkened stage, thumping out his protest songs in rasping cockney, Billy Bragg speaks for millions. At the Labour party Conference, the troubadour of the Left gives the activists a message they all unconsciously share. Conflating the multitude of Establishment horrors, 'the courts, the secret handshake, the Stock Exchange and the Old School Tie', Bragg's roll-call of conspiracies ends with the one demon common to both right and left, the civil service. Elected governments come and go. But the bureaucracy goes on forever.

The functionaries at the top of the civil service are, by this account, like the eunuchs of ancient Byzantium. Without the presence of these emasculated males, the business of the empire could not have been carried on. Not only was every position in state service open to eunuchs, many of the highest posts were actually reserved for them. Sons of the great patrician families offered themselves for castration to become eligible.

Ever since the Victorian reforms of Charles Trevelyan and Stafford Northcote, the bureaucracy of Britain has persuaded many of the universities' finest brains to forswear the pleasures of the flesh for the service of the state. The professional civil service was the creature of Oxford and Cambridge, and Gladstone was in no doubt that in making entry to the bureaucracy dependent upon talent rather than cronyism, the reforms would 'strengthen and multiply the ties between the higher classes and the possession of administrative power'.[1] Before the Northcote-Trevelyan reforms, many government posts had been a sought-after sinecure, openly bought and sold through advertisements in the columns of *The Times*, with those involving least work commanding the highest fees. But the new civil service, drawing its entrants from reformed universities and burgeoning public schools, was to be a meritocratic profession, selecting from the cream of university graduates and making them custodians of public polity.

How different a picture the bureaucracy presented as it entered the 1990s. It had been under attack for the best part of two decades and morale was as low as anyone could recall. Not only had almost 167,000 jobs disappeared (out of a total of 732,000 in 1979), but those who remained felt undervalued and unloved. In some government departments, the trail from Whitehall to the finance houses of the City was so well worn that it could almost be read on the pavements. During 1988, almost one third of the economic advisers in the Treasury disappeared to double their salaries by becoming in-house consultants or journalists. In the Inland Revenue, tax inspectors could treble their pay by taking their expensively-taught skills to the private sector.

The civil servants who survived found little public sympathy, not least because for three decades or more, the bureaucracy had been a whipping boy for Britain's relative industrial decline. The Left blamed them for the persistent obstruction of Labour government attempts to create a socialist Utopia, while for the Right the fact that Britain had a dramatically less dynamic economy than her competitors proved the unwordly incompetence of the Oxbridge generalists who administered the state. 'Disparaging the civil service has become a national pastime, rather like throwing beer bottles at football matches,' Lord Rothschild said in the 1970s. A decade later, beer bottles were banned from football terraces, but the assault upon the traditions of the civil service had advanced beyond popular abuse to become an item of government policy.

Although the organization of the modern civil service dates from the reforms of Sir Warren Fisher after the First World War, it is really the creature of its Victorian forebears. Lord Macaulay concluded in the 1850s that the best possible education for an administrator was in the liberal arts, then dominated by classical studies. The influence of Macaulay's brother-in-law, Trevelyan, and Benjamin Jowett, later to become master of Balliol College, Oxford, provided the opportunity for the universities to take on a new role. The civil service was 'a new profession at the time when the old ones were overstocked', in the opinion of the master of Marlborough. A higher civic calling, providing entrants to the civil service, became part of the universities' *raison d'être*. Relations between Whitehall and Oxbridge remained close for generations. Not only did the dons at the ancient colleges harvest the finest brains for the service of the state, they provided an informal reservoir of advice, served on commissions of inquiry and in later life the luckier civil servants might expect to pass their retirement in the comfort of an Oxford master's lodge.

In professions like the law or medicine there is a specific task to be discharged and a confidential relationship between practitioner and client to be maintained. In the civil service, the fiduciary ethos found its expression in a sense of custodianship of an idea of Britain. Senior bureaucrats became what one of them calls 'guardians of the nation's morals'. Lord Sherfield, who served as deputy head of the Foreign Office and joint head of the Treasury before retiring as chairman of the Atomic Energy Authority in the sixties, has the intellectual insouciance to state the underlying self-confidence with no embarrassment. 'We attempted to moderate the more extravagant demands of ministers,' he told me. When I asked on whose authority, he answered, 'In the interests of what one saw as sound policy.'[2]

For ministers, elected to translate manifesto promises into action, running up against talk of 'sound policy' was a source of constant exasperation. One set of political memoirs after another chronicles the frustration of politicians at the resistance of the bureaucracy to change. Most such recollections are full of self-serving justification, and the civil service provides a convenient scapegoat for the failure of ideas which have not been properly thought out. But retired ministers are right to notice a feeling within the bureaucracy that the civil service represents a continuum, while elected governments ebb and flow.

'That's all right, we can leave it for a day or two to the automatic pilot,' Churchill said as he prepared to leave on an overseas visit.[3] The automatic pilot in question, Sir John Anderson ('Old Jehovah', to his awestruck subordinates) was one of the outstanding heads of the civil service this century, but there is a sense in which the whole organization considers itself to be performing the same function as he.

Occasionally, we get flashes of the direct political influence of mandarins. During the 1974 miners' strike, the head of the civil service, William Armstrong, was tendering strong advice to Edward Heath to resist demands for conciliation. Jim Prior recalls that 'he told us that what was at issue was the sort of society in which his grandchildren would be brought up, and that it was imperative that the rule of law must not be flouted.'[4] Prior was deeply impressed, as apparently was Heath, the more so since overt political advice was so rarely given. Another senior civil servant recalls how they gathered by the light of the Cabinet Office emergency generators, working feverishly to devise ways of offsetting the three-day working week which resulted. 'There was a feeling that it was up to us to keep the country going,' he told me, recalling the time as one of the bureaucracy's battle-honours.

Such occasions are rare. For the most part, mandarins like to think of government as a big country house, in which they are the butlers, showing new tenants how the place is run. It is a characteristic metaphor, speaking of an age of elegance and suggesting, without actually stating it, that the permanent status of the staff gives them a better sense of the fabric of the place than mere passing tenantry. On the other hand, the sin of which the civil service stands pre-eminently accused is that in its administration of the country it has an institutional bias against radical initiative which might have saved the nation from economic decline. Large expanses of the mountains of literature chronicling the decline of Britain in the twentieth century deal with the inadequacies of the amateur British civil service.

It is hard to deny that in countries like France and Japan the civil service played a far more effective role in promoting industrial development. In Britain, the argument goes, the steady stream of young people coming out of the universities into Whitehall stood aloof, committed to Edwardian ideas of their role which had nothing to do with promoting enterprise. Simultaneously, the model of a 'respectable' career Whitehall held up attracted disproportionate numbers of graduates into administering the products of wealth when they might have been generating it.

This is not entirely fair. While it is true that the greatest years of the modern bureaucracy occurred during the Second World War, when it sucked in talents from all over the nation, this was at a time when government, of necessity, played a central role in running the economy. The bureaucracy should have been reformed at war's end, to take account of the greatly changed circumstances, but the opportunity was missed (partly, it has to be said, by design).

There was, however, a dignity of purpose among many of those who joined the administration in the postwar years which has been wilfully misunderstood by many of their enemies. Sir Derek Mitchell, who joined the Treasury in 1947 and rose to become deputy permanent secretary, recalls it clearly. The son of an elementary school headmaster who won a scholarship to St Paul's and thence to Christ Church, Oxford, he admits to a bias against business. But not for entirely unworthy motives.

> We just felt public service was much more honourable and challenging than to dirty one's hands in trade ... Of course, I have a higher regard for the profit motive now, but we sincerely felt that it was a more proper use of one's talent to put it to the use of the community as a whole.[5]

But in the postwar Welfare State, with increasing areas of the economy, from the mines to the hospitals, under government ownership, the task of the bureaucracy was no longer one of pure administration, the drafting of legislation and so on. Much of it was really about management. But the civil service was still recruiting in the same old pattern. Soon after Sir Claus Moser was asked to become head of the Government Statistical Service in 1967 he was invited to lunch by one of the permanent secretaries. As drink loosened the two men's tongues, they began to swop life stories, Moser recalling how he had arrived in Britain as a thirteen-year-old refugee from Germany. His lunch companion disclosed an education at Eton and Oxford, then suddenly clapped him on the shoulder and exclaimed, 'You know, it's a remarkable tribute to this country that somebody with your background has become a permanent secretary!' Moser was one of the most distinguished statisticians of his day. What the Etonian meant was that it was surprising that he should have joined the club.

In fact, the caricature figure who has slid effortlessly through Winchester or Eton and then Christ Church or Balliol and on into the public service is largely a myth. Despite the succession of an Etonian (Robert Armstrong) by a Harrovian (Robin Butler) at the head of the civil service in 1988, most of the permanent secretaries are clever state school pupils or the products of minor public schools. In 1941 one of the mandarins asked the rhetorical question 'what sort of young man enters the civil service?', and answered that he was likely to be cleverer and more industrious than his fellow students at university, and that

> many of the entrants are poor and without family influence – the sons of country parsons or small tradesmen or widows living on tiny incomes who for years have made sacrifices in order that their clever boys may not be robbed of a university career and the chances it offers. A young man of this origin must earn his living from the moment he leaves the university ... In any case (his family) can do nothing for him and he knows it.[6]

It is an indulgent portrait, but in terms of background it has become increasingly true. They are largely the children of the middle class. 'Today's mandarins tend to come from families of great diligence and a little prosperity, rather than great prosperity and a little diligence,' decided two authors who studied their backgrounds in 1980.[7] Since the war, the proportion of public school products at the top of the bureaucracy has been in steady decline. In 1960, of the twenty-eight senior civil servants, eighteen had been educated in the private sector. By 1990, the proportions had dropped to fourteen out of thirty-six.

But the mandarinate remains largely the preserve of bright Oxbridge types. Between 1900 and 1919, sixty-three per cent of permanent secretaries had been at the ancient universities. In the twenty years between 1965 and 1986, the proportion of Oxford and Cambridge graduates, rather than dropping, had actually grown, to seventy-five per cent.[8] Every single head of the service since the war has been a graduate of one or other of the ancient universities. For years, the selection process was designed to choose people with administrative skills who were also clever enough to have gone on to become professors. It is a culture which places the highest of premiums upon the ability to digest information fast and then to argue a case successfully. It is a world in which they value the good opinion of one another more than the approbation of the public. It is precisely the environment in which conditioning influences will be most powerful.

The civil service spent most of the eighties trying to change the stereotype mandarin, while simultaneously arguing that the Oxbridge dominance did not represent an institutional bias. As salaries in the bureaucracy looked progressively more miserly by comparison with the riches to be earned elsewhere, they needed to broaden their graduate intake anyway. The First Commissioner, Dennis Trevelyan, an avuncular roast beef and two veg character whose official task is to be 'responsible to the Queen and the Privy Council for keeping unqualified people out of the civil service', visited every university and polytechnic in the country to try to drum up interest among new recruits. By the late eighties, his efforts were showing in the proportion of what he calls the 'golden boys and girls' chosen as potential future mandarins who had been educated outside Oxford and Cambridge. In 1982, seventy-five per cent of them had been educated at Oxbridge. By 1987, the figure had dropped to fifty-four per cent. It is still a disproportionately large number, but when the two universities are attracting a disproportionate number of the best students, it would be perverse to try to manipulate the selection process against them. The selectors still seek much the same skills, although they tend to qualify their observations, slightly too hastily, with remarks about the need to pick people who have potential management skills as well. In doing so, they reflect the mood of the times.

By the time that Mrs Thatcher moved into 10 Downing Street, the self-confidence of the civil service had been badly dented. When so much of industry was in the state sector it was inevitable that the management bureaucracy would look inept. One misjudgement after another, like developing in Concorde a supersonic passenger aircraft which could never hope to recoup its development costs, shot great holes in Whitehall's claim to be packed with infallibly wise policy-makers.

The most trenchant criticism of the civil service, that it is staffed by amateurs, has been repeated time and again. As Thomas Balogh remarked drily in 1959, 'in a planned economy, the crossword-puzzle mind, reared on mathematics at Cambridge or Greats at Oxford, has only a limited outlet.'[9] Victorian reforms had created a selection process with an instinctive bias against socialism, and one in which 'positive knowledge and imagination, assertion of the social against the public interest, were obviously not looked for.'[10] The examiners chose instead extroverts, conformists, above all amateurs, who made White-hall 'the apotheosis of the dilettante'.

It was damning stuff, which Balogh's friend Harold Wilson took seriously enough when in government to set up a committee under another pal, the Vice Chancellor of Sussex University, Lord Fulton, charged with investigating the civil service system of recruitment and training. Fulton also concluded that the civil service was 'too much based on the philosophy of the amateur,'[11] that the driving principles were anti-creative, and that the whole organization was resistant to change. He recommended sweeping changes, including the creation of a Department for the civil service, the abolition of distinctions between different classes of civil servants, greater interchange with the outside world, and an extension of opportunities for scientists, engineers and other specialists. In the event, the Fulton report, although accepted by Harold Wilson, was pretty thoroughly suffocated by the civil service.

The Thatcher criticisms of the service were of a different order.

Her suspicion had been evident from the moment that she first achieved cabinet office under Edward Heath. Appointed Secretary of State for Education, she bowled into her office to meet her permanent secretary, Sir William Pile. He recalled the encounter with a shudder:

> Within the first ten minutes of her arrival, she uncovered two things to us. One is ... an innate wariness of the civil service, quite possibly even a distrust; and secondly, a page from an exercise book with eighteen things she wanted done that day. Now these two actions were quite unlike anything we'd come across from predecessors and later on, I think, we saw that this was only the beginning of the relevation of a character that we'd have to get used to and that we hadn't run into before.[12]

The focus of the criticisms had changed. Now the complaint against the amateur had been translated into an argument that the bureaucracy was inefficient, extravagant, cynical, too academic. The incoming government in 1979 had no shortage of policies; when about half the economy was under state control what was needed from the bureaucracy was management skills. By the end of the Thatcher decade she had set in train a series of reforms designed to bring about what a permanent secretary in the Cabinet Office described as 'the most profound changes for over a century'.[13]

To bring the disciplines of private enterprise to bear on the bureaucracy, Mrs Thatcher recruited Sir Derek Rayner, Managing Director of her favourite firm, Marks and Spencer, to run an Efficiency Unit. 'Rayner's Raiders' set about their task of increasing efficiency with a vengeance, and within eight years were reckoned to have saved £1 billion.[14] It was Rayner's successor, Sir Robin Ibbs, a businessman borrowed from ICI, who produced what was hailed as a blueprint for a bureaucracy of the twenty-first century. Behind its stunningly dull title *The Next Steps*, Ibbs' report contained ideas which could have had long-dead mandarins rising up from their graves in horror.

The report had concluded that the most fundamental problem with the civil service was not so much its ethos as the task it was expected to perform. *The Next Steps* proposed that all Whitehall functions which could be categorized as 'managerial' be transferred to largely autonomous agencies, free of ministerial control, and free, within their budgets, to run themselves as they saw fit, hiring and firing senior staff exempt from the old Whitehall jobs-for-life culture. All manner of government tasks could be delegated in this way, from licensing cars to collecting taxes or paying social security benefits. The idea of

separating executive responsibilities from central government had
been developed in Sweden. The Ibbs report had in fact largely been
written by three civil servants, Kate Jenkins, Karen Caines and
Andrew Jackson, who, if their proposals are ever fully implemented,
deserve to be as well-known as great figures like Trevelyan, Northcote
and Fisher. In the months which followed their completion of the
report, all hell broke loose among their colleagues.

For the Treasury, the idea was anathema: for six decades, they had
set the budgets and therefore exercised control over every other
department in Whitehall. The Thatcher years, with their commitment
to tight control of public expenditure, had actually seen a consolidation
of the department's authority. Truly independent agencies would have
lessened the Treasury's power considerably.

The critical discovery of Sir Robin Ibbs' three investigators was
that despite all the talk of a revolution having swept through Whitehall
after seven years of Thatcherism, precious little had really changed.
Between them, the Treasury and the Cabinet Office were still in
control; despite all the rhetoric about a 'can do' mentality having
taken hold, things were really much as before. The organization was
still over-preoccupied with policy advice, encumbered by red tape,
and short of management skills.

By the time that the Ibbs report finally saw the light of day early in
1988, there were already signs of a Treasury fight-back. The number
of agencies to be set up in the first of the 'Next Steps' had been
whittled down to a dozen institutions, including such controversial
outfits as the government Stationery Office and the Meteorological
Office. Most of the chief executives hired for the first new agencies
came not from industry but the existing civil service and the man who
would implement the policy, Peter Kemp, was a Treasury official
himself. Mr Kemp declared that he would be very disappointed if
three quarters of the staff in the civil service were not eventually hived
off to independent agencies. We shall see.

All sorts of factors militate against the transformation of the upper
levels of the civil service into a ruthlessly efficient business. Whatever
the claims of a change of heart, institutional traditions are immensely
strong. In a closed culture like that in Whitehall, experience even of
other parts of the country, where most industry is located, is minimal.
Locked into a tiny area of the metropolis, hired in their early twenties
and expected to continue for nearly four decades, the pressure to
conform to the existing stereotype is enormous. Patterns of recruitment

inevitably attract those who have a sense of public service rather than a commitment to management – if they wanted to become managers they'd join Unilever or ICI. A culture of official secrecy is the enemy of efficiency. And even after the best part of a decade in which civil servants have been encouraged to take secondments to industry, the total number of all grades of civil servants attached to outside organizations in 1988 had only reached the underwhelming total of 311.

And if the civil service does end up with most of its functions being performed by semi-autonomous agencies, the consequence of separating the management functions from policy advice will be to leave a rump of bureaucrats in Whitehall, which will include, of course, the great majority of those hired from the universities to join the fast-track administrative stream. Their main function will be policy advice.

'Promotion comes to them,' Richard Crossman observed of his difficult-to-manage top civil servants, 'not from the minister – he has virtually nothing to do with it – but from the standing which they have in the eyes of the Treasury and the head of the civil service.'[15]

Admission to the 650 posts in the marshalling yard at the top of the bureaucracy is at the discretion of the Cabinet Office. Separately, like courtiers at the deathbed of a Florentine prince, each department is constantly reassessing its own succession plans in case its permanent secretary should fall under a bus, or – more commonly – just live long enough to collect his inflation-proofed pension at sixty.

In order to be considered, the anointed few must first win the approval of the Senior Appointments Selection Committee. The advantage of this system, which was only established in 1968, is said to be that it gets around any temptation to croneyism. But the committee is made up entirely of existing permanent secretaries, it takes its initial recommendation from the permanent secretary who is to be replaced, and then 'takes the minister's views into account'. In practice, the process means that permanent secretaries are appointing other permanent secretaries whom they have known all their working lives.

Like so many other plums, the final decision on who gets appointed to a vacant department is with the prime minister, who makes a choice from the Committee's short-list, presented by the head of the civil service. The justification for the entirely internal process which has taken place up to this point is that it distances the appointment of mandarins from day-to-day politics.

But by 1990, every single permanent secretary in Whitehall had been appointed by Margaret Thatcher. The situation was inevitable, given the length of her premiership, but the suspicion is that, just as with powers of patronage in everything from the chairmanship of regional health authorities to membership of the Arts Council, those who got promoted were those who were 'one of us'. It would be most surprising if she had taken less interest in senior appointments in the civil service than in, say, the trustees of national museums, where her influence was considerable, and one senior official was candid enough to admit that she was the most interventionist prime minister on such questions since Lloyd George. Some senior members of the Labour party are convinced that any incoming Labour government will have to conduct a purge of permanent secretaries. Even sympathetic academics like Dr William Plowden, of the Royal Institute of Public Administration, are bothered. In the third Thatcher term he decided the influence was more insidious:

> a perverse process of politicization, which is that some civil servants are not giving the best policy advice because they are not giving all the pluses and minuses of a course of action because life will be easier if they shade their advice ever so slightly.[16]

Perhaps the Labour party are being too alarmist about the apparent politicization of the bureaucracy. Even Tony Benn when a postmaster general in Harold Wilson's 1964 government had decided that the civil service was not an environment conducive to dynamic management.[17] One mandarin explained the change which had come over the top of the civil service by saying that 'Our job now is to tell the minister how to achieve what he wants to achieve.'[18] Considering that previous Labour ministers have complained repeatedly that in the past the civil service has done precisely the reverse, Margaret Thatcher may have created an environment in which an incoming socialist government could find a bureaucracy willing and able to carry out its wishes.

Despite all the upheavals, the mandarinate remains one of the finer Victorian institutions. Most work hard for more meagre rewards than they could get elsewhere. They are not financially corrupt. The policy advice is well rounded and thought out. Even though it is still wedded to unnecessary secrecy, the ethos of the profession still places the highest regard on the common good.

But they are well removed from the rest of British society, and the links with the remains of what used to constitute the Establishment are pretty attenuated. Having served in the wartime civil service, the men who ran the civil service throughout the fifties, sixties and seventies had a range of friendships which spanned national life, from the universities to the merchant banks. Even those who had the most non-Establishment backgrounds, like Sir William Armstrong (he was the son of Salvation Army officers, and joked that if he'd shown any ability at the triangle he would never have ended up in Whitehall), had acquired a network of people in positions of power and influence with whom they were on first-name terms.

But Sir William Armstrong was one of the last of that generation. By the time his namesake, Sir Robert Armstrong, took over, the last of the Old School were on the point of retirement. One immediate consequence was that the civil service was more cut off from the rest of society, most at home in the endless grey corridors of Whitehall. The men at the top in the eighties and nineties had had little or no experience of life outside Whitehall, unless they had spent a brief interlude on one of the civil service's exchange schemes. As one retired permanent secretary put it 'they simply have no imaginative understanding of how other people live and work'.[19]

Other characteristics were noticeable, too, particularly a certain lack of self-confidence among the younger staff. 'They've been told for a decade that being a public servant is a second-rate occupation staffed by second-raters,' was how one permanent secretary put it to me. They were creatures of their time, and as belief in the role of the state had waned, so had their own belief in their role. 'They're a very different type of person now,' another senior official said.

> When you put the best of the previous generation in a room with, say, a group of bankers, they seemed intelligent, articulate, often iconoclastic. They'd dominate the conversation. But nowadays they seem less interested in conceptual matters, and if you put a group of them in a room with a group of bankers, it'll be the bankers who make the running. It's the bankers who seem the iconoclasts, and the civil servants who seem to be the mechanics.[20]

Part of this is the inevitable consequence of working for a government which took office determined that, whatever else it did, it would not get bogged down in civil service advice. Supplanted as advisers by a profusion of policy consultants and zealots, the upper reaches of the bureaucracy have lost part of the role they had performed since Gladstone's day.

There are practical steps which could be taken to restore some of the morale of the domestic bureaucracy, which would not involve abandoning the principles of Northcote and Trevelyan. There seems to be no justification for the fact that permanent secretaries can carve up top appointments between them, and no reason why all senior jobs in the bureaucracy should not be advertised and open to all. In the longer term, the civil service could abandon the idea that it can reliably choose bright-eyed young graduates in their twenties and pay for the privilege of backing its judgement until they retire. Open to talent at all levels, and properly rewarded, the civil service might genuinely be more in tune not only with business realities but with the rest of society. It might also recover some of its *esprit de corps*.

Of all government departments, none is grander than the Foreign Office. More than almost any other major institution of state, apart perhaps from Buckingham Palace, the Foreign Office somehow has managed to preserve its old identity. Uniquely in Whitehall there still exists an identifiable Foreign Office 'type'. No similar creature exists elsewhere; at the Treasury there may be a distinctive style, but it is hardly a type, and a discernible Trade and Industry or Environment type is almost unimaginable. Can it really be the case that the qualities needed to represent the government to foreigners are so different to the qualities needed to represent the government to its own people?

To this day, no functionary has more self-assurance than the Foreign Office official. There is a glorious aloofness about many of them. Part of it comes from a lifetime spent at cocktail parties and diplomatic receptions, part, perhaps, from their connections with the Court. Ambassadors serve as the Queen's representative and, although constitutionally this obviously means the government in power, their despatches are still delivered to the Palace daily.

The connection with the crown expresses a more profound attitude. 'For some reason,' a minister who came to the Foreign Office after serving at one of the great domestic departments told me, 'there is an ethos in the Foreign Office that foreign policy is a highly skilled thing, which ministers really oughtn't to get too involved in.'[21]

The *hauteur* of the Foreign Office seeps out of the walls of the place. When Palmerston commissioned Sir Gilbert Scott to design a building properly reflecting Britain's imperial pomp, the architect originally came up with plans for the Gothic wonder later dusted off and recreated as St Pancras station. Palmerston preferred a mock Italian palazzo, adorned with statues, frescoes and sweeping staircases, to impress visiting foreign emissaries. In the late 1980s the building underwent extensive renovation and cleaning which failed to remove altogether the fingerprints of generations of civil service janitors. But the long corridors still feel as if they ought really to ring with the tap of the malacca cane of a plenipotentiary despatched across the globe to demand agreement with the British Empire.

The particular circumstances of the Foreign Office make the *déformation professionelle* more acute than at any domestic department of state. Where civil service officials elsewhere are constantly dealing with legislation to be put before the House of Commons, and therefore need to develop political antennae, their counterparts in the Foreign Office are working on papers to be read only by their colleagues and ministers. They have spent years in a series of overseas postings where social and professional life revolves around the same tiny circle of colleagues and acquaintances. It was only relatively recently that the idea of formal training was introduced; the previous system inevitably emphasized the importance of informal absorption of the wisdom of the place. Those marked for greatness in their early thirties – the 'flyers' – are those who have 'pure white files', scarcely the surest sign of originality or independence of mind. Few achieve real responsibility until they are within a decade of retirement. The hierarchical structure of the organization then ensures that ministers have too little to do with brighter, younger staff, and too much to do with those who have spent a lifetime steeped in the culture of the place.

Perhaps the most surprising thing about the foreign service is that it has retained its allure while its real importance has been declining irreversibly for years. It is not merely that Britain no longer has either an Empire or, often, the military means to back up a diplomatic threat. Nor is it even that the speed and impact of the mass media means that governments can witness events unfolding in front of their eyes as quickly as the local chargé can file his despatch. The whole business of being a diplomat has become less significant. In an age of instantaneous high-quality telecommunications between capital cities, who needs a local man-on-the-spot? Questions which have the most frequent and direct impact upon British citizens are pre-eminently connected with the European Community, where policy considerations are an extension of domestic concerns – food subsidies are the business of the Ministry of Agriculture, terrorism of the Home Office.

But almost every time there is an attempt to mount an investigation into the possibility of changes within the Foreign Office, it gets blown out of the water. In the early sixties, Lord Plowden remarked upon the general amateurism and lack of specialization, but to no great effect. In 1969, the industrialist Sir Val Duncan observed that much internal accountancy was 'in or near the quill pen era'. In 1975, the 'Think Tank', wondered whether the job could be done with fewer staff, in smaller missions, and why, for example, did the British embassy in Paris need eleven official cars when the French embassy in London had only one?[22]

What happened to the Think Tank investigation continues to serve as an awful warning to anyone who dares to challenge the collective wisdom of the Foreign Office. 'That proposal should have gone straight into the poisoned chalice file,' the head of the Tank, Sir Kenneth Berrill, remarked ruefully afterwards.[23]

The Tank's six investigators split into teams of two and hared off around the world to find out how British diplomacy operated. The missions followed a set pattern – a meeting with the ambassador, discussions with staff and talks with the foreign service of the host country. Tessa Blackstone discovered that inside the embassies the pattern was usually the same. 'There were a lot of overqualified and well-paid people sitting around with not enough to do.'[24]

Berrill kept the three most important missions, in Paris, Moscow and Washington, for himself. Moscow was fine, but in Paris he was met with ill-concealed hostility from the ambassador. Washington, with its village-sized community of six hundred staff and families, was the worst experience of the lot. Sir Kenneth was invited to explain himself to the Diplomatic Wives Association, at a mass meeting. For so genteel-sounding an organization, Berrill found it 'the most hostile audience I have faced in my entire life.'[25] The confrontation ran with bad feeling. One diplomatic wife after another got to her feet and lectured him on how hard life had been on previous postings in Kampala or Kathmandu. Why didn't he have any appreciation of the work their husbands had been doing for the nation? To put it bluntly – an old Foreign Office chestnut this – what could an outsider know of the delicate business of diplomacy?

Worse was to come when the Foreign Office mobilized to fight the report on publication. The researchers had concluded that one of the common suppositions about the Foreign Office was largely true – it was out of touch with domestic political conditions, too adrift from the departments in the home civil service whose interests they were supposed to be promoting abroad. They considered several possible solutions, but always found themselves asking the same question they had posed right at the start: did Britain really need an entirely separate Foreign Office? The more they thought about it, the more the answer seemed to be 'no'. The Tank decided the solution was to merge the Home and Foreign services, and to create within the new body a Foreign Service Group.

This was anathema to an organization steeped in a sense of its own history, and the diplomats now engaged in outright manipulation of sympathetic journalists to fight their corner. Before their conclusions had been published, anonymous diplomatic service sources were telling the press that 'the report will very likely be absurd.'[26] When finally it appeared, *The Times* managed on one day to attack the report on three separate pages. In one particularly stinging column, Lord Chalfont suggested that the report was 'an example of what happens when you send little boys (and littler girls) to do a man's job,'[27] conveniently ignoring the fact that the average age of the team – 39 – was the same as that of the Foreign Secretary, David Owen.

The recommendations on the British Council, the cultural wing of British diplomacy, also didn't go down well. Miserably underfunded though it is, the Council had acquired a reserve army of artists, writers and academics it had sponsored on overseas lecture tours which could be called out in times of crisis to do battle in the letters columns of *The Times*. This regiment was sufficiently well-connected even to have persuaded Buckingham Palace that the report was recommending something akin to the invasion of the Visigoths. On more than one occasion the Queen herself questioned the wisdom of the proposals.[28]

After this furious lobbying, the central proposal, that the foreign service be merged with the civil service, was rejected. The Foreign Office reluctantly accepted a compromise suggestion that some diplomats should spend time on secondment to relevant departments in the civil service, and that some postings, particularly within the European Community, should be open to domestic civil servants. But the organization remains as proudly independent today as when Palmerston commissioned its offices.

Part of this is due to the distinctive recruitment pattern for the Foreign Office. For generations, the occupants of Sir Gilbert Scott's palazzo remained the best connected of all Britain's public servants. While the domestic bureaucracy increasingly selected the products of homes of 'great diligence and a little prosperity', foreign policy remained the more-or-less exclusive preserve of aristocrats. The excuse

for continuing to employ nobility to represent the country abroad
was that they could mingle comfortably with the kings, presidents
and prime ministers of the quaint little nations to which they were
accredited, at ease in the drawing rooms where affairs of state were
settled. So while the rest of Britain succumbed to the demands of
the popular vote, the Foreign Office remained grandly aloof, rooted
in that pre-lapsarian world where public life and Society were undivided.

The Victorian radical John Bright had exclaimed in the middle of
the nineteenth century:

> When you come to our foreign policy you are no longer Englishmen, you
> are no longer free; you are recommended not to inquire. If you do, you are
> told you cannot understand it; you are snubbed, you are hustled aside. We
> are told that the matter is too deep for common understanding like ours –
> that there is a great mystery about it. We have what is called diplomacy.
> We have a great many lords engaged in what they call diplomacy. We have
> a lord in Paris, we have another in Madrid, another in Berlin, another in
> Vienna, and another lord in Constantinople; we have another in Wash-
> ington – in fact, almost all over the world, particularly where the society is
> most pleasant and the climate most agreeable, there is almost certain to be
> an English nobleman to represent the English Foreign Office, but you
> never know what he is doing.[29]

When I first read this speech, in 1987, I checked the list of the top
dozen British ambassadors. One hundred and thirty years later, there
were still two lords among them, Lord Bridges in Rome and the Duke
of Richmond's son, Lord Nicholas Gordon-Lennox in Madrid. In all
the other cities, Britain was represented by a mere knight. Whatever
they think of them at home, the British still have a taste for titles
abroad, like an impoverished duchess who wears her tiara to disguise
the fact that the roof is falling in.

Even after the Northcote-Trevelyan reforms had initiated the idea
of a professional civil service, diplomacy remained the preserve of the
upper classes. To be considered as a candidate for the foreign service
in the early years of this century, an applicant had to be nominated by
the Foreign Secretary. The pool of potential ambassadors was further
restricted by the fact that for the first two years of his career the
diplomat was expected to support himself as an 'honorary attaché',
which demanded an income of at least £400 a year.[30] It was not until
the end of the First World War that this last requirement was
dropped, although when proposals to reorganize the service were
being mooted in 1918, the Diplomatic Secretary, the Hon. Theo

Russell dashed off a quick note to his chief clerk on the subject of the new selection process. 'We shall also have to decide,' he wrote, 'the composition of the Board of Selection ... How to exclude Jews, coloured men and infidels who are British subjects, [and] if a public school education is obligatory.'[31]

No formal ban on infidels or others was ever brought in, but the new selection process tended to discriminate in favour of a certain type. The language requirement, in particular, gave those who could afford to pay a crammer a head start. The new Foreign Office, while no longer the exclusive fiefdom of the aristocracy, retained many of the aristocrat's predilections, including his disdain for trade; instead of assisting with the vital business of promoting British exports it left that job to the Department of Overseas Trade.

A chap's personality was at least as important as the quality of his mind, and when, in 1939, the Diplomatic service was faced with proposals to amalgamate with the Consular service, it fought back again by stressing a certain style. In a paper dripping with FO superiority, Sir Hughe Knatchbull-Hugessen, the designated ambassador to Turkey, explained that, since a diplomat had to 'fraternize with the governing class in no matter what country', a certain type of background was essential.

> Though we would be far from suggesting that personality, 'address' and savoir-faire are not of great importance in the Consular service, it is in the Diplomatic service that these rather intangible qualities are most essential ... This means that all suspicion of an inferiority complex must be absent from [the diplomat's] make-up.[32]

Knatchbull-Hugessen would not, he said, dream of suggesting that such self-confidence was exclusive to certain public schoolboys, but ...

The Second World War, and the subsequent election of a Labour government, finally forced a limited change upon the Foreign Office. Bevin had no prejudice against aristocrats *per se*, and even told the headmaster of Eton 'to keep sending Etonians, because diplomacy couldn't do without them,'[33] but he wanted to get rid of 'the limited Court Circular society',[34] with which the Foreign Office seemed to be so preoccupied. The reforms he and Anthony Eden introduced were supposed to open the service to all candidates, regardless of their background or the depth of their pocket.

Appearance, belief and fact can be three very different commodities in this area of background and style. Henry Fairlie's central thrust against the Foreign Office, in his famous 1955 article, was that it was intimately plugged into the social network which continued to exercise power and influence:

> Somewhere near the heart of the pattern of social relationships which so powerfully controls the exercise of power in this country is the Foreign Office. By its traditions and its methods of recruitment the Foreign Office makes it inevitable that the members of the Foreign Service are men . . . who 'know all the right people'.[35]

The criticisms drew immediate protests from the FO's defenders. John Sparrow, a distinguished Oxford don who sat frequently on Foreign Office selection boards angrily told him that 'candidates from grammar schools, and from working or middle-class homes have (to say the least) as good a chance of success as others.'[36] Yet the recruitment figures hardly endorse this picture. In the five years from 1955 to 1959, 87.6 per cent of successful applicants to join the élite administrative grade of the Foreign Office came from public schools.[37] If working-class candidates genuinely did stand as good a chance as anyone else, there must have been remarkably few of them, and they of pretty low calibre.

Fully one third of the permanent secretaries between 1900 and 1986 had no university education,[38] presumably on the grounds that formal qualifications mattered less than a capacity to mix easily in the courts and chancelleries of the world. The new selection tests at Stoke d'Abernon, a country house near Leatherhead which had been acquired for the purpose after the Second World War, were intended to discover intellectual as well as social skills, although even thirty years later – by which time the tests had long been moved to London – the impression persisted that the selectors were as interested as anything else in whether applicants ate their peas off their knives. A certain style of education now became a substitute for breeding. While fewer recruits got into the Foreign Office without higher education, the dominance of Oxford and Cambridge persisted. When Michael Shea was recruited into the Foreign Office in 1963, he was the first graduate of a Scottish university to be selected for eight years, and one of only three who had not been to either Oxford or Cambridge.

Between 1900 and 1985 the cream of the British foreign service was represented by her ambassadors to Washington, Paris, Moscow, Berlin/Bonn and Rome. Vienna was also a top posting before the First World War, and since 1945 the United Nations and NATO have had similar status. All told, these eight posts were held by 110 individuals.

A quick scan of their backgrounds gives a good indication of the twentieth century Foreign Office élite.

To begin with, there is not a single woman among them. On parental background, the picture is necessarily inadequate, since a full forty-one failed to give details in their entries in *Who's Who* at the time. But of the remainder, no less than forty had titled fathers, dividing roughly half and half between hereditary peers and knights or baronets. Sixty-nine were graduates of Oxford or Cambridge. Twenty-eight – one quarter – were Etonians, a further fifty-three had been at other public schools.

To be fair, the numerical dominance of the public schools has declined in recent decades. The proportion has been dropping steadily, from eighty-seven per cent in the late fifties, to sixty-six per cent in the late sixties, and sixty per cent by the end of the eighties. But the Foreign Office is still terrain where the Oxbridge public schoolboy ranges free.

More even than the domestic civil service, once recruited, they tend to stay on the payroll. It is a practice which Sir Hamilton Whyte, the retiring High Commissioner to Singapore, argued in 1987 was 'plain crazy'. He was too diplomatic to cite any examples to support his case, but might have had in mind the British ambassador in Europe who survived in post despite being an alcoholic, his colleague whose wife could be discovered at embassy receptions in the bath with a bottle of gin, or the representative in Latin America who passed his tour in the paralyzing grip of a homosexual infatuation with a local political leader.

Sir Hamilton – 'Ham' to all and sundry – proposed an 'up and out' system of early retirement, to dispense with those who had outlived their usefulness. He might also have suggested the recruitment of mature men and women from industry, the universities or the media as a way of bringing the service more into tune with the rest of Britain. As it is, the selection process is largely unchanged, and the complexion of the future Foreign Office can be gauged by examining the new recruits.

About twenty candidates pass the rigorous selection tests for the Administrative grade each year. Despite the vast expansion of higher education, between 1985 and 1989, sixty-five per cent were products of Oxford or Cambridge. One third were women and less than one fifth were scientists. Not a single successful candidate belonged to an ethnic minority.

So the ranks of younger diplomats advancing steadily towards ambassadorships are still a pretty homogeneous lot. In 1988, among the eight hundred members of the Administrative group, men outnumbered women ten to one. Of the 667 whose educational records were available, 484 had been to Oxford or Cambridge. In only one of the three previous years had an applicant from a polytechnic managed to win a place in the Foreign Office. The eight hundred included one black person.[39]

So the men at the top of British diplomacy have a quite predictable look to them. The Foreign Office declines to list missions in order of importance, but judging by their strategic significance to Britain and the cost of the post (Lagos is the sixth most expensive embassy in the world), one arrives at a tally of the following seventeen significant British overseas missions: Bonn, Canberra, the European Community, Johannesburg, Lagos, Madrid, Moscow, NATO, New Delhi, Ottawa, Paris, Peking, Riyadh, Rome, Tokyo, the United Nations and Washington.

In view of the long institutional prejudice against women, it is not surprising that in early 1990 all the posts were held by men. (The five British overseas missions led by women included places like Luxembourg, the Ivory Coast and Chad, none of them exactly in the front line of international diplomacy.) Every single one of the men in the seventeen major missions was a graduate of Oxford or Cambridge. Three of the sixteen were Etonians and three were former pupils at the great London school, St Paul's. All the rest attended other public schools. It is hardly an earth-shattering change.

Margaret Thatcher was not the first prime minister to arrive in power deeply suspicious of the Foreign Office. Its history, culture and style had antagonized many before her, not because of its grand self-confidence so much as a perceived willingness to surrender to foreign governments. 'A cowardly lot of scuffling shufflers', Churchill called them, in a particularly grumpy mood. As Foreign Secretary, David Owen discovered that when going into important negotiations, the Whitehall tom-toms would knock out a message to all relevant ambassadors, who would send back suspiciously well co-ordinated advice:

> The thrust was always the same: 'The Foreign Secretary's got to give way,' 'There's simply no alternative,' 'The roof's going to fall in.' A long catalogue of woe, just two days before you're due to discuss something crucial. It was all just unbelievably co-ordinated.[40]

To many of Margaret Thatcher's closest allies, the Foreign Office was a beast to be tamed. The attitude found its most pithy summary in the words of Paul Gore-Booth that 'the object of policy' was to 'ensure that a great nation could stop half-way down and establish itself as a second-level power with real tasks to perform and obligations to fulfil.'[41] This was a perfectly sensible strategy, but it implied surrendering 'a place at the top table', which might be taken by someone else. Norman Tebbit put it more bluntly: 'The job of the Ministry of Agriculture is to look after farmers. The job of the Foreign Office is to look after foreigners.'

A more old-fashioned cabinet colleague put it slightly differently:

> She hates the Foreign Office because she hates foreigners. Foreigners are an inevitable but unacceptable complication: she wants to put Britain right, and while she quite likes to be seen parading around with Gorbachev, she never liked 'abroad'. She doesn't consider America abroad, but the rest of it she thinks is pretty bloody awful.[42]

This might have been a sufficient drawback, but there was another factor. Not only did she arrive in Downing Street with a distrust of foreigners, she also detested compromise. Since the business of the Foreign Office was compromising with foreigners, her contempt was more-or-less inevitable.

One Foreign Office minister snorted angrily when I asked about relations with the Prime Minister:

> The Foreign Office is, of course, concerned with abroad, and has to spend its time getting on with foreigners, and try to get the best deal for Britain, because nowadays we're all dependent upon one another. She thought that anybody who spent too much time with foreigners, and got on with them, was anti-British, or wet, or feeble. Since the Foreign Office is solely concerned with that, she took against them. She thought they compromise: she's right. Of course they compromise. How the hell do you expect them to behave? To get their own way all the time?[43]

No other department of state, with the exception of the Treasury, puts such invisible preconditions upon the sort of person who can become foreign secretary. It is just inconceivable that certain politicians, eminent though they may be in other fields, would be allowed to take charge of foreign policy. The departmental theology permits only a limited range of practitioners. Of the four men to serve as Foreign Secretary during the eighties, none was on the wilder shores of Thatcherism and three were old Etonians. Two, Lord Carrington and Douglas Hurd, had served with British missions overseas before going into politics: the department welcomed them back as its own.

The Foreign Office's self-confidence derives from a sense that they represent not merely the government of the day, but the nation. 'Political parties come and go,' one ambassador once told me, 'but British *interests* go on forever.' This is true enough, but it largely depends upon foreign affairs being a matter of consensus and assumes that there are few, if any, alternative policies to the ones being pursued. Possible alternatives do exist, in all sorts of areas. The phenomenal success of public appeals for development aid in the 1980s indicates only one area where official policy and the aspirations of the people are clearly out of kilter.

But the Foreign Office does not welcome other ideas about policy. When a Labour government appointed the distinguished philosopher Stuart Hampshire to be a special adviser, to get at the raw material of decisions before the Foreign Office had come up with an authorized version, he found himself frozen out. His name was put on the list of people in the private office to whom incoming telegrams from ambassadors should be sent. It was simply crossed off by the senior private secretary, and the words 'not necessary' written beside it.[44]

Is there any justification for this Foreign Office superiority? The catalogue of cock-ups is lengthy. It remained over-obsessed by a glorious past, aloof from a uniting Europe, too attached to an empty Commonwealth, and over-valued the Atlantic Alliance. In the postwar period, the list of misjudgements begins with advice against accepting the Volkswagen manufacturing plant as war reparations from the Germans, through to being caught on the hop by one crisis after another – Rhodesia's illegal declaration of independence, the overthrow of the Shah of Iran and the Argentine invasion of the Falkland Islands.

There were voices within the organization which recognized the deficiencies, but usually, the blame was laid elsewhere. In his valedictory despatch in 1979, Sir Nicholas Henderson, retiring ambassador in Paris, penned one of the most eloquent appraisals. It was a downcast message. When he had become a diplomat, one quarter of the world's population belonged to the British empire or Commonwealth, while Churchill, Attlee and Bevin dealt on equal terms with Stalin and Truman. But British industrial performance had been miserable ever since, and the situation had only been made worse by serious errors of judgement, like the British refusal to get involved in Jean Monet's early ideas for European co-operation. It was, he suggested, just a little embarrassing to be representing a country whose pretensions to power were now so far removed from the dreadful reality of her second-rateness. What's more, he said, the foreigners knew it.

This was an interesting perspective from a man occupying an eighteenth-century palace on the Rue Faubourg Saint Honoré, the more so since he had been one of the leading campaigners to have the Think Tank's suggestions for a more in-touch service drowned at birth. The standard Foreign Office response to suggestions of failure is to argue, with Bevin, that if the country produced more coal (or oil, cars or washing-machines), she could have a more vigorous diplomacy. The problem with assessing the Foreign Office is that in the business of diplomacy, profit and loss accounts are far harder to read than in any commercial enterprise.

Diplomatically, Britain walks on water. The Foreign Office can take some of the credit for the fact that Britain has a greater voice in world affairs than can be justified by her material or military might. 'Your guys are just damn good, there's no other explanation,' an American diplomat once told me. Economically, the United Kingdom is now merely in the second division, and not even at the top of it. In diplomatic terms, however, she is still reckoned one of the great powers.

Partly this is because so much of the diplomatic world is still cast in the mould of 1945, and the permanent seat on the United Nations Security Council and the rest are the legacy of an imperial past. As the years pass, the British ship of state settles lower and lower into the water. Economically, the Japanese now carry sufficient clout to rank way above other non-superpower nations. Even the 'special relationship' between Britain and the United States is a weaker thing, as France and West Germany continue to develop their pre-eminent positions in a European Community to which British governments seem incapable of giving wholehearted support. So if Britain is taken more seriously than she might be, it is largely because British diplomats are good at their job. But the most substantial criticism that can be levelled at the Foreign Office diplomats is that they are too attached to the old order to be able to forge the new.

Yet the influence of the Thatcher years upon the Foreign Office was profound. Her own personal standing in the world made the job of representing Britain easier, and the perceived improvement in the state of the UK economy helped too. But, committed to a future in

Europe, the Foreign Office had begun the eighties a little embarrassed by the European Community budget disputes in which the Prime Minister had banged on about getting back 'our money'. And, as with most prime ministers, the longer she stayed in office, the more she liked to cut a dash on the international scene. As time passed, Downing Street took a growing role in foreign policy, so that by the end of the decade increasing numbers of decisions, from policy on Europe to South Africa, were really being made in Number 10.

In a series of skirmishes – on sanctions against South Africa (which she opposed, but the Foreign Office supported), on allowing British bases to be used for the American bombing of Tripoli (in which she overruled Foreign Office objections) and on a range of compromises with the European Community (which she almost always opposed and the Foreign Office supported) – Margaret Thatcher got her way. Even decisions about how the British ambassador would cast his vote in sessions of the United Nations General Assembly were made in Downing Street.

'When I was Foreign Secretary,' remarked David Owen, 'we'd scarcely have mentioned things like that to Jim Callaghan. So there was an enormous erosion of the Foreign Secretary's power. The Foreign Office was just by-passed.'[45]

This is something of an exaggeration. It does not necessarily follow that because foreign policy in the Thatcher decade was, truly, 'Thatcher-ite', the Foreign Office has lost its power. It is an organization in which the business of strategic compromise is bred in the bone. By the 1990s, the Foreign Office was talking a new language. Much is made of increased efficiency and glossy handouts are produced to illustrate the way in which more countries are covered with fewer people than fifteen or twenty years ago. (As regards reducing the numbers of overseas staff, the Thatcher government did no more than continue a policy introduced in recognition of changing political and technological realities by previous Labour and Conservative govern-ments.[46]) But for all its retrenchment, the Foreign Office remains almost twice as large as the diplomatic service of West Germany, whose economic performance is so much better.[47] Twice as much time is now said to be spent on commercial activities, promoting British trade and so on, as is spent on political analysis. Trade work is now said to consume one third of the Foreign Office budget.

But the gilded path to the top remains through political work; administrative trainees spend most of their first eight years engaged in it and have little or nothing to do with commercial activity until they are thirty. Thereafter, those marked for greatness are almost invariably those who have shown the most acumen in political assessment.

Many of the differences between Downing Street and the Foreign Office were really questions of style rather than substance, anyway, and the fact that Margaret Thatcher was internationally the best-known British Prime Minister for decades actually made life easier for many British diplomats. In a perverse way, she had given them a stature and a self-confidence which had been missing before she came to power.

They had anyway a depth of institutional pride which it would be hard for any individual to dent. When Mrs Thatcher attempted to block Foreign Office wisdom on eastern Europe by consulting the eccentric one-time International Brigade volunteer turned monetarist, Alfred Sherman, her exasperated Foreign Secretary, Lord Carrington, cajoled her into visiting the Foreign Office, to hear the views of the experts.

Carrington assembled two senior figures from the Foreign Office planning staff, Rodney Braithwaite and Christopher Mallaby, both of whom had served at the Moscow embassy. Before the Prime Minister arrived, he warned them of her tendency to dominate any conversation. 'If she tries to interrupt, you keep going,' he is said to have warned Mallaby, a tall, languid Old Etonian. When the Prime Minister arrived, Mallaby sat down, crossed his legs and began his lecture on the Kremlin. Sure enough, the Prime Minister immediately started to break in. Mallaby sailed on, oblivious. Mrs Thatcher was first astonished, then bemused, and finally impressed. That was the Foreign Office style at its most ineffable.

CHAPTER SIX

Floreat Etona
(and Her Little Brothers and Sisters)

> Jolly boating weather,
> And a hay harvest breeze,
> Blade on the feather,
> Shade off the trees
> Swing, swing together
> With your body between your knees.
>
> Rugby may be more clever,
> Harrow may make more row;
> But we'll row for ever,
> Steady from stroke to bow;
> And nothing in life shall sever
> The chain that is round us now.

– *Eton Boating Song* William Cory

'THE CLASS SYSTEM has never recovered from Rab Butler's Education Act of 1944, and its condition is now terminal,' the headmaster of Eton confidently asserted at the close of the 1980s.[1]

It is an idiosyncratic view, to say the least. Over forty years after the legislation which opened secondary education to all, the public schools account for seven out of nine of the army's top generals,[2] two thirds of the external directors of the Bank of England, thirty-three of the thirty-nine top English judges,[3] all the ambassadors in the fifteen most important overseas missions, seventy-eight of the Queen's eighty-four lord lieutenants and the majority of the bishops in the Church of England.[4] Even the bold, thrusting entrepreneurs who have become such folk heroes have failed to cast aside old money: of the two hundred richest people in Britain, thirty-five were educated at a single school, Eton.[5] Reports of the death of the class system have been greatly exaggerated.

One hundred years after their heyday, the British public schools are doing very nicely thank you, their ancient buildings renovated, their waiting lists bulging, their status undiminished. It would be hard to overstate their influence upon the institutions of power in Britain. It is not merely that they provide a disproportionately large part of the élite in so many areas of national life. The very shape of organizations, from the financial institutions of the City to the Church of England, reflect in some way the structures and mores of the public schools. The internal hierarchies, the requirements for promotion, the assessment of excellence, the masculine clubbiness, the rewards for loyalty, are all instantly recognizable to a product of Winchester, Eton or Harrow.

The public schools are a means of absorbing dissent, challenge and change. The self-proclaimed advocates of enterprise who so denigrate the traditional ruling class will send their children into its embrace at the earliest opportunity. Parental aspirations are married to free-market arguments about choice and a form of ambition inflation occurs. The process follows an unerring pattern, of which the Thatcher family themselves are a perfect example: although she herself attended a state grammar school, her husband Denis was at the minor north London public school, Mill Hill. They chose to send their son, Mark, to Harrow. 'What they don't realize is that in doing so, they're being trapped by the spider's web. They're reassuring the Establishment that all is well. And the Establishment gets its own back through their children,'[6] observes Dr John Rae, former headmaster of Westminster, another school which takes large numbers of children of influence.

Every nation has its élite, but the distinctive quality of the British élite is the way in which it is still dominated by the products of a tiny number of schools, which made their selection at the age of thirteen, and for attendance at which – scholarships aside – the *sine qua non* is parental wealth. The terminological contradiction of the British public schools – that they are not public at all – is, of course, what gives them their allure. They account for only seven out of every hundred children of school age. Winchester and Eton, fourteenth- and fifteenth-century foundations intended for both rich and poor, now demand annual fees from most of their pupils of up to £8,000 or more. The *grandes écoles* may dominate the élite in France, but their entrants are at least chosen by open, competitive examination. Of course, the children of wealthy parents have a better environment in which to study than the son or daughter of a Citroën assembly-line worker, but at least they are in the same school. In Britain, the first instinct of wealthy parents is to remove their child from the state sector of education.

The model for the schools was set in the latter half of the nineteenth century. The great expansion of public school education at the time was directly attributable to the growth of a middle class prepared to spend money on the educational alchemy which would turn their unprepossessing offspring into aristocrats *manqués*. This process had little to do with academic achievement, as Lord Clarendon's famous Royal Commission discovered in the 1860s, after three years' inquiry into the education provided at Eton, Winchester, Harrow, Westminster, St Paul's, Charterhouse, Merchant Taylors, Rugby and Shrewsbury. *The Times* summarized their verdict on the education available at these schools as 'a failure even if tested by those better specimens, not exceeding one third of the whole, who go up to the Universities.'[7] Not much was being taught. Even less was being learned.

The Commission had practical suggestions to make about how standards might be raised, including the introduction of French and German, mathematics, a natural science, some history and geography and drawing or music. This syllabus now became the model for a whole raft of schools, and all of the Clarendon schools remain prominent in their field, the first five continuing among the best in Britain. Their importance in the perpetuation of an élite lay not merely in their academic achievements – although the standards at some are very high – so much as in the creating of a social network based upon shared beliefs. These schools, wrote Clarendon,

> have been the chief nurseries of our statesmen ... men of all the various classes that make up English society, destined for every profession and career, have been brought up on a footing of social equality, and have contracted the most enduring friendships, and some of the ruling habits of their lives; and they have had perhaps the largest share in moulding the character of an English gentleman.[8]

Not only, then, did the public schools produce an élite in which those born the sons of tradesmen had by the age of eighteen acquired the manners of the gentleman, but the two prerequisites for an Establishment – shared beliefs, and the social contacts to ensure that they were transmitted into society – had been created by the time they ended adolescence.

But what were these values? Parents did not send their sons off to regimes of cold baths, bullying, buggery and rough-house sports to turn them into intellectuals. Old Squire Brown had a good idea why Tom was being despatched to Rugby:

> I don't care a straw for Greek particles, or the digamma, no more does his mother. What is he sent to school for? Well, partly because he wanted so to go. If he'll only turn out a brave, helpful, truth-telling Englishman, and a gentleman, and a Christian, that's all I want.[9]

Rugby's headmaster, Dr Arnold – only one among several great reformers shaking up places like Shrewsbury, Charterhouse or Uppingham – certainly seemed to share this idea of the function of the school. The advice he gave his prepostors (prefects) was clear: 'What we must look for here is, first, religious and moral principles; secondly, gentlemanly conduct; thirdly intellectual ability.'[10] The creation of the Christian gentleman was the main business of the late nineteenth-century public schools. Some of the new institutions set up to cater to the middle classes had particular markets in mind – Marlborough had special facilities for the sons of Church of England clergymen, Wellington was intended for the sons of army officers – but they all shared the same ideals. No fewer than seventy-seven of the schools in the present Headmasters' Conference were established between 1840 and 1900. Nine out of ten of the preparatory schools which supplied the public schools were founded in the hundred years after 1850.

The period between the Clarendon Commission and the outbreak of the First World War was the golden age of the English public schools; it mattered not that what was being taught, with its disregard for science and research, its contempt for industry, its blind respect for authority, was actually accelerating the decline of empire while purporting to be its protector. The boys largely ran the institutions themselves, organizing the mundane domestic duties which kept them ticking over, guardians of a precise hierarchy of petty privileges which kept everyone in his place. Life revolved around frequent hymn-singing in Gothic school chapels, and even more frequent compulsory attendance on the cold and muddy sports fields. (This last addiction was one of the more idiosyncratic, the cliché that 'the battle of Waterloo was won on the playing fields of Eton' having passed into common wisdom, despite the fact that Wellington probably never uttered the remark: there were no compulsory games during his time at the school.[11]) The products of the public schools knew how to play a straight bat on Dean Farrar's 'cricket-field of life', and they emerged gloriously free from any possible taint of intellectualism. Noël Coward caught them perfectly:

> We know how Caesar conquered Gaul
> And how to whack a cricket ball:
> Apart from this our education
> Lacks coordination.[12]

A. C. Benson, a housemaster at Eton and later Master of Magdalene, spoke more in sorrow than in scorn when he observed in 1904 that

> it makes me very sad sometimes to see these well-groomed, well-mannered, rational, manly boys all taking the same view of things, all doing the same things, smiling politely at the eccentricity of anyone who finds matter for serious interest in books, in art or music.[13]

But that was the point of the public school system: it produced solid, reliable men who could be counted upon to administer an empire: an appreciation of the finer points of metaphysical poetry was scarcely essential for a life likely to be spent as a district officer in rural Bechuanaland. The public schoolboy soon became the stuff of myth – honest, upright and God-fearing, the only white Christian in a sea of black heathens. Take the hero of Henty's *With Roberts to Pretoria*, sixteen-year-old Yorke Pemberton:

> a typical public schoolboy, straight, and clean-limbed, free from all awkwardness, bright in expression and possessed of a large amount of self-possession, or, as he himself would have called it, 'cheek', was a little particular about the set of his Eton jacket and trousers and the appearance of his boots; as hard as nails and almost tireless; a good specimen of the class by which Britain has been built up, her colonies formed and her battlefields won.[14]

Every headmaster of the latter half of the twentieth century has had to address the question of how to make relevant an institution whose primary purpose was to turn out chaps to run an Imperial regime which demonstrably no longer exists. A close reading of the registers produced by a sample of schools for the year 1875 confirms the centrality of the Empire to the schools' purpose. The class of 1875 from Harrow, Charterhouse, Winchester, Marlborough and Rugby, together with the Eton upper school Vth form lower division, produced 950 young men. Of their subsequent careers 845 are traceable. Of these, by far the greatest number, 168, joined the army. A further eighty-eight either emigrated or joined the colonial service. Only eighteen joined the civil service, half of them Etonians. Eighty-six of them became Church of England clergymen. Not surprisingly, for the products of a regime which placed little value upon science or modern languages (in 1884 Eton employed twenty-eight classics masters but no modern language or science teachers), there are few academics or teachers. Fourteen of the group became MPs. There are two other noticeable characteristics. Contrary to popular myth, a relatively large number did go into business or commerce: there are eighty-two businessmen, forty-eight financiers, and fifty-three merchants in the group. The other striking feature is the number who joined the professions. Twenty-one became doctors, but a further 125 – the second largest number in the whole sample – became lawyers.

There were of course cads, bounders and dissenters among these products, but by and large, the best of them had imbibed much the same set of values as Squire Brown had sought in young Tom. They were gentlemen. They were loyal to Crown and Empire. They thought there were few problems which couldn't be solved over a brandy-and-soda.

These beliefs were tested to destruction in the mud of Flanders. When the Public Schools Club examined their membership list at the Armistice, they found that eight hundred members had been killed in action.[15] Even those who survived the years of senseless trench slaughter with their beliefs in the Christian gentleman, leadership and self-sacrifice untarnished returned to a world in which the Imperial purpose would have less and less need for them.

Once Labour had supplanted the Liberals as the main opposition to the Conservatives, far from being seen as the nurseries of a necessary administrative class, the public schools began to look out-of-touch bastions of privilege. In 1923, George Bernard Shaw thought Eton, Harrow, Winchester and their imitators should be 'razed to the ground and their foundations sown with salt.'[16] George Orwell had the cosseted and outdated milieu to a 't':

> The year is 1910 – or 1940, but it is all the same. You are at Greyfriars, a rosy-cheeked boy of fourteen in posh, tailor-made clothes, sitting down to tea in your study in the Remove passage after an exciting game of football ... The King is on his throne and the pound is worth a pound. Over in Europe the comic foreigners are jabbering and gesticulating, but the grim grey battleships of the British Fleet are steaming up the Channel and at the outposts of Empire the monocled Englishmen are holding the niggers at bay ... Everything is safe, solid and unquestionable. Everything will be the same for ever and ever.[17]

This world, so vividly parodied by Orwell in 1940, was preposterous then, yet it survived into the sixties and seventies. Go to one of the major public schools today and the ambience is little changed. The stone-flagged corridors still echo to the shrieks of Bunter and the characteristic smell is an incense of burned toast and sweaty rugby shirts.

But, far from stagnating, the public schools have grown in size and confidence. Over the last forty years, membership of the Headmasters' Conference has swollen. Part of the development can be explained by the decision of Grammar Schools funded by direct government grant to opt out of the state system, but the old-fashioned public schools have also expanded to meet increased demand. Some of the Clarendon Commission schools have grown by as much as a quarter over the last few decades. Part of the growth in some of the second-division schools can be explained by the fact that they now admit girls, but many might have expanded further, had they not been restricted by ancient buildings. In the case of a school like Eton, the increase in demand for private education has, if anything, tended to emphasize its exclusivity.

In the last decade, the expansion of the private sector has been even more marked. While the total number of children in secondary education fell during the eighties, because of a lower birth-rate, the number in independent schools rose, so that a higher proportion of the school population was being educated outside the state sector. Figures published in 1988 by the Independent Schools Information Service show that, over a ten year period, the proportion of pupils in private schools rose from 5.8 per cent of the school population, to seven per cent.[18]

Throughout the postwar years, the left has vacillated between arguing for their outright abolition and a pious belief that they would wither on the vine, if only state education could be made good enough. By the 1960s it was obvious to all that the latter idea was pie-in-the-sky. The Labour Government returned in 1964 was committed to tackle the issue, but Harold Wilson took the line of least resistance, and turned the problem over to the Great and Good. After five people refused the poisoned chalice, a well-meaning educationalist, John Newsom, was persuaded to chair a commission to decide what was to be done. Two public school headmasters agreed to sit on the committee which was supposed to devise ways of burying them. As Harold Wilson had by now not the slightest intention of acting upon anything they proposed, the whole thing was, in the words of one of the team, Lord Annan, 'the most gracious and complete waste of time of my life.'[19] The committee's first report, produced in April 1968, was a masterpiece of Great and Good fudge, of which A. P. Herbert would have been proud. It recommended that the public schools make half their places available to an ill-defined group of children who would 'benefit from a boarding education'. In yoking together two separate ideas, the egalitarian undesirability of private education and a supposed pool of disadvantaged children who needed to be sent away to boarding school, it was a nonsense which satisfied no-one. The report was ignored by the cabinet and promptly given the last rites by the party conference.

Conveniently forgetting that they had done nothing about them when in government, the Labour party continued to huff and puff about the public schools when back in opposition. 'I must, above all else,' the Shadow Education Minister, Roy Hattersley, told a conference of preparatory school headmasters in September 1973, 'leave you with no doubts about our serious intention to reduce, and eventually to abolish private education in this country.'[20] When Labour did regain power, in 1974, these 'serious intentions' turned out to be some half-baked ideas about removing the taxation benefits of their charitable status, which soon drowned in a swamp of practical difficulty and political indifference.

The public schools, meanwhile, had organized themselves into a lobby, renaming themselves 'independent schools'. It was an astute move, simultaneously distancing the schools from the old sport and psalm-singing tradition, and implying that anyone who attacked them was also an enemy of free choice.

In the event, it was the direct grant grammar schools which were killed off in the seventies. So-called because they were funded with money from central government, the great direct grant schools had been one of the glories of the British educational system, where a sliding scale of fees gave equal opportunity to the children of rich and poor. Manchester Grammar School had produced a stream of luminaries from the Marks and Spencer families to leading lights in the Royal Society. The second in command of the Treasury at the time of the abolition of the direct grant status, Sir Leo Pliatzky, and the permanent secretary at the Ministry of Defence, Sir Frank Cooper, were both past pupils of Manchester, while the Chancellor of the Exchequer in the cabinet which made the decision, Denis Healey, had been at Bradford Grammar School. It was undeniable that, by operating a policy of selection at eleven, the grammar schools were divisive. But it was a curious epitaph for a Labour government that the main effect of its policies upon the independent schools of Britain was to increase their number.

The fees demanded by the grammar schools – £2,600 a year at Bradford Grammar in 1990 – are enough to put them beyond the reach of most parents.[21] Yet they are cheap by comparison with the old-fashioned public schools. Between 1966 and 1980 the average annual fees rose by 404 per cent, an increase almost identical to the rise over the previous half century. Such schools now cost about £9,000 per year, disregarding uniforms, travelling, additional tuition, pocket money and so on. Parents with three children at such schools therefore have to find up to £30,000 per year, *after* paying tax.

What is it for which they are prepared to pay so dearly? Parents think their children will receive 'a better education' at the fee-paying schools than they would get in the state sector. In practice this means a belief they will achieve better exam results than would have been the case had they gone instead to the local comprehensive school. The ambitious middle-class saw the 1970s decision to abolish selection at eleven as an abandonment of old grammar school standards in order to pander to the less able. The fact that many of the new comprehensive schools had to have enormous numbers of pupils in order to offer a reasonable spread of subject choices, and that some of the staff were wedded to radical theories of education were quickly seized upon by those elements of the press ready to proclaim that the change had been a disaster. Within little more than a decade, it had become received wisdom for many that the whole upheaval had been a mistake; Bernard Levin in *The Times* called it 'wickedness'.[22]

Those who can afford to pay to escape this egalitarian swamp expect their children to perform better than would have been the case had they stayed in the state sector. A 1988 survey by the Headmasters' Conference showed that the number of A grades in the national GCSE examinations increased by five per cent in the sample of seventy independent schools, while the national improvement was two per cent. The independent schools' proportion of A, B and C grades increased by four per cent, twice the national level of improvement. These schools educate only about one child in fifteen, but they account for more than one in four of the university students in Britain; at Oxford and Cambridge the proportion is even higher. At the more distinguished public schools, the great majority of boys now go on to higher education. At Harrow, seven out of ten boys continue to university, including approximately twenty per cent to Oxford or

Cambridge. Winchester produces forty or fifty Oxbridge undergraduates each year, and sends a further forty or fifty to other universities.[23]

Most parents who can contemplate the fees demanded by such schools are likely to be naturally competitive figures who have been successful in their chosen careers. The majority will have been at secondary school in the fifties and sixties. They may not have attended a public school, but the grammar schools of their day were still largely fashioned on the Clarendon schools. If they are in a position to pay the heavy fees demanded today, they are likely to feel that their education served them well, and unlikely to be sympathetic to much of the claptrap talked by educational radicals about the harm done by competitive sport and the rest.

And the mystique of the English public school survives more-or-less intact. *Tom Brown's Schooldays* is still in print, in five separate editions (there's the enduring power of myth!), although the morals and escapades of his tormentor, Flashman, have proved more in tune with the times, selling steadily year after year and translated into half-a-dozen European languages, including Portuguese and Finnish.

Tom Brown's old school, Rugby, smeared in orange brick across the dreary Midlands town which shares its name, exudes the characteristic self-confidence of the public schools, although it has slipped from its former prominence to become merely one of the bunch of also-ran schools. Groups of boys saunter the streets in out-at-the-elbow tweed jackets, their books slung on their hips, in that distinctive rolling gait of the public school. By the age of fifteen, they have that imperturbable air, only skin-deep perhaps but there none the less, of the ascendancy.

But the appearance of unchanging tradition is wrong. Like almost all the schools which have survived into the nineties, Rugby has been transformed. It is a business nowadays. A quarter of the pupils are the sons of old boys, but it is a declining proportion, and marketing is the name of the game. Apart from its recruiting sergeant, the school has a press officer and employs a firm of public relations consultants. The prospectus is impressive – facilities for art and sculpture, biology and physics, music and languages, as well as the inevitable range of sports from fives and fencing to hockey on the school's own floodlit astro-turf. Chafed by the persistent claim that they were largely responsible for Britain's industrial decline, the public schools try to appear less prejudiced against industry, by promoting links with companies, and attempting to make their careers staff slightly less out-of-touch.

Rugby even has a retired ICI manager employed as 'industrial liaison officer'.

What the successful public schools offer now is a service industry, which they are happy to have judged not by their own standards, but by the agreed yardsticks of the rest of society. In return for several thousand pounds, they say, we will give your child a better chance of gaining admission to university or to the profession of his choice. The parents at schools like Rugby are drawn from the professional classes: they believe headmasters when they say that the public schools are better at operating the Oxford and Cambridge admissions procedure than their state-run counterparts.

And then there are the people they meet. Rugby is a second division school, yet at various meetings during 1988 the boys of Rugby had the chance to question six serving or former government ministers, one chief constable, two bishops, seven university professors, the editor of the *Spectator*, one general and the director of Friends of the Earth. Even Labour MPs happily accepted the invitation to speak to groups of senior boys. It is hardly surprising if they emerge from their schooldays with a different map of the way around the institutions of power to that given to the sixth-formers of a comprehensive school in inner-city Liverpool.

At Eton, the list of visitors is at least as impressive. Gladstone accepted an invitation to speak at the school because 'he considered himself bound to anything for Eton',[24] and feelings of obligation, curiosity or deference continue to draw leaders of society there every year. At no other school are boys able to saunter down to one meeting or another to hear Alexander Solzhenitsyn, the NATO secretary-general or firebrand radical politicians. A talk to a few hundred privileged children below voting age can hardly be the most immediately productive way for such distinguished figures to spend their time, yet the school draws them in, like moths to a flame. During the academic year which ended in the summer of 1989, in addition to visits by the representatives of organizations like the RSPCA and the Probation Service, the boys of Eton were entertained in a concert by Dame Janet Baker, heard Dr Henry Kissinger expound on international relations, Nelson Mandela's lawyer on the state of apartheid, and listened to the chairman of the Conservative party, the director-general of Fair Trading, the chairman of Scottish and Newcastle Breweries, the director of Oxfam, two bishops, one junior minister and a Cabinet minister.

The visitors are only one reason for the sheer worldliness of Eton, its most distinctive characteristic. The scale of Etonian involvement in the running of twentieth-century Britain is staggering. Between 1900 and 1985 there were just over 1,500 ministers of all parties. No less than 343, over one fifth, had been at school at Eton. (The next highest totals, Harrow with eighty-three ministers in the period and Winchester with fifty-four, came nowhere even remotely close.) Sitting beneath the walls of Windsor Castle, the boys still feel part of a small community in which the royal family are fellow villagers.

The Provost of Eton, Lord Charteris, the Queen's former private secretary, believes that its size (with nearly 1,300 pupils it is twice the size of most boarding schools) is part of the explanation for Eton's intensely political nature. But why should that make any difference, I asked him. 'Because it's a hot-bed of intrigue,' he replied with a laugh, pouring a gin-and-tonic in his panelled house inside the school. 'The boys discover very early that they've got to get round people to get their way. It's the ideal training ground for statesmen, politicians, entrepreneurs. And pirates.'[25]

There are other reasons too. Eton is packed with children of the rich and powerful, who have spent their lives in an environment where cabinet ministers, international bankers or diplomats are regular houseguests: it would be surprising if they did not have grand ambitions. The profusion of plaques in the college chapel commemorating a score of prime ministers, the obsessional interest of the press, the gawking of tens of thousands of tourists, bear in upon the thirteen-year-old the privilege of his position.

The school's current headmaster, Dr Eric Anderson, has spent only the last decade at Eton, having previously taught at two Scottish schools, Fettes and Gordonstoun, and been headmaster at Abingdon and Shrewsbury. With his straight dark hair falling across his high forehead, the dark jacket, the clerical tabs below his white bow tie, he looks vaguely like a Wesleyan preacher:

> Ninety per cent of the most lively and interesting boys I've met have been Etonians, and so have ninety per cent of the nastiest boys I've met (although the latter category is of course much smaller).
>
> They're politically aware and well informed, which is quite unlike any other school I've ever taught in. Most would describe themselves as Conservatives, and politics is still an ambition many of them have, although nowadays they would tend to add 'if I'm good enough'.[26]

The tendrils of the Establishment ran out through the shared schooling of most of its members. Although the influence of the old boy network has been exaggerated for many years, as Lord Charteris admits, it still counts for a good deal among Old Etonians:

> The world is run on knowing the right people, actually. I'm sorry, but it is. Generations ago, if you were an Old Etonian, if you were a member of the aristocracy, you knew the right people. Well, it's just the same now really. It's just a lot bigger.[27]

But even Eton is raising its academic standards, and casting its net wider than it did. Over the last thirty years the number of pupils who are the sons of former pupils has dropped by half, from almost two thirds of the school population to just over one third. The new generation of self-made men and women who have risen within the Conservative party may bridle at the Etonian's effortless disdain, but it remains their devoutest wish to kit their sons out in the tails and tabs and have them acquire the distinctive ascendancy swagger. Two out of every three put down by their parents (often at birth) will be rejected from the provisional entry list which will yield the final 250 to be admitted.

By virtue of its great size (in some respects it functions more like a university), its position and its tradition, Eton is atypical, and, as we have seen, there are fewer old boys prominent in national life. It is the dozens of less well-known schools which have found themselves the main beneficiaries of the boom in demand. Over half of parents with children at independent schools are products of the state sector. Which brings us to what the customers want.

Squire Brown in *Tom Brown's Schooldays* didn't 'care a straw for Greek particles or the digamma', and no more so do his modern counterparts. But they do care deeply about exam results. Ninety per cent of Rugby pupils go on either to university or polytechnic, twenty per cent (about thirty every year) of them to Oxford or Cambridge. There is a certain desperation in the conversation of sixth-formers, aware that their parents have spent forty thousand pounds on their education in the hope that they will do better than if they had gone to the school on the corner. Half-a-dozen boys I questioned were all obsessed by what grades they would get at 'A' level, and showed a neurotic fear that the colleges at Oxford and Cambridge for which they were aiming would expect better results because they came from a public school. By comparison with the vision of nineteenth-century idealists, there was a frankly selfish streak to their view of the world.

The question 'Does the idea of service mean anything to you?' drew only bewilderment.

Old Squire Brown had expressed the hope that 'if he'll only turn out a brave, helpful, truth-telling Englishman and a gentleman and a Christian, that's all I want.' Contemporary parents may not have such ambitions any longer, but they do care about 'standards'. It is a big selling point: as the guide to independent schools puts it:

> Heads and staff at independent schools aim to teach children to work hard and to take a pride in their work; to pay attention to detail; to have good manners; to consider other people's feelings and to grow up into a responsible adult who will be an asset to the community.[28]

(It would be interesting to try to find a headmaster in the state sector who did not share this list of ambitions: one suspects they only exist in the fevered imaginings of leader-writers on the *Sun*.) When I asked Rugby's hulking, tuba-playing headmaster, Richard Bull, the order in which he would place Arnold's three objectives – moral principles, gentlemanly conduct and intellectual ability – his reply was surprising. He still saw morals as the primary objective on the grounds that 'someone's got to hold out for these things, otherwise things would be even more chaotic than they are already.'[29] Rugby pupils are still required to turn out for compulsory chapel on three weekday mornings and once on Sunday. But it has become an empty exercise in many schools.

'Don't fornicate in old school braces' was the resounding dictum with which some Etonians were sent out into the world in the fifties,[30] and the schools have never been much good at sexual morals. But the chapel, and a distinctly Anglo-Saxon Christianity, was at the core of the schools. In the stained-glass windows at Radley the school buildings were painted into the background of the Last Supper, almost as if Christ wore the old school tie. It was a decidedly muscular form of religion. During the First World War, the headmaster of Abbotsholme School in Staffordshire actually rewrote the Beatitudes, so that 'Blessed are the meek' became 'Blessed are the manly'. General Sir Charles Carmichael Monro was typical of many public school products in considering himself a devout Christian, although he didn't much care for the Psalms because of their 'whining' attitude; 'always asking God to smite the enemy instead of going and doing it oneself.'[31]

It was inevitable, then, that chapel attendances would become a focus for the dissent which swept many of the schools in the late sixties and early seventies. Though they never reached the machine-gun fantasies of Lindsay Anderson's *If*, rebellions centred on acts of worship – perhaps taking the form of a mass silence during hymns – left the staff, most of whom had gone from school to university and then straight back to school, completely bewildered.

Combined with the external political threat, the protests had the effect, however, of ushering in a new era into the schools. The absurd privileges of hierarchy – who could or could not wear their jackets unbuttoned, sport a coloured handkerchief or wear brown shoes – were largely dismantled. The petty barbarisms of the school disciplinary code have been reined back. One Rugby sixth former spoke almost regretfully of the fact that none of the junior boys had been 'wedged' (hung upside down by his underpants) for ages. At most such schools corporal punishment has been stopped altogether and personal fagging has been scrapped. Not only do members of staff address boys by their first names, but the boys use first names back to some staff members. Bleak, dark corridors and studies have been renovated and the dormitories boast not merely quilts and central heating, but even – unheard of – a measure of privacy. The greatest change, however, has been the introduction of girls to many of the schools, where they have raised academic standards and acted as a civilizing influence throughout the institution.

All of these changes have made the schools more appealing to parents ('getting the mothers' vote' was how one headmaster described it). But something has been lost in the process. The secret of the success of the schools is that they act as a sophisticated crammer, yet their strength is supposed to lie in their moral values. Parents make a simple commercial decision about their children's education, and expect the staff to provide the moral framework which simply doesn't exist at home. 'What heads, deputy heads and those who run boarding houses spend most time doing,' says the headmaster of Gordonstoun, 'is trying to instil in teenage boys and girls a real sense of decency, straightforwardness, common sense and loyalty.'[32]

It can be a Sisyphean task. The dilemma is simply stated: is it the function of the schools to reflect the values of society or to form them? Many try to fudge the issue. There is plenty of talk of 'Christian values', but few have any idea of what they mean in practice, and they recognize that too rigorous a moral code will merely exaggerate the gulf between the schools and the outside world. After one session of the Headmasters' Conference in the early eighties which was greatly preoccupied with discussion of 'Christian values', the headmaster of Westminster, John Rae, came away observing bleakly that 'we didn't have the slightest idea what we were talking about!'[33]

The parents appear to want the schools to pass on something they eschew or disregard in themselves. After meeting one demanding parent after another, David Newsome, headmaster of Wellington, was candid.

> When I observe the shallow materialism of some of the homes from which our boys come, and the glib expectation that a school such as mine will provide the culture, sensitivity and spirituality that are so flagrantly inconspicuous in the domestic *mise-en-scène*, I feel a twinge of despair.[34]

It is scarcely surprising there is widespread agreement that the current generation of public school pupils suffers from an inner spiritual emptiness and a lack of intellectual curiosity. It is quite different training young people for the old role of 'serving society' and training them to make a lot of money. A bishop who is a frequent visitor to several major schools often gets the feeling that he's being taken around as a relic or reminder of the old values. 'The idea of Vocation has almost disappeared,' he says. 'It's quite frightening how selfish the pupils have become. They are overwhelmingly out for themselves.'

The pupils, consumers of a dearly-bought service, demand the opportunities for which their parents have paid. Dr Rae has sadly observed the way in which the schools have adopted new values.

> Whatever their private misgivings, the schools endorse the priorities of the age: every man for himself in the competition for good 'A' levels, a good university, a well-paid job and red Porsche to roar up the school drive, scattering your former teachers like nature's rejects in the race of life.[35]

In their sales-pitch to prospective parents, the schools concentrate upon things they think they can readily explain. Hard on the heels of the promises of examination results come the bastard children of Dr Arnold. They boast of their discipline. There is much talk of 'service'. This last, perhaps the finest Victorian value, is the most empty claim of all. On close examination, the social service advertised in the prospectus means only digging old ladies' gardens, or the occasional afternoon when, released from military training, the boys will help out in a school for the educationally subnormal. The nineteenth-century ideal of self-denial in obedience to the needs of the less fortunate survives only in the platitudes of headmasters.

Approaching fifty years since the introduction of 'free, high-quality secondary education for all', the public schools seem as secure as ever. What is in danger of disappearing is the shared sense of values which gave these privileged places any claim to moral respectability.

CHAPTER SEVEN

Money by Degrees

> Don in Office, don in power,
> Don talking on Woman's Hour,
> Don knocking up a constitution,
> Don with ideas on prostitution . . .
> Don brassy, don belligerent,
> Don tipping off for ten percent,
> Don christian-naming with the stars,
> Don talking aloud in public bars
> Remote and ineffectual Don
> Where have you gone, where have you gone?

– Thoughts on rereading Belloc's famous lines on dons A. N. L. MUNBY

I N THE SUMMER of 1988 the West German president, Richard von Weizsäcker, was invited to Oxford to receive an honorary degree. It was one of those glorious, sunny afternoons when the ancient universities appear perfectly timeless. After the ceremony, with its Latin invocations, its pomp and good humour, he took tea in the magnificent garden at St John's, Oxford's richest college. As he looked at the sea of red gowns standing on the lush turf beneath a cloudless blue sky, he turned to the Warden of St Anthony's College, Professor Ralf Dahrendorf. 'There's only one thing I wonder,' he said. 'What *is* going on inside all these brilliant heads?'

'That's very simple,' said Dahrendorf. 'Only one thought. Money.'

Dahrendorf had plenty of first-hand experience of the dons' obsession. Like the bloated and impoverished Cyril Connolly lying in his bath moaning 'A million pounds! What I could do with a million pounds!', money is *the* topic in every senior common room. Where previously dons might have discussed over the port transubstantiation or the advice they would give ministers on relations with Mongolia, now they tried to dream up new ways of squeezing funds out of potential sponsors. Unlike Connolly, who could sell his talents as a journalist, most of the dons had no practical skill they could market.

The better scientists knew that they could raise money to conduct the research which interested them. Privately, they grumbled about the amount of time they had to spend soliciting sponsorship, but they acknowledged that they might as well get on with it. The difficulty lay in devising an overwhelming argument why International Sludge Incorporated should sponsor research into, say, Byzantine theology. Everyone, including the professors of Byzantine theology, had now heard the message from Whitehall: the state was no longer some ever-indulgent patron. The universities had to 'get into the marketplace' and find alternative sources of finance. When industrialists had been obliged to sit through Mrs Thatcher's homespun homilies on business they had enough practical experience through which to filter her ideas about how to run their affairs. Dons were another matter. They took it at face value. Confronted with diminishing government funds, they dutifully took their cue, and began attempting to solicit money from industry. In most cases it was a waste of time.

A year after his exchange with the German president, when he had sat through dozens more grumbling conservations over the dinner table, Dahrendorf remarked drily, 'My dons are always going on about money. They haven't the slightest idea what they're talking about.'[1]

When Lord (then plain Professor Fred) Dainton moved from having been vice chancellor of Nottingham University to take up a professorship of chemistry at Oxford he was invited to a series of welcoming dinners. At meal after meal he was subjected to the same supercilious greeting, most perfectly encapsulated by the overbearing archaeologist Dame Kathleen Kenyon, one evening at St Hugh's College.

Turning to him, she exclaimed in a Maudie Littlehampton voice, 'How nice it must be, Professor Dainton, to come back to Oxford from the provinces!'

An ability to husband borrowed *bons mots* is an essential aid to High Table survival and Dainton was able to dredge up the relevant riposte, coined originally thirty years earlier by the Manchester historian Sir Lewis Namier.

'Yes, principal,' he said, and paused for a moment, 'I find the transition from the provincial to the parochial quite interesting.'[2]

The hauteur of Oxford and Cambridge is not based upon their popularity (universities like Manchester are more sought-after), but upon longevity and their chumminess with power. As one Oxford graduate remarked, 'if you go to Oxford or Cambridge, you're given a different class of map of the world. It has a different projection. Instead of looking up at the institutions of power, you look down upon them, and you can see the way into them, the links between them.'[3] This perspective produces an insouciant self-confidence that seems to make it easier for Oxbridge graduates to get on in the world. Whitehall, the banks, the Diplomatic service are all dominated by alumni of Oxford and Cambridge. The 1945 Labour Government of Clement Attlee contained only five Oxbridge graduates, easily the lowest postwar total. But in the following three decades, a majority of every cabinet had been at one or the other university.[4] Of the 650 MPs elected in the 1987 General Election, 204 had been students at Oxford or Cambridge (of which 166 were Conservative and thirty-two Labour), more than all the other universities put together.[5] Oxford and Cambridge continue to fashion the ruling élite.

The Oxford and Cambridge selection procedures, with their emphasis on interviews, inevitably favoured articulate public school products, but the state schools were remarkably efficient at scalping the talent of the nation and packing it off to the ancient universities (and one or two other places, like the London School of Economics). Once there, the institutions moulded the intelligent children of modest homes to a distinctive pattern, enabling them to acquire the codes of dress, thought and often of speech of the ascendancy. Macmillan, for example, was fascinated by his Cabinet Secretary, Norman Brook, on the grounds that although 'he had no background', he possessed remarkably sound judgment. An explanation of sorts was given later by Maurice Bowra, who had taught Brook when he arrived at Oxford from Wolverhampton Royal Grammar School. 'Very quick, Brook,' recalled the great classical scholar. 'Learned the tricks, learned the tricks. Came up with a front pocket stuffed full of pens. Soon disappeared inside. Learned the tricks.'[6] The state sector might provide many of the best brains, but the public schools still set the social tone.

Of the two places, Oxford remains the most worldly. It was no accident that led Cecil Rhodes to choose the university for the site of his scholarships, a bold attempt to create a worldwide Establishment. The last Cambridge Prime Minister was Stanley Baldwin, since when Oxford has produced seven. Physically close to the centre of England, the college which most sums up Oxford's relationship with the nation

is Balliol, where for a century the emphasis has been upon public
service and temporal success. Cambridge was locked away in the
Fens, on the way to nowhere, turning out scientists. If Oxford was
about the application of knowledge, Cambridge was about pure
thought. This is a simplistic distinction and ignores the significant
contributions of each in other fields – Cambridge in literary criticism
and Oxford in medicine, for example. The current Master of Balliol,
Baruch 'Barry' Blumberg, is a Nobel Prizewinner for his work on
hepatitis and liver cancer. But still something of the stereotype
remains true.

'In Cambridge, you have to make excuses for going up to London.
In Oxford, people are surprised if you haven't got work to do there,'
commented one don who had taught at both places, and of the two
universities, it is Oxford, urbane, witty and somehow passionless,
which is most firmly plugged into Whitehall and Westminster. 'I
often tell undergraduates "Write an essay as if you're writing a brief
to a minister",' a Balliol politics tutor said in 1984. When an undergraduate asked why, he was told sharply, 'because that's the way you'd
do it in the civil service.'[7]

In sharp contrast, Sir Kenneth Berrill, when a fellow of King's
College, Cambridge in the late sixties, needed three attempts to
persuade the Governing Body to invite an alumnus who had become
a cabinet minister to dine at High Table. No Oxford college, alive
to the political world beyond Paddington station, would need more
than the merest hint that such an invitation might be favourably
received.

Increasingly, though, the differences between the two universities
are less significant than the similarities, and the distinctions are more
between Oxbridge and the rest of higher education. However much
they might protest it, the public image of the two universities is still
set some time in the 1930s. Both have had to work hard to combat the
image of braying frivolity beloved not only by the popular press but
by the small, most privileged sector of the undergraduate body.
Precisely because they appear to belong to a gilded world in which
youth is put on first-name terms with influence, they are consciously
avoided by many who might easily pass the entrance requrements.
But once inside, the cosiness, the seriousness with which frivolous
pursuits are taken, the brittle common room manner, provide the
ideal orientation for Westminster or Whitehall.

It was Henry Kissinger who observed that student politics are

vicious precisely because the stakes are so small, and the back-stabbing
and intrigue of the Oxbridge political clubs and debating societies
have for years provided the perfect training ground for Parliament. Of
the young men and women who filled the single office of president of
the Oxford Union in the first eighty years of this century, fifty-three
became politicians, including thirty-three ministers.

At a time when the brightest young people in the land were
predominantly being drawn to two major universities, it was inevitable
that figures in each generation would arrive at influential positions
with a network of acquaintances already established. The phenomenon,
most observable in the 1950s, persisted throughout the 1980s. Sir
Maurice Shock, the chairman of the Committee of Vice Chancellors
in the mid-eighties, had for nearly twenty years been senior treasurer
of the Oxford Union Society. As a consequence, when dealing on
behalf of the Universities with the Department of Education, he
already knew almost everyone who sat across the table from him. The
Permanent Secretary, Sir David Hancock, had been at Balliol; Robert
Jackson, the higher education minister, had been president of the
Union, and although his predecessor, George Walden, was a Cambridge man, before him the chair had been occupied by Peter Brooke,
also president of the Union, and his predecessor had been William
Waldegrave, yet another president. The Education Secretary in the
mid eighties, Kenneth Baker, had been secretary of the Oxford
Union.

In the Labour party the Oxbridge influence is declining, as new
MPs arriving at Westminster are increasingly drawn from the provincial universities and polytechnics. A steadily growing number of
Conservative MPs are graduates of other places, but the great majority,
and some of the most influential, continue to come from the political
nurseries at the ancient universities. Sometimes, the profusion of MPs
from one generation almost suggests a freemasonry. The tireless
Edwina Currie, who arrived at Oxford from Liverpool Institute for
Girls, entered Parliament in 1983. She discovered that sixteen of the
other MPs returned in that election had been fellow students at
Oxford.[8] No less than fourteen members of the Conservative Association at Cambridge in the early sixties went on to enter the House of
Commons. Many became prominent in the party, including Leon
Brittan, 'one of the most ambitious men I've met', in the opinion of
one contemporary; Kenneth Clarke, remembered for his addiction to
jazz; Norman Fowler, a certain coldness beneath the bonhomie; John

Selwyn Gummer, his childlike face shrouded by the hood of his duffel coat; Michael Howard, attempting to swallow the last traces of his natural Welsh accent; Norman Lamont all Brylcreemed hair and natty jackets.

This dominant position held by Oxford and Cambridge graduates in public life cannot last. The question is by how much and how quickly it will be watered down. Oxbridge graduates are already greatly outnumbered by the products of other universities, and by the millennium, the imbalance will be even greater. The vast majority of pupils at state schools never even consider either Oxford or Cambridge, largely because so few of their teachers have attended either place.

But behind this issue is another, more profound one. It is about the universities' relations with power.

The common rooms of Britain's universities were the repository for the values of the Establishment. The world of the High Table might have been remote, privileged, bitchy, but it nurtured that certitude which underpinned the higher professional classes. The values that were unconsciously imbibed at Oxford and Cambridge had an important influence on a majority of the leaders of twentieth-century Britain and their resonance has spread far beyond these shores.

The core of the Great and Good came from academia, trundling down on the train from their regius professorships to serve on one royal commission or another, to give a minister informal policy advice, or just to mingle in the clubs. A. L. Rowse once observed of his colleagues at All Souls College in the fifties that

> One thing dominated them all – the sense of public duty; there was nothing they would not do if they were convinced it was their duty. This was the air they breathed; I never ceased to admire them for it. It always seemed to me characteristic that when old Lang [Cosmo Gordon Lang, Archbishop of York and Canterbury] was struck down by a stroke, in the street, on his way to a meeting of the trustees of the British Museum, his last words were 'I must get to the station'.[9]

Of all the Oxford and Cambridge colleges, it was All Souls which took its civic role most conscientiously. With its immaculately maintained green lawns, its rich yellow stone quadrangles, the elaborate wood panelling and persian rugs upon the floor, the college is a congenial enough place for a bright – and they are all very bright – young man or woman to spend a few years wrestling with their intellect. There

are no tiresome undergraduates to be taught and the few eccentric
duties of the fellows are scarcely onerous. At college gaudies they are
required to sing a song in honour of their sacred bird, the mallard,
often with new verses made up for the occasion, and once every
hundred years, at the turn of the century, all the fellows process
across the roofs by torchlight behind a dead duck on top of a pole. It
is a life in which rose-tinted spectacles are handed out at the porter's
lodge. 'In a very imperfect world it seems to me that of all human
institutions, the University of Oxford, and in it the College of All
Souls, comes nearest to perfection,' Rowse remarked on another occasion.[10]

The achievement of All Souls was to be simultaneously the most
cloistered and the most worldly of colleges. Each year the college
elects two or three of the brightest graduates in Oxford to become
'Prize fellows', a process which ensures that the place is bristling with
the ambitious and the competitive. The rest of the college, comprised
of professors, research fellows and former prize fellows, is leavened by
the presence of 'London Fellows'. Formally known as Distinguished
Fellows, it is this group which gave the college its unmistakably
Establishment air. In 1990, the London Fellows included the former
cabinet ministers Lord Hailsham and Lord (Keith) Joseph; the distinguished Law Lord, Lord Wilberforce; retired diplomats Lord Sherfield and Sir D'Arcy Reilly, and Sir Jeremy Morse, chairman of
Lloyds Bank and member of the Council of Lloyd's. It was noticeable
that, with the exception of Lord Jay (formerly the Cabinet minister
Douglas Jay), the Labour party was not well represented, reflecting
either the fellows' capacity for choosing people of a kindred political
outlook, or a socialist distaste for the comfortable quadrangles. In
recent years as well as the eccentric Lord Joseph, All Souls has
produced a number of Tory ministers of a younger generation in
William Waldegrave, Robert Jackson and John Redwood. The leader
of the Conservative group of Oxford dons, Jonathan Clark, is also a
fellow.

College convention, which decrees that fellows speak on their feet
at college meetings, is good training for a political career, but All
Souls' role in public life is minimal now compared to the 1930s, when,
together with Cliveden, the country home of Lord and Lady Astor, it
became one of the main centres in which most of the Establishment
succumbed to the collective delusion of Appeasement. 'It would be
difficult to overestimate the damage done to this country by that

disastrous dinner table,' wrote Robert Boothby later.[11] In fact the
fellows were split, with many of the younger dons, including Douglas
Jay, Isaiah Berlin, and A. L. Rowse, all passionately anti-appeasement.
But the senior figures, like Geoffrey Dawson, editor of *The Times*,
were another matter. In Jay's opinion:

> If ever a man believed sincerely in the establishment of Church, State,
> Eton and Empire as they existed in the 1920s and 30s, it was Geoffrey
> Dawson. Unfortunately, neither Hitler nor unemployment fitted into the
> picture, so they were blithely disregarded.[12]

Scarcely a significant area of British public life was unrepresented at
the All Souls dining table. It included bankers, bishops and
cabinet ministers, with loose connections to the two Foreign Secretaries, Halifax ('all hunting and holy communion' in Attlee's memorable phrase) and Sir John Simon. Douglas Jay recalls that 'If you even
suggested that Hitler was likely to make war, they didn't answer you
with arguments. They just shook their heads, and looked sad and dis-
believing.'[13]

The influence of this All Souls group was profound, although
probably less than that of the sometimes overlapping Cliveden Set.
That there is, mercifully, no comparable group today, is due to a
number of reasons – shortage of leisure time and the fact that many
married fellows prefer to spend time with their families, to name but
two. The catastrophic failure of the collective wisdom of appeasement
also had something to do with it. Certainly, by the 1950s, when
Jeremy Morse was a young prize fellow, All Souls was noticeably out
of step with the rest of the country. Leaving Fleet Street for dinner at the
college on the day that British forces went into action over Suez, the bus
to Paddington Station was abuzz with jingoistic excitement at the
prospect of 'teaching the arabs a lesson'. The Oxford train was similarly
alive with nationalistic tub-thumping. It was when he walked into All
Souls that he understood the separateness of the place. The college was
cast into gloom, convinced – with the exception of a single classics
professor – that the whole venture was a ghastly, imperialistic mistake.

By comparison with its earlier days, the college now seems much
less grand. All Souls is much larger than it was: when full there are
twice as many fellows present as in the days when Dawson and the
rest met there. A higher proportion of the prize fellows stay in
academic life instead of making their careers elsewhere, which means
the college has a diminished diaspora. The Warden, Sir Patrick Neill,

still belongs to the corps of the Great and Good, somehow finding time during the eighties to serve as vice chancellor of Oxford, chairman of the Press Council, an appeal judge for the Channel Islands, to lead an investigation into the scandal at Lloyd's, serve as vice-chairman of the Committee of Vice Chancellors and Principals, be an independent director of *The Times* and to be the first chairman of the Council for the Securities Industry. But when the London Fellows meet now at college dinners, the gatherings have a different air about them, according to one participant. 'It's more like a rather up-market old-folks dinner-club,' he said.[14] Some are regular visitors; Lord Hailsham used the college a lot after becoming a widower. Most months of the year you can still find senior politicians and civil servants picking their way past the porter's lodge and across the quadrangle to dinner, and the college still organizes discrete lectures and seminars at which the academic and political worlds rub shoulders. But it is hard now to imagine any gathering around the college silver (all of it marked with the sign of the mallard), concocting a policy which would bear down upon government and nation.

But then All Souls and the ancient seats of learning, still overawed by Keynes, provided little of the intellectual drive of the eighties. 'Anyone who had spent their academic life in the major British universities would have had no idea of what Thatcherism was about', one of the new generation of policy advisers said, with only a touch of exaggertion.[15] Largely ignored by the new policy-makers, the collective wisdom of the old universities just collapsed like a sad soufflé. The new dynamic came from other universities in other places, like Chicago, and from right-wing policy institutes.

Mrs Thatcher dealt with the dons' collective wisdom in the most effective way possible. She ignored it. With no Royal Commissions being set up, there was less for them to do anyway, but there was something else, too. 'If you already know the answers,' one professor asked tartly, 'what need do you have to listen to scholarship?'[16] Not that hers was a government which eschewed a role for intellectuals. By comparison with other Conservative governments there was a positive lust for them. But they were different in character: instead of trying to temper the wishes of government to received wisdom, they provided fresh ideas. Their ceaseless industry was one of the reasons that, however unpopular the Thatcher Government may have become, it was never short of radical plans for legislation.

'What we have achieved could never have been done without the leadership of the Institute of Economic Affairs,' Margaret Thatcher admitted in 1988,[17] paying tribute to the essential role of the organization in the development of her policies. The Institute had been set up thirty years earlier under Professor Ralph Harris, who listed his hobby in *Who's Who* as 'conjuring and devising spells against over-government'. There were numerous other outfits which sprang up to provide an alternative wisdom to that available within the universities. The foundation in 1974 of the Centre for Policy Studies by Sir Keith Joseph (with money from a plastics manufacturer, Nigel Vinson) was a tacit admission of the Conservative party research department's own contamination by consensus. It was these irregular outfits which challenged the basis of Keynesianism and laid the ground for an assault upon collectivism.

This little coterie of kindred spirits was distinguished not only by their shared ideology (the profession of almost *any* ideology beyond a belief in the post-war consensus was abhorrent to many of the old school). They also, unlike the academics previously drafted in as supernumeraries to government, believed in change. Show them one of the institutions of the corporate state, and, like hounds with a fox, they instinctively wanted to tear it to pieces. With the exception of the 'Peterhouse Mafia', the little group of bone-dry former acolytes of Maurice Cowling, it was noticeable that many of them had learned or practised their trade away from the traditional ivory towers. Ralph Harris had gone to the Institute of Economic Affairs from St Andrews University. David Green, the head of the Institute's health policy group, had a Ph.D. from Newcastle University. Digby Anderson at the Social Affairs Unit got his doctorate at Nottingham. The two founders of the Adam Smith Institute, Eamonn Butler and Madsen Pirie were also alumni of St Andrews.

Within Downing Street, her economic adviser, Alan Walters, was a graduate of Leicester University. Of her close political allies, some, like Norman Tebbit, had no degree; others, like David Young, had studied in provincial universities. Those, like Keith Joseph, who had roots within the mainstream academic community were so seized of the rightness of the new ideology that they were happy to wade into battle against the tenured complacency of former colleagues. Professor Brian Griffiths, who ran the Downing Street Policy Unit through the third election and government, was an LSE man. Others who drifted in and out of the enclosed world around the Prime Minister, while they might have been educated at ancient seats of learning, delighted in their roles as heretics. To be 'one of us', you were most definitely not of the academic Great and Good.

British intellectuals have complained for years about the fact that no-one listens to them: the very notion of the intellectual seems somehow inimical to the pragmatic cultural tradition. But the new disregard was something else. There was a feeling almost of contempt among the new Downing Street insiders. Even after a decade of Thatcherism, despite all their attempts to make themselves seem wised-up to the realities of the market economy, the universities still looked unworldly.

Professor Sammy Finer, who had taught at Keele, Manchester, and half a dozen European and American universities before returning to Oxford, thinks the distinctive thing about the two ancient English universities is their bookishness. 'I can only call the prevailing pattern in Oxford one of civility. It is a cast of mind in which, even if the student himself isn't bookish and learned, he comes to respect learning and bookishness.'[18]

This sort of life did not cut much ice with the new men at Number 10. British higher education had proved the enemy of enterprise, and while a few managers in the rustbelt industries might have retained some deference, in the younger, brasher businesses, there was near-derision. The advertising industry, dominated by once-sharp young men who had started life as messengers, clerks and teaboys, felt it particularly strongly. Tim Bell, who briefly considered further education as a way of fulfilling his teenage ambition of becoming a reporter with ITN, discarded the idea because 'the students were all blokes in duffel coats, listening to trad jazz and being irritating.' (He preferred modern jazz, slick suits and nightclubs.) Bell, who became Thatcher's main adviser on presentation, has come to see the universities as impractical, cosseted, irrelevant. His contempt may be unsophisticated and crudely put, but it speaks volumes for the cast of mind of the little group who enjoyed access to Downing Street throughout the eighties:

> The universities sidelined themselves, with their totally archaic way of working. They spend a lot of time teaching useless subjects. They operate a ridiculous, old-fashioned élitist society, which still has that old British Empire thing of 'it's better to get pissed than learn anything.' It's all potty.[19]

The universities watched their rustication from Whitehall with growing despair. Professor Sir Richard Southwood, Oxford's vice

chancellor, held a visiting post at Cornell, and experienced the transatlantic difference at first hand:

> When I go to America, the universities are appreciated. They're still part
> of that common framework, and businessmen understand, and value, their
> role. Here, they just snipe at us.[20]

The record of British academia, notably at Oxford and Cambridge,
did, after all, justify a degree of self-confidence: Trinity College,
Cambridge alone has twenty-eight Nobel prizes; France has forty-
four. But popular attitudes to higher education were markedly different
to those in other European countries. Resentment against the cosseted
world of the dons, in which they could get elected to a comfortable
cloister in their twenties, and remain there for the rest of their careers
had been latent for years. Now, the disdain of Downing Street gave it
licence.

It was around this time that Margaret Thatcher met Professor
Dahrendorf. With the directness and lack of small talk for which she
is famed she turned, looked him straight in the eyes, and said, 'the
universities have failed Britain. You have failed us.'[21] Even Dahren-
dorf, an eloquent sociologist, was temporarily silenced by this outburst.
On another occasion, Mrs Thatcher told a gathering of backbench
Conservative MPs that she had made a study of British millionaires.
She had made the startling discovery that not a single name which
came to mind was a graduate, least of all of Oxford or Cambridge.
Ergo, Oxbridge was anti-business.[22]

Certainly, the universities were rooted in the old corporatist world.
They were led by men who had entered academia when Britain was a
very different country. Sir Maurice Shock, Rector of Lincoln College,
Oxford, an undergraduate contemporary of William Rees-Mogg,
Robin Day, Dick Taverne and others, observed of them:

> Whatever their politics, there really wasn't a pin-head's worth of difference
> between them. There was a prevailing Fabianism, like the nineteenth-
> century assumption about the all-conquering tide of liberalism. They
> thought the future lay with meritocratic Fabianism.[23]

By the end of the 1970s these beliefs had been tested to destruction,
and dissolved in acid by failure.

In other times, the conferring of an honorary degree upon the prime
minister by the University of Oxford would have been an unremark-

able event, a rite of passage marking simultaneously both respect and acceptance by one of the pillars of British society. Previous graduates who had gone on to Downing Street had been similarly honoured, and Mrs Thatcher, who had studied chemistry at Somerville College between 1947 and 1951, was undoubtedly the most famous alumna of the university in the twentieth century. An honorary doctorate would have been a means of shaking hands across the chasm opening between the universities and Whitehall. It would also have rather tended to confirm Oxford's misty grandeur.

In the event, the Thatcher degree demonstrated how great the gulf between the old and new orders had become. The Prime Minister was one of six distinguished candidates, including the President of Italy and the opera singer Sir Geraint Evans. The vote confirming the award of a degree should have been a formality, but for weeks beforehand flysheets had been circulating around the university arguing that she should be denied the degree because (like almost every other part of the public service), the universities had had their budgets cut. For Oxford, to give the degree would, said one waggish don, 'be feeding the hand that bites it'. In fact the dreaming spires had suffered from the Thatcher cuts less than most places – universities like Salford, which was less than twenty years old, had been far more savagely hit. The fundamental objection, however, could not be quantified in monetary terms. What the dons really objected to was the government's whole attitude to higher education, which appeared to see it only in terms of training for jobs, a rejection of the spirit which had animated higher education for a century or more.

On the appointed day at the end of January 1985, over a thousand lecturers and professors crammed into the Sheldonian Theatre to cast their votes. Most had never before been to a meeting of Congregation, the university's obscure governing body. The outcome was predictable from the start. The 'no' exit of the building was still jammed with voters long after the final 'yes' had been registered: the final figure 738 against, 319 in favour. The only other person to have been snubbed in a similar fashion was the Pakistani President Zulfikar Ali Bhutto, who had been rejected a decade earlier by a majority a fraction of the size, on the grounds that he shared responsibility for massacres in Bangladesh.

The affair of the honorary degree had been handled with staggering ineptness from beginning to end. Why an honorary degree was not proposed when Mrs Thatcher became leader of her party in 1975, or when she became Prime Minister in 1979, but suggested only when she was at her most unpopular in academic circles is a conundrum. How a campaign led by a professor of government and an authority on ancient Greek homosexuality could have mobilized the university's scientists and doctors to pack the Congregation is a mystery. Why the dons who voted to snub the Prime Minister thought they would engender public support instead of appearing rude, petty-minded, and spiteful, is a wonder. It would, altogether, be hard to conjure up a more politically incompetent exercise.

There was, in theory, no absolute reason why the funding and administration of the universities should be any less the business of government than the running of the road network or the Forestry Commission. The arms' length relationship between politicians and the universities was one which the academics relished, for obvious reasons, since it gave them both an assured income and relative freedom of action. But as they largely existed at the taxpayer's expense, the government was quite within its rights to exercise its authority in an attempt to make them more 'relevant'. The problem was that the universities had come to think of the old system as immortal.

The most ringing proclamation of the role of the university, which many still cite as *the* manifesto, remains that of Cardinal Newman. In 1852, after his break with Anglicanism, but long before he had been offered a cardinal's hat, Newman was invited to deliver a series of lectures in Dublin, arguing for the foundation of a Catholic University. The theory which Newman expounded in his addresses (although all were published, some were never actually delivered), became the credo of academia for a century.

In short, knowledge was an end in itself. In a moral sense it was undeniably wholesome: the student acquired civilized values which would colour his entire outlook on life:

> He apprehends the great outlines of knowledge, the principles on which it rests, the scale of its parts, its lights and its shades, its great points and its little, as he otherwise cannot apprehend them. Hence it is that this education is called 'Liberal'. A habit of mind is formed which lasts through life, of which the attributes are freedom, equitableness, calmness, moderation, and wisdom.[24]

When the first fifteen youths arrived at the new university in November 1854, Newman elaborated on the difference between what they would learn at the university, and the sort of knowledge they would have acquired had they decided instead to study for a profession. The education 'does not make physicians, surgeons or engineers, or soldiers, or bankers, or merchants, but it makes *men*'.[25]

The utilitarian objections to this philosophy a century or more later are obvious enough. Newman justified the privileges of the minority in terms of 'raising the intellectual tone of society'. The system turned out people confident in their own opinions and judgement:

> It teaches him to see things as they are, to go right to the point, to disentangle a skein of thought, to detect what is sophistical and to discard what is irrelevant. It prepares him to fill any post with credit, and to master any subject with facility.[26]

It is a soaring manifesto in defence of the generalist. But it is deeply flawed. It had no great vision of creative genius. It ignored – scorned – science, and provided an easy prop to generations of university professors, civil service commissioners, gentlemen in the City, in their apologias for the cult of the amateur.

Yet Newman's philosophy survived almost unquestioned through most of the succeeding century. The ancient universities cast such a shadow across higher education that other institutions could not grow. Since the politicians and permanent secretaries were themselves usually products of Newmanite Oxbridge colleges, they paid too much attention to the demands of admissions tutors about secondary schooling. The liberal education, which encouraged students to see problems from all aspects, was a deterrent to the sort of creative or heretical thought upon which businesses are built. And while only a handful would go on to become permanent secretaries in Whitehall, the sons and daughters of business people and tradesmen emerged from Oxford and Cambridge prepared only to consider a narrow range of acceptable careers, the families thereby translated from generators of wealth to consumers of wealth in one generation.

But Newman's ideal of the civilizing role of the university knitted easily into a vision of postwar Britain in which opportunity should be open to all, regardless of means. Between 1945 and 1990, the number of universities almost trebled from seventeen to forty-seven, teaching well over 300,000 students. Another 300,000 attended the thirty Polytechnics. The guiding principles of university expansion laid down by Lord Robbins in the early sixties were based upon impeccably liberal principles. Instead of going in for manpower planning, education was to be available to all who reached the requisite standard.

True, he suggested an expanding proportion of students should study science and technology subjects, but it fell far short of any tight, centrally directed quota system. The expansion was supervised by the remote old dons on the University Grants Committee, which controlled all aspects of development, from staff salaries to the amount which might be spent on an office chair.

In 1963 Albert Sloman, the newly-appointed Vice-Chancellor of yet-to-be-built Essex University, delivered the Reith Lectures on BBC Radio. The new 'plate-glass' universities on American-style campuses were to be the most dramatic symbol of the Robbins era, created by the finest British architects, like Sir Basil Spence, or Denys Lasdun. The Vice Chancellor's aspirations soared. The universities would be big enough to sustain sophisticated research departments: Essex was planning to accommodate ten thousand students, rising to twenty thousand. Individual departments might have up to ten professors. He made all the right noises about how the university would plan ahead to meet the future manpower needs of the nation, about collaboration with industry, about how students from all disciplines would learn a foreign language, and would not specialize too early.

Not much of it happened. The 1963 Reith Lectures represent a vanished vision. This is now seen, and talked about, as a Golden Age. There was the will to make things happen: the Essex campus had been thrown up on the outskirts of Colchester and students had moved in within three years of the university being established in 1964. For the next few years, the universities glistened brightly, invitations to an exciting new style of higher education. But the dream was never realized. Albert Sloman's Essex entered the 1990s scarcely larger than it had left the sixties, with a population of just over three thousand students. The accommodation looks what it is, a series of bleak tower blocks on Essex wetlands. The concrete and steel which was to give form to the ambitions of Robbins today looks grubby, bleak, and in some cases is physically falling apart. The ambitions seem similarly flawed.

You can almost see where the money ran out. The limitations to the liberal ideal became clear early on. If you allowed students to follow their own choice of academic study, absurdly large numbers chose courses like sociology and psychology, which had little or no practical benefit to the rest of society, who were, after all, footing the bill. The sudden expansion brought into university life lots of second-rate lecturers, who because the universities granted them 'tenure', could not be shifted or sacked, and just grew paunchy, lazy and ever more inept. These were practical problems, which demanded practical solutions. The practical steps, though, would have the effect of shaking the philosophical pedestal upon which academic life rested.

There was an almost audible intake of breath throughout the universities when, in 1985, the Education Secretary, Keith Joseph, produced his Green Paper on higher education. It was a bleak, narrow-minded and uninspiring document. Where Robbins had larded his report with references to Confucius and the Old Testament, the Green Paper was written in the plodding language of an accounts clerk let loose on a typewriter. The universities had been 'too academic', the research had been 'non-cost-effective', and insufficiently 'profitable'. The government had specific, mechanistic demands of higher education. But it had no broad vision of what function it was to serve in a civilized society.

The innate sense of longevity in the Oxbridge common rooms meant that initially they felt able to ignore this vulgar intrusion: they would still be there long after it was dead and buried. But their inability to defend the old values and their failure to generate any public support for their campaign of resistance revealed how threadbare their ideas were becoming.

The new systems proposed by Joseph and the education ministers Kenneth Baker and Robert Jackson – all of them Oxford men – at least had a clarity of purpose about them. Jackson in particular, the aridly dry minister with specific responsibility for higher education, rapidly became the most loathed man in academe. He had the knack of the uncomfortable question. Why were the dons so obsessed with maintaining a student ratio which was lower than at distinguished places like Stanford? Why did they need to spend half the year on vacation? What was the value of so much of the research they said they were pursuing? The department wanted to see universities setting objectives and carrying out management appraisals, ideas the dons felt belonged more properly to the working practices of encyclopaedia salesmen rather than their authors. Implicit in all of the ideas was the thought that learning could be judged by standards other than its own, and that the dons were not to be trusted.

There was one new policy idea after another. Fees for overseas students were doubled: numbers fell. Budgets were to be cut, then came the announcement that student numbers were to be increased. Staff were offered early retirement, then, when talented young scientists rather than dusty old professors of Sanskrit took the money and ran, more funds were made available to hire new staff. To the universities, this to-ing and fro-ing did not look like a coherent policy. 'Most of us are suffering from varying degrees of shell-shock,' remarked Lord Flowers, Vice Chancellor of London University.[27]

Money was the key to control. The University Grants Committee, the mechanism for preserving an arm's length relationship between government and higher education, although founded in 1919, had been an essentially Edwardian institution. It was clearly not going to survive the new approach. It had lasted so long because Edwardian figures dominated public life well after the era had passed. (Sometimes literally – in 1937 the UGC had nine members, all but the chairman over sixty and five of them octogenarians.) A new University Funding Council, to be a roughly balanced mixture of professional academics and businessmen would now decide how money should be spent. Its new chairman, Lord Chilvers, an engineering don, company director, and well-known Conservative, had soon antagonized most of the academic community by suggesting, in an interview with *The Times Higher Education Supplement*, that not only would universities have to find funds elsewhere, there was a lot to be said for students paying their full fees, and leaving the state to pick up what he called the 'charity' bill only for the really poor.[28] Plans for a student loan scheme seemed to complete the abandonment of the old vision of the universities as a benefit to be available to all who had the talent.

The delicate, mutually respected relationship between Whitehall and the universities had been smashed. Not only were the universities now expected to parade themselves before industry in the hope of having a few thousand pounds stuck down their gowns, they also found themselves drawn into a series of ad hoc relations not merely with the Department of Education but with an entire cross-section of the bureaucracy, from the Treasury and the Department of the Environment to the Department of Health (on medical school matters), and the Department of Trade (on industrial matters).

Of all the British universities, none appeared to have a less desperate need of £220 million than Oxford (except, perhaps, Cambridge). But it was Oxford which led the way in trying to tap sources of finance. To drum up funds (the Bodleian Library alone was said to be short of £10 million), the university hired an American fundraiser with mutton-chop sidewhiskers, Dr Henry Drucker. In October 1988, an unlikely waggonload of well-lunched worthies descended on the university to launch the appeal, in a train donated for the day by British Rail. They included the Archbishop of Canterbury, three dukes (Norfolk, Wellington and Atholl, all Oxford graduates), and numerous politicians, including the former prime minister, Lord Home. Other members of the appeal committee included the Queen's former private secretary, Lord Charteris, the recently retired head of the civil service, Lord Armstrong, the former master of the rolls, Lord Denning, a trio of judges, a smattering of showbiz glitterati (Magnus Magnusson, Sir Robin Day and Dudley Moore), the Secretary-General of the Commonwealth, Sir Shridath Ramphal, half a dozen bankers and industrialists, a similar number of knights from the Foreign Office, the General Secretary of the Trades Union Congress, novelists like Iris Murdoch and Anthony Powell, the actress Dame Peggy Ashcroft, the conductor Jane Glover, and token outsiders like Rupert Murdoch and the former American defence secretary Caspar Weinberger.

It was as reasonable a cross-section of the Great and Good as could be gathered together. It is a fair bet that, asked whether they felt that more public funds should have been made available, many, perhaps most, would have answered 'yes'.

In his last year at Oxford, Robert Armstrong went to seek advice about his career. The son of the distinguished musician, Sir Thomas Armstrong, his had been a seemingly effortless progression – the Oxford forcing-house the Dragon School, then Eton, and now an undergraduate at Christ Church. The man he sought out, Sir John Maud (later Lord Redcliffe-Maud) was a fellow Etonian, a bishop's son of whom someone once remarked 'you must take the smooth with the smooth'. Maud, an outstanding wartime civil servant who ended up in the Master's Lodge at University College, Oxford, had spent his career in effortless moves between academia and the mandarinate. Now he told Armstrong that in his view he should apply to sit the exams for entry to the civil service.

Maud had spotted a natural, and Armstrong rose through the bureaucracy, until he emerged at the top as Cabinet Secretary. Then the memoirs of former M.I.5 man Peter Wright provoked the *Spycatcher* fiasco, with Armstrong being shuttled from London to Sydney in a frenetic, comically doomed attempt to prevent publication. He ended up, in the opinion of the most acute Whitehall-watcher, 'the most famous public servant since Cardinal Wolsey.'[29] It was a role he cannot have foreseen, for the world he had chosen was one in which well-drafted discretion was the better part of power. The interesting thing about both Maud and Armstrong is how little thought either of them gave to any other career – the public service just seemed the natural thing to do.

The links between Whitehall and the masters' lodges are under more pressure now. *The Times* remarked in 1988:

> Vice chancellors and permanent secretaries used to be men of the same Establishment clay. Once upon a time they hobnobbed in the Athenaeum. They struck bargains, the universities sending their best and brightest into Whitehall, retired permanent secretaries moving out into college headships and honorary professorships ... that cosy relationship has gone for good.[30]

This is a considerable exaggeration. Both the institutions are waiting and watching, in the hope that the nineties may prove less traumatic than the eighties. What was indisputable was that the combination of comparatively low pay and a poor public image made the civil service look less than glamorous to many graduates, at the very time that alternative careers were opening in consultancy, the professions, or the City. Looked at in ten-yearly intervals at only one of the ancient universities, the collapse of the public service as a career is startling.

In 1958 Cambridge supplied 103 graduates to the public services, including local government, the health service and the nationalized industries. By 1968, when both the university and the bureaucracy were larger, the figure had risen to 178. By 1978 there had been a decline to 129. But the real crash occurred at the end of the 1980s – by 1988, the figure had dropped to a mere forty-nine.[31]

These figures would doubtless make enjoyable reading to those who thought the decline of Britain was the result of too much talent being diverted into an unproductive bureaucracy. But the emerging Cambridge graduates were no more prepared to get their hands dirty than their predecessors. The number going into industry fell throughout the last years of the eighties, until by 1988 it had dropped to only 229, nine per cent of the total: three years earlier it had been fifteen per cent. These figures are surprising, if only because industrial demand for graduates had been increasing, while the 1960s prejudice against industry is said largely to have disappeared. Part of the blame for the poor showing of industry can be attributed to unattractive rates of pay and to companies' inept handling of graduate recruitment. (Bill Kirkman, who ran the Cambridge appointments service for over twenty years, remarked that with the exception of concerns like Unilever or Shell, 'I wouldn't even know who's responsible at a lot of companies, some of them household names.'[32]) But it is hard to escape the conclusion that the values and culture of the liberal education still provide a deterrent.

The figures can hardly have made inspiring reading for education ministers who had spent so much of the eighties moaning that the universities were failing to produce the technocrats and managers who would revive the economy. All that seemed to have happened was that more Cambridge alumni had chosen comfortable bolt-holes in the professions and commerce. According to the Institute of Manpower studies at Sussex University, between 1979 and 1987, demand for graduates from banking and insurance rose by 310 per cent. The number becoming lawyers increased by ninety per cent in the same period, the number of accountants rose by half.[33]

The largest firm of accountants in Britain, Peat Marwick McLintock, in 1988 recruited over 1,200 graduates, the equivalent of the entire output of a medium-sized university. Firms of solicitors which had once taken on perhaps five or six graduates were now looking for fifty or sixty. Even the Bar began to stage 'presentations' in Oxford and Cambridge, hoping to lure new recruits. But accountancy represented the most sustained growth of all the professions, with six, seven or eight per cent of graduating students choosing to enter an occupation which a decade earlier had been a byword for unfashionability. Some join to acquire a qualification which they hope will lead on to wealth and influence in commerce. But many others are signing up in an army of clerks. Large companies need spiralling numbers of graduates as their businesses become more complex and information-based. Many which had previously never considered recruiting people with degrees now draw them in by the bus-load. We are on the way to the Ph.D. proletariat.

One don after another complains that students see degrees merely as opening the door on a lucrative career. The principles of Newman may not have been abandoned by the academics, but to many of their students, they are increasingly irrelevant. The salaries offered to new graduates going into the City are already sometimes twice as high as those offered to young people prepared to work in the public sector, with professions like teaching suffering badly. As the competition for graduates gets more intense, the disparity looks set to grow. It is summed up in the bleak observation of one recent graduate who spent years at Cambridge and emerged with a good degree that, 'Nobody pays you to do anything worthwhile nowadays'.

If students are able to earn more than a regius professor within two or three years of graduating, it is scarcely surprising that the universities' own recruitment is suffering. The Vice Chancellor of Oxford, Sir Richard Southwood, thinks that graduates are less prepared to start on an academic career if it seems that the universities don't have the trust of government: 'People like to join a winner.'[34] Already, universities are finding it hard to fill posts with adequately talented people. In areas like mathematics, accountancy, computing and electrical engineering, where jobs in commerce were creaming off many of the better graduates, the problem was particularly acute. 'There is a strong signal of a decline in quality,' a committee of vice chancellors observed in 1988.[35]

'It's inconceivable that Wittgenstein would be offered a lectureship today,' one bitter Cambridge don told me over tea. 'I mean, what would his business plan look like?'

He was, he admitted, exaggerating. But by the 1990s the dark cloud over the quadrangles had been stationary for years. 'The universities have reached a point of near total acquiescence and despair,' said Ralf Dahrendorf. 'I can't think of another country in the civilized world where the universities are as demoralized as they are here. They expect the worst.'[36]

It is, as Clausewitz observed, the speciality of intellectuals to indulge in indignation. More worrying was the fact that many were voting with their feet. Regius professors unable to afford a house in Oxford discovered that if they were prepared to make the trip across the Atlantic they could literally triple their salaries and halve their workload. To the evident disgust of some American professors, who resented the thought that their universities should become 'the new Victorian punjab of academia, designed to provide outdoor relief to the British academic classes,'[37] some of the brightest names in British academic life left the country during the closing years of the 1980s. The philosopher Bernard Williams, Provost of King's College, Cambridge, announced in 1987 that he was sick of 'rallying the troops, fighting the cuts and carrying out a public relations exercise'[38] and left for Berkeley, aged nearly sixty. Professor Christopher Ricks, a distinguished English don at Cambridge, went to Boston; Professor Peter Hall, Britain's foremost authority on urban planning, went to Berkeley. Sir Michael Howard retired from the regius professorship of Modern History and went to Yale. Alan Ryan, a political scientist, went to Princeton. Simon Schama, who went to become a professor at Harvard in 1980 and subsequently produced two dazzling works of history, explained that at Oxford he had had to spend most of his time getting students through exams, 'knowing that not many of them were particularly thrilled to be doing it – they were just waiting for the inevitable interview at the merchant bank.'[39]

British dons who kept in touch with colleagues who had decamped abroad regarded them wistfully. Norman Stone, Professor of Modern History at Oxford, spoke for them all:

> When you get given a secretary, a library from which you're allowed to borrow books, and students who turn up for lectures (none of which is true at many British universities), you tend to look at academic life more kindly. Particularly if, in addition, your wife doesn't have to give tupperware parties so you can pay the mortgage.[40]

Ministers produced a stream of figures to try to show that the 'brain drain' was a myth, that there were as many academics coming to Britain as were leaving.[41] But the bare figures, which showed a couple of hundred academics coming or going each year, did not give the whole picture. Several surveys suggested that the academics who were coming to Britain were less experienced and less talented, while it was the better home-grown ones who were leaving – this was the important, and undermining, thing. During the fifties and sixties, Britain could lay claim to pre-eminence in great areas of scholarship: as a result intellectual life in Britain had a truly metropolitan feeling. Now, there were signs that much of British academic life was merely a province of America.

Meanwhile, the function of higher education was being redefined. At the end of the eighties, plans were under discussion for expansion; by the end of the next quarter century, one third of the school population would be going on to further education. The archives of the Department of Education and Science are littered with similar promises which have been made in the past. But this time, the talk is of a qualitative as well as a quantitative change. In a speech which signalled that the battle for the survival of the liberal education had hardly begun, the Education Secretary observed in 1989 that

> we shall have to be careful not to generalize about 'quality' on the basis of traditions of cultural exclusiveness which belonged to the world of three per cent participation in higher education and which are neither appropriate nor sustainable in a world of thirty per cent participation.[42]

The writing was on the wall.

In many places, shortage of funds had already forced universities to embrace a new type of sponsor. Oxford had prised enough money out of Nissan to set up a centre for Japanese studies, Sussex had persuaded Toyota to sponsor engineering research. A new breed of vice chancellor was emerging, appointed on fixed term contracts, politically more acute, diplomatically more skilled, and with a manner calculated to please potential donors. Like other areas of the élite, they tend to be more heterogeneous in their background and more businesslike in their mission. A surprising number are engineers, like Graeme Davies at Liverpool, an able New Zealander. It remains, however, an occupation dominated by men, and their encounters at the Athenaeum, their chosen scheming ground, are less about how to fill professorships than how to raise money.

In the past, the universities, taking their cue from Oxford and Cambridge, have always been the places in which the values of the Establishment were refined, where the networks were formed, and where the custodians of the national well-being retreated for sustenance. Intellectuals in Britain have rarely formed a disaffected caucus within the state on anything like the scale to be found in other parts of Europe. They became adornments instead to the complicated filigree of royal commissions, committees of inquiry, public authorities, arts councils and broadcasting authorities. Called upon to perform these tasks less frequently, feeling their very way of life under threat, there came prolonged whines of discontent from the Fellows' Parlours.

They have not really taken to heart the message that higher education could not continue indefinitely on a model laid down over a century ago, and for the most part the experience of being besieged gave rise merely to a feeling of bitterness. The universities most penalized by the severest cuts were those places – the universities of Aston and Salford for example – which were most attuned to the commercial world. None of the universities was allowed to go to the wall, but the real growth of recent years has been the expansion of polytechnics, which now educate as many students as the universities, thereby easing the pressure for change.

If the spirit of Newman is alive and well in the ancient universities, it is because no alternative manifesto has been laid out. All they have heard instead is a lot of carping. In the older universities, which set the tone for most of academia, nothing much has really changed. The dons learned a new language, but altered none of their basic beliefs about their role. Some more students are being taught practical subjects, but many of the better brains have fled the country, leaving more room for second-rate ones.

A new vision of the function of the universities will only take hold when it is backed by the money to make it realizable. Because further education is still regarded as the preserve of a small élite, British schools continue to disgorge over forty per cent of their pupils with no educational qualifications. This shameful waste of talent belonged to the nineteenth century, when industry needed unskilled labour, rather than to the needs of the twenty-first century. It is the flip side of Newmanism, and it cannot be overcome – as it must be – until a fresh concept of higher education is expounded and then supported.

CHAPTER EIGHT

God Save the Church of England

> God bless the Church of England,
> The rectory lawn that gave
> A trodden space for that bazaar
> That underpinned the nave.
> We must dip into our pockets
> For our hearts are full of dread
> At the thought of all the damage
> Since the roof was stripped of lead.
>
> – JOHN BETJEMAN

THE 1990s VENTURE beyond the gates of Marston Hall in Lincolnshire at their peril. There is no radio, no television. No newspaper is delivered. The only periodical brought through the great Tudor doors is *Country Life*.

The Reverend Henry Thorold is almost the last remaining squarson in England. A gangly, unkempt figure in tubular trousers, threadbare clerical collar and patched tweeds, he commutes from the ancestral home to the local churches in an elderly Bentley, simultaneously the local squire and parson. It is not a role he relishes. 'I don't *like* duties,' he mutters testily as we pause beside the church to admire the oldest and biggest laburnum tree in England.

It was in the villages and hamlets of rural England that the Church was once most vibrantly alive. The Church of England, bells tolling from the ivy-clad tower to summon the labourers to Harvest Festival, is part of the folk memory of the summer of British greatness, a pastoral counterpoint to stories of wars, conquests and colonies. Each community had its own bucolic parson and its own Church school. Since the last World War, as the rural population dwindled away, replaced by tractors or seduced by city wages, the Church has retreated from the countryside too. Where once each village had its own priest, each priest now has up to ten villages. In rural counties like Herefordshire, the number of clergy has been cut by half within a generation; in the diocese of Salisbury the number of rural clergy has dropped by forty per cent. The traditional heart of the Church beats but faintly.

The Thorold family, who still own large tracts of the county, first came to Marston in the fourteenth century. Generation after generation they produced their quota to become county lieutenants, MPs, justices of the peace, army officers, and clergy. Henry Thorold, being the younger son of a younger son, took holy orders, and avoided loathsome parochial responsibilities by serving first as a naval chaplain and then as a housemaster at a minor public school. After fifteen years, he retired to the family manor house at Marston Hall. His cousin, the fifteenth baronet and deputy Lieutenant of the county, lives a few miles away at Syston Hall.

The plumbing and wiring at Marston appear to have been modernized around the time of the last war. On a warm summer's evening, it is a full ten or fifteen degrees cooler than most modern houses, and in the drawing room heavy embossed wallpaper hung with cobwebs covers the places where damp has broken through in brown stains. Clocks chime every quarter of an hour. If it seems surprisingly late, it is because they are chiming twenty minutes early. Henry Thorold wears no watch, and likes to be sure that he has plenty of time. Dinner is a Marks and Spencer's chicken pie, eaten off the family silver, and accompanied by an excellent claret. 'Nowadays, I dine at Lord Sieff's sideboard,' he says. The candlelight throws a gentle, flickering light on the Reynoldses, Lelys and Poussin on the walls.

The Church of England lay at the heart of the idea of the Establishment; 'Prosperity to the Establishment and confusion to all Enthusiasts,' was the toast of Henry Thorold's predecessors in the early years of the nineteenth century.[1] They were referring to Nonconformists, but they might as easily have been damning enthusiasms of all kinds, for the Church of England saw itself lying deep and steady beneath the nation, the ballast which kept the ship of state on an even keel.

The special privileges of the Church of England, the Queen as its head, the squad of bishops in the House of Lords, the pre-eminence of the Archbishop of Canterbury above all other non-royal citizens, were the visible signs of the Church's unique appanage. Its particular strength derived from the fact that it existed in the territory which lay at the heart of the Establishment, the area where public life and private morals collided. If the Establishment was about shared values, the Church of England was the arbiter of what those values were.

The close relationship between the Church and the Establishment was consolidated by the family ties between the clergy and the gentry. They were generally one and the same. Although the Reformation stripped the Church of much of its secular power, once the monarch had become its head, the local parson was invested with a new social status. Where previously, the clergy had often been the sons of artisans, as the pulpit now became a channel of communication from government to people, increasing numbers of them came from the aristocracy. (So eagerly did the Thorold family embrace religion that not only did they spawn Anglican bishops, an aberrant gene produced Jesuit priests as well.)

The Reformation also meant the end of the clergy's pre-eminent role in most of the professions, apart from education. The physicians denied them the right to practise medicine and within one hundred years they were largely gone from the civil service and the great offices of state. Archbishop Laud, beheaded on Tower Hill in January 1645, was the last cleric to hold a senior office of state, and the last ecclesiastical diplomat died one hundred years later.

By then, however, the Anglican parsonages had taken on their distinctive role in the political culture of Britain. Writing in 1830, Coleridge saw them as beacons of light in a benighted land. By their very presence every village and hamlet acquired

> a germ of civilization . . . this unobtrusive, continuous agency of a Protestant Church Establishment, this it is, which the patriot and the philanthropist, who would fain unite the love of peace with the faith in the progressive amelioration of mankind, cannot estimate at too high a price.[2]

In the year that Coleridge expressed these views, half of Church appointments were in the hands of private sponsors – Lord Fitzwilliam had twenty-eight livings at his disposal alone – which further consolidated the links between the Church and the gentry. Today, the appointment of clergy in most parishes is a matter for the bishop.

But the country parishes have been low on the Church of England's list of priorities, starved of vicars and money on the grounds that since Britain is a largely urban nation they have a less urgent call upon the Church's resources. The most dramatic social initiative of the Church in the eighties – *Faith in the City* – focused on the specific problems of the inner cities. A later report on the difficulties of country parishes was commissioned only as an after-thought, and owed its existence to the fact that the Archbishop of Canterbury was an amateur pig-breeder. (The Duke of Westminster – 'I wouldn't say I'm religious, I belong to the Church of England' – ran into the Archbishop while he was exhibiting his sows at the Royal Show and over tea offered to put up £100,000 to pay for the report.) But talk of the crisis in the inner cities does not find a sympathetic ear in Lincolnshire:

> It's complete nonsense. I was at Southwell [Minster] when they read out the Archbishop's letter on the inner cities. It completely ruined an otherwise elegant and educated sermon. What about the crisis in the countryside? Why did this parish have no priest for six years?

Perhaps there's a shortage of clergy, I suggested.

> Shortage? Shortage? If there is, it's because the Church is spending money on bureaucrats. I met a former pupil of mine recently. Impressive young man. He'd become a clerk in Holy Orders. I asked him what he was doing. He told me he was diocesan education officer, whatever that is. He'd no parish, you see. That's what the Church is spending money on, and that's why – all these canons and others with no proper job – they haven't got any parish priests.

The light from the two triple candelabras flickered across the canvases on the walls. The complaint of bureaucracy, indifference and the unrepresentativeness of the governing General Synod is heard in rural parishes across the land, a chorus from within the Church's soul that it has been betrayed. Beyond the mullioned windows an owl hooted.

And what of the family? What of the tradition which had seen generation after generation producing at least one clergyman?

'That's all over now,' he said bitterly and sadly. 'This family had been in love with the Church. But it's at an end. What does the Church of England stand for any longer?'

It is a question asked with despairing frequency by many of the Church's former friends. Being 'Established' means more than the formal privileges of the Church of England. It defines what the Church is. Historically, the fact that it was born not merely out of the Reformation, but out of nationalism has been more important than any questions of dogma. The Church abounds in such a bewildering number of different factions, each rejoicing in its own idea of Anglicanism – Evangelicals, Conservatives, Liberals, Anglo-Catholics, High-Churchers and Low-Churchers – precisely because its position as the Established Church allows it to be all things to all people. It is, before everything, the Church where the pragmatic good chap gets on his knees.

And still, each week in churches across the land, the special relationship between the Church of England and the nation is re-affirmed in prayers for the Queen and the government. Yet the Church has surrendered much of its privileged position, almost un-noticed. One cannot imagine that the coronation of the next monarch will be conducted without a prominent presence from the Roman Catholic and Nonconformist Churches. The Archbishop of Canterbury still has the right to be called to speak in the House of Lords before anyone else except for the party leaders, but few of the bishops would fight with any vigour to retain exclusive rights to their couple of dozen seats there, and most would like to see a Roman Catholic Cardinal Archbishop there too.

Go to Westminster Abbey, and you see the frailty of the tradition. Every day at noon, surrounded by the tombs of the heroes of the British Empire, a white-haired clergyman ascends to the pulpit and invites the congregation to join him in prayers for the state of the world. As he recites the Lord's Prayer through a loudspeaker, hund-reds of tourists, chattering, chewing, giggling, ignore him. Three and a half million visitors traipse around the nave of the Abbey each year. Exactly one third of that number attended Church of England services on the average Sunday in 1986. All the statistical indicators support the picture of an organization in relentless decline. In 1914, there were 22,000 Anglican clergy. By 1987 the figure had more than halved, to 10,500.[3] In 1930, of every ten children born, seven were baptized. By 1986, it was true of only three in every ten, and in some parts of the big cities, almost half the parents could not even be bothered with the inconvenience of getting married beforehand. Be-tween 1969 and 1989, 1,215 churches were shut down or demolished.[4]

Faced with this bleak picture, one is inclined to share Swift's view:

> The Church and clergy here, no doubt,
>   Are very near akin;
> Both, weather-beaten are without;
>   And empty both within.

It seems as if the Church of England has lost its sense of purpose.

Historically, the Church's privileges extended far beyond matters like the coronation of the monarch or the appointment of bishops. For three hundred years, subscription to the Thirty-Nine Articles was a precondition of admission to Oxford and Cambridge. Abolition of the requirement in 1871 inevitably weakened the link between the Church and the educated élite, although the Church retained a disproportionate influence through the appointment of college chaplains and university professors. The Church continued in comfortable alliance with the status quo. In 1848, as the Chartists marched to demand universal male suffrage and the reform of parliament, the hymnist Mrs Alexander was blithely reciting the natural arrangement of things:

> The rich man in his castle,
> The poor man at his gate,
> God made them high or lowly
> And ord'red their estate.[5]

A century later, the rich men's castles had all been requisitioned for war use, and the poor man had left his gate to vote in a socialist government. The Church had to grapple with the challenge of making itself relevant to the new world. In retrospect, however, the creation of the modern Welfare State, for which its leaders had lobbied vigorously, can be seen as the point at which the Established Church succumbed to the process that will end with its disestablishment. They actively promoted the instruments of their own irrelevance. Ministering to the poor and the sick, educating the young, were now the responsibilities of government. While maintaining that its spiritual role was undiminished, the Church voluntarily surrendered many of its social and practical responsibilities. As a result, it quickly became less visible, and in some cases invisible. Many who before the war might have joined the ministry because they wanted to act out their Christian beliefs found they could do so more easily working as state-employed teachers, social workers or doctors.

Still today the modern churchman most admired by senior bishops is Archbishop William Temple, who had been a pupil at Rugby while the school was still in the shadow of Dr Arnold, and took his injunctions about 'service' into action. He had joined the Labour party in 1918, possessed of a burning desire to improve the lives of the poor. When the opportunity came to translate belief into deed, he was one of the main architects of the 1944 Education Act (so close then were relations between Church and state that on one occasion, R. A. Butler and Temple got down on their knees together at the end of a meeting.) The Act surrendered control of Church schools in return for an undertaking that all state schools include an act of worship and some religious instruction. Over the following decades, however, this requirement became increasingly meaningless. By the 1970s 'religious instruction' was a few superficial talks on the difference between

Buddhism and Judaism. By the 1980s, opinion surveys were showing
that 'Christian' children increasingly doubted even the existence of
God.[6] The Church of England had become the Established Church of
a society which had quietly become Godless.

Nowhere was this gulf between the notional role of the Church and
the true situation greater than in the inner cities. If the strength of the
Church of England has traditionally been in the countryside, the great
conurbations have been its weakness for generations. The drift of the
population away from the land and into the city was ignored by most
of the clergy, secure in what Gibbon called 'the fat slumbers of the
Church'. It was the Methodists and Roman Catholics who rose to the
challenge of the new, rootless urban working class. By the 1980s, with
many of its responsibilities now taken on by the state, the Church of
England's presence in many urban areas was almost vestigial. Not
only was the Church absent from the areas of most pressing spiritual
and social need, its claim to represent the soul of the nation was
outlandish when all that it encompassed was the suburbs and the
countryside. The attempt had to be made, at least, to regain the cities.

The social problems of the British inner cities had been recognized
by the Labour Government during the 1970s, and they seem to have
been seriously aggravated by the first few years of Thatcherism. The
restructuring of the economy, the 'painful medicine' which the new
cabinet administered, had its worst consequences in the older cities,
where unemployment, poverty and crime all rose. One weekend in
April 1981, police in Brixton, South London, faced stones, bricks and
petrol bombs in full-scale rioting of a kind most citizens could
recognize only from scratchy archive film of the early days of the
Ulster crisis. Other cities followed. In 1983, Archbishop Runcie
appointed Sir Richard O'Brien, a distinguished industrialist, to lead
an inquiry into the problems of the inner cities, and 'the challenge
which God may be making to Church and Nation'.

Sir Richard was one of the finest men of his generation, a war hero
who had been awarded the DSO once and the Military Cross twice
for gallantry. A modest, quiet and friendly man, he had subsequently
worked in industry where he had come to have a high regard for trade
unionists, some of whom he considered represented 'the very best of
British virtues'.[7] The rest of his commission comprised a couple of
liberal bishops, several urban priests, academics, teachers and a trade
unionist. It was not the sort of body likely to produce recommendations which would please Downing Street.

'We have been deeply disturbed by what we have seen and heard,' they said in their report. The inner cities were rotting from within, as a consequence of poverty. Poor people felt powerless, the gap between rich and poor was widening, and the poorest minority was increasingly shut out from national life. The report was unambiguous about the need for urgent action:

It is our considered view that the nation is confronted by a grave and fundamental injustice. The facts are officially recognized, but the situation continues to deteriorate and requires urgent action. No adequate response is being made by government, nation or Church. There is barely even widespread public discussion.[8]

The commission knew that what they had to say would shock. A press conference to launch the report was called on a Tuesday. All members agreed they would say nothing beforehand. As a matter of courtesy, since they listed sixty-one recommendations, twenty-three of which were calls for action by government, Sir Richard delivered a copy to Downing Street on the previous Thursday. He soon discovered that the good manners which had previously underpinned relations between Church and government had been abandoned. Downing Street set out to discredit and destroy the report. The next day selected journalists, eager for any crumb to fill the Sunday papers, were presented with a gift. Unnamed government ministers were quoted in the press describing the report as 'pure Marxist theology'.

Sensational though these claims seemed at the time, in retrospect they mainly reveal how out-of-touch the government had become. In the case of the inner cities, it was the poor old Church of England which had its finger on the pulse. Initiatives which were decried and ridiculed at the time, later became the basis of government, or government-endorsed policies. *Faith in the City* was nothing like Marxist propaganda, merely a forcefully-argued – if at times naïve – call for action. The report was particularly hard on the Church itself, which it described as irrelevant to the needs of the urban poor. But it was distasteful to the government both because of its expressions of horror and its revelation of the Church of England's continuing attachment to the Welfare State.

The attempt to sabotage *Faith in the City*, from which it never fully recovered, was little short of scandalous. The Church of England, long accustomed to the parodies of the Left, had been lumberingly slow to recognize the sea-change which had taken place within the Tory party. The commission had been politically inept not to realize that calls for the state to spend money on social programmes could be made a lot more appealing to Downing Street if they were combined with notions of self-improvement, individual initiative and family discipline of the sort which Mrs Thatcher loved to express at the first glimpse of a reporter's notebook.

'Christianity is about spiritual redemption, not social reform,' Mrs Thatcher told the Church of Scotland, when she came to explain her religious beliefs in May 1988. Expanding upon her text, she quoted her favourite hymn, 'I Vow to Thee My Country'. The crux of Christian belief, she suggested, was summed up in the verse 'soul by soul and silently her shining bounds increase'. The inference was clear: it was not collectivism which provided the animus for Christian initiative, but individualism. In this context, the fact that her government squeezed the Welfare State was less an assault upon the poor and more a means of enabling them to achieve individual self-realization.

But for the Church the implications of government policy were altogether more serious. The idea of a commonwealth of common interest was intrinsic to the idea of the established position of the Church of England. If the philosophy was to be disregarded, the position was altogether harder to justify. The Thatcherite view, wrote *The Times*' religious affairs editor in one of the more perceptive observations on the subject, 'denies the Church of England's implicit claim to be of the essence of this mystical idea of "England" by being its common faith, its very heart, soul and conscience.'[9]

The most discreetly influential figure in the Church of England's governing body for the last decade was a Dickensian character to be found in a large, gloomy office inside the smoke-blackened portals of Church House, just around the corner from Westminster Abbey. Derek Pattinson enters the room at a precisely regulated walk, his grey hair escaping all over his collar and ears. The only hint of an impish personality is the red lining to his black jacket. Otherwise, all is clerical drab, striped trousers, black jacket and waistcoat, detached stiff collar with a silver stud showing beneath his huge Adam's apple, a walking parody of the Victorian clerk. There is a gold pocket-watch on a chain across his paunch. In silhouette you wonder how such an enormous head could possibly balance on two such thin legs.

'A glass of sherry?' he asks, and a young man pads into the room with a silver salver, a couple of glasses and a decanter.

Derek Pattinson was the Sir Humphrey Appleby of the Church of England. He had been a civil servant at the Treasury before being recruited to become secretary-general of the General Synod, the Church's ruling body. His successor, Philip Mawer, expected to take the church up to the second millenium, had abandoned a promising career in the heart of government, at the Cabinet Office. The recruitment pattern is instructive, for the General Synod has increasingly taken on the character of the MPs seated only a few hundred yards away in the House of Commons.

Looking down upon the circular pale wooden benches, with the bishops seated in a splash of purple in the centre, the elected clergy and laity ranged behind them, this does not seem a cross-section of the Church. It is a sea of grey flannel. True, there is a good representation of women, a smattering of monks and nuns, and two black faces.

But, whatever its pretence, the Synod is not representative. The previous governing body of the Church, the Church Assembly, was replaced in 1970, partly on the grounds that, with over seven hundred members, it was too big to function efficiently. But since most of the Synod's eleven days of conference each year take place midweek, it is dominated by those who can afford to take time off work – professionals, the higher salariat and political busybodies. They are chosen by the deanery synods, which in turn tend to be selected by vicars who ask the question, 'who's got a car and doesn't mind going out at night?' There tends to be a liberal smattering of clergy wives. By the mid-eighties, no skilled or unskilled worker had ever been a member of the General Synod.[10]

Conservatives tend to see the Synod as a ferment of left-wing agitation, the source of much of the rot in the Church. One particularly trenchant attack described its 'joy at exclaiming "mea culpa"', as a consequence of its middle-class composition. Charles Moore wrote in 1986:

> There is a disposition to see all poverty, unemployment, crime, racial
> hatred and urban decay as the result of the callousness of the rich. The
> Christian injunction to show a special reverence for the poor is elided with
> a quasi-socialist belief that their sufferings are produced by 'the oppressive
> structures of society'.[11]

In fact, by comparison with the hierarchy of the Church and the majority of new clergy, conservatives had a disproportionately loud voice in the Synod through the eighties. Anything less like a bunch of social or theological revolutionaries would be hard to imagine. The real problem with the Synod is that it has emphasized the numerous divisions within the Church and given the impression that all matters of doctrine can be sorted out by voting on them. They cannot. On matters of belief there is little or no room for compromise. As the former Bishop of Birmingham has pointed out, the Synod:

> fosters the impression that the Church should work like a parliamentary democracy. It is not an appropriate form of government for an episcopal church. The people of God should have a say, but bishops should take the initiative.[12]

Few of the Church's conservative critics would find a reassertion of the authority of the bishops any reassurance. They believe most of them to be members of a 'lilac ascendancy'[13] who care as much about 1960s sociological quackery as about the message of the Bible. But such a transfer of authority would at least have the merit of calming things down. The General Synod was born of a desire to involve ordinary members of the Church in the making of Church laws. But if you bring together 250 lay people who think they have a message, 250 clergy whose life is the Church, and fifty-three bishops who've sat through all the arguments a dozen times before, and then invite them to overturn four hundred years of history on momentous issues like the ordination of women, you have a recipe for tumult.

Mervyn Stockwood, the former bishop of Southwark, looked at the Synod and declared it 'a disaster, a playground for bureaucrats or bores'. The bores are doubtless well-intentioned, and in a small, vigorous Church which had no formal relationship with the state, their legislative role would be all very well. But their activities not only emphasize the divisions in the Church of England; they challenge its relationship with the state.

Time was when the Church of England was known as 'the Tory party at prayer'. No-one would make the claim today. Archbishop Runcie was asserted to have voted Social Democrat but much of the estrangement of the Church from the Conservatives is a consequence of the change within the party. The Church has continued to articulate an idea of society which was rooted in a philosophy the Conservative party discarded, bag and baggage, in 1979.

In the House of Lords, it is not unusual for the bishops to be divided on ethical questions though they tend to be consistently liberal on social questions like reform of the divorce or abortion laws. The justification for these stances, which so frequently seem to be at variance with strict Biblical injunctions, is that they are trying to ease the causes of tension within society. Few Tories objected strongly to the bishops' well-organized resistance to government plans to legalize Sunday Trading: what happens on Sunday was obviously a legitimate concern. But it was their critical stances on other pieces of government legislation, such as the bill to abolish the Inner London Education Authority or to replace the domestic rates system, which really antagonized the right-wing.

Contempt for the Church of England is most vocal among the more boorish element on the Conservative backbenches, but it is by no means confined to them. A hereditary Tory peer remarked that he had stopped paying attention to the bench of bishops because 'they're just a bloody nuisance, generals without an army'. A charming old knight from the shires told me over tea at White's that whereas he always used to consult the local bishop on social legislation, 'I stopped talking to him when the clergy all became bloody social workers'. A young MP remarked wistfully that 'I've just lost faith in the Church of England'.

So deep does the disillusion run that some members of the House of Commons now consider themselves better custodians of the Church than the Church itself. Decisions by Synod have to be ratified by Parliament, where, because of the ambiguity inherent in the Church's established position (does ultimate authority lie with the General Synod? with Queen in Parliament? with her bishops?), there are politicians prepared to defy the will of the Synod. Proposals to establish 'team ministries' of clergy, to modernize procedures for ratifying the appointment of bishops and to allow the ordination of divorced clergy, have all run into parliamentary opposition. In the summer of 1989, this last issue proved so contentious that it was voted down at half-past-three in the morning by a determined group who argued that it amounted to an abandonment of the Church's teaching that marriage was for life. It was eventually passed some months later, but the message had gone out that there were points beyond which Parliament would not allow the Church to tread. Sooner or later, a confrontation over the question of Establishment seems inevitable.

It is one of the curiosities of the fact that the Church of England is Established that its most senior appointments are made not by its bishops or the Synod, but by the prime minister, who need not even be a practising Christian. Several prime ministers have used their position to try to change the complexion of the Church. Both Ramsay MacDonald and Attlee intervened in the process, to try to ensure that the bench of bishops reflected the new Britain they wanted to see emerging. But Harold Wilson felt it was simply none of his business, and in 1976 James Callaghan agreed to an arrangement under which Downing Street's choice would be limited to a short-list of only two candidates, prepared by the Church's own committee, the Crown Appointments Commission.

The joke in higher levels of the Church of England during the Thatcher years was that if you wanted to have the Prime Minister appoint your first choice, you made sure that the second name on the list was that of the Area Bishop of Stepney, Jim Thompson. Thompson, a big, kindly man in the tradition of sporty churchmen, had been appointed to Stepney in 1978, clearly marked for high office. Having spent the best part of twenty years in the East End of London, Thompson was sympathetic to the poverty-stricken and also to homosexual clergy, as well as being in favour of women priests. As a regular broadcaster, his liberal ideas were well-known to Downing Street.

The Appointments Commission, made up of members of the General Synod, the archbishops and the diocese in question, meets in secret conclave for two days. On the first day the Church bureaucracy presents them with a dozen or more names, which by the end of dinner on the first evening has generally been whittled down to four or five. Having slept on it, the committee resumes next morning and by the afternoon has reduced the list to two names. It is from these two that Downing Street must make its choice. A gentleman's agreement decrees that the prime minister will select the first of the two names, unless advised by the committee that they had had difficulty in choosing between the two.

When the bishopric of Birmingham fell vacant in 1987, Thompson's was the first name on the Commission's list. Mrs Thatcher picked instead the Bishop of Kensington, Mark Santer. When the see of London had become available in 1981, the Commission was split seven votes to five on whether to appoint John Habgood, the Old Etonian Bishop of Durham, or the more conservative Bishop of Truro, Graham Leonard. Mrs Thatcher picked the second choice, Dr Leonard. Although the whole process is shrouded in secrecy, it is hard to resist the feeling that these were decisions of pure politics.

If so, Downing Street has been haunted by the law of unintended consequences. While Thompson might be said to have been more left-wing on social issues, he was not opposed to the bomb. Mark Santer won himself no friends in Downing Street by campaigning for unilateral nuclear disarmament. And losing the bishopric of London meant that John Habgood was free to be appointed to the more influential Archbishopric of York two years later.

The problem with trying to change the episcopacy is that the pool from which it is drawn is much of a muchness, committed to the same moral/political beliefs which have dominated the higher levels of the Church for years. The Downing Street appointments process deals only with candidates who have advanced through the liberal orthodoxy to become suffragan bishops or something similar. What has happened with other senior appointments in the Church, like deans and some cathedral canons – positions solely in the hands of Downing Street – rather confirms the difficulty of effecting any radical change.

It is a world full of ecclesiastical intrigue. The functionary responsible throughout the eighties was the Prime Minister's Appointments Secretary, Robin Catford, one of the few senior civil servants who can claim to have begun his bureaucratic career amid the bulrushes on the banks of the Nile (he worked for the Sudanese civil service).

His job would be instantly recognizable to any reader of Trollope. The moment it seems that a deanery is about to become vacant, the appointments secretary will travel the country from cathedral close to cathedral close, making discreet enquiries of bishops and lord lieutenants, inclining an ear here, nodding his head there. His presence sets the place on edge: everyone knows why he's there, but they can hardly begin a conversation with 'Appointed any good deans recently?' At the end of his 'soundings', in the words of one cleric 'a fog descends', as a short-list of two or three names is prepared for the Prime Minister. Since Mrs Thatcher wouldn't know most of the candidates if they lay down on the Downing Street doormat, each name is accompanied by a short pen-portrait. Canon Snodgrass would be a popular choice, but the job involves a great deal of expense and he perhaps couldn't afford it. Dr Cuttlefish looks well qualified, but his wife is having an affair with the gin bottle. Professor Popplethwaite would offend no-one, but is deaf.

It is hard to believe that the appointments secretary's little biographies are anywhere near the top of the Prime Minister's in-tray.

Doubtless they lie at the bottom of the despatch boxes delivered to the Prime Minister's flat in the evening, and are reached sometime around three o'clock in the morning. However anxiously decisions are awaited, they must make light reading after the latest ambassadorial telegrams from Moscow and Peking.

The fact that most deans appointed continue to be liberals suggests that Downing Street has failed to make much headway in its campaign to turn the Church into the paths of right-headedness.

It was, after all, Margaret Thatcher who appointed David Jenkins to be Bishop of Durham in 1984, from which post he rocked the boat more than all the other bishops put together. But it seems the Bishop of Durham was a mistake. Of the two names on the list presented to Mrs Thatcher, Jenkins, a theology professor at Leeds University, was unknown to her. His thumbnail biography – a wartime commission in the Royal Artillery and a career spent as an academic – appeared to offer little cause for concern. Downing Street realized its error almost immediately. During the bitter miners' strike in the year after his appointment, the Bishop repeatedly accused the government of 'not caring' and of deliberately penalizing the poorest members of society. Later suggestions that the resurrection might have been a spiritual rather than a physical occurrence, led one backbench Conservative to demand his excommunication. Within Downing Street, Church gossip has it, Mrs Thatcher remarked, 'Right, the next five are ours.'

If the remark was made, she was less than conspicuously successful. Because choice is so limited, and the gap between Church and state so much wider than previously, Margaret Thatcher made less of an impact on the Church than on most of the institutions whose appointments she had anything to do with. On one occasion soon afterwards, having presented the Commission's two names to the Prime Minister and awaiting formal notification, the senior cleric involved was astonished to be summoned back by Mrs Thatcher. For a full forty minutes she subjected him to close questioning as to why other names, of people she found more congenial, were not on the short-list.

There is some evidence that the appointments commissions are becoming more conservative – on two further occasions Jim Thompson's name was put forward by a diocese looking for a new bishop, only to be struck off by General Synod representatives. On another occasion the Archbishop had second thoughts about both the names to emerge from the committee, and told them to start again from scratch. But in general, the bishops are a liberal lot, and with

Downing Street's choice limited to two names, there is little that the Prime Minister can do to change things.

The Chief Rabbi was much more congenial to Prime Minister Thatcher. About twenty per cent of the electorate in her constituency was reckoned to be Jewish,[14] and the community's philosophy of self-improvement chimed perfectly with her own ideas about the importance of private enterprise and individual initiative. When the Archbishop launched *Faith in the City*, with its explicit criticism of government social policy, the Chief Rabbi pronounced that instead of drawing state benefits, people should learn from the Jewish experience and drag themselves up by their bootstraps. 'Cheap labour is better than free dole,' he claimed. This was music to Mrs Thatcher's ears, and she made Immanuel Jakobovits first a knight and then sent him to the House of Lords, where his prophetic white beard provided a counterpoint to the bishops' white surplices.

Slowly, the pedigree of Church of England bishops is changing. In the first sixty years of the twentieth century, the proportion who had been educated at independent schools never dropped below seventy per cent, while the number who had been at Oxford or Cambridge remained at over ninety per cent.[15] By 1987, of the forty-three diocesan bishops in England, two thirds had been to public school, and three quarters were graduates of Oxford or Cambridge.[16] Three years later, the proportion of bishops who had been educated at state schools had risen to half, although the proportion of Oxbridge graduates remained the same.

But a trend is under way. The bishops are distancing themselves from much of the rest of the country élite. They have lost, or abandoned, the grandeur and style which marked their social position in the past, and nowadays most of them look like nothing so much as rather civilized corporate businessmen. By comparison, they are paid remarkably badly, getting an average of only £17,000 or so per annum. The appurtenances of their positions, the palaces, the robes and mitres, the chauffeur-driven cars, lay them open to attack by the Left, even though inside the palace the bishop is more than likely sitting in the kitchen in a thick sweater eating bangers and mash. And while the Left resent him for being privileged and out of touch, the Right lay into him for not being sufficiently like his predecessors. He is seen as part of a woolly-minded liberal conspiracy, when he ought to be acting like an old-fashioned bishop, the natural ally of the lord lieutenant, the judges and the gentry.

But the disengagement looks set to continue. Only one third of the bishops belong to London clubs, only five of them to the Athenaeum, their old stamping ground. Of the new entrants to the Church of England clergy, most no longer come from the public schools. Out of the 320 candidates for the priesthood accepted into theological college in 1987, three quarters came from state schools, a far lower figure than the caricature picture of the Anglican clergy would suggest. They still tend to be better educated than most – almost seventy per cent had some form of higher education[17] – and the links with the social services are emphasized in the fact that a growing number have had some previous job, often in one of the 'caring professions'. They are increasingly politicized and whatever may be true among the laity, the ordinands seem to be mainly Labour voters. 'They hold forth with passion about apartheid, the poll tax, the under-funding of the NHS and the need for a redistribution of income as they might once have debated transubstantiation,' observed one horrified conservative visitor who spent time at several theological colleges.[18] The fact that they are increasingly drawn from suburbia gives little comfort to those campaigning to save the rural heart of the Church and their liberal feelings about homosexual and female priests makes a further drift away from the old social Establishment almost inevitable.

History will be kinder to Dr Robert Runcie, the 102nd Archbishop of Canterbury, than his political opponents were. He is an unlikely hate-figure. Crinkle-haired and compassionate, he had fought through the Second World War as a tank officer in the Scots Guards (William Whitelaw was a brother officer), winning the Military Cross for 'courageous leadership and magnificent marksmanship', by taking out German artillery positions while exposed to enemy fire.

It had always been understood that its established position did not oblige the Church of England to give blind support to the government of the day. For example, in the sixties, the then Archbishop of Canterbury, Michael Ramsey, had astringently laid into the Labour government's immigration policy. The personal animosity said to exist between Downing Street and Lambeth Palace in the eighties was greatly exaggerated, but the two places did stand for radically different visions of Britain. Downing Street exhorted the nation to celebrate British victory after the capture of South Georgia in the Falklands War; in the St Paul's Cathedral service after the campaign, Archbishop Runcie spoke of 'a shared anguish [which] could be a bridge of reconciliation'. During the 1984 miners' strike, he criticized government policies which had created 'unprecedented unemployment, poverty, despair and helplessness', and refused to come out for one side or the other.

It was not, as some of the more hardfaced Tories like to suggest, that Robert Runcie and the rest of the bench of bishops are gently-born paternalists, while the new breed of Conservative is self-made and competitive. The Archbishop's background was scarcely more prosperous than that of Margaret Thatcher; after an upbringing in suburban Liverpool he had only been able to afford the Oxford fees with the help of two scholarships. But whereas Mrs Thatcher had immediately joined the University Conservative Association, Runcie signed up with the Labour Club and even toyed with the idea of becoming a communist. Returning to the University after war service, Runcie had acquired a profound dislike of any form of totalitarianism, and joined the Conservatives as well as the Labour party. He was sacked from the post of college secretary for the Tories because the party, including Margaret Thatcher – a contemporary – thought he didn't take politics seriously enough.

Where others had ideology, Runcie had tolerance. A deeply spiritual man, he had the misfortune to lead a Church committed to consensus for the first postwar decade in which the country was led by a government which emphatically rejected it. Coinciding with the escalating differences on such fundamental matters as women priests, his instinct was to stress areas of agreement rather than difference, and, in the parlance of the Church, to 'hold the ring'. The 1988 Lambeth Conference, in which almost single-handed he managed to prevent six hundred Anglican bishops from all over the world falling out in serious disagreement, was a personal triumph.

But it was Runcie's style of leadership which led to the most tragic and sordid episode in recent Church politics, when Canon Gareth Bennett wrote the traditionally anonymous preface to the 1987 *Crockford's*, the biennial directory and companion to the Church of England. It was an articulate and waspish exposition of Anglo-Catholic despair at the state of the Church, accusing the Archbishop of taking the line of least resistance on each issue.

> He has the disadvantage of the intelligent pragmatist: the desire to put off all questions until someone else makes a decision. One recalls a lapidary phrase of Mr Frank Field that the archbishop is usually to be found nailing his colours to the fence.[19]

The furore which followed the *Crockford's* affair, with the enormous press interest aroused (even *The Sun* discovered that it had a religious affairs correspondent, a member of staff whose previous duties had been far from onerous), was all the Synod arguments writ large. Just before he was to be unmasked as the author of the words, Canon Bennett connected a rubber pipe to the exhaust of his car and gassed himself.

Canon Bennett's idiom may have been that of the university common room, but he was speaking for a substantial body of opinion, who believed the Church of England was being run by a comparatively ruthless group of like-minded liberals. They detested going to church on Sunday, finding no familiar hymns, being invited to shout 'Alleluia', shake hands with total strangers and stumble through services which seemed to be rewritten every three months. A wholesale retreat was in progress, they felt, from the liturgy, the very beliefs, which had kept the Church together. They demanded a return to the Book of Common Prayer, which within a generation had almost been abandoned in favour of 'alternative' (they dubbed them 'abominable') orders of service; clear, orthodox public stances on questions of sexual morality (i.e. opposition to homosexual acts, etc.); less power for the General Synod, which they saw as dominated by unrepresentative liberals, and outright opposition to the ordination of women.

The difficulty for the Archbishop was that he stood squarely within the liberal Anglican tradition. It is a church whose instincts are to include rather than to exclude. It has no history of pursuing its beliefs to the point of persecuting dissenters. The idea of excommunication is almost incredible. The Anglican Communion, of which Robert Runcie was the *primus inter pares*, included probably seventy million members in over four hundred dioceses spread across 164 countries. Because of this diversity, because of the Church of England's relationship with the British State, it simply cannot be run like the Roman Catholic Church. Yet, because there is no hierarchy of authority, there seems to be no clear vision.

In fact, some of the most important decisions about the future of the Church have already been made. To say that they had been arrived at clandestinely would suggest something too Machiavellian. It is more that they have happened by benign muddle.

Take the ordination of women, an issue which threatened to provoke a schism. A manpower crisis is about to hit the Church, which may only be resolved by a female priesthood. In the early 1990s, many of those who entered the clergy in the surge of idealism after the Second World War will retire. To replace them, the Church needs a steady supply of between four hundred and 430 young ordinands each year. In the dying years of the eighties they were only able to find three hundred or fewer suitable male candidates.

The Church was also training seventy or so women. As they could not be given parishes, this seemed a curious policy. When I asked Canon Timothy Tyndall, who was in charge of training, about it, he replied, 'We've a feeling God will work it out.'

In fact, regardless of rulings by Synod, the whole drift of Church thought has been towards the ordination of women. Having decided that there is no theological objection to their being created deacons, it is hard to see how the pressure for the full ordination of women can be resisted indefinitely. The overwhelming reason, however, is practical: many of the most outstanding candidates for theological college are women, and without them there just won't be enough clergy to staff the parishes.

The divisions within the Church do no more than reflect divisions within society. Even those who don't set foot inside a Church building from one year to the next have views on questions like the ordination of women. It is the price that the Church of England pays for being Established. The diversity which was once seen as its strength is now seen as its weakness.

No-one doubts the greater influence given the Church of England because it is the Established Church of the nation. Not only does it confer certain statutory rights upon bishops and vicars, it invests them with an authority by which they can command the attention of press and television on any subject from water pollution to the rights of man. It draws the Church into a whole series of informal relations with government departments in which its views are sought on all manner of impending pieces of legislation. But this position is bought at a price. Its freedom of movement is restricted, as is its capacity for fresh thought about its role and for new ideas in its ministry.

'The more the clergy are felt to be part of the social scene, the more the values they are seen to represent, and the values of society itself, will be regarded as fundamentally in harmony,' says the Archbishop of York.[20] The differences between the government and the Church which emerged during the eighties were the consequence of the

Church continuing to defend the values it had endorsed for most of the postwar years. Some clerics, despairing of the prospects of reconciliation with government, began openly using the expression 'the loyal opposition' to describe their role. 'One is endeavouring', according to the Archbishop of York, 'to be critical and yet supportive: if we have swung in a critical direction, it is because we have an ideologically motivated government.'[21] A change of government, and the source of friction will change.

The more profound question is not whether the Church of England is, as a whole, out of sympathy with a particular government. It is whether it any longer represents and speaks for some deeper purpose within the nation. Certainly, the cultural homogeneity upon which it is based has gone. The other religions grow apace – getting on for two million Moslems, 300,000 Sikhs and Hindus, and 400,000 Jews, to say nothing of the rapidly growing army of the Godless.

The justification for the fact that the Church of England is 'by law Established', beyond the constitutional paraphernalia is the assumption that it is the embodiment of something in the national soul. Cosmo Lang expressed the idea in a question in 1913:

> whether just there, in that inward region of the national life, where anything that can be called its unity and character can be expressed, there is or is not to be this witness to some ultimate sanction to which the nation looks, some ultimate ideal which it professes. It is in our judgement a very serious thing for a state to take out of that corporate heart of its life any acknowledgement at all of its concern with religion.[22]

On an average Sunday about 1.1 million people attend Church of England services, a tiny proportion of the population. It is probably no longer even true that the Church of England has the largest number of churchgoers in the country, as the average Mass attendance in Roman Catholic churches in England and Wales is almost 1.4 million. But, confronted with a form requiring a statement of religious adherence, official estimates suggest that up to sixty per cent of English people will still fill in the words 'Church of England'.[23]

Many of the younger clergy believe that existing as so vague a badge of cultural identity holds the Church back from its real tasks, precisely because it assumes that the community is Christian. They say that to rediscover a sense of purpose, the Church needs to escape from the foggy world it currently inhabits, and deal only with true, active, believers.

Where once the commonest Anglican Sunday morning service was

Matins, now it is the Eucharist or Family Communion. Those who take a full part are doubtless more highly motivated than many who would have attended the old service. But it is an exclusive form of worship, and demands a commitment which those who might attend for the Harvest Festival or Service of Remembrance cannot give. Even those who still make the effort discover that prayers and forms of service familiar to generation after generation have been discarded.

Then there is the question of births, deaths and marriages, another signal of the way in which the Church of England is changing from being the Established Church to being merely one British denomination among many. A small but apparently growing caucus within the clergy is campaigning against what they call 'indiscriminate baptism'. Increasing numbers of parents who approach the local vicar asking to have their child baptized – surely a citizen's legitimate expectation of an Established Church – are subjected to close questioning about the precise nature of their beliefs and practices. Although the General Synod, the governing body, has reaffirmed that the Church has a duty to marry those who request it, many vicars are noticeably hostile to the idea of performing weddings for those who are not regular communicants. Senior churchmen like the Archbishop of York are alive to the potential dangers; it is, after all, the only one of the three rites of passage – baptism, marriage and burial – when the participants are in a position to be aware of what's going on, and so one of the few points where huge numbers of ordinary people encounter the Church. 'If the practice of restriction became more widespread, I think the notion of our being the Church of the nation would become more and more tenuous,' he told me.[24]

But the claim is already getting pretty tenuous. For the time being at least, there is no great head of steam to try to get the Church of England disestablished. It is a cause restricted to a small band of eccentrics. The last formal attempt was made by Tony Benn, as the House of Commons dozed through debates on obscure Church of England doctrinal measures in the summer of 1988. It was defeated by Conservative MPs brought scurrying from the bars and restaurants, and exhorted by the Whips to 'Save the Church of England! Save the Church of England!' as they were sleepily ushered in to vote down the proposal.

But the question of its Establishment is one the Church cannot ignore for ever. The constitutional consequences – getting rid of the bishops from the House of Lords, allowing the monarch to be a Buddhist, Baptist or run-of-the-mill agnostic, and, perhaps, the return to the Church of its massive estates – would be significant but do not provide insuperable obstacles. The other possible consequences, such as the emergence of political parties in explicit or discreet alliance with the Church, and the reactions of others which were against it, would be likely to make it a more narrow, doctrinaire and somehow less English Church.

But, if it does not happen through schism or revival, sooner or later it could happen through apathy.

CHAPTER NINE

Stand Uneasy

Blood understood the native mind.
He said: 'You must be firm but kind.'
A mutiny resulted.
Standing upon a mound,
Blood cast his lethargic eyes around,
And said: 'Whatever happens we have got
The Maxim Gun, and they have not.'

– HILAIRE BELLOC

ONE THOUSAND RED tunics stand motionless on the gravel of Horse Guards beneath a cloudless blue sky. A single word of command, caught in the echoes of the old stone buildings, causes an instant stiffening, a flex of the knee, the smack of hand on rifle and the stamp of brilliantly polished boot upon the ground. A slight breeze catches the white feathers in the hats of the mounted staff officers. The Queen's foot taps to the marching tunes of three hundred massed bandsmen as the Colour of the First Battalion Coldstream Guards, emblazoned with three centuries of battle honours, is trooped down the still lines of bearskins. Every movement is timed to perfection, the Horse Guards clock chiming the quarter hour in the still intervals between the complicated wheels and turns. The sun glints on the cuirasses of the Household Cavalry on three hundred horses, and, in little more than an hour, two and a half months of training and rehearsal are finished with. Saloon bar wisdom has it that no nation on earth does this sort of thing better, and the belief is well-founded.

But it is not only the tourists gawping at the Trooping of the Colour who consider the British Army a spectacle. The same is increasingly true of the British people. It is over forty-five years since Britain last fought a major war, and not only are there fewer men in uniform than before the outbreak of the Second World War, but they make up a considerably smaller proportion of the total population.[1] Thirty years after the ending of conscription, the army exists as a small, professional élite: unlike other European nations which retained national service, in Britain the military experience is confined to a tiny sector of the population. The number of retired officers serving on county councils has been decimated in the last three decades,[2] and when retired cavalry officers march through Hyde Park at the beginning of May to remember their fallen comrades, stiff in their bowler hats, well-cut suits and tightly-rolled umbrellas, they mark events which increasing numbers simply cannot remember, like emissaries from the other side of history.

Even inside the army there is a sense of increasing remoteness and purposelessness. With a stranger present in the Coldstream Guards officers' mess, the talk turns to grumbles as soon as the roast beef and Yorkshire pudding have been served.

'The army's finished,' moans one young subaltern, far too short a time in the Guards to have any yardstick by which to make a proper comparison. Others are quick to take up his theme, one after another, down to the youngest, fresh out of Sandhurst, who also seems to think that a terminal decay is rotting the army from within. There is something particularly disconcerting about such gloomy views coming from such young, fit and handsome faces.

But the belief has taken hold and it cannot be shifted. Many are the sons and grandsons of former officers, who have filled them with tales of the high old times they had when the army was the agent of Pax Britannica. Now, it all seems dull, penny-pinching and visionless.

Their fathers too have felt the contraction, as their watering holes closed their shutters for the last time. The United Services Club auctioned off their silver and surrendered their magnificent Nash building years ago. Only a third of the members of the Naval and Military Club have any connection with the services. The Guards and Cavalry have been forced to amalgamate. The Army and Navy ('the Rag', after a nineteenth-century member complained that the food was no better than 'rag and famish') continues to serve second-rate food in a dreadful concrete building on the corner of St James's Square, and the Royal Air Force Club, near Hyde Park Corner, is functional, unpretentious and reasonably financially secure. But the world the clubs typified, where military service was a shared experience among the nation's decision-makers and opinion formers, is long gone.

Ancient regiments with long family traditions have been amalgamated, and even in those which survive sons are no longer following in their father's footsteps, as the attractions grow more meagre, the overseas postings more infrequent. The top military men are shadowy figures, unknown to the general public, rarely featured in the newspapers. The person in the street could name the senior bishops of the Church of England or the captain of the West Indies cricket team before he could guess at the identity of the chief of the defence staff. Even the generals are increasingly advising their sons against making a career in the army. County towns may maintain their formal links with the local regiment, but the occasional parade by a regimental band does little more than emphasize the gulf: the martial culture is more enclosed, more removed, than it has been for decades. Codes of dress and speech, no less than of manners, seem unworldly and anachronistic: off duty, the young officers of the smarter regiments are identifiable at a hundred paces, marked out by their bearing, their manners, their haircuts, their clothes and the shine on their shoes. The public schools, which have for generations provided the nucleus of the officer corps, continue with diminished cadet forces, but it is increasingly difficult to find masters with even the most elementary knowledge of soldiering to take charge of them and military training is attractive mainly as a source of potential university sponsorship. Even the caricature braying major, cravat at his throat, whisky-red face, has largely vanished from satire, so completely has the military disappeared from public view.

Yet military service was at the heart of the Establishment. It was not only that the honours system began as a means of rewarding loyal service to the Crown, but the values of the officer class were a continuation of the idea of knighthood. The classic British Army officer was, first and foremost, a gentleman. His background was in the land, his interests were sporting, his education was privileged, his manners were perfect. He was conservative with a small c, but beyond an atavistic tendency to harrumph at socialism, he was apolitical. He took his oath of loyalty to the Crown seriously, loved the monarchy and took pride in his regiment. He had the paternalistic virtue of concern for his 'chaps', and, whether subaltern or colonel, would do his best to care for them. He was courageous and, when the chips were down, selfless to the point of self-sacrifice.

It has been one of the blessings of life in Britain that her citizens do not fear the military. The last time the army intervened directly in political life was during the Glorious Revolution of 1688: the list of charges against James II at the time of his expulsion from Britain accused him of 'raising and keeping a Standing Army within this

kingdom in time of Peace without consent of Parlyament and Quarter-
ing Soldiers contrary to Law.'³ The idea of a standing army was
unpopular not only because the citizenry disliked having to foot the
bill for its existence, but also because it was an engine of royal
despotism. The Declaration of Rights made a standing army illegal
unless it was authorized by parliament.

But legal constraints apart, the other important reason for the
relatively benign role of the British Army was the nature of its
officers. It made political sense to have the army run by representatives
of the class which had most interest in preserving the status quo. One
nineteenth-century historian wrote:

> The danger of entrusting an armed host to the will and pleasure of one
> man in time of peace has hitherto been recognized in Parliament, and this
> evil can by no better method be averted than by having the officers,
> subordinate to the Commander in Chief, drawn from that social class, the
> members of which are most likely to lose than to gain by military aggres-
> sion.⁴

The greatest providers of officers for the army were the great estates:
in 1838, fifty-three per cent of the officer corps came from titled or
landed families, including three-quarters of the full generals.

The ability of these figures to buy themselves commissions had led
the Duke of York's adjutant-general to observe despairingly half a
century earlier that, 'out of fifteen regiments of cavalry and twenty- six
of infantry which we have here, twenty-one are commanded literally
by boys or idiots.'⁵ It was the tide of professionalism sweeping
through Victorian public life which finally got rid of the purchasing of
commissions and translated the army into a notional meritocracy.

The modern British Army is a largely Victorian creation: it was
then that the regimental system was elevated into the basis of the
army, that the great garrison towns like Aldershot were built, and that
many of the modern dress uniforms were designed. As the civil
bureaucracy was to pass from placemen to scholars, so military service
was to become a true profession of arms. Predictably, it was the sons
of the 'higher' professions – civil servants, lawyers, clergymen and,
notably, army officers – who now flooded into the army. There was a
vast new pool of talent available in the rapidly expanding corps of
public schools. The Duke of Cambridge, commander-in-chief of the
army, welcomed these hearty young men because although 'the education may be defective in some respects, it is the education of the best
class of English gentleman.'⁶ The public schools duly churned out the

cadets which the army required, and by 1913 over half the officer corps were public schoolboys.[7]

Above all, the officers of the new army tended to be the sons of past officers (surveys of the time show that there were up to ten times as many Sandhurst entrants from military families as from any other background),[8] which meant that the military were already showing the disposition which would make them an isolated tribe. But in style the new professionals aped the manners of the old rural upper class. The life of the officer continued to be based around polo and hunting and grand balls, which meant that to participate fully, it was desirable to have a private income. The gentleman remained the ideal. Major-General J. F. C. Fuller, who was gazetted in 1898 and went on to become the most original tank warfare theorist of his day, recalled his fellow Sandhurst cadets vividly:

> It was an aristocratic army, feudal in the sense that it was grounded on leadership and fellowship, in which, with few exceptions, the leaders were the sons of gentlemen, and more frequently than not eldest sons – the privileged son. When I went to Sandhurst we were not taught to behave like gentlemen, because it never occurred to anyone that we could behave otherwise. We were taught a lot of obsolete tactics, as in every army of that day; did a tremendous amount of useless drill; but never heard a word about 'responsibility', 'loyalty', 'guts', etc., because – so I suppose – those were held to be the natural prerequisites of gentlemen.[9]

The other ranks of the time were also a distinct caste:

> A rough lot, simple, tough, illiterate; largely recruited from down-and-outs, men who had got into trouble, vagabonds, with a sprinkling of the sons and grandsons of NCOs and private soldiers – military families – who generally became NCOs.[10]

Of the two groups, it is the second which has changed most. Today it is to the formerly 'drunken soldiery' that we look for exemplary behaviour; the hooligans are in civvies. The increasing sophistication of modern killing machines demands a level of literacy and numeracy which old boneheaded privates could never have reached. By comparison, many of the conventions of the old officer corps remain largely untouched.

Throughout much of this century the army continued to draw its officers from a tiny sector of British society: of six thousand Sandhurst cadets trained between 1947 and 1958, two thirds came from public schools, including nearly four hundred from Wellington and over three hundred from Eton. Although the cliché that the academy only recruits from a handful of public schools has not been true for twenty years, the entrance statistics hardly reflect society at large. Figures from Sandhurst in 1989 show forty-seven per cent of cadets coming from fee-paying schools, forty-three per cent from non fee-paying schools, and ten per cent from Welbeck College, the army's technical academy. Among graduates, forty-eight per cent had been to fee-paying schools, and fifty-two per cent to state schools. To be representative of society at large, the figures would have to be in the order of ten per cent and ninety per cent. Attempts to discover from Sandhurst how many black or Asian British cadets have passed through meet with the response that 'no records are kept',[11] so we are little the wiser on how ethnically representative the officer corps is, although figures from the Ministry of Defence show that in 1988 thirty-six blacks applied for commissions, almost all of them in the Royal Air Force. Only one applied for an army commission. Out of the thirty-six, one was successful.

Sandhurst aims to teach 'leadership', a quality they find hard to explain in language comprehensible to a layman. In 1959 Simon Raven decided that although the Academy was by then choosing one third of its intake from the state schools, it was still trying to turn them into fully-plumed gentlemen. He enumerated the qualities the Academy set out to instil. 'Guts' were so important that the officer cadet 'would never admit to physical inadequacy until he dropped dead or unconscious.' Enthusiasm, of a casual, indiscriminate kind was closely allied to guts: 'a blind, uncritical application to any task, however silly or futile.'[12] Loyalty – to Queen, country and regiment – was also instilled, as were initiative and 'sociability', which came to imply 'an unquestioning deference to the convenience and opinions of one's military superiors.' Presiding over everything was the quality of responsibility: 'like the Holy Ghost, it is supposed to be every-where.'

Whatever they had been like when they began this total immersion, the men who emerged were all of a distinct 'type'. They may have started as butcher's or plumber's sons, but they all acquired an unshakeable belief in their new identity. 'Where I had expected to find a professional officer corps,' Raven commented, 'I found a caste rooted in its own conception of superior, God-given status.'[13]

This was decidely not the sort of thing that the army wanted to hear at the time, and thirty years on, mention of Raven's article still sets the temples throbbing. When I mentioned it to General Simon Cooper, the intelligent angular commandant at Sandhurst at the time, he wrote me a seven-page rebuttal of Raven's thesis. He concluded:

> I find his interpretation trite and dishonest. I question his entire philosophy that qualities which have stood the test of time and battle, qualities found in soldiers from many backgrounds and walks of life, are merely the tools used by a cynical military hierarchy, generation after generation, to produce an officer clone in an image of uncaring, officious, self-satisfied superiority.[14]

The General's indignation is understandable, and large sections of the officer class are now broader in background and accent than was once the case. Fourteen per cent of officers have seen some service in the ranks, and without them the edifice would collapse. But there is still a sense in which the process does its damnedest to turn its cadets into ersatz Etonians, reflected in the nickname some of the squaddies have given the place, 'the Rupert factory'. The chasm between the British officer and his men is wider and deeper than in other European armies. A distinguished psychologist examining the officer caste in the mid-seventies remarked that 'all that remained of his training in the mind of each recipient was faulty syllogism: Officers should be gentlemen; I am an officer; therefore I am a gentleman.'[15] More recently, a Sandhurst graduate returning to visit his alma mater discovered that, although cadets came from all sorts of different social backgrounds, the officer-model to which they were tailored was still based on old-fashioned ideas of the public school gent. He observed that 'the assumption made by the army planners of the late 1980s, and widely held throughout the army, is that men will only respect their officers if they appear to be members of the middle or upper-middle classes.'[16]

In the context of the pervasive British class system the approach is understandable. The problem is that the mould to which the young officer cadets are being fashioned was smashed in the outside world twenty or more years ago: the army's social engineering predates the discovery of the populist wheel. The gentleman has become an endangered species, supplanted by others whose morals are less clear-cut, whose style is more informal and whose accents are more varied. As a consequence, the military 'type' is more conspicuous nowadays than ever. Aware that they are to some extent out of step with the rest of us, conventional wisdom in the army has it that society has 'slipped'. Looking at how much of the City behaves it is hard to disagree. The army's belief is the justification for preserving customs, manners and modes of thought which are increasingly anachronistic. Of all the sections of the old ruling class, the military have changed least.

Major-General Sir Christopher Airy, commander of the Household Division in 1989, and a man who still makes a point of walking to the front of the train after a railway journey and saying 'thank you' to the driver, was frank about it:

> About fifteen years ago, there was this great cry that the army was part of society, and reflected that society. But if society's slipping, it would be appalling to slip with it. You can't afford to let standards slip, or you become sloppy, less effective on operations, and you become something people would no longer wish to look up to.[17]

'Something to look up to' lies at the heart of it. The rest of society has handed responsibility for our defence to a relatively small and very self-contained organization which can make its plans for the future only upon the basis of what it knows worked in the past. Regiments have traditional patterns of behaviour which stretch back as far as their battle honours, and they must prepare for the unknown on the basis of the known.

The difficulty is that in the outside world, the previously clear-cut division between an educated officer and an uneducated soldier no longer exists. During the high unemployment of the early eighties in particular, all the services were able to raise their entry standards for the junior ranks. But peacetime officering rarely attracts the very able, which is why thirty years ago, General Sir John Hackett, then commandant of the Royal Military College of Science, asked whether 'the service of the Crown in this country's land forces (is) to be left in the hands of those whom industry would reject, young men too dull to get into Shell, or ICI, or Glaxo?'[18]

Three decades on, it is the boast of the army that nearly half of the cadets recruited now have some form of degree, a higher proportion than in either the navy or the air force.[19] 'Some form' is the critical phrase: many are the army's own internal awards. A quick look at the amount of time devoted to different areas of study reveals that academic enterprise is considered no more important than drill, and less than half as important as sport.

During the successive retrenchments forced upon Sandhurst by the

Training periods on the Sandhurst Standard Military course.

Drill	6%
Physical Training	6%
Academic study	6%
Exercises	27%
Signals	4%
Map Reading, etc.	2%
Skill at Arms & Fieldcraft	10%
First Aid, etc.	4%
Sport	13%

(Remainder spent in organization, travel,
kit cleaning, military law, etc.)

Treasury, academic work has been reduced time and again. It is now strictly utilitarian, divided into communication studies (how to deal with that contemporary ogre, the reporter on the streets of Belfast, among other things), defence, international affairs and war studies. Instructors observe that, like other products of the British secondary school system, the cadets are less proficient at English and maths than their predecessors, yet fuller of self-confidence (however questionably founded). Recent highlights of the communication tests have included a demonstration by one cadet of how to take the top off a champagne bottle with one sweep of a cutlass, and debates between different military leaders, two of which have resulted in a convincing victory for Adolf Hitler.

Bizarrely, for an army still being trained to fight in continental Europe as part of a largely European alliance, there are no language lessons whatsoever.

The distinctively British thing about the military élite is the way in which two parallel hierarchies exist. Most armies respect their doughtiest fighters, and a deference is shown to the Special Air Service (and the Royal Marines Special Boat Squadron, although technically part of the navy) and the Parachute Regiment. But there is a social hierarchy within the army which is every bit as rigorous. The model upon which the British officer is fashioned finds its apogee in the messes of a handful of regiments. At the top of the heap are the smart regiments – Cavalry units like the Lancers or the Hussars, and the Guards, who, because of their three-hundred-year responsibility for the protection of the royal family, 'seem to think they're bloody royalty themselves', according to an officer in another regiment. The

Royal Green Jackets, who reckon themselves the most intelligent regiment in the infantry, and whose passage into one top job after another has earned them the nickname 'the Black Mafia', also have a less than diffident idea of their own prowess. All these regiments look down upon the ordinary infantry, the county regiments and the men of the line.

Nowhere is there a sense of loyalty to something altogether more mystical than passing governments than among the 450 officers of the five regiments of foot Guards and two Cavalry regiments of the Household Division. Apart from providing the escort for state ceremonials (in which the Queen takes a close personal interest, to the point of suggesting changes to the drill), the commanding general calls at Buckingham Palace at least three times a year, to supplement his written six-monthly report to the Queen. Confronted with proposals to change their status, to reduce their size, or alter their postings, the regiments are provided with the most influential lobby in Britain. It may be deployed by the Queen's private secretary writing to the permanent secretary, although one Ministry of Defence general I questioned recalled how the Queen had personally expressed her displeasure over a planned posting for one of the regiments, because it would reduce their availability for ceremonial duties. The proposal was promptly dropped.

The 1989 Queen's Birthday parade was the last to be commanded by Major-General Sir Christopher Airy, a tall, slim Scots Guards officer who the following year went on to become private secretary to the Prince of Wales. During his time in command of the Household Division you would find him, like his predecessors and successor, dressed in a dark pinstripe and mirror-bright toecaps, seated at the same desk in the same room occupied by the Duke of Wellington when he commanded the entire British Army. Perched above the archway on Horse Guards, looking out across the parade ground and down through the lakes and lawns of St James's Park to Buckingham Palace, the office has one of the finest views in London. The General's walls are painted sludge-green, the mouldings picked out in white. Two ten-foot replica Gainsboroughs hang on either side of the door. Wellington's desk is oval-shaped, inlaid and, like everything in the Household Division, polished like glass. Even a cheap government-issue carpet cannot spoil the room.

I wondered whether the Guards were really necessary any longer.

'Good heavens yes,' replied an astonished General, as if it was the first time he had heard the suggestion.

Why?

'Because we hope to be the best soldiers in this country, and indeed the world.'

Deeply resentful of the charge that they have become 'chocolate soldiers', the Guards constantly stress their combat roles. And, to be fair to them, the Household Division has produced great *esprit de corps*, and some of the finest fighting men in the British Army.

But a cross-section of society they are not. During the 1989 Trooping of the Colour, four of the five company commanders were Etonians. There was not one black or Asian face to be seen on the entire parade ground. Although the policy of official discrimination has been formally abolished, it is clear that things haven't changed much since Denis Healey raised the matter with the Colonel of the Life Guards, Major-General Lord Michael Fitzalan Howard:

> He simply didn't understand what I was on about. He pointed out that there was once a black man who had played the big drum in one of the Guards bands – no doubt he thought the leopardskin made that appropriate. But he found the idea that black men should serve in a Guards fighting unit was so preposterous that his mind simply refused to encompass the idea.[20]

The few black people who have since won places in the Guards have found themselves the victims of petty bullying and bigotry, and not a single black or Asian officer exists in the division.

The élite regiments have traditionally drawn their officers from a very small pool. General Sir James Glover, who ran military intelligence during the Falklands campaign and later became Commander in Chief UK Land Forces, was educated at Wellington, a military public school, continued his education at Sandhurst and later joined the Royal Green Jackets. He recalls how 'a great stream' of his contemporaries went into the army from Wellington. At that stage, the Green Jackets were recruiting the majority of their officers from scarcely more than half a dozen schools. By the 1980s the regiment had trebled its catchment area. But even so, it comprised only about twenty main schools. Sir James, as Colonel Commandant of the regiment, suggested they make a positive effort to find a broader range of officers from different backgrounds. However:

in the end I was persuaded that if you can manage to draw people from the same background, without lowering standards, it strengthens the family bond. And that sense of family in turn makes for reliability when you're facing bricks and bullets.[21]

In the Household Division, the business of selecting officers begins early. A commission in the Division is still sufficiently sought-after that the adjutants receive eager letters from new fathers requesting that their sons be 'put down' for a possible commission while putative ensigns are still in nappies. Each regiment maintains a 'puppy list', whom they will invite for interview when the boy is in his last year at school. But it is no longer true (it was always an exaggeration) that only Etonians and Harrovians get commissions in the Guards. Of the thirty-eight boys on the Scots Guards puppy list of potential officers between 1989 and 1991, the two schools with the largest number of candidates (four apiece) were Milton Abbey, a minor public school in Dorset, and Glenalmond College in Perthshire. There were two candidates from Eton and two from Harrow, two each from Fettes, Sherborne and Worth schools.[22]

There were twenty-six schools represented, which appears to suggest that the Guards regiments are no longer the closed élite they once were. But the Scots Guards, naturally, recruit much more heavily from Scotland than regiments like the Grenadiers or Coldstream. And the possible candidates had one overwhelming characteristic in common: out of the thirty-eight boys, there was only one from a state-funded school.[23] Because of their preoccupation that the regiment function as a family, the overriding consideration of the colonels who interview the boys is whether they're 'the right sort' and are likely to 'fit in'. The conclusion is inescapable that boys from less privileged homes are deemed unlikely to do so.

In the Household Cavalry, the picture is even more vivid. At the beginning of 1989 the regiments held a list of ninety-six potential future officers on their 'puppy lists'. Not a single state school was represented, while Harrow with eleven candidates and Eton with nine dominated comfortably. Ampleforth, Wellington and Millfield had five candidates apiece.[24]

In 1939 new officers joining the Guards were given three pieces of advice by their commanding officer:

On no account are you to marry until you are at least twenty-five, you are to hunt in Leicestershire at least twice a week, and you are never to wear a grey top hat before the June race meeting at Epsom.[25]

For decades, those who have most enjoyed a commission in the Household Division have been those lucky enough to be possessed of a private income. In the nineteenth century, this was understandable; the uniform cost hundreds of pounds, and there were two black chargers to be bought as well, to say nothing of the considerable expense of the London social scene. When military conditions of service are appreciably more comfortable than those for most civilians, accommodation is provided and salaries are guaranteed by government, one might wonder whether a private income is any longer a necessity.

Necessary perhaps not. But desirable, certainly. The young officer next to me at lunch was planning to spend the following day (Wednesday) hunting, getting back in time to pack up for exercises in Kenya. To get by without an additional source of finance can be a struggle. 'I had no private income for twenty years,' one colonel told me. 'It just meant that when people invited me to shoot, I said "thank you" and went gratefully. One had a cheaper shotgun, a rotten pair of skis, and travelled by the cheapest trains in Germany.'[26] General Airy supported himself on his pay throughout his career in the Guards, but his response to the question of whether the majority of his officers had a private income suggested that his case was far from the norm.

'I don't know. There's no reason why I should know. Absolutely no reason at all. But I'm pretty certain that there's *a fair proportion* these days who don't.'

Early in the 1970s a young naval officer was posted to the Ministry of Defence. The posting was an early indication that the admirals had marked him down as a potential leader of his service; experience as a Whitehall Warrior was an essential step on the road to a senior 'flag' command. Like most such officers he was resentful at being away from the sea and the task for which he had been trained. Whereas the services operate on vertical chains of command, the Ministry of Defence runs on horizontal, diagonal or wavy lines of influence, not easily comprehensible to a bluff sailor.

One day he received a call from a senior civil servant. The mandarin asked him to rehearse the arguments in favour of the Polaris nuclear missile system, in order that he could familiarize himself with any new naval theories. The officer concentrated upon the enhanced capacity of the missiles to penetrate anti-missile defences around Moscow. The assistant secretary stopped him. 'Look, young man,' he said, 'you've got the wrong idea. The enemy isn't Moscow. It's the Air Force Department.'

Every Whitehall Warrior has stories of the campaigns fought, the alliances forged, the victories won in the endless tussling over defence budgets. For men who have emerged from the enclosed world of service life, entering the Ministry of Defence is like taking tea with Machiavelli. The more outstanding senior officers make an effort throughout their careers to mix with people from outside the defence community. But the majority have joined the forces at the age of eighteen (usually directly from all-male schools), and will not leave it until they retire. It does not make for great breadth of vision.

Britain's good fortune in having a military élite who abide by democratic controls has rarely been questioned by senior officers. The only occasion in recent times when there has been talk of discontent verging on the mutinous came during the crisis after the illegal declaration of independence by the white minority government in colonial Rhodesia in November 1965. Feasibility studies indicated that a military operation to seize the vital institutions of government was viable, providing it was launched quickly. Such an operation would have involved British troops fighting against men they regarded as brothers-in-arms: all had sworn loyalty to the Crown; Rhodesians had fought alongside British soldiers in the Second World War; the two forces frequently exercised together and many were personal friends. Rumours began to circulate of discontent in the messes. In retrospect, one suspects that the closest the officers came to dissent was the sort of attitude expressed by Air Marshal Sir Michael Beetham, then commanding RAF Khormaksar in Aden from which an invasion would be launched:

> Reinforcements began pouring in. And we were thinking 'Oh Christ, we can't go and fight our chums down there.' But I do not believe that if there had been a properly constituted order to go we would have refused. Unless, of course, the Queen objected. So, I think we would have gone, but we'd have done it with a great deal of reluctance. No-one would have had their heart in it.[27]

Most of those involved are now retired or dead, and none has confirmed suggestions of what would have been a potential mutiny. If it seems improbable that the officer corps would have defied the will of parliament, it is equally improbable that the unease of the forces was not brought to the attention of the defence secretary. Similarly, a decision in the future suddenly to withdraw from Northern Ireland would worry many senior army officers, although it is hard to imagine anything approaching outright defiance of orders. And any government elected with a promise to rid the country of nuclear weapons would throw the chiefs of staff into disarray, since nuclear weapons have been the cornerstone of British defence policy. Faced with a disarming defence minister, they would almost certainly exercise their right of access to the prime minister, and possibly also to the monarch, and would doubtless make sure that the fact they were doing so was leaked to the press. Refusal to implement orders seems unlikely, resignations less so.

'The arrogance is simply beyond belief,' says one former defence minister of his attempts to deal with the generals in Whitehall on other matters. The senior officers' pledge of loyalty to Queen and country is to some deeper notion of Britain than mere politicians express. If the generals say that something is in the best interests of national security, how can the politicians, mere amateurs, disagree? The size of the defence budget, the complexity of defence theory, the confident authority of senior officers accustomed to being obeyed and the intractability of the enduring military conundrum – the desire to do twice as much as the country can afford – put any politician arriving at the Ministry of Defence at an immediate disadvantage.

The chiefs of staff, by contrast, are regarded by their thousands of officers as the custodians not merely of the nation's security, but of the very heritage of their service. Politicans and governments may come and go, but the country will always need the army, the navy or the air force. They have spent a lifetime in the service and have arrived in their posts as a result of an appointments system in which like chooses like*. In wartime, the brilliant commander is often the maverick. In peacetime, the maverick is just a bloody nuisance. There are understandable reasons for this conservatism: if they get things wrong, people die. Inevitably, they tend to cling to what has been proven to work. 'We're navigating into the future on a fix taken years ago, in the last war,' is how Admiral Sir James Eberle puts it.[28]

But if politicians criticize the defence establishment for its comfortable sense of superiority and resistance to change they largely have themselves to blame. Political discussion of defence issues is confined

* There are also an awful lot of them. By comparison with allied armies and navies the British forces are top-heavy. The proportion of admirals and generals to troops is roughly four times greater than in the United States, and three times as high as in France or West Germany. The Royal Navy has as many admirals as it has ships in its main surface fleet. The British Army, which is smaller than the United States Marine Corps, has one 'two star' general for every 2,230 soldiers. In the US Marine Corps – which includes as many combat aircraft as the RAF – the ratio is one for every 6,900.

to the most simple-minded sloganizing at elections and a few poorly-attended parliamentary debates for the rest of the time. As the House of Commons fills with MPs who have no personal experience of the forces, their ignorance deepens. In 1988, eight out of ten MPs were unable to name either the NATO Supreme Commander or the organization's Secretary General.[29] Defence Ministers come and go with revolving door rotation. Between 1945 and 1986 there were twenty-two of them, an average stay of under two years, less time than it takes to build a warship. In the period betwen 1979 and 1989, the minister in charge of defence procurement, with a budget of over eight billion pounds, changed six times, a here-today, gone-tomorrow speed which one former permanent secretary describes as 'beyond disgrace.'[30] Since new weapons projects can take ten years, it is hardly surprising that military men can be inclined to take ministers less than seriously, particularly when some junior ones ('the bottom of the sock' in the words of one general) seem to know next-to-nothing about the subject. Air Marshal Sir Michael Beetham recalls:

> You spend months getting them all briefed up, showing them British Forces Germany, RAF Strike Command and other service establishments at home and overseas. And they're usually intelligent people, and they learn about it. Then you find that they've been moved to another job. And you've got to start all over again with another one. You just despair.[31]

The confrontations between ministers and military men take place inside the Ministry building, an ugly grey slab running from the Thames halfway up Whitehall. Above the main entrance two massive reclining nudes, uncannily like the sort of Stalinist memorials to foundry-workers you find in Moscow, are decaying gently in the acidic rainfall. It is a functional and uninspiring place, only the airlock security doors and notices warning of the danger of IRA bombs giving any clue to its activities. Recently the gloomy corridors have been repainted (for the first time, according to one disgruntled insider, in seventeen years), colour-coded in greys, blues and browns to tell lost souls on which side of the building they are wandering. Old tribal loyalties are still proudly proclaimed, a board on the second floor listing all the Masters General of the Royal Ordnance since 1414. Of all the departments of state, the Ministry of Defence is the most unnecessarily secretive and the most smug.

The headquarters staffs, some 22,000 of them, include about three thousand serving officers and men, who arrive in Whitehall uneasy at the tatty surroundings, the scarce support staff and the prospect of endless paper-shuffling instead of the command of men, ships or aircraft. Shambling security guards in ill-fitting blue serge are the only figures in uniform to be seen inside the building, for unlike military headquarters like the Pentagon, British military men prefer to work in civvies. The officers may find it an uncongenial life, battling their way through the carnage of the 7.14 from Haslemere, in constant danger of ambush by one bureaucratic stratagem or another, and always fighting the same defensive campaign against the carpet-bombers of the Treasury, but service in Whitehall is a prerequisite for the highest posts.

All the figures are huge. The Ministry employs the largest number of bureaucrats and is the third largest landowner in Britain. The £8.26 billion spent on equipment from bombers to bearskins during 1989 make it the single largest customer for British industry: apart from the 350,000 jobs dependent on direct contracts, almost another 150,000 or so are sustained by overseas sales of British defence equipment. Without the Ministry of Defence, whole sectors of the British economy, from shipbuilding to aerospace, would collapse. But there are no market forces to discipline this operation, and unlike other government departments such as Health or Transport, which can measure their achievements by the number of patients treated or the miles of road built, there is no easy yardstick by which to assess the efficacy of it all.

Money, or the lack of it, is the repetitive, nagging backdrop to all British defence thinking since the last war. The elephantine collective memory of the services recalls the cuts of past years as if they were yesterday. The 1957 decision by Duncan Sandys, in the first of the great post-war retrenchments, to slash the size of the air force, reduce the navy and to force the army to amalgamate historic regiments, is still remembered like some humiliating battleground collapse. 'We're only now beginning to repair the damage caused by that man Sandys,' said one officer, who could only have been in short trousers at the time. The cancellation of TSR2 and the withdrawal from East of Suez imposed by Denis Healey in the sixties, which provoked the resignations of the First Sea Lord and the minister for the Royal Navy, are still fresh in the mind.

The characteristic way of ducking demands that money be saved is for projects to be 'moved to the right', a way of buying tomorrows which ensures that new tanks or missile systems enter service years after the forces had claimed they could not get by without them. When a figure emerges who is prepared to confront the difficult choices head-on, he is likely to find that the political intrigue of which the services are capable will, in the words of one former minister, 'make the palace of Westminster look like child's play'.

John Nott was the first defence secretary too young to have fought in the war, although he had served as a lieutenant in the Gurkhas during the early fifties. His predecessor, Francis Pym, had failed to find ways of saving the large amounts of money which would be needed to leave funds to pay for the Trident nuclear submarine programme and the new Tornado aircraft for the Royal Air Force. Nott, a banker by profession, was more resolute. He instructed each of the service chiefs to draw up a list of priorities, so that sensible decisions could be made about where budgets might be cut. They all wrote back saying that everything was vital. 'He'd asked a lot of sensible questions. Trouble was, he didn't get any sensible answers. He'd bowled them a straight ball, and they smothered it as if it was a googly,' a cricketing admiral explained later. Nott realized that he would have to make a choice himself between cutting the size of the British Army of the Rhine or reducing the navy still further. The Royal Navy had been watching their fleet being pared away for thirty years. At the end of the Second World War it included over one thousand major warships, among them fifteen battleships and battle cruisers, over fifty aircraft carriers, 130 submarines and almost five hundred destroyers and frigates. Now, the entire fleet was down to 150 ships, including fifty in the critical force of destroyers and frigates, which they claimed was the absolute minimum necessary for the protection of the eastern Atlantic. Nott concluded that the surface fleet should be cut still further.

The admirals were horrified, but they had met people like John Nott before. When asked for suggestions on how they could make the required cuts they immediately offered up two ships which could be lost without doing serious damage to national security. The first was the Royal Yacht, *Britannia*. It was, they said, one of the few vessels they felt able to forgo. This is a regular Navy gambit: the royal yacht appears in the list of fleet vessels as 'royal yacht/hospital ship', although on the last occasion on which a hospital ship was required, during the Falklands War, she was kept thousands of miles away from the action. Britannia costs the navy some £7 million pounds a year to run, but only a minister with a death wish is going to torpedo the vessel. Like every defence secretary before him, John Nott laughed at the admirals' cheek and rejected the idea.

As to their second suggestion, the ice patrol vessel, HMS *Endurance*, Nott was more sympathetic. It was in the Falklands, eight thousand miles away from the main British theatre of operations, and the Argentine threat was only fourth on the list of intelligence priorities. The Foreign Office were arguing that the ship was a signal of British resolve, but they didn't have to foot the bill – a meagre £2 million – (although Nott invited them to do so). The decision was referred to the cabinet Overseas and Defence Committee, where Nott won the day. The announcement that *Endurance* was to be withdrawn, which was to be taken by the Argentines as a sign of lack of commitment to the South Atlantic, was made on 30 June 1981.

Faced with a determined minister, the navy organized one of the most effective military lobbies seen at Westminster for years. In theory, service chiefs are subject to the control of their political masters, while retaining the right of access to the prime minister. In practice, they have at their disposal a well-oiled machine of back-bench MPs and Lords, a network of newspaper and television correspondents and a diaspora of retired generals, admirals and air marshals who are delighted to see their names in the newspapers. The admirals mobilized their lobby. MPs in a hundred constituencies received letters from worried voters. A junior minister, Keith Speed, a former Royal Navy officer, resigned. There were letters to the local and national newspapers from retired officers, and unattributable press briefings by serving ones.

In the event, it was the Falklands invasion, which had, ironically, been made more likely by the *Endurance* decision, that saved the Navy. After it was over, £1 billion was spent on new warships, not merely to replace those lost in the campaign, but because the war had demonstrated the need for a long-range nautical capability. The 1967 Labour Defence White Paper had announced that Britain would finally relinquish her imperial role by 1971 and thenceforward British military energies were to be directed more-or-less exclusively in Europe. Now the residue of British Imperial history had again rescued the forces from the chill winds blowing through all other government departments. At the start of the nineties, apart from the tens of thousands of troops and airmen in West Germany, there were garrisons or naval bases in the Falklands, Cyprus, Hong Kong, Brunei, Gibraltar, Belize and the Indian Ocean. 'The divergence between

Britain's shrunken economic state and its overextended strategical posture is probably more extreme than that affecting any other of the large powers, except Russia itself,' remarked Paul Kennedy, historian of the great powers in 1987. Within three years, the Soviet Union had begun withdrawing troops from the remnants of its Empire and was trying to find ways of reducing its other commitments. Even without the collapse of Communism in Eastern Europe, the British military would have had to find a way of doing something similar. Sensible decisions are hard to reach from the shadows of past glory.[32]

The power of the individual services within the Ministry has been steadily diminishing for years, valiantly though they have struggled to keep their independence. After the war, not only did each service have its own department and cabinet minister, it retained great autonomy. By the mid-sixties, a reorganization knocked out in only six weeks by Lord Ismay and Lieutenant-General Sir Ian Jacob had brought the services together in a central Ministry. Ismay and Jacob's plan was full of radical ideas, most of which were never implemented, including even the possibility of a common uniform. (This idea was later taken up by the Canadians, who speedily decided it had been a mistake.)

But the row which followed the Nott defence review, with each service fighting its own corner regardless of national defence priorities, showed how relatively impotent the ministry and minister could remain. In a demonstration of the power of brevity to move mountains, the then chief of the defence staff, Lord Lewin, wrote a two page letter to the defence secretary arguing for a stronger, unified central staff. In the event, it was Michael Heseltine, Nott's successor, and another man who had not fought in the war, who brought in the most far-reaching reforms, involving a dramatic erosion of the power of the individual services. Real power now lies with the chief of the defence staff, chosen on a principle which all the services strenuously deny is 'Buggins's Turn', and his central staff, made up of officers from all services.

These 'purple' officers – this being what someone imagined the light blue of the air force, khaki of the army and dark blue of the navy would look like if they were merged – are supposed to forgo previous loyalties and view the defence of the realm from a central, Whitehall, perspective. (Internal surveys show that army officers have much greater difficulty than either sailors or airmen in adjusting to the idea of an integrated ministry.) In theory, virtually no area of national defence is immune from the deliberations of these teams of officers drawn from all three forces. But there is little evidence so far of truly radical initiatives emerging from the teams. The main principles of British defence remain unchanged. The existence of three separate services and the relationship between them is largely unquestioned. Since all papers produced by the teams must be circulated to all interested parties, there is little chance that a proposal that, for example, the RAF abandon operating helicopters, will survive the RAF's own revision.

The military have repeatedly demonstrated their ability to out-manoeuvre their political masters. Indvidual ministers may serve at the Ministry for only two or three years at a time, but the service has a life of its own, and the instinct for survival replicates itself in one generation of Whitehall Warriors after another. Looking back over a lifetime career in the Ministry of Defence, Sir Ewen Broadbent reflected in 1988 that 'Even where radical decisions for future phasings out were taken, as over aircraft carriers in 1966, or the amphibious capability in 1981, they were soon modified.'[33]

So British defence continues to rest upon the idea of 'balanced forces'. The British Empire is no more, and the Soviet Empire is a shambles, yet the cake continues to be cut in roughly equal thirds between the services. Drastic steps are rarely contemplated and scarcely ever taken. A decision to plump for a 'continental' strategy at the expense of a 'maritime' strategy, for example, or vice versa, which would be a way of making inadequate funds more effective, would provoke apoplexy in one or other of the services. All of which explains why we have largely the same mix of forces now as we had twenty years ago. 'What we have nowadays is defence by sacred cow,' says Sir Frank Cooper.[34]

But the money gets spread more and more thinly. The consistent pattern since the end of the Second World War has been one of steadily rising costs and steadily decreasing numbers. A dozen good arguments can be produced for not abandoning a balanced surface fleet in favour of coastal defence or submarines, or for not giving up aircraft in favour of missiles, so strategy is dominated by the one constant factor, money, or the lack of it. The demand of the defence professionals that Britain maintain 'balanced forces' means a form of salami-slicing on all of them. If carried to its natural end, it would mean that Britain would eventually be defended by one tank, one ship and one aircraft.

Anyone who spends a few hours in many a British Army mess becomes aware of the way in which this attitude has infected the forces. In the belly of the army, the rumbles are growing. Despite the protective cocoon of service life, the most commonly heard complaint is that the 'quality of life' has got worse. When pressed for an explanation, moaning majors cite everything from the fact that they did not get a foot on the housing ladder early enough to 'contractorization' of support services, which means there isn't an army cook standing by to prepare a meal at any hour of the day or night. They complain they don't have afternoons free for sport any more.

Moaning has always been a speciality of the military. But underneath these apparently trivial complaints is a deeper malaise, a sense that 'the army isn't what it was'. A dozen or more officers must have mentioned in conversation that they wouldn't recommend their sons to follow in their footsteps.

As military experience becomes rarer, so the obligations of service life seem greater. In the navy, reduced numbers of ships look likely to mean longer periods at sea, which can only increase the strain. The best that many army regiments can expect is a succession of tours in Germany and Northern Ireland, interspersed, if they're lucky, with the occasional exercise somewhere warm. The Falklands Campaign, in which British forces were seen winning a notable victory against the odds, did wonders for their self-esteem and for recruiting. But the Falklands War was probably the last imperial spasm, and is fading into memory: much more commonplace is yet another few months in the wet slums of West Belfast or Londonderry: some units have now been posted to the province a dozen times or more. Officers' wives with careers of their own are increasingly unprepared to follow their husbands from Britain to Germany and back again every few years, and also reluctant to take on the traditional responsibilities for the wives and families of the soldiers.

The constituent nations of the United Kingdom, English, Welsh, Scottish and Irish, have always had a more distinct sense of their own racial identity than the blanket term 'British' suggests. Through one round of defence cuts after another, the army has fought to keep individual, locally based, units alive. This obsession with regimental cap badges meant the survival of almost a dozen more individual units than common sense dictates; by 1990 some 'regiments' contained no more soldiers than an average company. Their continued existence was due partly to the persuasive lobbying of retired officers, but also to the fierce loyalty of local people to a fighting machine with which their community has historically identified.

Collectively, the army into which these individual units were merged was one of the essential elements in defining what it meant to be British. The national preoccupation with 'heritage' is in large part an obsession with past battles and military pomp. Britain's perception of herself internationally is shaped by a martial history in which a small group of islands imposed Pax Britannica upon the world.

Throughout the decades since the Second World War, the armed forces have been in decline, and the diminishing significance of the military in national life cannot be separated from the widespread sense of aimlessness which overtook much of the rest of British society. Dean Acheson's aphorism that Britain had lost an empire and not yet found a role hit the forces less acutely than it hit foreign policy makers because the real and ever-present threat from the Warsaw Pact provided a ready justification for the existence of the military. Now that the Warsaw Pact has collapsed, further reductions in the army's strength, the dissolution of more historic regiments, are inevitable. Increasingly, the forces seem not merely isolated and misunderstood. They are in danger of looking unnecessary.

CHAPTER TEN

The Unexpected Return
of Samuel Smiles

'Heaven helps those that help themselves.'

– *Self Help* SAMUEL SMILES

I T IS A perfect summer Sunday, bright sunshine, a few feathery
white clouds high in the sky. The grass on the Guards' Polo Club
in Windsor Great Park is a rich green beneath the polished black
boots of the Household Cavalry band, who are, as usual, playing
bouncy themes from television series. Soon, the 25,000 spectators will
watch two English teams, one of them led by the Prince of Wales, in
combat with teams from North America and Australasia. The competition for the Coronation Cup, and the less important Silver Jubilee
Cup, promise the most exciting polo of the summer.

But the *paparazzi* are uninterested in anything happening on the
sixty thousand square yards of well-kept turf. They are buzzing round
a marquee at one end of the pitch, pushing past, or over, the white
picket fence, motor-drives whirring. 'This way, Cybill!' 'Over here,
love!' Cybill Shepherd, a minor soap opera star enjoying her fifteen
minutes of fame smiles, twirls a parasol, embraces a bewildered
companion, does whatever they ask.

Suddenly, the photographers are gone, leaving Miss Shepherd and
her escort sipping free champagne, with the awkward look of turtles
washed up by the tide. But everyone else looks out of place too, for
the marquee is filled not with the friends of the players, nor even with
friends of the spectators, and most certainly not by polo enthusiasts.
They are all here because somebody in the public relations department
of the jewellers Cartier sent them an unsolicited invitation to a day of
drinks and food at the company's expense.

They are an odd mixture of starlets, fading showbiz 'celebrities',
corporate businessmen and the occasional insignificant aristocrat. An
unstated deal has been done: Cartier will provide them with lunch

(smoked salmon, stuffed veal, peach and passion-fruit salad), as much champagne as they can drink and a grandstand seat alongside the Royal Box. In exchange, they will parade themselves before the cameras of the drooling photographers. The pictures will be printed in the middle-brow press, promoting the fiction that Cartier International Polo, or 'The art of Polo by Cartier', as the programme for the afternoon modestly puts it, is '*the* most glittering day in the polo calendar'. The cost of this piffle to Cartier is £1 million a year.

On the polo ground, the four-man England team, working their way through two dozen lathered-up ponies, are leading the Australasians six goals to five in a match which gallops from one end of the ground to the other. The England back, Lord Charles Beresford, sends the white ball soaring towards the goalposts, to ensure an England victory. At the presentation of the cup by the Queen, a little man in a beard and bilious green suit will be hovering inescapably within the photographers' field of vision. This is the president of Cartier, Alain D. Perrin, the beaming benefactor as the Queen presents her son with his trophy: the monarchy by courtesy of Cartier.

The Coronation Cup polo tournament is a sponsor's delight. It has the great merit of associating rather vulgar jewellery with one of the most exclusive sports in the world. Played in the grounds of Windsor Castle, with all the attendant flummery of military bands and be-medalled soldiery, it is operetta brought to real life. Above all, the virtually guaranteed presence of at least one major royal means it simply cannot be surpassed for image-making.

But almost all the sporting events of the English summer season have now succumbed to the corporate party-givers. Like a vast besieging army, their tents now surround, and often engulf, the event itself. Even competitions like tennis at Wimbledon or cricket at Lords, where grandstand seating might be expected to exclude corporate hospitality kings, have succumbed. Events like the Henley Regatta have almost disappeared in a sea of white canvas. Enthusiasts complain that the whole ambience of such events is being changed, that while the sponsors help to raise money, it is achieved at the price of putting well-oiled and often semi-comatose clients on the spectators' benches.

But without their help, many of the events would simply cease to function on any grand scale. The prejudice even of the artistic community against industry is increasingly concealed, aware that without its sponsorshop, theatre companies and art galleries would go under.

It is these captains of enterprise who are held up as role-models for the rest of Britain. They were to be the major beneficiaries of a decade of new-style Conservatism, indeed, the whole purpose of Government policy was to make life easier for them. Swashbuckling characters by their very nature, they arrived at wealth and power uncontaminated by the prejudices of the university common room or the professions. They were the one sure constituency upon whom Margaret Thatcher could count in her assault upon the old order. Indeed, there was a good chance that at some time they would have been on the receiving end of the class prejudices of the higher professions. Most were 'one of us' without a second thought.

By the start of the nineties, their Panglossian musings on the inherent superiority of free enterprise were beginning to look a little threadbare, as their favourite analogy, 'Great Britain plc', produced balance sheet after balance sheet in which social liabilities – homelessness, crime and general grime – loomed ever larger.

But a new ethic had taken root, replacing the commitment to the Welfare State. It was recognized that pledges to reduce the burden of taxation and the role of the state had inevitably left a gap in social provision which somehow had to be filled. As the New Right held that a century of prejudice against industry had been responsible for Britain's more-or-less ceaseless decline, they looked to Victorian capitalism to provide a model of how to meet the needs which were no longer being met by the state. The biscuit baron Sir Hector Laing, a close personal friend of the Prime Minister, was quick to take up the challenge. Although not a self-made man himself, Sir Hector shared the aspirations of the Victorian magnates.

'If you look at what people like Lord Leverhulme, or the other City fathers did, their achievement was enormous,' he told me. 'We can fulfil the role of the City fathers today.'

When I suggested that he was recommending a return to nineteenth-century paternalism, he was unembarrassed.

'We've never put anything better in its place,' he said. 'And besides, someone's got to help people to help themselves.'[1]

'Someone's got to help them to help themselves.' The words might have fallen as easily from the lips of any one of the great Victorian industrial philanthropists clutching his copy of Samuel Smiles' tract *Self Help*. 'Where men are subjected to over-guidance and over-

government, the tendency is to render them comparatively helpless,'
he wrote,[2] expressing a sentiment that might equally well have come
from the lips of any true-believing Thatcherite. The most enlightened
of the nineteenth-century industrialists had recognized that the process
which was drawing labourers off the land and into the smoke-belching
cities placed a distinct social responsibility on their shoulders. Where
the local squire had once provided housing on his estate, built or
maintained the local church and provided land for the local playing
fields, they realized that the needs of the vast new industrial proletariat
were every bit as acute.

Lord Leverhulme, Sir Hector Laing's hero, had been given a copy
of *Self Help* on his sixteenth birthday and retained his enthusiasm for
the book throughout his life, handing out copies to youngsters in
whom he took an interest, and doing his bit for the book's phenomenal
sale of 150,000 copies. Leverhulme's monument is Port Sunlight, 'a
new Arcadia, ventilated and drained on the most scientific principles',
as its first historian put it.[3] Even today, when the urban sprawl has
encircled the place, the houses clustered around Lever's giant soap
factory retain a distinctly calm, clean and well-scrubbed feel. When
the breeze blows from the right direction, the air is still scented with
the whiff of Lux, Surf and Lifebuoy. There is not a scrap of litter nor a
scrawl of graffiti in sight. The broad avenues, the fairy-tale version of
history written in its jumble of architectural styles, the temperance
hall now transformed into the 'Famous Olde Bridge Inn', with its
'New Traditional Style Restaurant', are more like a film set than a
housing estate.

Port Sunlight, like Sir Titus Salt's model village, Saltaire, near
Bradford, or the Cadbury's Bournville suburb in Birmingham, were
all attempts to recapture the lost rural idyll in the new industrial
cities. They went hand-in-hand with a certain authoritarianism. Leverhulme dismissed the idea of a profit-sharing scheme in 1903 on the
grounds that his workers could not be trusted not to spend the money
on 'bottles of whisky, bags of sweets, or fat geese for Christmas.'[4]
There was a weekly dance, but young women wanting to date men
were required to make application through the social department, to
be checked for suitability. (At Bournville female workers automatically
lost their job when they married.) Sunlighters were discouraged from
spoiling the view by hanging around on their doorsteps chatting to
neighbours, and washing was only to be hung on the line on certain
days of the week.

In return, Port Sunlight saved them from the horrors of the industrial slums, gave them a solid roof over their heads and decent sanitation. The workers tended to stay loyal to Lever Brothers. Inevitably, it was an introverted place. One visitor wrote:

> The whole village was dominated by the spirit of soap. All its occupants were employed in the industry; not only were they engaged in it all day, but it was a constant source of conversation at night. You could no more escape from its influence than from the odour (not at all an unpleasant one) permeating it from the great factory plant.[5]

Trade unions found organization an uphill struggle. 'No man of independent turn of mind can breathe for long the atmosphere of Port Sunlight,' the secretary of the local branch of the Engineering Union wrote to Lever.[6]

However commercially congenial this pliancy may have been to the Levers, the industrial philanthropists were not uniquely men of the right. Many of the great British industrial families were barred from the Establishment of the day by virtue of their background and occupation, to say nothing, in several cases, of their religion. Indeed, it is interesting to note that while modern industrialists make political donations almost entirely to the right wing (£2.5 million in an average, non-election, year like 1986), the Victorian entrepreneurs so frequently held up as their models were quite often liberals. George Cadbury, for example, became so frustrated by the jingoism associated with the Boer War that he financed the *Daily News* as an organ for his liberal ideas. He also campaigned hard for old age pensions and against sweated labour.

It is easy to glamorize the philanthropists. Many of the industrialists, notably in sectors like mining or steel, comfortably lived up to their hard-faced, hard-hearted caricature. The importance of the better ones was the model they provided for others. But once governments had accepted that providing housing, health-care and the rest were their responsibility, the role of the employer was bound to diminish. Apart from anything else, they were being taxed to pay for the welfare benefits.

The finest examples of paternalism occurred within companies which remained in family ownership. But the demands of taxation, wages and international competition meant that these old firms had to expand way beyond their roots if they were to survive. The early family entrepreneurs usually found they could only keep the business intact by importing talent into the management of the company, at the same time as stock market flotation diminished direct family control. The subsequent division between gentlemen and players worked satisfactorily for a while, but in the end, the gentlemen were just not up to the challenge. The Courtauld family textile firm is a case in point.

Samuel Courtauld III had similar paternalist instincts to those which motivated Lever to build Port Sunlight. He expected obedience and he exercised benevolence. Ruthless when threatened with industrial action, he none the less spent generously on schools, houses and libraries in the depressed Essex countryside where the firm was based. By the time of its second great expansion, with the patented discovery of Rayon in 1908, the firm had become a joint-stock company, and passed into the hands of his great-nephew, Samuel Courtauld IV. This was the member of the family who amassed the great impressionist art collection which can still be seen in the Tate and National Galleries and at the Courtauld Institute. Courtauld shocked his fellow directors at one stage by recommending that workers be appointed to the board, and R. A. Butler, who married his daughter (he thought he had been accepted by the family for two reasons; 'first that I was a member of the Carlton Club; and second that when carving I could make a partridge do six'[7]), believed that Courtauld represented the finest sort of 'humanized capitalism'.

Courtauld's successor, Sir John Hanbury-Williams summed up part of what this meant by remarking in 1952 that 'there has been a gentleman's club atmosphere in the boardroom and I believe it true to say that over the years this has spread to all the departments of our business.'[8] Hanbury-Williams was certainly a gent himself; trained as a diplomat, a gentleman-usher to King George, and married to a Russian princess. But his firm was less than awe-inspiring. The company which had been so phenomenally successful in the early years of the century had just sat back under its gentlemen-directors and let the grass grow. Its rival, Imperial Chemical Industries (ICI), by contrast, had continued to invest heavily in new ideas and products, and had passed from the cultured paternalism of the founding Mond family into the hands of a succession of self-made men. By the 1960s Courtauld's was a plum ripe for the picking. If the plum had not entirely rotted beforehand.

In the event, the ICI takeover bid failed, but it served to wake up the firm to the fact that times had changed. The new boss, Frank Kearton, was the son of a bricklayer and a trained scientist: with him the company had passed from the gentlemen to the players. Full of rhetoric about turning the firm into the 'Hong Kong of Europe', he went for a strategy of rationalization and vertical integration, streamlining the whole process of production from the original yarns to final garments. Although he became the industrial hero of his day, Kearton's tactics did little to abate the chill winds which continued to whistle around the company throughout the seventies.

The chairman for the eighties, Christopher Hogg, reflected the new grim mood which came to pervade British industry. Although he seemed to be hewn from the old timber (Marlborough and Oxford), he proved completely ruthless when it came to restructuring the company. He said later:

> I put one single, absolutely clear restriction on everyone. I simply said that every manager had to make a twelve per cent return on capital employed. In cash. Above all, it was a standard by which everyone could succeed, because even a manager who was losing twenty per cent on sales could halve his operation, take out the working capital, and there was the cash. He had to worry about what happened next year, but he had succeeded.[9]

To anyone trying to build up a company, remarks such as this last one would have sounded an awful warning. But Hogg and his like were concerned with managing, not building, with finding immediate answers to immediate problems, the most pressing of which was how to rescue the capital of investors who had put their money into a declining industry.

By the end of the eighties, Courtauld's had been separated from its roots. In 1989, the 'unbundling' strategy resulted in the original Samuel Courtauld business being sold off to the Japanese. Courtaulds' British workforce, which had stood at 95,000 in 1979, was down to only 39,000 ten years later. 'The job losses ground away at his finely developed social conscience,' an admirer wrote of Hogg, 'but he did not flinch from involving himself in the harsh details.'[10]

The pattern of command at Courtauld's – from harsh paternalist through humanitarian aesthete and gentleman to a technologist and finally an unbundler – demonstrates a pattern common to much of beleaguered British business. It has behaved like a demented piano-accordion, expanding and contracting to no apparent benefit. To satisfy investors, once the initial energy or idea has been used up, managers must buy to create the impression of growth, or sell to give the impression of productivity and profit. No doubt, Courtauld's old 'humanized capitalism', which R. A. Butler had praised to the skies in the fifties as the model for British industry, wasn't up to the challenge of international competition. Nor was Courtauld's unique: the early years of the Thatcher government forced every sector of British industry to make harsh choices.

By then, the family firms which had been such fine models were unrecognizable. Much of British industry was owned by pension funds, insurance companies and the like. In 1957, they held eighteen per cent of the country's ordinary shares. By 1973 the proportion had risen to forty-one per cent. Ownership had been divorced from control, which now resided with professional managers, a breed eulogized even by prominent figures within the Labour party, like Anthony Crosland.[11] By now, the heavy involvement of the state through nationalized industries and government contracts was bringing about a new breed of board member, the state sector barons. One minister or civil servant after another made the apparently effortless transition from Whitehall to boardroom.[12] That they were no match for a new, more ruthless breed of predator beginning to stalk the stock exchange was powerfully demonstrated by Lord Chandos at Associated Electrical Industries (AEI), a popular minister, One Nation Tory and patron of the arts, who presided over a period when profits were appalling. Chandos and AEI succumbed to the pounce of the up-and-coming tycoon, Arnold Weinstock, like tethered goats.

AEI was only one of many losses of the old order. Between 1954 and 1966, thirty-two of the top 120 companies disappeared. Industrial production became concentrated in fewer and fewer hands. In competitor nations like France and Germany, a much greater proportion of the national wealth was generated by small or medium-sized companies. In Britain, the top 100 companies, which had produced sixteen per cent of the nation's manufacturing output in 1909, had increased their share to forty-one per cent by 1970.

There was another consequence. The takeover, particularly the threat of the hostile takeover, concentrated minds all round. Unfortunately, it concentrated them upon short-term results. To let profits slip in the short term in the interests of long-term benefits was a risk which many would just not take: if you let profits, and the share price, drop, you might not have any long-term in which your policies could come to fruition.

By the end of the eighties, the two industrialists most highly rated by British businessmen were Lord (James) Hanson and Sir Owen Green.[13] Both presided over companies which had shown spectacular growth throughout the decade, Hanson forging an empire which straddled the Atlantic, Green becoming a figure to strike fear into the hearts of family businesses across the nation. They were restless men from whom silence was taken as a sign not of contentment but of plotting. They were not uniquely products of their age – Weinstock and the other sixties predators were their spiritual ancestors – but while the takeover merchants and asset-strippers of those days had been feared and rather distrusted, men like Green and Hanson were feared and admired.

At nine o'clock one January morning in 1985, Owen Green strode into the elegant St James's headquarters of the Dunlop corporation, demanded admittance to the office of the chairman, Sir Michael Edwardes, and handed him an envelope. Then he turned on his heel and left. The bid contained in the envelope was sufficient to acquire the company for Green's BTR group. One of the first things Green did as Dunlop's new owner was to sell the entire office building in which the confrontation had taken place.

The incident is typical of Green's style – audacious, ruthless and practical. In the 1980s he raised his profits from £42.5 million to £819 million, and his share price by 863 per cent. During the relentless rise of BTR from its modest beginnings as the Birmingham Tyre and Rubber company, Green consistently applied the same principle. The only thing that matters is the bottom line. 'He has an almost evangelical hatred of the corporate culture, where everyone arse-licks the chairman and has a roller,' one of his disciples crudely explained in 1987.[14] The first thing to be sold off when Green takes over a company is the valuable real-estate housing the corporate headquarters. Dunlop lost their premises in St James's, and Thomas Tilling, another acquisition, found their Mayfair mansion sold to the Kuwaitis. Green's own corporate base was in a grimy backstreet of Vauxhall, where few journalists were granted interviews, and the single sheet of information handed out by the company reveals only that the chairman served in small boats during the war, has three children, and is a 'bad golfer, good reader'. He claims to pass unnoticed in a crowd.

Hanson, by contrast, was instantly recognizable. Six foot four, thin and angular with a long swooping nose, he was once described as having a passing resemblance to a giraffe. His receding thin hair emphasizes a high forehead, and he retains the good looks that once attracted Hollywood actresses (he was engaged to Audrey Hepburn for most of 1954). Like Green, Hanson distrusted the flabbiness of many established British companies, almost as much as he disliked the nationalization policy of the socialist government which had taken over the Huddersfield haulage business developed by his father and grandfather. When he began the Hanson Trust in the sixties, his company was worth £300,000. By the nineties the stock market valued it at over £11 billion. Hanson himself was rubbing along on an annual salary of £1,263,000.

The similarity between Green and Hanson – they both make big profits and are heroes to their peers – disguises a significant difference. Green is an old-fashioned Black Country businessman who seems to think that overheads start south of Coventry. His management ideas are clear and simple – concentrate on the product, manufacture it efficiently and cut out wasteful things like plush corporate headquarters and fleets of executive limos. Hanson is a different kettle of fish altogether.

The City of London, Hanson's partner, Sir Gordon White, once quipped, 'is full of people just waiting for us to lift their wallets and rape their wives.'[15] Each Hanson company was expected to make a return on capital of twenty per cent, and to increase profit by twenty per cent annually. In the early years after acquisition, it is a simple enough matter to sell off plush headquarters and the rest, but the process cannot continue indefinitely. Weinstock killed off thousands of jobs after taking over AEI, and Hanson followed much the same pattern. What became of the battery manufacturer, Ever Ready, is a case in point. The company was in bad shape when Hanson bought it in 1981, but it had sales of £241 million, sixty per cent of its production was exported, and it employed 2,658 people. Two years later its sales were worth £132 million, only twenty per cent of production was exported, and the workforce had been cut to 1,061. Factories in Nigeria, Italy and West Germany had been got rid of. Even the company's latest 'Gold Seal' technology, which was being developed at the German plant, had been sold to a rival. Profit levels had soared to 24.4 per cent. To investors Hanson's arrival must have looked like the coming of Father Christmas. But by any social evaluation, this was hardly a record of triumph.

But social considerations do not appear to weigh heavily upon these men. Green's South African subsidiary of Dunlop has been branded one of the worst foreign employers in the country by the Congress of South African Trade Unions. In a rare interview, Green laid bare his contempt for those who worry about anything other than getting a return for the shareholders:

> Those educated postwar have been taught – brainwashed – that it is socially undesirable to make much money. So they combine other objectives, that it is just as important to have a good personnel policy, decent factories, to play a significant social role. They blur the issues – the key is the bottom line.[16]

The growth of their empires is directly related to the mercurial personalities of Green and Hanson, but they had sound business ideas too. They have a knack of picking duff companies and making them work. Both men encouraged their subordinates to take decisions and to run their divisions on their own initiative, although few members of the public could name their products. British Gas, after all, supplies gas, BP supplies petrol. But Hanson? In fact, the products ranged from gold and shovels to hot-dogs and artificial flowers, while Green's BTR produced tyres, concrete, beds and artificial legs.

Not long ago people like Hanson would have been considered cowboys, or rather, bandits. When Harold Wilson first put forward Hanson's name on his honours list, eyebrows were sufficiently raised at the Palace for him to get a knighthood rather than the peerage originally suggested. When Mrs Thatcher resubmitted his name in 1983, the peerage went through without a murmur.

It is noticeable that he enjoys something of a charmed life. When both he and United Biscuits bid for Imperial Tobacco, his opponent's offer was referred to the Monopolies Commission. His wasn't. Rudolf Agnew's Consolidated Goldfields spent months fighting off a bid from the Minorco Consortium, led by the hapless Michael Edwardes, only to succumb to Hanson's charms, after a chat one evening in the summer of 1989.

Figures like Hanson and Green brought a sense of vigour back to British business life, which had grown steadily more complacent, inefficient and uncompetitive through the postwar decades. British unease about ruthless businessmen, summed up in the resonant remark of a Conservative MP in 1919 about 'hard-faced men who had done very well out of the war', underlay the preparedness of much of industry to collaborate with their regulators. The new generation of predators were unafraid of being called 'hard-faced'. When James Goldsmith, Jacob Rothschild and Kerry Packer emerged sleekly into the limelight in the summer of 1989 to announce they were laying siege to BAT with a £13 billion takeover bid – three times bigger than any bid previously seen in Britain, although later withdrawn – there was scarcely a breath of criticism.

Yet none of these three men was actually in the business of making anything. Sir James had begun his business career with £8,000 won on an accumulator bet at Eton and then gone on to make one fortune after another by putting together and taking apart large companies. Jacob Rothschild was well-known as the most ruthless member of the banking dynasty. Kerry Packer, the pug-faced Australian, was reckoned the richest man in the continent after a lifetime of deal-making. Between them they had 120 years' experience of wheeler-dealing. But they were not industrialists in the mould of a Lever or a Pilkington, or even of a Richard Branson. BAT itself had grown plump, expanding way beyond its core business of selling cigarettes, by succumbing to the same takeover mania, spending £7 billion in the process during the previous ten years. The raiders' promise was to liberate separate divisions of BAT from the stifling hand of corporate bureaucracy.

The takeover fire was fanned by all sorts of factors, not the least of them the fact that City merchant banks had corporate finance departments which only survived as long as they could keep finding targets for corporate raiders to attack. Managers of ever-larger pension funds who might previously have been prepared to stick with a company for long-term growth now come under perpetual pressure to deliver short-term results. The enormous fees sloshing around mean that banks, stockbrokers and a raft of associated advisers, negotiators and administrators stand to make a fortune from the bids. Goldsmith was prepared to spend £165 million in professional fees for the BAT takeover. It is a lot of company cars.

However happily brokers and bankers may have looked on the endeavours of these men, the promiscuous suit of one business after another represented an idea of what business was about altogether different to that of the great Victorian companies upon which British industrial wealth was based. The classic confrontation between the two philosophies occurred in November 1986, when Green's BTR attempted to take over the glass manufacturers, Pilkington Brothers. If such a thing as an industrial Establishment exists, then Pilkington are in the heart of it. Like other nonconformist family businesses, a charitable trust set up by the firm spends millions each year on care for elderly former employees, from meals-on-wheels to digging their gardens or arranging holidays. But unlike so many similar businesses,

the Pilkington family managed to continue producing new generations
to run the firm efficiently, and it remained in family control from its
foundation in 1826 to 1970.

Free of the pressures of shareholders clamouring for short-term
profits, the company invested heavily in the early fifties in a new
manufacturing process, float glass, devised by Alastair Pilkington, a
distant relation. It took seven years and £7 million (at 1950s prices) to
get it right, but eventual success translated the firm into the biggest
glass manufacturers in the world. Licensing the process meant that
fewer workers were needed at the factories in St Helens, but the
company succeeded in halving its workforce from fifteen thousand in
1970 to seven thousand in 1986 without any enforced redundancies
and without strikes.

Then along came Owen Green. The previous year he had told the
British Institute of Management that

> We have never seen the ethical need or material need for placing research
> and development to the forefront of our activities. Research does not seem
> to fit easily into the cut and thrust environment of industry and com-
> merce.[17]

Now he laid siege to Pilkingtons, who responded with horror. Anthony
Pilkington, the chairman, speaking with the authority of the fifth
generation, declared that

> this bid is about the future of all British companies who believe in the
> creation of wealth and the pursuit of excellence . . . rather than the poverty
> of cashing in the future for short-term gains.

The company launched a public relations offensive to prove that it
was not the sort of clapped-out concern which needed the benefit of
BTR's restructuring. The family still held twenty per cent of the
shares, employees perhaps another ten per cent. Horrified at the
prospect of the arrival of the avenging angels from BTR, the trade
unions joined the campaign against the takeover. In the end, they
won. One victory for the old order in a war generally going the way of
the new.

It was Pilkington Brothers which provided the model for the organization which has come to represent the acceptable face of capitalism,
Business in the Community. Faced with the need to lay off thousands
of workers, Pilkington's agreed to set up the St Helen's Trust and to

back it with £35million. The Trust was a spectacular success, generating an estimated six thousand jobs through the promotion of small businesses in the area. Contemporary histories of Business in the Community tend to gloss over the fact that the Trust partly owes its origins to concessions won by the trade union movement. When the recession of the early eighties hit the country, the St Helen's Trust provided a working model of how an enterprise agency worked. The idea appealed immediately to Sir Hector Laing, who had met Margaret Thatcher in the seventies when both were houseguests of Jim Prior, the avuncular Suffolk MP later to become employment secretary. Thatcher's talk of 'getting government off the backs of the people' struck a chord with Laing. When he saw the consequences of cuts in government spending, the St Helen's Trust seemed to him to show how the gap might be filled.

The headquarters of Business in the Community are in a walk-up office above a branch of the National Westminster Bank in the wilderness between the glitter of the West End and the grime of the East. Outside, heavy lorries thunder down into Shoreditch, inside it hums with good-humoured enthusiasm. Since its foundation, it has become the organization for businesses with a social conscience; nearly two-thirds of *The Times'* top one hundred British companies are members, and two hundred smaller firms. Hanson is a member. BTR is not. Prince Charles is a highly active president, and the directors and advisory committee have become industry's Great and Good.

It was the April 1981 Brixton riots which made Business in the Community. Two hundred and seventy-nine policemen were injured, nearly thirty buildings wrecked by fire, as alienated young men – the great majority, although not all, black – rampaged, burned and looted. This was clearly not the ideal environment in which to be selling washing-machines or personal computers, and it looked as though the disaffection which had inspired the riots would spread.

Stephen O'Brien had at one time or another considered becoming a vicar, a social worker and a politician, and ended up as an international money broker. O'Brien was approaching fifty, with the looks and enthusiasm of a Corinthian football coach. In the early seventies he had set up Project Fullemploy, which aimed to apply private sector management techniques to public money and in the process generate jobs for unemployed young black people. He was the natural choice to lead the new venture which aimed to act upon the ideas of Laing, Pilkington and a handful of others.

Business in the Community was a distinctively 1980s phenomenon, born of the collapse of consensus, the inefficiencies of the welfare state and the retreat by central government from many of its previous responsibilities. Twenty years earlier companies had begun to sponsor artistic and sporting events: now lower levels of taxation gave them more money to spend on activities other than direct investment in their businesses. But while business involvement in the community began as philanthropy, it soon developed into something else. 'Regardless of what you manufacture, you're going to sell more of it to a community that's prosperous,'[18] was the argument O'Brien began to deploy with increasing frequency. The advertising director, Tim Bell has a pithy summary:

> We live in a capitalist society. Capitalism is founded in the pursuit of self-interest. The Victorian philanthropist gave to charity because he'd made a lot of money, and he felt he ought to put something back. The modern philanthropist does it because it makes it easier for him to earn more.[19]

This philanthropic end of business is still dominated by the old bastions of British enterprise, like the Whitbread brewing dynasty. A slim, friendly man, Sam Whitbread the sixth, the current chairman, is firmly entrenched in the beerage: Eton, national service in the local regiment, chairman of the Bedfordshire Conservative Association, prominent in the local church, High Sheriff, a member of the county council and deputy Lord Lieutenant.

The Thatcher years were kind to the brewers. They survived the recession relatively unscathed, and by the end of the decade their combined turnover represented a staggering two per cent of the entire Gross Domestic Product. Confronted with proposals from the Monopolies and Mergers Commission to curb their power and redistribute pubs to smaller companies outside the six giants in the industry, they mobilized a devastatingly effective lobby. The Trade Secretary, Lord Young, having announced that he was 'minded to implement the recommendations' of the Commission, was first abused and then humiliated by Conservative back-bench MPs in cahoots with the brewers. He capitulated. The brewers emerged from it all with their power and their profits substantially intact. It was an object lesson in how powerful businesses can bully government.

Whitbread, like many of the brewers, works hard at its image. Among its better known sponsorships are the annual Whitbread Books of the Year award, the Round-the-World Yacht Race, Rugby League internationals, the Badminton Three Day Event, the Whitbread Gold Cup, the Stella Artois tennis championship and, through its Beefeater Gin subsidiary, the Oxford and Cambridge Boat Race. The recipients are carefully chosen to associate the company's products with health and wellbeing – the literary award had its genesis in rather whimsical notions of a good pint and a good read being ideal companions on a winter evening – and sponsorship is intended to provide maximum publicity for the firm.

But the Whitbread Community Programme is another matter. In the tax year ending in April 1990, the company planned to give over £2 million, one per cent of projected profits, to charity. Like many of the rich companies based in the East End of London, within the shortest of distances from the Whitbread headquarters are pockets of poverty and squalor as bad as any in Britain. The company, the most enlightened of its size, had heard of a scheme in Boston where rich downtown bankers had developed a partnership with local schools, under which they would guarantee employment to school-leavers, in exchange for the schools undertaking to produce students with the requisite skills. For the employers, the programme had the benefit both of upgrading the local labour pool, and breaking down barriers between business and local people. Whitbread applied the scheme in Tower Hamlets and Hackney, two of the most deprived boroughs in London, with a pledge of employment for three hundred local young people. The idea has since been adopted by government, and has spread across the country. The company, meanwhile, developed other projects, to provide work for unemployed graduates, supporting enterprise agencies and the Prince's Business Trust, and sponsoring awards to recognize individual doers of good.

Whitbread is a particular case. It is still quite a paternalistic employer and likes to characterize the company as a family: when, each January, the chairman writes to company pensioners outlining pension rates for the coming year he gets between five and six hundred letters in reply. Despite making his fortune from the manufacture of cheap intoxicating liquor, the company's founder, Sam Whitbread, was a devout low-Churchman. One of the main board directors and supporting staff are solely engaged in community works. The first Whitbread would instantly recognize the decisions being made by his descendant.

'I see it as a commercial investment,' he told me. 'We're operating all over the country, and wherever we have invested in the community programme, there's always been a very visible commercial return.'

It presumably doesn't make them drink more beer, so I asked how the commercial return showed itself.

> It attracts the right sort of employee – people feel they'd like to work for a company that does good things. And it brings you into very close contact with the local authorities, the social services and the police. And without putting too fine a point upon it, that does help in giving the impression of a caring company, which in turn results in getting planning approval quicker than we might, or a vendor being more prepared to sell a good site to us than to somebody else.[20]

'Heaven helps those that help themselves,' Samuel Smiles said, and other industrialists quietly admitted they could not afford to remain uninvolved simply because of the amount of business which resulted when people got together to discuss charitable initiatives. I found it impossible to be unimpressed, however, by the ideas and energy of Business in the Community. If the end is positive, who cares about the motivation?

Yet the gulf between the community and business, which the charity aims to bridge, is often the consequence of the very takeover mania which created the industrial heroes of the postwar years. The reason so much of British industry came to be seen as something other, separate from the main realm of people's lives, was because each time a business was taken over by a larger conglomerate, out went the local chap and in came the men in suits from head office. Companies which had previously been part of the town or county became branch offices or outstations, run from a headquarters miles away, whose only concern was the bottom line.

The tactics of Business in the Community have become increasingly sophisticated. Instead of developing a bloated headquarters staff, it has aimed to get smaller. To help develop a black professional class, plans were made for companies to offer young black people work before they went to university, to provide additional training during the vacations, and then to guarantee them jobs once they graduated. 'Target teams' were created, under the chairmanship of distinguished industrialists, to tackle specific problems, like ways of giving work to hard-core inner city unemployed, or developing links between schools and companies. Another, under the chairmanship of Sir David Scholey of Warburgs, addressed the question of how to raise relatively small amounts of money for would-be entrepreneurs who have no record upon which existing institutions would take a risk.

The organization attempts to encourage companies to base decisions about how and where to invest, recruitment and training policy, on considerations other than harshly commercial factors. They try to promote the integration of social initiatives into mainstream company policy, such as the idea that secondment to work on social projects is an alternative to study at business schools.

The model for many of these initatives is the United States, where for twenty years or more professional skills have been used to run entrepreneurial-like operations not for profit but for a social objective. By comparison with the United States, however, the generosity of British firms is decidely circumscribed. Taken out of context, the figures for charitable giving by British companies can look impressive. In 1988, British Telecom spent £11 million on community projects of one kind or another, BP gave £7 million to charity. No-one would call these figures peanuts, but they look less than impressive when set alongside profit figures. The three hundred most philanthropic companies belong to the Per Cent Club, pledged to devote half of one per cent of pre-tax profits to charitable works, hardly a great risk. And many other companies seem less than wholeheartedly committed. In 1988, BTR's charitable giving amounted to 0.0173 per cent of profits. In 1989 Hanson made profits of £1.064 billion, as well as spending £3.5 billion to buy Consolidated Goldfields. Dividends to shareholders came to £447 million. The total amount of money spent worldwide on community and charity projects came to £1.6 million.

Though they are fond of citing the Victorian city fathers as their models, the new generation of industrial paternalists have yet to create anything similar. In Port Sunlight, the windows of many of the houses have discreet 'For Sale' notices behind the glass, despite Lord Leverhulme's wish that they should never be sold. The managers decided to allow in the estate agents in 1979, in recognition of the changed social climate. Old 'Sunlighters' are still in a majority, but their days are surely numbered, as houses are increasingly sold at prices beyond the reach of Unilever workers. One villager recalled the sound of thunder which greeted factory closing time, as thousands of nailed boots plodded home. The noise of today is the whine of Ford Fiestas each on separate journeys to work.

Times change, and however enamoured they may be of their Victorian role-models, the new generation of industrial philanthropists will never be able to reach the same levels of achievement. It is absurd to expect that charity can fill the gap left by reduced government expenditure, partly because, by comparison with public spending, the sums of money are tiny, but more importantly because their share-holders won't allow it. The great paternalists owned their companies and could do with their profits what they liked. The present managers are there on the sufferance of the pension fund managers and the corporate financiers. If they fail to deliver, the takeover sharks are waiting.

The 1980s were the kindest climate for businessmen for decades. Three separate pieces of legislation shifted the balance of power away from the trade unions and in favour of the bosses. Top taxation rates were slashed. A surging stock-market made it relatively easy to raise money, and if more was needed, there were plenty of venture capital firms in the City happy to supply it. Small wonder that by the nineties captains of industry had a greater self-confidence about them than they'd had for years.

They still complain at things like an education system presided over by teachers with a scarcely-concealed contempt for industry, turning out teenagers who frequently don't meet the standards necessary for employment. But the popular heroes of the eighties were self-made men and women (a third of self-employed entrepreneurs are now women), and their triumphs were saluted in the popular press.

But what of their influence? No Downing Street reception was complete without the occasional self-made millionaire, but their inter-est in politics was pretty restricted. The procession of ministers and civil servants from Whitehall to the boardrooms of big companies was scarcely diminished, but they were less influential in a world in which the rules had been rewritten to allow the market licence. The vulner-ability of companies to takeover meant that people once regarded almost as permanent fixtures could disappear overnight.

The new takeover kings, like Lord Hanson, exercise a less specific influence than the proprietors of the individual companies which he has taken over, simply because the range of his interests is so broad. But Hanson has no false modesty about offering the Conservative party advice on how it should conduct itself, and it is some indication of the way he regarded the relative status of himself and members of the Thatcher cabinet that while its members generally accepted his invitations to lunch, he considered his time too precious to attend many of theirs.

Sir Hector Laing claims he hardly sees a civil servant or minister nowadays, whereas:

> in the seventies, we were seeing ministers at least once a month on one damn thing or another. The other morning I asked 'Who is the permanent secretary at the Min. of Ag.?' And no-one had a clue. That gives some indication of the drift of companies away from government.

Not that such distance necessarily implies total ignorance of the mandarins.

'But presumably you still know senior civil servants?' I asked.

'No,' he replied instantly, then thought for a moment and corrected himself.

'Well, I know Robin Butler [head of the civil service], Clive Whitmore [head of the Home Office], Nigel Wicks [Second Permanent Secretary at the Treasury] and Andrew Turnbull [another senior Treasury official].'

This is about as distinguished a cross-section of the bureaucracy as you could come across.

'They were all private secretaries to Margaret. She always brings one of them with her when she comes to stay. So if you're asking do I know them well enough to ring them up and ask, "Hi, what's going on?" the answer is yes, I do.'

But the traffic tends to be in both directions nowadays. Where once industry joined organizations like the Confederation of British Industry to have a corporate ear in a corporate state, in the eighties the influential voice was the iconoclastic Institute of Directors.

Allen Sheppard, the squat and pugnacious Chief Executive of Grand Metropolitan, summarized:

> Throughout the seventies everyone believed that all social and economic problems had to be solved by 'they'. We'd become overwhelmingly institutionalized as a country. We'd given up our rights as citizens to the government, and apart from voting every five years, we spent the rest of the time complaining but doing sod all about it. But 'they' didn't achieve anything. So now we recognize it's got to be us. 'Theyism' has gradually died.[21]

Sheppard, the son of an East End engine-driver, entertains senior civil servants to lunch every three or four weeks, and senior politicians, notably from the Department of Trade and Industry, twice or three times a year. Previously, the businessmen were lending an ear to the bureaucrats: now it is Whitehall doing the listening.

But social prejudice against business has hardly diminished. The businessman is not commemorated by statues or monuments, there is no 'capitalists' corner' in Westminster Abbey. However much they are admired, people like Lord Hanson are still thought of as outsiders. There's something not quite *comme il faut* about the gold bracelet and the sheer predatoriness.

The Economist remarked in 1870 that

> it would 'pay' a millionaire in England to sink half his fortune in buying 10,000 acres of land to return a shilling per cent, and live upon the remainder, rather than live upon the whole without land . . . he would be a greater person in the eyes of most people,[22]

and much the same remains true today. The Pearson family, who now own *The Economist*, along with other profitable top-of-the-range products like the *Financial Times*, Château Latour, and Penguin Books, is considered respectable not because of the poshness of its products so much as for the fact that the founder of the family fortune, Weetman Pearson, sank the fortune he had made in construction and Mexican oil wells into the Cowdray Estate, which rolls across miles of Sussex, its yellow doors and window frames recognizable in village after village.

At the first chance, newly-rich industrialists still rush off to the country in their newly-tailored Norfolk jackets, clutching chequebooks. Some, like Roger Croft, who bought the forty-room Lockerley Hall, near Romsey in Hampshire, are at least open about their ambitions. 'I'd love to have been a nineteenth-century squire, and that is the way I am living now,' he boasts.[23] He is a property developer.

Lord Hanson's friend, Lord King, is every bit as ruthless. Ask him about whether business should be involved in inner-city projects, about the social responsibilities of industry, and he answers that the responsibility of an industrialist is to his company, his shareholders and his workers. Charity is the responsibility of the individual, not the company.

King's career in industry – heavy engineering and latterly the saviour of British Airways – is as impressive as any in Britain. But his sole everlasting regret is that he did not plant more trees during his lifetime. Having begun his business life in a Yorkshire pit village, where the three activities were 'liquorice, glass and poverty', his estate is his obsession. With his fat cigars, gold watch-chain and bulldog neck, Lord King looks a caricature Victorian industrialist. His speech is slightly slurred, still with the faintest trace of a northern accent, but the pinstripe suit is bespoke, and the cufflinks are woven gold. Yet his ambition is to be accepted as a country gent.

'You become part of the Establishment if you succeed,' he observes from behind his desk – empty but for a brass lamp, two ashtrays and his cigar lighter. 'But if you fail, they don't want to know you.' Lord King is successful all right, but, despite numbering the Prime Minister and a couple of dukes among his personal friends, along with membership of White's and Pratt's and the Mastership of the Belvoir foxhounds, he is still something of an outsider.

Lord King's greatest private worry is who, after his death, will be Master of Wartnaby, the estate at Wartnaby in Leicestershire, first acquired over thirty years ago, and gradually added to, until it now covers two thousand acres. One of his three sons is in business on his own account in the Carolinas, but in the usual pattern of British enterprise, both his twin sons have entered the professions: one is an accountant and the other a solicitor.

For all the talk, the British have yet to change their ideas about the gentleman and industry.

CHAPTER ELEVEN

Bowler Hats and White Socks

Nobody did a secret deal
Nobody was for sale
Nobody bent the rules at all
And nobody went to jail

And all of them were honest men
As white as driven snow,
And lived on a higher plane
And shat on those below

— *All Clear* ROGER WODDIS

THEY ARE THE sacristans of high capitalism. Tense, excitable, intently watching screens winking jumbles of incomprehensible figures, suddenly screaming into a telephone, then collapsing back in their chairs, the rite celebrated. Candidates for a heart attack at thirty-three, or, if they're lucky, mere redundancy at thirty. Cocky young things earning more than their fathers or mothers dreamed of, up early, drinking late, like Canute's courtiers denying the truth that they're really creatures of a dealer in Tokyo or a computer in New York.

In this dealing room there are six hundred of them, recruited at nineteen or twenty, washed up ten years later. Survivors say they can tell when the end is coming, when the stress is all getting too much, when the six-thirty briefing and the in-house breakfast offers not so much the prospect of a racing pulse but a sinking heart. Then the victims avoid the two company nurses, unsure of their loyalties.

But they cannot escape the electronic touch on the collar, as somewhere on a higher floor a superior hacks into their account and monitors, day by day, how much they're making for the firm. In some places the end comes fast. You go out to lunch, and they don't let you back in the building when you return.

They wear the dark suits, striped shirts and spotted ties of the gentleman banker, but this is a breed whose natural clothing is white socks. The City of London doesn't know any longer whether it belongs to them or to the two remaining top hats of the gentlemen bill brokers ambling across to their Thursday afternoon visit to the Governor of the Bank of England.

For generations, there was no doubt about it. The City of London was the financial wing of the Establishment, the socially acceptable face of capitalism. Railway magnates might seize the first opportunity to buy a country estate and acquire respectability, but usury was a job for those already gentlemen. Apart from anything else, it allowed a degree of leisure, a vital commodity for anyone aspiring to a quasi-aristocratic way of life. Bagehot wrote in 1888:

> The calling is hereditary, the credit of the bank descends from father to son. This inherited wealth brings inherited refinement. Banking is a watchful, but not a laborious trade. A banker even in large business can feel pretty sure that his transactions are sound, and yet have much spare mind. A certain part of his time, and a considerable part of his thoughts, he can readily devote to other pursuits.[1]

For those not fortunate enough to inherit a bank, to be 'something in the City' was a recognized, and often more congenial, substitute for finding an American heiress to restore family fortunes.

The aristocratic connections continue to the present day: the Queen's Lord Chamberlain, Lord Airlie, came to the job from the chairmanship of Schroder Wagg, the merchant bank, and happily combined his duties at Court with being chairman of insurance and investment companies. Sir John Riddell was appointed Prince Charles' last private secretary from a career as a City banker. It is hard to imagine a plastics millionaire gliding as easily into the royal palaces.

The solid, imposing buildings, the torrents of ants surging down the narrow streets at beginning and close of business each day, add to the sense that this is the powerhouse of modern Britain. Not that there is any entity to correspond to the coherence implied in the term 'The City'. It has fragmented geographically, dispersed to Docklands, Edinburgh, Norwich and half-a-dozen other cities. And it is fragmented functionally. Banks bank, insurance insures, brokers bargain. Those employed there might work for organizations in direct competition with one another, but the thing they all have in common is a love of money and deals. 'The City' survives as a state of mind.

Surprisingly wordly people can misunderstand the skittish wisdom of the place. 'Edward Heath got it completely wrong,' one eminent banker told me, referring to the beleaguered Conservative Government in the early seventies. 'He seriously thought there were perhaps two or three people in the City who had the key to a button marked "confidence". He was furious when he discovered they didn't exist, and he never forgave us for it.'

Heath's mistake was understandable. What little the outside world knew of the place was confined to such evidence as had emerged in inquiries like the Bank Rate Tribunal of 1957. The Tribunal produced half a million words of evidence on whether skulduggery had been involved in the selling of gilt-edged securities immediately before a rise in Bank Rates, but none of it was more revealing than the impression which emerged that the financial affairs of the nation were sorted out between chaps on their way from Threadneedle Street to the grouse moors.

'Of course, Rufie's not very bright,' said the second Lord Kindersley of Lazards about the second Lord Bicester, then of Morgan Grenfell, 'but we all like doing business with him.' Analysis of the relationships between the top people in the City showed a remarkable survival of the same old families – the Smiths, Rothschilds, Barings and others – who had run the money markets for generations. Eton seemed to have a stranglehold on most of the top jobs: almost a third of the directors of the clearing banks had been at the school, as had a third of the top merchant bankers and a third of the directors of the Bank of England.[2]

They knew each other, they trusted each other, and they could generally fix things between them. 'Look here, Rufie,' said Lord Kindersley at one point during the Bank Rate crisis, 'is it too late to stop this business or not?' To outsiders, it all looked terribly cosy.

But to those who inhabited it, the advantages of this clubby world were obvious. Handling vast sums of money – other people's money – was a great deal easier if the City's adage 'My Word is My Bond' could be believed. You didn't cheat other members of the family, and you knew from schooldays who was and was not to be trusted.

In the leisurely days of the fifties it was easy to draw a simple yet relatively precise map of power in the City. It looked like a series of concentric circles. At its centre was the Bank of England, solid, incorruptible, permanent. In the first circle around the Bank were the twelve Discount Houses, which dealt with the Bank's treasury bills and bills of exchange every morning and afternoon. The second ring was the seventeen merchant banks which made up the Accepting Houses Committee. A little further out was a third ring, comprising a number of the more important stockbrokers. Finally, so far away as to be almost falling off the edge, came the fourth ring, the financial institutions – the commercial bankers, the pension fund managers, the insurance companies. One of the reasons for the remoteness of this outer circle was that the institutions were largely run by functionaries who had worked their way to the top.

This globe was clear and simple and everyone knew where they stood. But over the next twenty years borders became fuzzier, as the divisions between different styles of institution were broken down and the cartels came under increasing pressure to adjust to the market. The globe finally imploded on 27 October 1986, as deregulation pricked the last untouched cartel – the Stock Exchange – and competition broke in.

The guarantor of the City's probity, upon which the prosperity of the City depends, remains the Bank of England. Public institution though it is, a visitor knows instantly that he is not in the civil service. To begin with, the characteristic shiny trouser-bottom and Whitehall shuffle are out of favour in Threadneedle Street. In place of the elderly porters in baggy blue serge, the central lobby is staffed by portly beadles in pink tail coats whose disdain is almost tangible. The Governor runs a pretty tight ship. Starting salaries are higher than for Whitehall civil servants, although less than intelligent young graduates might earn in many other places in the Square Mile. They are judged not merely by their executive ability (in fact they have precious little chance to make really important decisions until they are ticking off the years to retirement), but also on their drafting skills, their diplomatic abilities, even their dress sense. The wearing of trousers by female members of staff is still frowned upon, but they don't seem to find the restrictions too irksome and the Bank is less troubled by leaks than some Whitehall departments – a sign of a reasonable level of loyalty.

At the top of the Bank sits the Court, the board of directors. The Bank of England Act of 1946 lays down only that no more than four of the directors may be employees of the Bank, but says nothing of how the other twelve are to be chosen. In practice, the selection process is, in the words of one member, 'pure Old Boy Network'. Candidates to replace those who have retired or died in office are neither interviewed nor even formally discussed among the existing Court. Most are grand City figures, although intimate knowledge of how the economy works is not, apparently, essential. The token trade unionist, Gavin Laird, admitted his ignorance with a frank grin. 'What the hell do I know about international finance or the money market? Nothing.'[3] Like other outposts of the Great and Good, final appointment to the Court is made on Downing Street's recommendation, but it has remained largely the preserve of the governor and his deputy. Before the reign of the long-serving Montagu Norman (who had first been elected to the Court in 1907 and retired on grounds of ill-health in 1944), it had not been unusual for directors to be elected in middle age and to stay there until they died – a few even served several decades. This was hardly a recipe for dynamism, and most of the present generation are at least all well below retirement age. Seating at the Thursday morning meetings is, however, still arranged by longevity, so they rotate around the Sheraton table. The new boy (there are no women, or any black or Asian faces, for that matter) takes his seat on the Governor's left hand. The longer he serves, the further around the table he moves, until he becomes the most long-serving, seated on the Governor's right.

They can hardly do it for the money. Each receives £500 a year for his services, a figure unchanged for forty years. 'One is making a contribution to the system,' one told me. 'It's a chance to get into important action: the Bank is a catalyst in the City,' a banker director said, and several were frank enough to admit that both vanity and business considerations played a part: as one put it, 'the kudos is good for business.'

In March 1990, the Court had seventeen members, drawn from the City, industry and the Bank's staff. The five industrialists included two who bore the Thatcher stamp, Sir Hector Laing and David Atterton, an engineering entrepreneur and a director of Marks and Spencer. The head of the Securities and Investment Board, David Walker, had a seat at the Court. Among the other City representatives there was just one Baring – a marked drop in the number of dynastic representatives from ten years earlier. There is a predictable dominance of Oxford and Cambridge among them (thirteen are Oxbridge products) and four of the seventeen were at school at Eton.

How much real power they have is another matter. Seated in their elegant pale green room beneath Irish crystal chandeliers, they hear a report on what has happened to the money supply over the past seven days, and the Bank's buying and selling of sterling. Every fortnight they discuss a paper from one of the in-house economists. Although the only things for which they have any direct responsibility are the internal affairs of the Bank itself, their association with the Bank gives them considerable influence in the City.

The crucial person remains the Governor. His office is on one of the busiest corners in London. Yet the loudest sound inside is the ticking of the two clocks kept wound up by one of the flock of pink tail coated attendants who stand silently outside his door like whiskered flamingoes. A computer screen on the governor's desk with the latest price of sterling is the only concession to the twentieth century. Otherwise, the perfectly-proportioned room, looking out on to his enclosed private garden ('the most expensive lawn in Europe') speaks of an age of imperial power when the pound was a byword for reliability. A Zoffany portrait of an eighteenth-century predecessor hangs on the wall. On his old wooden desk, twin crystal pots of black and red ink speak of his accounting role, a silver handbell recalls an age before secretaries could be summoned by telephone or squawk-box.

Robin Leigh-Pemberton, the man Margaret Thatcher put into the governor's office, looks a chip off an old block. At weekends and whenever possible at other times he retreats to his estate in Kent, where he has been chairman of the County Council (as a Conservative), and of which he is now Lord Lieutenant. 'The thing about Robin,' a colleague once remarked, 'is that he really does think being Lord Lieutenant of Kent is more important than being Governor of the Bank.' The style of the Leigh-Pemberton governorship was so laid-back as to be virtually horizontal. During the great stock market crash of Black Monday 1987, for example, he was on an official visit to Eastern Europe. During the Johnson Matthey banking crisis, Brian Sedgemore, the bright but brutal Labour MP, referred to him in the Commons as 'that appalling deadbeat'.

'Robin is a lot brighter than he pretends to be,' one of his colleagues told me, 'but he hides it well.' His background – Eton, Oxford and the Grenadier Guards – was decidedly not the sort of self-made meritocratic pedigree Margaret Thatcher prized in her courtiers. But the attraction of Leigh-Pemberton to her (he was then the non-executive chairman of the National Westminster Bank) was that he was not out of the City mould. He had originally trained and practised as a barrister. Succeeding the independently-minded previous governor, Gordon Richardson, his appointment was pretty roundly damned in the Square Mile. 'They say the world's divided into those prepared to give independent advice to the Prime Minister and those who have done so,' a senior City figure told me, 'but Leigh-Pemberton is in a third category. She's the one who gives the advice.' In the City his appointment had been seen as a deliberate snub. (It was greeted with the headline in the *Sun*, ACTOR TAKES OVER AT THE BANK, a reference to a bit part he had once had in a film comedy.) The *Financial Times* commentator Samuel Brittan, whose younger brother, Leon, was at the time chief secretary to the Treasury, called his appointment 'a major blunder'.

This was unfair to Leigh-Pemberton. The Bank of England's precise relationship with government is ambiguous. It has neither the constitutional independence of the American Federal Reserve or the German Bundesbank, nor the subservient role of the Bank of France, which is run by the Ministère des Finances. The Treasury is legally entitled to give instructions to the Bank of England, but the power has never been used. The relationship is much more subtle, based upon understandings, perceptions and 'a sense of common purpose', as one senior figure in the Bank put it. This means that personal relations are immensely important: the Governor sees the Chancellor once or twice a week, and they dine at each other's houses at least monthly. There is usually a very senior Treasury official lunching at the Bank every other week.

But however you explain it, the 1980s were not a distinguished decade for the Bank. It is at its strongest when governments have weak or vacillating economic policies, and whatever else the policies of the Thatcher years may have been, they were rarely open to influence. Leigh-Pemberton's relaxed style at the Bank, delegating major responsibilities to his deputy, Sir George Blunden (a figure of real influence in the City), won favour in Downing Street, and he was appointed to a second five-year term in 1988. It was only after reappointment that he began to incur Prime Ministerial displeasure, by demanding greater freedom over monetary policy and going soft on Europe. He is there until June 1993, when he will happily retire to Kent.

It used to be said that it was sufficient for the Governor to raise his eyebrows for dodgy firms to mend their ways, and his influence is still considerable. But in a world in which business was run by chaps who had all been to the same schools, this was a much simpler matter. The carefully cultivated image of the City's impeccable morals may be a myth, but self-interest dictated compliance with the Governor's wishes. The chairman of a bank would drop in for a cup of tea or a glass of scotch, and leave in no doubt about what the Bank thought of his firm's activities. If there was any doubt about whether the governor would be taken seriously he had only gently to remind the institution concerned of the Bank of England's capacity to grant or deny business to commercial banks.

But then the City was run almost as an offshore island, and the governor was a bridge to Whitehall. Now, the majority of firms in the City aren't even British. They take their orders from Tokyo or New York or Frankfurt, and the offshore island has become part of an archipelago in international waters.

Stanislas Yassukovich lives, it seems to his employees, with the gods. Where the old merchant banks were all mahogany and ancient retainers, Merrill Lynch is glass, plastic and steel. The elevator rises ten floors, up through the roof of the building and into a tower from whence you look down on prematurely grey salarymen sliding their security passes into turnstiles to get at their desks and make money for the world's biggest brokerage house. Then the lift doors open and you are in a world of fibre-optic Georgiana – reproduction prints, brass doorknobs and linen wallpaper. No vulgar noise or bustle of business up here. A pin-striped butler breaks the well-heeled silence with an offer to take your coat.

After thirty years in the City, Yassukovich, a Franco-Russian American, has acquired the patina of an English gent – the well-tailored dark suit, the signet ring on the little finger of the left hand. There are others in the Square Mile who have been similarly assimilated over the years. His colleague at Merrill Lynch, Michael Von Clemm, another American who first came to Britain to do a postgraduate course at Oxford, now sits on the boards of half-a-dozen good causes, particularly archaeological trusts. Sir Mark Weinberg, a South African who chairs Allied Dunbar Assurance, is a trustee of the Tate Gallery. Sir Kit McMahon, Chairman of Midland Bank, is a cultured Australian (he once taught English Literature at Melbourne University) who sits on the Court of London University and the Board of the Royal Opera House.

Although they may have begun as outsiders, these men are scarcely different to generations before them, and play by the same rules. But the business of the City is no longer the exclusive preserve of the British gentleman. It is the City's very statelessness which is the key to its prosperity. From the development of the Eurodollar market, to

London's position as the third partner, with New York and Tokyo, of a speculative triad, the Square Mile has acquired an international orientation from which it cannot escape without catastrophe. The dealing screens which wink at the traders are driven by forces on the other side of the world as much as by anything intrinsic to Britain. Of the 345 banks in the British Bankers' Association at the start of 1990, 282 were foreign. Even the family broking firm of Sir Nicholas Goodison, chairman of the Stock Exchange during Big Bang, and prominent in good works like the English National Opera and the National Art Collection Fund, had become a subdivision of the French bank Paribas. Many of the foreign operators in London spend only a fraction of their time dealing with British business, and they recruit their top staff indifferently from London, New York or Frankfurt.

Highly paid, aggressively capitalist and ruthless, they are technicians. The promises are immediate, the rewards handsome, the prospects uncertain. The organizations for which they work not only have their headquarters abroad, they are run by men sent from head office who often resent their time in London as years spent away from the strategic centre. Japanese companies in London talk of *dochakuka*, blending into the background. But their sheer size dwarfs the old City stalwarts. When the Japanese firm, Nomura, was admitted to the London Stock Exchange in 1986, it had twelve thousand employees worldwide and was generating profits of $2 billion. The following year it became the biggest Eurobond issuing house in the world.

The Bank of England claims the governor's influence is undiminished. 'The Americans prefer our informality to the legislative controls at home, and the Japanese really don't want to displease us,' an official told me. One wonders whether he will be so sanguine in ten years' time.

Thirty years ago, a visitor to the City found that

> At and near the top of office after office are men who went to the same ten or twelve schools. Anyone without their background is immediately aware how similar they seem — no doubt he exaggerates the similarity, but the long, easy vowels and the commanding style of speech do provide a uniform stamp. There's also the manner: a little casual, a little amateurish, never taking things too seriously: the English sense of detachment, of considering it bad form (another phrase still heard in the City) to get earnest and worked up about a matter of principle.[4]

While the most powerful institutions in the City may have changed their style and be run by stateless men at home in a dozen time-zones, the bosses of the British institutions are pretty similar. They make much of the fact that the City is open to all talents, but the division between officers and men in British firms persists. 'It's all right having barrow boys doing the dealing – they're good at it, it's what they understand,' one senior banker told me (like most of the senior figures I met, he would only speak off the record). 'But higher up, you've got to have people who are at ease in industrialists' drawing rooms.' Taking a handful of merchant banks at random from near the start of the alphabet, the bosses of Barclays De Zoete Wedd, Barings, Brown Shipley, Robert Fleming, and Hambros are all Etonians.

Scanning the directors of a few other City firms confirms the continuing prominence of Eton. Of the thirty-five members of the board of Barclays – the poshest of the clearing banks – in 1989, eleven were Etonians. Merchant banks like Rothschilds have a broader cross-section on their boards, but six of the sixteen directors of Hambros had been educated at Eton, and nine of the twenty-five at Kleinwort Benson.

They are men who went into the City around the time the Bank of England was advertising for recruits with the information that

> all-round ability, including personality, power of leadership, and keenness for games is given considerable weight in choosing candidates. A boy who, though not brilliant, is a good all-round type with character and a sense of responsibility is likely to be an acceptable candidate.[5]

It sounds laughable in an age of technocrats. But the 'good all-round types' are now in the boardrooms. The world they joined was a civilized, dozy sort of place where the princes of the City, with names like Brandt, Hambro, and Kleinwort still ran the firms their forefathers founded, where anyone who was anyone knew anyone else who was anyone, and there was time for a decent lunch. It is extraordinary that they have somehow managed to preserve the style, as if the job is just a way of filling in between shooting weekends.

Apart from places like the Baltic Exchange, where the chartering of ships and cargoes is still done in unhurried coffee-house style, most of the firms in the City have retreated to their own corporate headquarters. Places like the Stock Exchange used to serve much the same function as the agora in ancient Athens, a meeting place in which news would be swapped and common wisdom arrived at. But the hexagonal hutches on the floor have been deserted ever since Big Bang introduced direct dealing between member companies, so the face-to-face contact is gone. 'You didn't tend to cheat a man if you were going to be facing him every day,' says one retired stockbroker. A sense of community has gone.

'It's more a matter of where you've got to than where you've come from,' was the neat answer when I asked the chairman of one of the clearing banks how important schools were now. But inevitably, there was one exception. When I raised the matter after lunch with a merchant banker he replied straight away that, 'It doesn't make the blindest bit of difference where you went to school these days.' Then he paused for a moment and added, 'unless it was Eton. Etonians just seem to *know* everybody.'

Thirty years ago, the question 'what is the City Establishment' could have been answered simply and swiftly by a quick look at the members of the Accepting Houses Committee, the organization representing the most important merchant banks. Membership of the Committee was by invitation to named individuals speaking for, and committing, their company, and the list was dominated by the eponymous heads of family-run banks, like Walter Brandt (William Brandt's Sons), J.H. Hambro (Hambros), and Ernest Kleinwort (Kleinwort, Sons). In June 1960, the seventeen members included nine representatives of titled families. Six of the seventeen went to Eton. Two had close connections with the Foreign Office. It began, in 1914, with a Rothschild in the chair, and it went out, in 1988-9, in the same way.

By January 1990 the Accepting Houses Committee had been wound up and the number of merchant banks in its successor organization, the British Merchant Banking and Securities Houses Association ('Bimbo' for short) had risen to sixty-five, of which large numbers were foreign. The City had become so internationalized that Stanislas Yassukovich was now near the heart of the Establishment, although his organization was neither British nor an old-fashioned merchant bank.

Size was never the determining factor for membership of the old Accepting Houses Committee, and the clearing banks were never members. But as the old distinction between banking and the securities business has become blurred, the privileged position of the British merchant banks has disappeared. A quick look at the top twenty biggest banks in the City (excluding those which are subsidiaries of the clearing banks) shows how completely the family network has been elbowed aside. The three largest of them – Abbey National, Standard Chartered and TSB – did not feature at all in the old Accepting Houses Committee list. Several banks in the bottom half of the top twenty were foreign, including the Scandinavian Bank Group, the Saudi International Bank and the Banque Nationale de Paris. Only seven on the list are recognizable survivors of the old Accepting Houses,[6] pre-eminent among them Warburgs, the fourth largest bank in the group.

The rise of Warburgs has been *the* success story of the postwar City, and evidence of the dramatic change in domestic British banking. Founded in 1946 by Siegmund Warburg, a refugee from Nazi Germany, it has grown from an outfit once said to have been staffed by 'Jewish Wykehamist accountants' to the point where it is the most successful British merchant bank and its chairman, Sir David Scholey, is widely canvassed as a future Governor of the Bank of England.

When he started, Siegmund Warburg was despised by the old City establishment. They denied him co-operation, they advised their friends to have nothing to do with him, and generally conspired to make life impossible. Ironically, given how many of the existing banks had been founded by immigrants, he was despised because he was a German Jew. He refused to play by the rules, and in a rare interview recalled how they talked behind his back:

> 'Do you know this fellow Siegmund Warburg? He starts in the office at eight o'clock in the morning.' That was considered contemptible. Most of them came to the office at ten o'clock in the morning. I was awful. They looked down on me with the most awful snobbism.[7]

The turning point came with the Great Aluminium War of 1959, still talked about in the City, even by people who must have been in short trousers at the time. The details of the contested takeover battle for British Aluminium are unimportant. But the failure of the great City firms, including Hambros, Lazards and Morgan Grenfell, to protect the company from American takeover – 'saving British Aluminium for civilization' one of them called it – marked the 'beginning of the end of the old City ways', according to Lord Cairns, vice-chairman of Warburg's. 'Nothing quite like that could be done again after thirty years of almost continuous deregulation.'[8]

Warburg's had proved not only that hostile takeovers could succeed, but that City wisdom could be defied. Today, it is the most enterprising of the British merchant banks and indistinguishable from many of them in style. In the face of the Big Bang they pulled off an audacious merger with the jobbers Ackroyd and Smithers, the brokers Rowe and Pitman and the government broker Mullens.

Of the old elite, only a few banks survive in a recognizable form, protected by family shareholdings. Some, which ducked out of many of the opportunities of Big Bang and stuck to niches in the market, have made it on their own terms. No-one would give Baring's the title of 'the Sixth Great Power' (after Britain, France, Austria, Russia, and Prussia) which they won in 1818, but they have developed profitable new markets in the Pacific, and Sir John Baring remains one of the City's Great and Good, sitting on the Court of the Bank of England. In Kleinworts, the family stake is now down to twenty-five per cent. Hill Samuel quickly found itself out of its depth, grasped at the Union Bank of Switzerland, sacked the two bosses of its corporate finance department on discovering that the entire division was negotiating to move en masse to a competitor, and was finally swallowed up by the Trustee Savings Bank. At Guinness Mahon, the entire senior management team walked out and Guinness Peat Group were taken over by the New Zealand investment company, Equiticorp. Morgan Grenfell was swallowed up by Deutsche Bank in 1989. Samuel Montagu is owned by Midland Bank. The list goes on.

Both Rothschilds and Hambros were split by family feuds and have taken time to recover. In 1988 Rothschilds appointed an American, Fred Vinton ('the closest thing America will ever produce to a gent', in the characteristically condescending judgement of another of Rothschild's veterans[9]) as second-in-command. Hambros, still chaired by Charles Hambro, the tall, bald descendant of the Copenhagen banker who opened his London Office 150 years ago, can scarcely be called a bank at all any longer, half its profits coming from estate agency and insurance. It is not many years since he had to check whether Nomura was creditworthy. 'Sometimes I wonder whether we have been so clever after all,'[10] he remarked with some understatement towards the end of the eighties.

The smugness of the old City served neither the banks nor the country well. An air of effortless superiority persists among the survivors of the old inner circle. They like to compare themselves to the 1855 classification of claret, and think that the *crus bourgeois* – the foreign newcomers – will never overcome their sheer misfortune in being foreign.

In general, though, the British merchant banks are tiddlers in an international shark pool. In the early eighties there was not one which was even half as big as the fourth largest American investment bank. The lazy, comfortable years of the fifties and sixties had been too kind to them, and they failed to seize opportunities for expansion abroad. By comparison with an American bank like Morgan Stanley or a Japanese like Daiwa, they were short of money, short of markets and short of decent management.

Because so much of the City was run by people who had been doing business together for years, the newcomers from abroad had to be innovative to compete. The Americans and the Japanese have turned out to have imaginative ideas about the use of capital in highly profitable areas of merchant banking like the equity and corporate advisory business. 'You know, Goldman Sachs make a lot of noise,' one old British banker said comfortably after lunch, 'but they haven't broken through.' The British banks tend to have a better nose for domestic business, have better contacts and a keener awareness of nuances. They make a point of dealing with broking firms like Cazenove, almost the last remaining independent broker, because 'it's a question of trust. We speak the same language, use the same system, the same lawyers, the same style.'

But the old City establishment could not keep Siegmund Warburg down, and the rump of the Accepting Houses Committee will not be able to hold off the foreigners for ever. As markets become more international, clients will demand international firms. For the moment, the big Japanese and American banks have bigger fish to fry as they square up for the coming battle for domination of each other's markets, but if and when they turn their attention to London, the British banks will regret their insularity.

The strength of the British banks was their connections with the rest of the ruling élite. Now in a world in which the rules of a theoretical meritocracy apply, they have learned the American business of 'networking'. The very thought would have appalled their predecessors thirty or so years ago. Then, anyone running a merchant bank would have tended to know his counterparts in Whitehall and Westminster anyway. 'It's my *job* to know the major players in Whitehall,' the chairman of one of the British merchant banks told me when I asked him about the importance of social events. We were on the top floor of one of the startling new buildings erected in the City during the last ten years. He is a comfortable, well-suited figure, crested signet ring matching crested cufflinks.

His diary for the week lists three lunchtime receptions and four evening drinks parties or dinners, all of which he will attend. On those days when he has no formal outside engagements, he is likely to be entertaining in one of the several dining rooms designed into the building for that specific purpose. Watching a reception attended by these men can be like observing a rapidly changing pattern of molecules on a microscope slide. The chairman will work his way fluidly around, two minutes with another merchant banker here, three minutes with a Bank of England director there, five minutes with a government minister. In an hour he has touched base with anyone worth cultivating and is away in his Jaguar.

Those banks which worry about their contacts can get around the problem by buying the services of retired civil servants or ministers. Sir Douglas Wass, retired from his position as head of the Treasury and joint head of the civil service in 1983, was hired by Equity and Law insurance the following year, and by Nomura two years later. Sir Peter Carey left his post as head of the Department of Industry in 1983 and became a director, and later chairman, of Morgan Grenfell. Sir Michael Palliser went from being head of the diplomatic service to become a director of Samuel Montagu and later deputy chairman of Midland Bank. Japanese civil servants call this process of recruitment to lucrative private sector posts on retirement 'going to heaven'. One can see why.

But the greatest concentration of such figures, a positive coven of former mandarins, is at N.M. Rothschild. The bank has enjoyed close relations with government since Nathan Mayer financed much of Wellington's Peninsular Campaign. In the courtyard outside his descendant's ugly 1960s offices, a couple of hundred yards from the Bank of England, half-a-dozen chauffeurs stand and talk, occasionally dragging a duster over limousines whose engines are permanently warm for a quick run out to Whitehall or St James's for lunch.

Secreted away in offices inside the building are Lord (Robert) Armstrong, the last cabinet secretary and head of the civil service, in another room is Sir Frank Cooper, the sprightly former permanent secretary at the Ministry of Defence, in a third is Sir Claus Moser, one-time head of the government statistical service and subsequently warden of Wadham College, Oxford. The bank has a prosaic explanation of their role. 'Evelyn [Evelyn de Rothschild, the bank's chairman] likes to have a few non-executive people around he can talk to,' a director told me. The former mandarins themselves like to think they have been recruited for their management skills, an explanation which does not impress many of the staff, one of whom gave a more jaundiced view:

> They're here as business-getters, or as insurance. It's a few phone calls, a few warnings, and it impresses a few customers. It's usually a mistake: they're useful for six months or a year, while their contemporaries are still in place in Whitehall or industry, then they have little or no value. And they hang on, annoying everybody, before they vanish.

But Rothschild's have a sensitive political nose. When slavery was abolished, it was a Rothschild who raised the £20 million to compensate British slave-owners. When Disraeli wanted to buy control of the Suez Canal in 1875 they produced £4 million. In the 1980s they discovered privatization, experience which enabled them to advise the governments of Spain, Singapore, Chile, Malaysia and Jamaica on the same subject. Doubtless by pure coincidence, the bank has a well-developed network of contacts in the Conservative party, including the head of the international privatization division, Oliver Letwin, who previously served in the Downing Street Policy Unit. In the 1979 cabinet Lord Soames was a director of the bank. Norman Lamont, Chief Secretary to the Treasury in the 1987 Thatcher government, worked for Rothschild's for eleven years. John Redwood had also been employed by Rothschild's before going into parliament and becoming a minister. John Whittingale, appointed Mrs Thatcher's Political Secretary in 1987 at twenty-eight ('Meet Maggie's New Toyboy', invited the *News of the World*), is another Rothschild man. The bank's Vice-Chairman, Michael Richardson, is a longstanding personal friend of Margaret Thatcher (both, among other things, had sons at Harrow), sufficiently well-attuned politically to have been the best informed person in the City at the time of the nationalization of the steel industry in the 1960s, and chosen to underwrite the flotation of the same industry when it was prepared for privatization twenty years later. That's dexterity.

The clubs which sustained the old City Establishment, like the Accepting Houses Committee, were little more than cartels. But they had one great advantage. If you wanted to remain a member, you obeyed the rules. The shame of the City now is that it seems unsure how to maintain standards without the club. A sort of ethical Darwinism has taken hold.

The pressures were understandable. Faced with deregulation, small firms were swallowed up by bigger ones, stockbrokers by merchant

banks, merchant banks by clearing banks, blurring lines of command
and destroying previous feelings of loyalty. Where once new employees
joined a firm and expected to stay there for life, now not only can they
leave and start again elsewhere, active poaching and disloyalty is an
accepted fact of life. Where once the stiffer City firms would automatically reject any ambitious young applicant if he was also looking
for jobs elsewhere (which may go some way to explaining why they
ended up with such a lot of duds), now they compete aggressively for
the best talent available.

And the pressures from the customers have grown too. Previously
clients would place their business with a broker or merchant banker
and stay with them for life. Now they are constantly on the lookout for
the best deal. This switch from 'relationship banking' to 'transaction
banking' means the pressure is constantly on to find new business.

In the early eighties, one of the major clearing banks privately
admitted that they suffered no less than twenty thousand cases of
fraud every year. Only a small proportion were crimes committed
within the City itself, and most institutions are reluctant to concede
the scale of the problem. But assuming this example to be not
unusual, the total amount of crime in British financial services runs to
extraordinary levels. In the early eighties, the Bank of England even
had evidence that international fraudsters were moving to London
precisely because it was so easy to commit crime there. Most cases
were neither investigated nor prosecuted against. Of those that showed
any prospect of coming to court, disturbing numbers ran into the
sands.

As usual, a member of the Great and Good, Lord Roskill, the
Appeal Lord, was commissioned to discover what could be done. He
concluded in 1985 that

> the public no longer believes that the legal system in England and Wales is
> capable of bringing the perpetrators of serious frauds expeditiously and
> effectively to book. The overwhelming weight of the evidence laid before
> us suggests that the public is right ... While petty frauds, clumsily
> committed, are likely to be detected and punished, it is all too likely that
> the largest and most cleverly executed crimes escape unpunished.[11]

The Roskill Committee conducted their investigations *before* Big
Bang. The solution proposed by government was a raft of different
regulatory bodies with unidentifiable acronyms, like Lautro, Imro,
Fimbra and TSA. It was a well-intentioned enough plan, which at
least recognized the potential for corruption which deregulation would

produce. But the new institutions created were far bigger than the specialist companies they swallowed up, and therefore harder to regulate. And once a set of rules was in place, they tended to be honoured in the letter rather than in the spirit.

The new rules were unpopular from the start. The ill-fated Sir Kenneth Berrill was appointed chairman of the new supreme regulatory body, the Securities and Investment Board, in 1985. In a remarkably short space of time he had made himself the most unpopular man in the Square Mile. Berrill was an abrasive figure, clever but impatient, whose experience in academia and Whitehall rendered him, in City opinion, no more than a rampant bureaucrat. He had no first-hand experience of the City until he was past sixty, and soon acquired the nickname 'Berrill the Peril'. The SIB's task was to implement the safeguards outlined in the Financial Services Act, a hideously complicated piece of legislation designed to protect the investor in a deregulated City. Time was short, too: the whole thing was to come into force within two years.

The City detested the Act. 'We couldn't believe "our" government was doing this to us,' one banker recalls thinking, and they certainly didn't take kindly to being lectured on their duties by an academic civil servant. 'The foreign firms weren't so difficult,' Sir Kenneth recalls, 'they were used to regulation. The problem came with the British companies, and particularly the Clearing Banks.'[12]

Berrill was under pressure to produce results fast. But it was an impossible task. The Act was supposed to protect the individual investor, when the vast bulk of business in the City was professional, wholesale trade which would come under the same suffocating rules. And the Department of Trade and Industry were leaning on him to be even stricter than he was planning. When the SIB submitted a draft rule book to the DTI it came back with thirty added pages of extra rules.

The decisive issue came with Sir Kenneth's proposals for getting the big British retail banks to clean up the way they sold services like life assurance or unit trusts. Berrill told the banks that he was going to introduce a principle known as polarity, by which they would have to make clear whether they were offering genuinely independent advice or acting as a salesman for their own product.

The idea went down like a lead balloon. As the banks' directors grumbled away at their lunches and dinners, a common view was formed: Berrill had to go. The Governor of the Bank of England,

Robin Leigh-Pemberton, had previously been chairman of the
National Westminster Bank, and they thought him a natural ally.
Both sides were squaring up for a trial of strength, and the *Financial
Times* was in no doubt about its importance. 'The authority and
morale of the SIB will be weakened if the Government and the Bank
of England fail to renew Sir Kenneth's appointment,' it said in an
editorial.[13]

But the City Establishment was to have its way. A reorganization
among civil servants at the Department of Trade and Industry
removed some of Berrill's allies and a cabinet reshuffle brought in a
new Trade Secretary, Lord Young, who had begun his career as a
City solicitor, and had remained sympathetic to the place ever since.
Within weeks, curiously authoritative articles began to appear in the
newspapers averring as fact that Berrill would soon be leaving the
SIB. He was not totally surprised when at one of their periodic
meetings Lord Young told him that, reluctantly, the government felt
it was time for change.

The new chairman of the SIB, David Walker ('Walker the Talker'
they dubbed him), was the City's choice. An athletic former civil
servant who had served as executive director at the Bank of England,
he was widely credited with being the brains behind Big Bang. He
still hopes, with some reason, to see his intense ambition rewarded by
being made governor of the Bank in due course. The Walker appointment was more congenial, but by the time it was made, there was little
possibility of convincing the outside world that self-regulation could
be relied upon, in the light of what had been revealed at Lloyd's of
London.

In insurance, like banking, trust is everything. But Lloyd's had
started going rotten from within in the seventies as it desperately
sought business to make use of the rapidly growing number of 'names'
looking for a home for their money. When Syndicate 762, which
included people considered the very picture of probity like the Queen
Mother's equerry, or the secretary to Princess Margaret, got stung by
a group of American fraudsters for £40 million, sixty-three of them
refused to pay up and sued the committee of Lloyd's for neglect in
failing to spot the fraud. The incident demonstrated vividly how
fragile the old conventions were, once business grows to the point
where people no longer know each other. Other scandals followed, in
which it became clear that corruption was not confined to dubious
foreigners but had permeated even apparently honourable under-

writers, including those, like Peter Cameron Webb, considered the cleverest in the market. It was not merely that gentlemanly codes of conduct were inadequate to control non-gentlemen, but that the gentlemen themselves could no longer be trusted.

The Lloyd's affair had shown how the City's much-loved system of self-regulation was no longer up to the job. Yet the deficiencies of the new system were also glaring. Lord Shawcross has watched the change at first-hand:

> Under the old system, there were rules, unwritten rules, that people adhered to. There used to be an axiom that 'my word is my bond'. No-one operates on that principle today. And in the old days, they didn't rush off constantly to the lawyers to find ways of getting around the law or the rules. Now, of course, that's the first thing they do.[14]

One incident after another has demonstrated the Square Mile's capacity for ineptitude or corruption in the wake of the collapse of the old City order. A Department of Trade investigation into the takeover of the House of Fraser group and its flagship, Harrods, by the Egyptian Al Fayed brothers concluded that they had lied repeatedly about their background and their resources. Their claims to a vast business empire had been given credibility when repeated by their bankers, Kleinwort Benson. The firm had once been considered the picture of City rectitude and yet had failed to discover that the two potentates were in fact the sons of an Alexandria schoolteacher. Kleinworts maintained afterwards they had been duped. 'The City works upon trust,' a banker limply explained.

The Blue Arrow scandal, in which County Natwest, the merchant banking subsidiary of the big clearing bank, organized a share issue for the Blue Arrow employment agency and then kept the price high by illicitly holding many of the shares itself, was firmly pinned on a middle-ranking member of staff. But it still forced the resignation of the bank's chairman, Lord Boardman.

With the Guinness affair, scandal touched the heart of the City. Those charged in connection with an alleged illicit share-buying operation, designed to keep up the price of Guinness shares during their takeover bid for the Distillers company, even included a partner of Cazenove's, the most prestigious stockbroking firm in the Square Mile.

As the world of the clubs gave way to a new competitive jungle, firms offered ever greater inducements to young people to work for them. Salaries once reserved for men and women who had worked for fifteen years were being thrown at fresh-faced young things almost straight from university. For a while, it was a world lousy with Porsche-dealers and champagne bars. Dealers, paid by results, could earn absurd sums. The pressures, and the temptations, were greater than ever before.

The elderly Lord Benson, who spent nearly two decades specializing in City fraud, was troubled by the temptations of the new City.

> The present outlook puts tremendous importance upon short-term results. Annual salaries and bonuses are so often based upon short-term results. People have to perform against indicators. The result is that people are under enormous pressure to show results which are both better than indicators and better than last year. So the pressure is on to cut corners. And once one does it, they all do it.[15]

There was another factor, too. In the days before and after Big Bang young people had meteoric rises, reaching positions of power and influence in a fraction of the time their fathers would have taken. In a bull market, the average age of the decision-makers was bound to fall. Accustomed to the champagne days, they did not have the experience to cope when times got harder.

But even people who had been in the City for decades were unsure about where the limits lay under the new conventions. 'Insider dealing', now considered an offence, had been good practice in many broking firms for years. 'If you hear of anything good, put me into it,' investors would say, and expect it to be acted upon. Surprising numbers of even quite senior figures are reluctant to condemn some of the recent scandals. One almost senses a feeling of 'there but for the grace of God go I' from some of them. The new competitive spirit, the fear that if they don't try every trick in the book on behalf of their client, the client may sue, has led to a climate in which they are inclined to shrug their shoulders, mutter into their whiskies, and resolve to make sure they follow the letter of the law, regardless of its spirit.

The financial success of the City of London was one of the great growth stories of the eighties. In the process, being 'something in the City' is supposed no longer to be a trade for a gentleman. Certainly, the style and scale of City activity have altered dramatically, more than any other part of British life. The cultivated image of the Square Mile is of a place that never sleeps, as deals are closed with Hong Kong or Tokyo or Sydney.

The complaint of British industry for decades, that the City is obsessed by short-term results and cares little for the problems of real people making real things, remains as true today as ever. It is a one-sided representation of the misunderstanding, but it reflects the way in which business in the City becomes increasingly divorced from the real economy of Britain.

The City may come to rue its introverted preoccupations one day. A certain resignation persists in the Square Mile, when much of the story of the last thirty years is the tale of one missed opportunity after another. The British position as the financial centre for Europe will be lucky to survive the continual weakening of the British economy against that of West Germany, and the gap is narrowing constantly. Trade, and financial services, follow the flag.

In the heyday of the great merchant banks in the nineteenth century, the credit-worthiness of the great British financial institutions was underpinned by the power of the British Empire and British industry. Now, the importance of London to the world financial system depends upon a residual body of expertise and its position on the Greenwich Meridian, a time-zone it shares with Timbuktu. It is not the most awe-inspiring of manifestoes.

CHAPTER TWELVE

The Arts Tsars

'Of what use is culture to a labourer?'

– EMANUEL SHINWELL, 1923

SOON AFTER HE had been appointed Minister for the Arts, Paul Channon was at the Royal Opera House, Covent Garden. Of all the British institutions for the performing arts, Covent Garden is the most blue-blooded, and its opening nights bring together some of the most influential people in the land. Channon, tall, smooth, the son of Sir Henry 'Chips' Channon, member of the Guinness dynasty, product of Eton and Christ Church, Oxford, was at home. As drinks were produced by the Opera House management, he fell into conversation with Roy Shaw. Shaw had been secretary-general of the Arts Council since the seventies, and the two men knew each other professionally. Social relations were another matter. Roy Shaw was the son of a Sheffield steelworker and had won a place first at the local grammar school and then at Manchester University in the teeth of intense competition.

Channon explained that he would not be able to stay long, as he and his wife had to fly to Venice for a few days. Shaw politely murmured 'how nice', and inquired where they would be staying.

'The Gritti Palace,' said Channon, naming the palazzo on the Grand Canal generally reckoned one of the finest hotels in Europe. Shaw, who had been brought up in a terrace house where the closest thing to opera was the music-hall, drew breath and muttered something about how comfortable their stay should be.

'Yes,' said Mrs Channon. 'It's so nice staying there *now that one doesn't own it.*'

Few remarks could capture more perfectly the cavernous gulf between the practitioners of the arts and their patrons. Paul Channon's successor as Arts Minister, Lord 'Grey' Gowrie, another Etonian, resigned his post in 1985, on the grounds that it was impossible to live in London on a ministerial salary of £33,000 a year. It seems fair to

ask how easily someone in this sort of world could empathize with
artists, actors or musicians rubbing along on the occasional engagement
and the odd day's teaching.

But patronage of the arts was a traditional responsibility of the
aristocracy, and in the Welfare State, the Great and Good took on
their mantle.

The radical playwright Edward Bond once described culture as the
figleaf the ruling class puts on when it looks at itself in the mirror, the
necessary justification for exercising authority over the 'uncultured
mob'. In postwar Britain, this has a perverse consequence: 'The
English right-wing Establishment have put money into our most
successful cultural institution – the theatre – while its best dramatists
have passionately experimented in the creation of socialist art.' Is this,
Bond wondered, 'the first time a capitalist government has felt forced
to make an investment on which it knows it can't get a return?'[1]

British artistic life has always benefited from patronage in some
form or other, whether monarchical, aristocratic, ecclesiastical or commercial. A belief in the elevating power of culture was an item of faith
among the more enlightened parts of the aristocracy, which is perhaps
why the post of arts minister or chairman of the Arts Council retains a
social grandeur totally lacking from being minister of agriculture or
boss of the Sports Council. By 1980 twelve men and one woman had
held these two top arts posts; eight of them had been to school at
either Eton or Winchester.[2] But it is the taxpayer who provides the
subsidies which keep the arts alive in Britain. Bond's observation
misses the point about the commercial importance of British drama,
music and the rest, but it neatly sums up the schizophrenic nature of
the arts world, an extraordinary beast with two heads, which can
sometimes be heard whining or barking at one another, to the bewilderment of passers-by.

The Arts Council, the fairy godmother to succeeding generations of
would-be artists, was founded in 1945 out of the same desire to do good
by statute that underpinned nationalization, the National Health
Service and the Welfare State. The new Medicis on the Council were
a cut above most of the Great and Good. The composer, Ralph
Vaughan Williams, the art historian Sir Kenneth Clark, and the academic Sir Ifor Evans were joined on the 1946 Arts Council by eleven
others – writers, public servants and musicians. Not one of them was
a businessman. Sir Ernest Pooley, a classic Great and Good figure

who took over the Arts Council on the death in harness of its chairman, Lord Keynes, at the Treasury's insistence, was 'a man of bottom'. Clark noted that, 'having no interest in the arts, he could be relied upon not to press their claims too strongly'.[3] The Council donned the mantle of the aristocratic patrons easily, and appointment to it became a pinnacle of Quangoland. Suggestions – even from the Duke of Edinburgh – that it might be better as an elected body have never been taken seriously because no-one can imagine a campaign waged along the lines of 'Vote for Bloggs, and get a fair deal for concrete poetry'.

The first and best-loved of the postwar arts ministers, Jennie Lee, widow of the Labour party hero, Nye Bevan, personified the liberal enthusiasm of the new dispensation. Her attitude of profound respect, without any great specialist knowledge, was widespread both in the Labour party and among more liberal Conservatives. The arts were 'a good thing' in themselves, and judgements about whether an exhibition of Caravaggio deserved support at the expense of the Royal Ballet could be safely delegated to the Great and Good on the Arts Council. In practice, this usually meant the genial, mountainous presence of Lord Goodman.

A solicitor by training, Arnold Goodman had always had a rather more than amateur interest in the arts – he was passionate about the theatre and a modest collector of late-impressionist art. He embodied the good intent of the Arts Council and dominated the world of arts officialdom for most of the sixties and seventies.

He was an unrivalled fundraiser for deserving artistic causes. On one occasion, Lord Harewood, grandson of King George V and managing director of the English National Opera, telephoned Lord Goodman during one of their periodic cash crises. Over lunch, Lord Harewood – by his own admission 'absolutely hopeless' at fundraising – listened as Goodman dictated a letter.

'An interesting cause has come to my attention, which I believe it might be in your interest to support', he said, concluding the letter with warm personal good wishes. To Harewood's amazement, he then instructed his secretary to type up two separate copies of the letter, and to send them to two titled businessmen.

'But what happens if they both agree to support us?' Harewood asked, suddenly confronted with the possibility of sponsorship beyond the dreams of avarice.

'You will note', said Goodman, raising his enormous eyebrows, 'that I have not named the deserving institution.'

In the study of Lord Goodman's central London flat, a bust by Sir Anthony Caro matches another huge bronze behind the door. Each accentuates the distinctive characteristics, the heavy jowls, the beak-like nose, the eyebrows like an unkempt hedgerow. It is one of the most famously and easily cartooned faces in the gallery of the Great and Good. A watercolour by David Piper hangs on one wall, a sketch by Henry Moore on another. Three carriage clocks have stopped, each at a different time. The bookcases are packed with works on socialism, judaism and poetry. Three dejected houseplants are expiring through lack of light.

The Arts Council was yet another of those bodies which had been created to keep politics at arm's length and Goodman represents the liberal tradition of public funding for the arts. On one occasion he was summoned to see Viscount Eccles, arts minister in the 1970 Conservative Government. 'Ted [Heath] and I don't like all these dirty plays you're putting on,' said Eccles (among productions to benefit from public money were *Blow Job* and *Play for Rubber Go-Go Girls*). 'Public opinion demands you do something about it.' Whereupon Goodman answered, apparently innocently, 'But I thought you were elected to do something about food prices,' and changed the subject.

Once Whitehall had become the major patron of the arts, Bohemia became a province of the Welfare State. The notion depended upon a caucus of artists living at odds with the rest of the community. Its essence was unconventionality, but when the main patrons of the arts were the taxpayers and their agents – agreeable fellows like Arnold Goodman – the avant-garde expired. In its place was an attenuated Romanticism, a muddled social-democrat-to-libertarian-socialist view of the world. Michael Frayn had spotted the emergence of the tribe early on: the radical middle classes – 'the do-gooders; the readers of the *New Statesman*, the *Guardian* and the *Observer*; the signers of petitions; the backbone of the BBC. In short, the herbivores or ruminants.'[4]

'We're all children of the postwar generation,' is how Richard Eyre, artistic director of the National Theatre puts it. 'We're all children of the New Jerusalem. And we're all graduates of the disaffected seventies.'[5]

To the outsider, many of their beliefs have more of a 1960s air to them. They see the arts not as celebration but as dissent, challenge and provocation. They dislike the dominance of white, male, middle-class Londoners (although most of them fall into this category themselves), and want to see the arts as more pluralistic, culturally diverse and 'community-based'. They favour things like neighbourhood radio, theatre-in-education, 'outreach theatre' and community library initiatives. A liberal mandarin class has developed among them, as administration of the arts became a career in itself, and they are to be found directing regional arts associations, working as consultants, running theatre groups, an apparently inexhaustible pool of people sufficiently large to ensure that whatever the changes of government policy, the ideology survives.

Although they clearly belong to a social and political network (a remarkable number of the more talented theatre directors, for example, are Cambridge graduates), these figures are capable of towering rhetoric on the subject of the British class system. The subsidized theatre is generally characterized in the conservative press as riddled with subversives hell-bent on undermining civilization as we know it. But it almost seems to have become institutionalized itself. The shadow of Brecht, Osborne and Wesker is a long one, and it is hard to resist the sneaking suspicion that a sort of rebellious orthodoxy was arrived at in the late sixties and has remained unmolested since. They bite the hand that feeds them, certainly. But never hard enough for it to stop doing so.

In this process, much of the zest has gone from the subsidized theatre. While the commercial theatres of the West End were working their way through every permutation of musical known to man, it was the National Theatre, the Royal Shakespeare Company and smaller operations like the Royal Court and Joint Stock which provided the greatest challenge to actors and authors, the greatest opportunities for directors and designers. It was exciting for audiences to see common beliefs and assumptions challenged on stage. But after a while, the experience is somehow neutralized by repetition and environment, and when the audience re-emerge into the foyer of the National Theatre, a string quartet reassures them that everything is really all right.

The playwrights and directors, increasingly middle-aged, settled in comfortable homes in Holland Park, still affect contempt for the values of a society in more-or-less irreversible decline. David Hare, a scholarship boy at Lancing College before going to Cambridge, has consistently produced some of the most exciting drama to have emerged in the English-speaking world, most of it performed in the publicly subsidized theatre companies. His first theatrical venture, the Portable Theatre Company, a travelling ensemble, was, by Hare's own admission, an 'angry, nasty group of people who wanted to go around the country and tell people that it was in terminal decline.'[6]

The Arts Council, studiously stand-offish, gave Hare and his friends the wherewithal to lay into the way of life they despised. Indeed, at times it looked as though in the hands of lesser talents than Hare, the struggle had acquired its own pointless *raison d'être*, provocative because that was the artists' skill, yet endlessly repeating the same themes. The critic Bryan Appleyard observed in the early 1980s:

> Postwar welfare art felt that its sole function was to fight fights, make points and shout the odds. Indeed, the very existence of the Arts Council effectively endorsed the whole package from the beginning. Operating at arm's length means that you respond to what the artists do rather than make suggestions or direct creativity, so it was cash on the nail for the social pugilists.[7]

Theirs was the literature of betrayal and disappointment. Hare recalled:

> We were all extremely angry with Harold Wilson and his government. We felt that with him socialism had failed definitively. None of us were naïve enough to believe that there was going to be a revolution in England in the late sixties. But we did think that the country was on the verge of nervous breakdown, that its institutions were bankrupt and that plainly none of us would dream of spending our lives in them. We were waiting for civil violence.[8]

This was doubtless an easy enough belief for a fresh-faced twenty-year-old student to sustain, but it looks decidedly threadbare in a middle-aged father who proudly lists his subversive achievements over two and a half inches in *Who's Who*. As for not spending their lives in institutions, not only has the revolution not occurred, he and his friends have waited for it sitting in the plush comfort of the National Theatre auditorium.

Taxed with the criticism that there is a certain ambiguity in using the publicly subsidized theatre to attack the state, Hare has an answer prepared. He does not say – as he could with justice – that his writing is sufficiently distinguished to shout for a prominent performance, nor that much of the commercial theatre is in the hands of play-safe entrepreneurs who don't want to startle the coach-parties. Instead he argues that it is

> one of the healthier democratic traditions in this country that the National Theatre is a stage from which you can attack the government ... There aren't many countries in the world where you are free to do that, so for goodness' sake let's go on using that freedom.[9]

Much of which sounds as if it could equally well have come from an editorial in one of the conservative newspapers the literary left so despise.

Richard Eyre, a self-proclaimed socialist and closet republican, was closely associated with the work of playwrights like David Hare and Trevor Griffiths. His film attacking the values of Thatcher's Britain, *The Ploughman's Lunch*, more than made up in contempt what it occasionally lacked in finesse. In 1988 he found himself translated to become artistic director of the National, one of the first of his generation (he was born in 1943) to be trusted with a great national institution. He told me:

> It feels like an essential rite of passage, that you do eventually join the Establishment. You just long not to be treated as trivial and marginal and silly. My abiding motto is that Biff cartoon where an ageing hippy is looking out and saying 'We are the people we warned ourselves against.'[10]

Sir Claus Moser, the brilliant mathematician who had risen to become head of the Government Statistical Service in the late sixties, knew that he had finally arrived when, in 1974, he became Chairman of the Royal Opera House, Covent Garden:

> Until I became Chairman of the Royal Opera House, by which time I was fifty-two, I had never, but never, met anybody royal: now I was entertaining them month after month. Suddenly this new world had opened itself to me. When I was a frequent visitor to Covent Garden, or even on the board, some people would scarcely speak to me. Yet literally the day after my appointment as Chairman was announced, a very distinguished woman whom I would prefer not to name, who had previously cut me dead, rang up, to invite my wife and me to spend the weekend with them in Scotland. It continued like that for all the years I was chairman. From that moment onwards I saw a totally new layer of British life. If I had to choose, *that* is the British Establishment. It's a common class, a common schooling, a common frame of mind.[11]

No other cultural institution in Britain enjoys the status of the Royal Opera House. Its position near the centre of the network of professional, social and political connections in Britain makes it respected even by those who have little instinctive feel for theatre, painting or other forms of music. Nowhere do the potential contradictions of public subsidy and private pleasure show more starkly.

The astronomical fees commanded by international stars, the huge expense of maintaining a chorus and orchestra, have made opera so expensive that much of it is now the preserve of people who don't even know what they like, but know what they can afford. Even after spending over £15 million of Arts Council grant in 1990, the best seats at Covent Garden still cost £98:

> It was in the mid-1970s that what might be called the professional middle classes were finally priced out of the body of Covent Garden . . . [so] that opera, in London at least, is no longer for all, but for those who can afford it,

lamented the editor of *Opera* magazine, an enthusiast since child-hood.[12] It is hard to see the justification for spending large sums of public money in order that a small minority with a large disposable income should pay slightly less. Yet the only thing which would bring prices down to the level at which ordinary people could afford to attend regularly would be a massive increase in the block grant from the taxpayer – hard enough to justify when the Arts Council's own research shows that in a three-month period only one per cent of the British population attend an opera performance.

The Arts Council spends the money because it believes it is supporting a 'centre of excellence', without whose influence the whole cultural life of the nation would be impoverished. For the sixteen years before the Second World War, the Royal Opera House had been subsidized off-season by being run as a dance-hall where, for half-a-crown, Londoners could dance the night away to Jack Hylton. During the forties, it had been occupied by Mecca Cafés, which laid on the sort of entertainment which is supposed to lift morale during wartime, but with the return of peace it began losing money again. The new lessees, Boosey and Hawkes, approached Kenneth Clark to see whether the Arts Council would sponsor a series of concerts. To their delight, Clark suggested instead that the Council took over the whole building. He admitted frankly to the Treasury that he had no idea what it would cost to run. It has turned out to be by far the biggest consumer of Arts Council subsidy.[13]

The Royal Opera House has survived as the favourite child of the Arts Council partly because no other artistic institution is so well-connected. Lord Keynes, the first chairman, also ran the Arts Council, beginning a relationship which lasted for four decades (between 1946 and 1981, nineteen of the forty-seven trustees and directors of Covent Garden had direct experience of the Arts Council or its wartime pre-decessor).[14]

With Keynes' death, the post of chairman was taken by Sir John

Anderson, an association with the upper reaches of the civil service which continues to this day. There are four main boards at Covent Garden, for opera, ballet and development, as well as the board of directors. In 1990, the secretary of each one was a senior civil servant, all of them past or present officials at the Treasury.[15] The former head of the civil service, Robert Armstrong, graduated to a seat on the main board after serving for many years as secretary. He was to have been replaced as secretary by Robin Butler, then serving as a senior official at the Treasury. When Butler got Armstrong's job as head of the civil service, it was felt to be just too embarrassing for the connection to be so openly flaunted, and the post passed instead to Andrew Edwards, another high-flying Treasury man. Doubtless all these figures were recruited for the famed civil service minute-taking skills, but it seems clear that these connections with the highest levels of the mandarinate have contributed substantially to the special privileges of the Opera House.

This protected position can breed a distinct arrogance. The Royal Opera House finds it hard to accept the right of the Arts Council to assess their work, and on one occasion Lord Harewood, when a director of the Royal Opera House, stormed out of an Arts Council meeting because they had had the temerity to question the merits of a company production. Roy Shaw recalls that Sir John Tooley, general director of Covent Garden in the early eighties, simply refused to countenance inquiry by his paymasters:

> You didn't have to make a criticism of a production, perhaps just to suggest that they were building up too much of a deficit, or that the last season wasn't terribly successful, and they made you feel that you were committing *lèse-majesté*. They lived in a different world.[16]

In Jeremy Isaacs, the general director who succeeded Sir John Tooley in 1988, the Opera House chose a man of decidedly different kidney. Isaacs, a liberal Glaswegian whose distinguished career in television culminated in the fashioning of Channel Four, took over with promises to do something about the mediocre standard of most Covent Garden productions, but instead found himself preoccupied with the permanent funding crisis at the Opera House. As one director of the Royal Opera House observed, time was when they spent ninety per cent of their time discussing productions and ten per cent discussing finance, now it was the other way round. Isaacs persuaded the board in 1990 that they should just ignore the fact that their budget was inadequate, and go £5 million into the red. It was a cavalier gesture in which he was betting that Convent Garden was too precious to the rich and powerful to be allowed to go to the wall. He will almost certainly be proved right.

The board of directors of this indulged institution have customarily been among the grandest of the Great and Good. In recognition of their position, they had always been selected to give a spread of political opinion. They customarily included one Labour party grandee and one Liberal among the academics, musicians, and the rest. But by the start of the nineties, the board had begun to show a distinct shift of emphasis. Now, the retailer, Lord (John) Sainsbury had crowned over twenty years' service by becoming chairman and been joined by a property developer (Sir Christopher Benson), two industrialists (Sir Alex Alexander and Sir James Spooner) and two bankers (Sir Martin Jacomb and Sir Kit McMahon). This was a less than earth-shaking change in social background – five of the fourteen on the board were Etonians and ten were titled – but in terms of occupation it marked a metamorphosis which has been affecting all areas of the arts.

The increasing prominence of businesspeople was gleefully seized upon by the welfare-statists as another opportunity for withering scorn, particularly when it was revealed that one scheme to solve the financial crisis involved turning the area around the Opera House into a series of 'theme' fast-food joints, including a 'roaring twenties speakeasy saloon', and even something called 'Pagliacci's Porch'. (The plans were torn up by the rest of the board when they were leaked to the press.)

The changing complexion of appointments at the Royal Opera House was reflected elsewhere. Some two hundred posts in the arts and broadcasting are in the gift of 10 Downing Street. The conclusion is inescapable that during the eighties, the power of patronage was used to attempt to change the face of the arts Establishment.

It was not that Margaret Thatcher was exactly noted for her interest in the arts. Number 10 was adorned with various pictures and vases spotted on visits to national museums and later borrowed, although according to one former director of the Victoria and Albert, when he escorted her around the museum the only flicker of interest came in the conservation department, where 'she knew and recited the formulas for plastic fixatives, and indeed it was as though she was attached with plastic fixative to the room.'[17] (This sort of catty superciliousness was commonplace among those who had enjoyed three decades of state patronage.)

The bile which poured from the arts world against her was extraordinary. The publisher Carmen Callil exclaimed that 'she terrifies me, she repels me, and I think she's ruining everything that is best about this country.' Dr Jonathan Miller went further, and found her 'loathsome, repulsive in almost every way', particularly disliking 'her odious suburban gentility and sentimental, saccharine patriotism, catering to the worst elements of commuter idiocy.'[18]

Mrs Thatcher had done little to enhance her standing among the intellectuals by such indiscretions as admitting to an interviewer that she was *re*reading Frederick Forsyth's second-rate thriller *The Fourth Protocol*. But what underlay the differences were conflicting attitudes to money. Committed to reining back public expenditure, Margaret Thatcher saw no reason why the arts should be immune from the cuts which faced almost all government departments in the early eighties. Her disenchantment with her first arts minister, Norman St John Stevas, was clear early on. 'Oh, Norman,' she told a visitor to Downing Street, 'he's the last of the big spenders.'

As in social spending, deficiencies in public funding were now to be made up by private sponsorship and greater efficiency. It followed that the new breed of appointees to great public artistic institutions would be businessmen who understood productivity and how to raise funds. Soon after the Conservative victory in 1979, Downing Street decided to send the construction millionaire Alastair (now Lord) McAlpine to the Council. McAlpine was no philistine; his Garrick Club tie proclaimed his presence at a thousand first nights and private views. But he was also deputy Chairman of the Conservative party. Roy Shaw vainly objected to the Minister, Norman St John Stevas, that it would be 'like putting an atheist on the bench of bishops'.[19] Stevas shrugged his shoulders, said the suggestion had come 'from a very high source', and made the appointment anyway.

Patronage of the arts has been one of the traditional pleasures of successful businessmen for generations, and there was nothing particularly novel about putting them on the boards of the great national institutions. Apart from anything else, they were some of the few people who had time to devote to the job. But it was the scale and frequency of appointments that lead to allegations of political bias.

In 1982 Richard Hoggart, author of *The Uses of Literacy* and a former assistant director-general of UNESCO, was unexpectedly dropped from the post of vice-chairman of the Arts Council. No-one questioned Hoggart's ability, and he was universally regarded as a skilled administrator. But he was also a socialist and made no secret of the fact. Hoggart was a close personal friend of the Secretary-General, Roy Shaw (they were both working-class boys from Yorkshire), who demanded a reason why from the minister. The minister looked sheepish, gave a schoolboy grin and said, 'I'm afraid Number Ten doesn't like him.'[20] Later that year Number 10 announced their choice to become the new chairman of the Arts Council. It was that great Lord High Everything Else William Rees-Mogg, recently knighted for his work as vice-chairman of the BBC Governors.

Where Rees-Mogg was chosen by Downing Street for one job after another, Sir John Burgh experienced a similar series of rejections. Sir John was precisely the sort of timber from which the old-style Great and Good had been hewn. One of the stable of civil servants to serve as secretaries at Covent Garden, he had retired from the post of director-general of the British Council in 1987. His mistake had been to lay into government policy. His valedictory address attacked the budget cuts suffered by the Council since the 1979 election, and appealed for more public spending on the promotion of British culture overseas. The nation spent half or one third of the amount devoted to the cause by France or Germany. 'The amazing demand for our language, culture and education must be seized and not lost through lack of vision and imagination,' he said. It was hardly the sort of speech to send rioters storming the barricades, but it got a few paragraphs buried away in the serious papers. It appears that that was enough to seal his fate. He had made the same point to a parliamentary committee the previous year, and Downing Street had marked his card.

Sir John was telephoned one day by the director of the Tate Gallery, inquiring whether he would be prepared to become a Trustee, should they offer him an invitation (protocol dictates that people are required to accept invitations before they are issued, to avoid embarrassment). After volunteering that he was no fine art connoisseur, Sir John was enthusiastic, even more so when it was explained that the intention was that he would go on to succeed the distinguished architect Richard Rogers (designer of the Pompidou Centre, Paris, and the Lloyd's of London headquarters) as chairman. Burgh's name was then sent to Downing Street for approval. There was silence from Number 10 for three weeks, at the end of which the Tate was brusquely informed that they had better find someone else. Burgh was not acceptable. 'Are we at the court of Henry VIII? Or of Stalin?' asked Sir John's old friend, Bernard Levin.[21] Nursing his snub, Sir

John retired to the presidency of Trinity College, Oxford, where they still played by the old rules.

The Burgh case is unusual because the way in which such appointments are made usually guarantees discretion. The pool from which names are plucked is very small (so small that one recent member of the Arts Council was appointed simply on the grounds that he had once been locked in a television hospitality room with the arts minister, where they had got gloriously drunk together). The group of distinguished figures asked to suggest names tend to keep their own counsel, but they became increasingly aware of other, political, considerations coming into play. Lord Goodman recalls that, 'several times in the eighties I was asked for suggestions for arts appointments. I'd put forward names, and then they were, I'm afraid, ruled out because they weren't the right political colour.'[22]

The political point is hard to prove, and Conservatives might well object that Goodman himself was a personal friend of Nye Bevan and Jennie Lee and a well-known associate of Harold Wilson. Goodman points out that the very first person recommended by Jennie Lee for appointment to the Arts Council was a Conservative MP and that he (Goodman) backed the nomination of Max Rayne as chairman of the National Theatre, 'and he's about as socialist as my late lamented mother's pekinese.'[23]

But a clear pattern of appointments did develop in the eighties. Richard Hoggart called the new Downing Street appointments system CPPE – Concentrated Personalized Preferment and Ennoblement.[24] It is unfair, and inaccurate, to suggest that the people who benefited from the new arrangements were all political sympathizers. Some of them were supporters of the right-wing of the Labour party, and others were attached to the centre. But the most fashionable had one thing in common; they tended to be businessmen, or had a businessman's view of the world. There seemed to be a view that not only were the skills of the entrepreneur universally applicable, they were also in some sense superior to the wisdom of academics and welfare-statist professionals. 'She goes for the millionaire of the moment', one Downing Street source said of the new appointments policy. The explanation for the apparent political bias may be less dramatic than it seems: successful capitalists believe in free enterprise, which was bound to put them at odds with most of the Welfare State artists.

Generous patronage of the arts is a sure means of buying a knighthood and businessmen have always been associated with great cultural institutions. The Tate Gallery, for example, was founded by the sugar king Henry Tate in 1897 (he was rewarded with a baronetcy the next year). What was different about the 1980s was that the businessmen being parachuted into the boards were not always distinguished by any lively existing interest in the arts. Robert Sainsbury, who had served fourteen years as a trustee of the Tate, was a noted collector. But Dennis Stevenson, the gallery's new chairman, a self-made millionaire and the boss of fifteen companies, was not. As other bankers and businessmen, like Sir Mark Weinberg or Gilbert de Botton joined the board of trustees, the number of artists dropped from four out of ten to three out of eleven, the bare minimum permitted by the gallery's constitution. The Tate's director, Nick Serota, said in 1989:

> I have the feeling that if I wanted to have Professor Richard Wollheim – who is, after all, an outstanding philosopher and art theorist – on the board of trustees, I think the chances of Number Ten choosing him would be quite slight.[25]

This rise of the businessman board-member seemed irresistible. Nearly half the board of the Victoria and Albert Museum were from commerce and industry, provoking howls of indignation from the old Great and Good, who argued that the custodianship of great national art collections demanded different skills to those applicable to running a business.

The view from Mount Parnassus was argued by Sir Richard Southwood, chairman of the Natural History Museum:

> I don't believe you can make billions over a short period of time without being an outsider. You may not actually break the rules. You may not get submerged in illegality. But you are galloping along at the edge of the waters. And for the museums and universities, which the Establishment looks after, one always wants people like Caesar's wife, who are above reproach.[26]

But the only weapon the old priesthood possessed was their scorn. And they used it. Sir Roy Strong, Director of the V&A for thirteen years until retiring to tend his garden in 1987, went on television to deliver himself of this forthright view of the new breed of trustees:

> One really wonders if they've ever read a Dickens novel. One really wonders if they know the difference between Van Gogh and Rembrandt. And some of them, I'm sure, think Jane Austen is a brand of underwear.[27]

With Sir Roy's retirement in 1987, it was the V&A which provided
the most dramatic example of the impact of the new-style worthies
chosen by Downing Street. Although still the world's foremost
museum of decorative arts, its management style owed more to the
Keystone Cops than to the Harvard Business School. In the mid-
eighties it emerged that no-one even had a precise idea of exactly how
many objects the museum possessed. Part of the English silver collection went missing. An Algardi bust was dropped and smashed, as was
an ancient marble figure from Korea. The museum discovered one of
its paintings had been stolen only when the police turned up to return it.

The new Chairman of the trustees, Robert Armstrong, arrived at
the V&A fresh from attempting to apply the disciplines of the
marketplace to the civil service: he saw need of the same medicine at
the museum. Fellow board-members included the chairman of the
Wimpey construction group, Sir Clifford Chetwood; the former managing director of the Mobil Oil Company, Sir Nevil Macready; City
grandees Ian Hay Davison and Sir Michael Butler (a former diplomat)
and the advertising magnate Maurice Saatchi. Unwilling to put up
with the old ways any longer, they argued the rest of the board into
accepting the need for dramatic change. A new Director, Elizabeth
Esteve-Coll, was hired to sort out the mess.

Mrs Esteve-Coll was part of a new breed of museum directors.
Previous generations had tended to be distinguished academics, but
while Neil MacGregor, the new Director of the National Gallery, had
at least been editor of the *Burlington Magazine*, neither Mrs Esteve-
Coll nor Nick Serota could summon a book between them. There was
nothing inherently undesirable about this change – after all they were
supposed to be running museums not delivering lectures – but it was
enough to earn them contempt. Mrs Esteve-Coll's sex and the fact
that she did not belong to the tight little coterie of curators and
historians who had trained at the Courtauld Institute (her background
was London University, Kingston Polytechnic and the University of
Surrey) put her at an immediate disadvantage in the war which broke
about her head when she implemented the board's new management
strategy. A predecessor at the V&A, Sir John Pope-Hennessy (Oxford,
Cambridge and the British Museum) was withering about the five-
page plan she produced. 'No such simplistic or imperfectly literate a
report would have been tolerated by any board with which I have
been associated,'[28] he proclaimed.

Mrs Esteve-Coll proposed separating 'housekeeping' from 'scholarship', a serious redefinition of the museum's role, and one which would require a new type of staff. She called in nine curators with a total experience of over 130 years and asked them to take redundancy. This was certainly decisive management – one interview is said to have lasted all of three minutes – made possible only by the presence of Robert Armstrong, who induced the Treasury suddenly to stump up additional resources to fund redundancy schemes without endangering the Museum's grant.

There was immediate uproar within the museum community: the distinction between the custodianship of great objects and the study of them was an artificial one, they argued. Directors of museums from Boston to Berlin wrote to protest. The dismissed keeper of Ceramics and Glass published the letter he had written, in 'sincerest contempt', to Mrs Esteve-Coll, accepting his redundancy and accusing her of bad faith, untrustworthiness and making the museum 'ridiculous'. There was an unattractive misogynist streak to the petulant performance of the ousted curators and they generated little or no public support.

But the changes at the V&A are part of a broader redefinition of the purpose of museums and galleries, as a result of the new commercial pressures. A year later, in April 1990, the Natural History Museum announced plans to purge itself of forty-six of its scientists and make itself more 'customer friendly'. 'Voluntary' admission charges – the absurd expectation that people should pay to see things they already owned – had been an early symptom of the transformation from nineteenth-century educational institutions open to all to a twentieth-century leisure industry for the affluent. Increasingly, the directors see their natural competitors as theme parks and tourist traps like Madame Tussaud's.

There have been undeniable benefits. Under the leadership of Neil Cossons, the Science Museum became much more user-friendly, with the staff taken out of their old blue serge prison warders' uniforms, put into blazers and encouraged to see the public as 'our customers'. At the Tate Gallery, some previous directors had felt so strongly that the pictures should explain themselves that they actually discouraged notices explaining what the contents of a particular gallery were. The new Director, Nick Serota, in his distinctive rimless glasses and silver bracelet, set out instead to proselytize and explain.

But if the policy is pursued energetically everywhere, the inevitable consequence will be that erudition, one of the distinguishing character-istics of a developed society, will eventually be diminished.

By the start of the nineties the new generation of Trustees had seized the commanding heights of the cultural landscape. The British Museum, where the trustees are nominated both by the Crown and the 'learned societies' (the Royal Academy, Royal Society, British Academy and the Society of Antiquaries), was largely unchanged and Lady (Mary) Soames, Churchill's last surviving daughter, had taken over the National Theatre, an appointment which seemed quite in keeping with the taste for nominating well-bred amateurs (she was, she said, 'staggered' by the suggestion). But the National Gallery was in the hands of the mercurial Lord (Jacob) Rothschild, a man so passionately devoted to collecting that at one stage he even bought the dealers, Colnaghi, but a brilliant businessman, none the less. Dennis Stevenson was running the Tate. The Royal Opera House was under the chairmanship of a Sainsbury grocery millionaire. Mrs Thatcher's favourite civil servant, Robert Armstrong, was in charge of the Victoria and Albert Museum. And the Arts Council was in the hands of Peter Palumbo, a multi-millionaire property developer and collector of Hockneys, Warhols, and Picassos. Whereas the original Arts Council of Lord Keynes had included no businessmen, in the Arts Council of 1990 they made up one third of the membership.

Whatever the howls of protest from the welfare-statists, these people have done pretty well. At the National Gallery, the Sainsbury brothers spent £30 million on a new wing and John Paul Getty gave £50 million for new acquisitions. Twenty per cent of the costs of the Royal Opera House were met by private-sector donations in 1990. The changing pattern of patronage of the arts, from the aristocracy to the state and now to a combination of business and the state, reflects the changing pattern of political power. In the process, questions about what the arts are for are getting new answers.

'Demoralized, cowed, sullen', were the words which dropped from Sir Peter Hall's lips when I asked him to describe the mood of the artistic community in Britain. They reflect failure. The struggle Hall and others have lost is not with any creative challenge but with their patrons. They have failed to change the world, failed to manoeuvre the arts into any greater centrality in national life, failed even to persuade government to provide the level of funding needed to keep them vigorous.

The arts professionals have never really abandoned High Victorianism. Privately, like Matthew Arnold, they see their role in an almost religious light. Press them on the subject of what the arts are *for*, and they get embarrassed. According to Richard Eyre:

> Ten years ago, it was possible to talk without self-consciousness about the arts being the antennae of society and poets being the unacknowledged legislators of the world, and about spiritual values. Nowadays, if you talk like that you feel just a bit evangelical. The pressure is on to talk about the arts in terms of a commodity. The argument is one of cost-effectiveness, investment, VAT and tourism.[29]

The justification for the arts can only be made in their own terms. But with the creation of an arts industry, the question of funding has come to be the pre-eminent issue. The plain fact is that after forty-five years of state sponsorship, we have reached a situation where we can no longer afford to pay the market cost of the arts. The deficit could only be made up by the creation of a new class of patron.

Industry and art are not natural bedfellows. The gulf of understanding is vast, and encounters between the jesters of the arts world and their commercial sponsors can be reminiscent of the meeting between the players and the court in Hamlet: sensitive, arrogant, fragile people face-to-face with hard-headed strategists. Outside the relatively small artistic community the notion persists that they are all anarcho-syndicalist adulterers. Richard Eyre encountered the force of ignorance when introduced to a retired brigadier a few years ago.

'And what do you do?' asked the old soldier.

'I work in the theatre,' Eyre replied.

'Hmm,' he pondered for what seemed like a full minute, and finally dredged up his one piece of knowledge on the subject. 'Must be a lot of fucking.'

They were obviously going to have to understand each other better, and the 1983 appointment of Luke Rittner to be Secretary General of the Arts Council gave the clearest signal of the way things were going to change. William Rees-Mogg, Arts Council Chairman, had met Rittner when he was director of the Association for Business Sponsorship of the Arts. By coincidence both men were Catholics and both Conservatives (Rittner had been a Tory councillor in Bath). Rittner's predecessor, Roy Shaw, thought he discerned the underlying strategy:

> Their attitude to public funding of the arts was rather like Lenin's attitude to religion, that if you created the right conditions, it would just wither away.[30]

This was hyperbole, but Britain was already spending proportionately less public money on the arts than any other country in western Europe. But in the absence of visible returns on investment and with numerous other more pressing calls upon public spending, some other source of funds had to be found. To some of the professionals homilies about 'getting into the marketplace' had a decidedly hollow ring to them. Anyone who had run a theatre or art gallery was painfully aware that they were there already: if the production flopped they had empty houses.

The Association for Business Sponsorship of the Arts (ABSA) had been acute enough to persuade Lord Goodman, now retired from the Arts Council, to be its first chairman. It was an inspired choice, but the two organizations had little or nothing in common. For over a decade Goodman steered ABSA to a more central role in British cultural life. In retrospect, he has regrets:

> I rationalized the belief into respectability in my own mind that it was a good thing for there to be a court of appeal from the Arts Council: it would be wrong to have only a place where decisions were taken about whether a play or an exhibition or an orchestra should get sponsorship.

But in the event, the existence of the organization, which drummed up £500,000 in 1976 and £30 million in 1988, changed the relationship between the Arts Council and its clients. Whereas previously suppliants might have been told that money was not available one year, but might be forthcoming the next, 'now they're told to go and beg for the money from other people.'[31]

And there was one absolutely crucial difference between the way that the Arts Council awarded its grants and the attitude of the burgeoning commercial donors. It was the difference between patronage and sponsorship, between disinterested long-term policy and the short-term needs of the market.

The literature produced by the Association for Business Sponsorship of the Arts makes the relationship between the new patrons and their clients quite clear. Whereas the private patrons of the Renaissance might have encouraged the arts for amusement, philanthropy, self-aggrandizement or the glorification of God, their modern counterparts do it as a form of advertising: the patron does not expect a return on his money, the sponsor does. A *Financial Times* headline once frankly described sponsorship as 'the art of getting cheap publicity'. In a guide to the tax implications of arts sponsorship prepared for the Association, the Inland Revenue requirements are spelled out: to qualify as a legitimate business expense, any thought of pure charity to deserving causes must be disregarded:

> It is important that advertising is seen to be the sole objective of the payment. If it is considered to be for a dual purpose, i.e. that of advertising and benefiting the body in question (or conceivably satisfying a personal whim of a director) the whole expenditure may be disallowed.[32]

It would be churlish and short-sighted to deny the benefits of much sponsorship, and some of it does seem genuinely disinterested. British Telecom's underwriting of the Lake District Music Festival, or W.H. Smith's support of young people's art can hardly yield great direct benefit to the company. But sponsorship does demand a return, as the franker businessmen confess. Grand Metropolitan, the hotel and catering chain, are sporadic donors to exhibitions and musical events. 'It is,' admits their no-nonsense Chairman, Allen Sheppard, 'to try to associate areas of good taste with our corporate image. We once sponsored an exhibition of paintings – I didn't much like some of them but they seemed to get acclaim. That was good for our image.'[33]

The sponsors certainly get a good run for their money. In relation to the overall sums spent on the arts, the money raised from business sponsorship is small, and most of it goes to established companies with established reputations. In exchange for sponsoring Covent Garden's summer season of cheap 'proms' the Midland Bank got their name emblazoned across the front of the Royal Opera House, despite the fact that early examination of the relative value of their sponsorship showed that it was worth *one seven-hundreth* of the Arts Council grant. Royal Insurance had their name and logo associated with the productions of the Royal Shakespeare Company in exchange for a donation of £1 million spread over three years. The Arts Council's grant was fifteen times larger, but was not marked by a similar advertising display.

But the real objection to an excessive dependence on the largesse of corporate patrons is that they manage simultaneously to be both fickle and cautious. Sustained planning is impossible when funding might be cut off at any moment because the latest set of results are disappointing or the new chairman doesn't believe in spending shareholders' potential dividends.

'We put on the sort of concerts that won't frighten the directors' wives,' John Drummond remarked of sponsorship when he was in charge of the Edinburgh Festival,[34] and the most contentious or difficult work finds it hardest to attract commercial patrons. Certainly,

the demands of business are often less than wholly appropriate to the
creation of great art. 'The questions sponsors ask are: what is our
product, how do we market it, are we getting value for money?' Mark
Fisher, the Labour Arts spokesman observed. 'These may not exactly
be the most relevant tests when considering how to improve the
standard of writing in Britain.'[35]

'It's inconceivable that we could raise sponsorship for *Look Back In
Anger*,' remarks Max Stafford-Clark, Artistic Director of the Royal
Court Theatre, where the play was first staged in 1956. 'You couldn't
get sponsorship for a new *Waiting for Godot*, if it came to that.'[36]
Financial uncertainty doubtless creates a more challenging business
environment. It does not necessarily do the same for creative enterprise, even at the greatest national institutions. 'You can't take risks
when you're teetering on the brink of insolvency,' says one National
Theatre board member.[37]

The changes brought about by the new attitude to the arts have
been most fiercely argued over in the world of theatre because it is the
most politicized of the cottage industries which make up the artistic
community in Britain. The Arts Council's subsidy policy had one
overwhelming advantage. By and large, it worked. The credit for
turning London into the theatrical capital of the world should go to
the British taxpayers. Whatever the later shortcomings, they provided
a level of support which produced the right environment for writers
and directors to take creative risks. The disciples of non-governmental
sponsorship are fond of citing the United States as a model. But the
American system has not produced a theatrical scene as lively as
London's, as many an American tourist will bear out. Also, a wealthy
man or woman there effectively has the choice between giving their
money to the tax authorities or to the New York City Ballet; the
choice does not exist in Britain, and it is hard to see challenging
drama proving as attractive if it did.

It is a climate which demands the Arts Council itself become
adventurous. But they have done the reverse. 'Nowadays, we tend to
give money to people we think we can trust,'[38] one member admitted.
Responsibility with public money is to be commended, but it makes
for conservatism. In the 1960s the Council was creating, or assisting at
the birth of, new opera and theatre companies, extending the facilities
of the metropolis to the provinces. Now, the mood is one of caution
and retrenchment. The theatre director Peter Brook discovered that if
he wanted to spend time experimenting with different forms of

theatre, the money would be forthcoming in Paris rather than London, and one cannot imagine the British Arts Council encouraging and supporting a composer, as the French encouraged and supported Pierre Boulez, while he experimented with music and orchestras.

So the arts struggle on, perpetually passing the hat like a hungry busker. At Covent Garden half the audience often seems to be there at someone else's expense, provided with free champagne and smoked salmon by a company keen to impress. They return from the intervals sleepy and bored and spend the second and third acts surreptitiously lifting their cuffs for a glimpse of the time, trying to read the programme in the dark, desperately trying not to nod off. Glyndebourne, Lord Harewood observes sourly, 'sells out regularly to people who have no idea whether what they're watching is any good or not.'[39]

The plain fact is that the arts on their present scale are just unviable: the national appetite is greater than the national capacity. The development of state sponsorship for the arts after the Second World War has been one of the many success stories of the Welfare State. But it not only created a caste of arts bureaucrat, it insulated the artist from the most basic fact of life, that to survive he or she must have customers.

Artists dependent on partonage have always written, painted or composed to please their sponsors. The Arts Council was the most benign of patrons, studiously refusing to interfere with the creative process. It distorted the natural relationship between the state of the economy and the conditions of the arts, allowing them to flourish while the circumstances of the nation continued to deteriorate. The numbers who took advantage of the sponsorship by attending plays, concerts or exhibitions grew.

If higher education were to extend beyond a privileged minority, the audience for the arts might grow sufficiently for them to become economically viable. But there is little sign of that happening, so the artists must look to the new breed of sponsors if they are to continue in business. On the record so far, it is not a recipe for great creative achievement.

CHAPTER THIRTEEN

Bring on the Comfortable Men

Many of the English,
The intelligent English
Of the Arts, the Professions and the Upper Middle Classes,
Are Under-cover men.
But what is under the cover
(That was original)
Died; now they are corpse carriers.
It is not noticeable, but be careful,
They are infective.

– *The English* STEVIE SMITH

I RECALL visiting London as a student. It was about three o'clock in the afternoon, a bright, late summer's day in 1970. The newspapers had been filled with the doings of the newly-elected Heath government. In St James's Park the last Whitehall late-lunchers were making their way across to the Treasury, Foreign Office or Ministry of Defence. As I turned into Pall Mall, down the steps beneath the gilded figure of Athene stepped a recognizable figure instantly familiar from the television pictures of the comings and goings in Downing Street. I could not recall his name, and at this distance it matters not, nor did I know the building from whence he emerged after lunch. Racking my brains as I continued down Pall Mall, I was astonished to see another unmistakable figure emerge from another building, identified only by its street number – this was a well-known bishop. Some thirty yards further on I ran across a Cambridge professor. Turning the corner up towards Piccadilly I was in time to see the general secretary of the TUC getting into his car, and shortly afterwards another government minister emerging from another grandly anonymous building.

I subsequently discovered that the building with the statue above it was the Athenaeum, and the other two nameless buildings were also clubs – the Reform and Brooks's. Like many of my generation, for years afterwards these buildings seemed to me the secret seat of British power, behind the high windows through which one could glimpse the gilt-framed portraits of Empire heroes and white-coated waiters serving coffee to balding heads in ancient armchairs.

How curiously anachronistic it all was. In the real world, the Empire was long gone and the architectural style of the times wasn't Barry's Palazzos but John Poulson's concrete shopping centres. The sexual revolution, rock-and-roll and the emergence of classless youth culture had swept like an incoming tide across the rest of Britain and left this little well-shod outcrop in St James's untouched.

In fact, behind those imposing façades, many of the clubs had had enough of a struggle just to find the members to keep going. Some of the more distinguished stayed in reasonable health – in 1968 the Turf, haunt of faded racing folk, numbered sixteen of the thirty-one British dukes among its members. But dozens of the others closed their doors and sold up. Between 1938 and 1978, the number of clubs dropped from 120 to less than forty. Yet those which survived still drew cabinet ministers, bishops, permanent secretaries and generals to St James's for their meals as assuredly as their school bells had once summoned them to identical food forty years or more earlier.

Designed to be as much like a chap's house as possible (Brooks's was once memorably described as being 'like a duke's house, with the duke dead upstairs'), the clubs had entirely the wrong image for the age of the Common Man. They belonged to the era when the country was still run by aristocrats: White's, for example, is older than the Bank of England. Macmillan, who was an active member of five London clubs simultaneously, had their inappropriateness made clear when, after the 1957 leadership election, he took his chief whip, Edward Heath, to dine at the Turf.

Macmillan felt that they were entitled to a quiet celebration of champagne and game pie, but had reckoned without the intrusiveness of the new medium of television, which delightedly filmed the two men emerging a couple of hours later. 'The food, the drink, and above all the place were seized upon with avidity as the symbols of a reactionary regime,' he remarked later.[1]

The difficulty was that to men of Macmillan's generation, the London clubs were just part of life. When R. A. Butler was summoned to Churchill's sickbed in 1951 to be appointed Chancellor of the Exchequer, his first action was to take lunch at the Athenaeum with the head of the Treasury and his private secretary. 'We sat at a table in the window and ate what remained of the club food after the bishops had had their run; for we were somewhat late, and the bishops attack the sideboards early,' he recalled.[2]

'Pratts's used to be the sort of place where bishops were made. Nowadays all you hear is people talking about their woodcock,' a member told me when I asked him about the influence of the clubs nowadays. But the decline is not evenly spread. Many have gone for good, others survived the hard times by sacking the mad majors who had until then acted as secretaries and engaging catering managers. The Oxford and Cambridge, once restricted to graduates from those two universities, took to advertising itself. The Travellers', while still insisting that its members have travelled at least five hundred miles from London – a requirement now fulfilled by any Ibiza package holidaymaker – became scarcely more than a civil service canteen. At the Reform, mandarins and politicians seem outnumbered by public-relations executives and advertising men.

Older members have found the change in the clubs baffling. Ten years or so ago, on being told that his club was providing increasingly frequent accommodation for 'commuters', one asked what they were. 'They've come in from Woking,' said the next armchair. 'From Woking?' asked the bewildered old buffer. 'Is there trouble out there?'

But at White's, where whatever the time of day you always feel you have just had a full-blooded lunch of roast-beef and Yorkshire pudding, the feel of power and wealth is still present. The only things more cushioned than the venerable armchairs are the members. The air is permanently heavy with stale cigar smoke. Beneath the pall, the slightly grubby cream walls are hung with monumental oil paintings of thoroughbred dukes and horses. Beyond the old leather chester-fields, a news agency printer is buzzing away, bringing Reuter reports from Delhi or Johannesburg and the latest stock market prices from New York and Tokyo. As the time for tea and hot buttered toast gives way to calls for bottles of champagne and large whiskeys, it could be any date in the last forty years.

The problem is that most people are just too busy to spend as much time in the clubs as they used to. Important figures in the City are likely to be taking a working lunch, often followed by formal dinners in the evening, and simply don't have time to travel across town to Pall Mall. The new professional politicians recognize the need to 'maintain contacts', but they arrive at Parliament with fewer friends or acquaint-ances outside the overheated world of politics, and have not the time to spend in the leisurely ambience of St James's. Their values, anyway, are individualistic and they have less time for the virtues of solidarity, companionship, clubbiness.

A handful of clubs retain some significance.[3] The Athenaeum and the Oxford and Cambridge for senior civil servants and vice chancellors. White's for the grander Tories and the Carlton for the parliamentary infantry. Lord Rees-Mogg told me that when he was editor of *The Times* in the seventies, where others might go to the pub to take the public pulse, he would make a point of visiting the Garrick as often as possible, 'to discover what was the story that people were talking about'. Malcolm Turnbull, the Australian lawyer who fought the *Spycatcher* case through the courts, claims to have gathered useful intelligence about the tactics of the British Attorney-General, Lord Havers, because the latter was in the habit of discussing the case in the urinals of the Garrick. On being appointed Cabinet Secretary and head of the civil service in 1988, Sir Robin Butler, who had previously belonged to the comparatively modest Anglo-Belgian club in Knightsbridge, was immediately put up for, and accepted by, the Athenaeum, Brooks's and the Oxford and Cambridge: membership is an accessory of the job, like the knighthood and the peerage on retirement.

For the most part, the St James's clubs are no more than occasionally convenient watering holes for powerful men who are uneasy in pubs. In an average week, there is no place where you are likely to find a wider cross-section of the British élite rubbing shoulders with one another. And beyond the grand St James's clubs, there is still some urge among the men who rise to the top of British society to get together in dining clubs. Prominent parliamentarians have Grillions, an early nineteenth-century dining club established so that politicians could fight in private, 'to see how far they need to fight at all in public'. The City has half-a-dozen members-only institutions, relics of the pre-Big Bang easy ways and still places where City wisdom is distilled. The Church of England has 'Nobody's Friends', mainly made up of High Tory and Athenaeum types (nine are prominent in the Conservative party, and none, as far as I can see, Labour politicians), the two Archbishops, fourteen other bishops, a few public school headmasters, almost a dozen judges and a few elderly aristocrats like Lord Home.

Only the conspiracist would argue that there was anything sinister about these gatherings. Their influence is altogether more subtly conservative. The dining clubs tend to emphasize those things members have in common at the expense of those things which divide. They make for a certain homogeneity and reinforce the boundaries of what is thought changeable.

One Tuesday evening every month a dinner is held at Brooks's, the second oldest of the St James's clubs. By comparison with others, Brooks's is famously apolitical (the most dramatic incident in the club's history occurring in 1913 when a baronet member tried to take dinner in the middle dining room without wearing full evening dress, and resigned in protest at being asked to leave), but on these evenings, it is playing host to the most exclusive dining club in Britain. It is called The Club.

I first heard about its existence by accident, when interviewing a very senior public servant. 'I suppose you could say The Club is the Establishment at play,' he remarked.

'Which club?' I asked.

'Oh gosh,' he gulped. 'Perhaps I shouldn't have mentioned it. I thought you knew already,' he said and changed the subject.

'Who's in The Club?' I asked.

'I'm not allowed to tell you.'

When it was founded by Dr Johnson and Joshua Reynolds at the Turk's Head in Soho, The Club had the reputation of being harder to get into than the Kingdom of Heaven. Early blackballed candidates included the Lord Chancellor and the Bishop of Chester, although Edmund Burke, Adam Smith and Charles James Fox all managed to get elected, the latter not without having to wait several years as a calculated snub by Johnson. Boswell describes the range of topics discussed over dinner as including the astronomical price of works of art, the difficulties of parliamentary opposition when the government of the day had such an overwhelming majority, the latest books and how they might be able to wangle some free claret.[4] The agenda can scarcely have changed.

Just over fifty people, all of them male, are entitled to attend. Although Gladstone is said once to have turned up for dinner and found himself alone, the average attendance is usually about a dozen or so. Among those with a right to attend in 1990 were the Cabinet Secretary, Sir Robin Butler; his predecessor, Lord Armstrong; the Queen's Private Secretary, Sir William Heseltine; the Archbishop of Canterbury; the Lord Chancellor; the Foreign Secretary; the Governor of the Bank of England; three prominent bankers, Sir Jeremy Morse, Sir David Scholey and Sir John Baring; the former president of the

European Commission, Lord Jenkins; the former cabinet ministers, Lords Whitelaw, Pym and Carrington; and a smattering of Conservative academics, like Lords Quinton and Blake. The Club is dominated by Etonians (six of the preceding group were at the school), and the joint treasurers are Lord Armstrong and his Eton contemporary Sir Anthony (Tony) Lloyd, a grand but jovial Appeal Court Judge who once ran the Mile for Cambridge.

This is precisely the sort of cast-list you'd come up with if you were looking for the heart of the Establishment: powerful, well-upholstered men confident in their authority.[5] It is hard to sustain the case that between them they fix things over their monthly dinners, partly because most have no idea in advance who the other diners will be and partly because society is now so much less easily manipulated. The membership of The Club has a slightly *ancien régime* feel. But its finespun influence, built upon having broken bread together, is none the less real for all that. And in its male exclusivity, it is also part of the explanation for the fact that so great a part of the upper echelons of British life still exclude women.

The clubs are the pinnacle of a culture, from the public schools through the professions to the judiciary and parliament from which half the population is automatically excluded. It is not the result of active discrimination so much as a series of unconscious assumptions about the corridors of power. The old Establishment may have fragmented, but the one thing you can confidently assume about powerful people in modern Britain is that still, the vast majority of them are men.

With the highly conspicuous exception of Margaret Thatcher, women have played a minimal role in recent public life. By 1990, there had been only two occasions since the end of the war when there was more than one woman in the cabinet. There were a record number of female MPs after the 1987 election, but the total of forty-one looked less than stunning when set against the twenty-four women members in 1945. So acute was the shortage of parliamentary women that on the 1986 Ministerial Group on Women's Issues, the chairman and three quarters of the members were male.[6]

In the judiciary, Britain entered the nineties with no female law lords, only one woman among the thirty lords justices of appeal, and one other among the eighty high court judges. As the majority of non-executive director appointments in business are made on the old boy network, company boards are dominated by men. Only twenty-one of the top 200 companies have women in the boardroom.[7] Less than one per cent of chief executives are female. In 1990 there was one woman (Dame Anne Mueller at the Treasury) among the thirty-five permanent secretaries in the civil service and only five female ambassadors – none at high-level embassies – among the 208 British overseas missions. Even in supposedly enlightened academia, of the 401 professors at Oxford and Cambridge, only twelve were women.

The influence of women cannot, of course, only be assessed by the number of influential posts they occupy, but it is a good enough measure. In the days when the worlds of power and Society interlocked, apparent male dominance was offset by the discreet, informal influence of women. Margot Asquith was a leading member of the Souls, the group of aesthetes and intellectuals formed in the 1880s, which included prominent political figures like Lord Curzon and A.J. Balfour. Beatrice Webb's influence on the foundation of the Welfare State was none the less real for being exercised indirectly.

But once the gentility had been taken out of politics and parliamentary life had begun to be divorced from the everyday doings of the already rich and powerful, the only effective way to measure the impact of women upon the governance of Britain was by the number who were actually involved in it. The all-pervading presence of Lady Violet Bonham Carter, to which Henry Fairlie took such exception in the 1950s, was noticeable precisely because she was the last refugee from the world of the pre-war hostesses.

Many of the formal obstacles which women have had to overcome in order to get their hands on the levers of power have been removed since then. But all the advances of women – from the first Doctor of Medicine (Elisabeth Blackwell) in 1849, to the first female MP (Nancy Astor) in 1919 and the first Appeal Court Judge (Dame Elizabeth Butler-Sloss) in 1987 – have been the products of single-minded determination as much as any change of climate. (Family background is also obviously a help. Nancy Astor entered the Commons by succeeding her husband as MP for Plymouth; Elizabeth Butler-Sloss is the daughter of a high court judge and sister to the former Attorney General, Lord Havers.)

The sheer maleness of much British life continues to present an enormous deterrent. It is at its worst in that most insulated of professions, the law. Only fifteen years ago women were excluded from some leading practices, and since then, admission to chambers, the essential first step on the road to success at the Bar, has been largely a matter of contacts within an overwhelmingly masculine world. Admittedly, there are signs of change – the proportion of practising female barristers has doubled since the 1970s (to fourteen per cent), the proportion of practising solicitors has almost quadrupled (to nineteen per cent). But the prevailing ambience of the law courts, as of the common rooms of the ancient universities and the Palace of Westminster, is neither female nor asexual.

Despite the opening of Oxbridge colleges to both sexes, women who have worked in American universities frequently remark upon the effort they must put into the business of getting on with their colleagues in Oxbridge common rooms, the struggle to be treated as just another colleague. In the vicinity of Westminster, the male atmosphere is overwhelming. 'Just try buying a pair of tights or a box of Tampax,' one female MP told me when I asked her how this climate showed itself.

The picture is changing only very slowly. In the old pillars of the corporate state, the civil service, the BBC and several of the nationalized industries, selection and promotion policies designed to encourage women are gradually producing a corps of senior middle-management figures who may one day succeed to the top posts. Even so, the projected outcome is less than awesome. The Treasury predicts that by the year 2016, nearly a century after the Representation of the People Act gave the vote to women, thirty per cent of senior civil service posts will be held by women. We shall see.

The ranks of the Great and Good continue to be dominated by men, and it sometimes seems that the appointments policy is designed to do no more than the bare minimum for the representation of women. Ever since the Postmaster General thought he could kill two birds with one stone by appointing a socialist woman to the board of Governors of the BBC, there has been at least one woman on that body. But to be truly representative, which is, after all, their function, half the governors should be women.

By the summer of 1990, the number of women on the BBC board of Governors had risen to three,[8] the result of a Downing Street policy which deliberately set out to increase the representation of women in public office. It had taken ten years since she took office for Margaret Thatcher to get around to insisting that one name on each short-list of candidates for public appointments be a woman, but it was a step in the right direction. Yet, however hard such policies may try to increase the number of prominent women, they are inevitably constrained by the fact that at the most important levels, ministers and civil servants appoint, in the words of one of them, 'chaps we know'. Unfortunately, the only women most of them, know are their wives, daughters or secretaries.

So if the pool of men is small, unexciting and unrepresentative, the pool of women in public life is tiny. Mary Warnock, an old-fashioned liberal if ever there was one, served on one committee after another, her most distinguished contribution being an inquiry into embryo research in the mid-eighties in which she had – literally – the right to define life and death. In commerce, Detta O'Cathain rose to public prominence from the unlikely springboard of the Milk Marketing Board and was soon in demand for service on the boards of the Midland Bank, the retailers Tesco and Sears, Channel 4 Television and the Industrial Society. Several others are political wives. Elspeth Howe, the most prominent of them, has worked hard to promote the cause of women, serving on the Equal Opportunities Commission and working as a tireless proselytizer for female advancement. Mary Baker, wife of the Conservative party chairman, Kenneth Baker, collects directorships the way others collect stamps: by 1989 she numbered Thames Television, Avon Cosmetics, Barclays Bank and the Prudential among her commercial interests; Bedford College and Westminster School in education; the London Tourist Board, the Women's National Commission and the Holiday Care Service in public works. Not bad for a mother and teacher. Jane, married to Jim Prior, holds non-executive directorships of the Trustee Savings Bank, and its subsidiary credit-card operation, as well as having a seat on the board of the sugar company Tate and Lyle. She also found time to act as governor to two schools and to sit on the council of Prince Charles' Youth Business Trust.

It is worth remarking on the scarcity of women in public life for the indication it gives of how little has really changed. The upper reaches of British society may no longer be the exclusive preserve of the upper classes. But the combination of upper and middle-class people who have replaced them still tend to have their style of education – and their sex – in common.

When Charles Wilson was appointed the twenty-first editor of *The Times* in 1985, he received 300 letters of congratulation. The only thing which staggered him more than the sheer volume was the contents of one of them. On Lambeth Palace notepaper the Archbishop of Canterbury had written in his own hand:

'Now that we are both members of the Establishment, perhaps we should get to know each other a little better.'

The Archbishop had a nice line in dry, clerical jokes, and his remark, the prelude to an invitation which Wilson never took up, can only have been made tongue-in-cheek. Time was when both men would have unquestionably been part of the Establishment, not merely by virtue of their position, but because most of those who occupied such posts tended to share much the same assumptions about the world. *The Times* was the journal of that tribe, the newspaper of St James's libraries, judges' robing rooms, fellows' parlours, officers' messes and the cathedral close. It is still to be found in many of them, but it is rarely there alone, and no-one pays it much more attention than, say, *The Independent* or the *Financial Times*. The altered state of *The Times* is a metaphor for what became of the Establishment.

The staff of *The Times* used to have an almost sacerdotal idea of their own role in the scheme of things. Lord Northcliffe, who owned the paper for fifteen years in the early part of the century, called the Oxbridge-educated leader-writers 'the Black Friars', and wanted to write over the portals 'Abandon Scope All Ye Who Enter Here'. They were often men of immense learning – Claud Cockburn claimed to have seen one of them once translating Plato into Chinese – in no doubt that in the words of its onetime editor, Geoffrey Dawson, *The Times* was 'the submerged half of the government'.

Nowhere was awareness of the paper's unique role more self-confidently expressed than in an anonymous thirty-nine-page memorandum written by senior journalists in the late fifties. Alarmed by plans to try to double the circulation, introduce a less 'ponderous' style of writing, give less space to leader columns and put news on the front page (instead of the personal columns), they delivered themselves of this conception of their readers:

Great Britain cannot function without a strong, educated, efficient, informed governing class. *The Times* is the organ of that class ... The existence of a competent governing class is rightly said to be absolutely dependent upon *The Times* because no other newspaper attempts to rival it in self-respect, impartiality, independence, range of significant news, capacity to reason upon the matter printed. No other newspaper possesses the space in which adequately to discuss, in leading articles and letters to the

Editor, the topical and national problems of today and tomorrow. This was true a hundred years ago and it is true today. A country like Great Britain depends for its administrative efficiency upon its politically intelligent and professional men; these in turn depend upon *The Times* for the material upon which to reflect, and ultimately, to act ... The Chief Proprietors of *The Times* are not engaged in the enterprise of publishing a newspaper interesting to the 'reading public'; they have never acknowledged among their duties that of providing a 'livelier' newspaper.[9]

There is a dash of both whimsy and confusion to this self-confident picture of the newspaper's readership, as if processes like the end of Empire had scarcely entered the coal-fired rooms where the leader-writers dreamed up their great thoughts for the next day's breakfast sideboards. The tightly-knit governing class was already dissolving, the distinctions between informed opinion and public opinion becoming more and more blurred.

The 1958 advertising slogan, 'Top People take *The Times*', which stuck with the paper for the next three decades, drew on the very image that the paper's management was at the time trying to dispel. It managed to offend both the old guard (top people who already took the paper didn't need the fact emblazoned on crude advertising hoardings) and the new populists, to whom it seemed to suggest that if you weren't a nob, the paper wasn't interested in you. The editor, Sir William Haley, disliked the campaign, but it worked none the less, and circulation began to build.

But the combination of selective influence and mass readership is a trick which can't be done. The paper repeatedly proved itself unable to decide which of the two beasts it wanted to be. Ten years after the revolt of the Black Friars, the paper planned another dash for growth, under the editorship of the young William Rees-Mogg. Again, there was an expensive advertising campaign, grandiose talk of doubled circulation, disquiet among the leader-writers, and a quiet return to a readership little larger than it had been when the paper proclaimed itself as belonging to the Top People.

Had it not been for the ludicrously expensive production practices connived at by both management and unions, the paper might have been able to continue defying one of the basic laws of capitalism: expand or die. As it was, it depended upon the indefinite patronage of a benign sugar-daddy, happy to support the most famous paper in the world because of its reputation as the paper of the ruling class.

When the Canadian tycoon Roy Thomson, son of a Toronto

hairdresser, bought the paper from the Astors in 1966, he reckoned it 'the greatest thing I have ever done'. This was not a business judgement – like the allure of an ancient stately home to a successful manufacturer, *The Times* promised status, respectability and constant bills. To satisfy the Monopolies Commission, that old howitzer wheeled out whenever an aggressive entrepreneur looks like upsetting the comfortable inefficiencies of vested interest, Thomson had to promise that he would not get involved in running the paper personally.

Under his protection, the presumption of intimacy with the élite survived. Peter Jay, the economics editor, was once assailed by a not-very-clever sub-editor laying out a piece he had written for the next morning.

'I can't understand your article,' he said, rather truculently.

Jay drew breath for a moment, then replied:

'You're not supposed to. It's written for three people. Two of them are at the Treasury and the other's at the Bank of England.'[10]

Eventually, it was the bloody-mindedness of the trades unions which exhausted the indulgence of the Thomson organization. When, in November 1978, the unions refused to countenance new working practices which might have ensured the paper's survival, Thomson just stopped printing, in the hope of administering a 'short sharp shock'. The paper stayed shut for almost a year. By the time, fifty weeks later, *The Times* restarted publication, something had gone. Beyond the £39 million which the confrontation had cost Thomson, was the damage done to the paper's standing: the journal of record had ceased recording.

The man who bought *The Times* from Thomson in 1981, Rupert Murdoch, was someone about whom it was impossible to nurse illusions. He already owned the *Sun* and the *News of the World*, two newspapers which plumbed depths of popular taste previously thought unfathomable. *The Times* itself had commented unfavourably on the antics of Murdoch's yellow press in the United States. The noticeable thing now was how muted was any serious talk about a colonial barbarian getting his hands on a great national institution, a reflection of the already diminished status of the paper.

Hannen Swaffer, the great Fleet Street polemicist, once described his job as being to print 'such of the proprietors' prejudices as the advertisers don't object to'. By the standards of some of the monsters who have stalked the British press, Rupert Keith Murdoch is a less interventionist proprietor than many. But he demanded that his papers support the Thatcher government and when his editors were too 'thoughtful' – a damning term coming from him – they were sacked.

In other times, when a different sort of Conservatism held sway, the Great and Good would have tried to moderate the Murdoch influence upon *The Times* through the 'independent' directors on the newspaper board. But in the changed climate of the eighties, the contest between the remnants of the Great and Good and international business was like watching a philosophy professor trying to discuss ethics with an armed mugger – there was no doubt as to the eventual outcome. The 'independent' directors of *The Times*, all of them appointed by Mr Murdoch, have included figures like his London banker, Lord Catto; the founder of that powerhouse of Thatcherism, the Institute of Economic Affairs, Lord Harris; and the man who taught Murdoch the skills of sub-editing, Sir Edward Pickering. Their powers were in any case terribly limited, and the only recent occasion on which they have raised an editorial disquiet with Mr Murdoch came when the *Sunday Times* appeared to have committed *lèse-majesté* by reporting an alleged row between Buckingham Palace and Downing Street.

Murdoch was canny enough to reassure the old guard on the paper that while he did want to increase circulation, it would not be done at the expense of its authority. This may have been sincerely meant, but it was so much hot air, as the experience of the two previous attempts to achieve the same objective had shown. On *The Times* of the fifties, feature or background articles scarcely existed, because it was assumed that anyone reading the paper already knew the background. To attract a new readership, Murdoch engaged a new editor, Harold Evans, who had turned the *Sunday Times* into one of the outstanding newspapers in the English-speaking world. Evans trebled the number of features, made bigger, bolder use of pictures and hired over fifty highly-paid new staff. He scored a notable triple triumph, alienating the old guard, failing to increase circulation more than minimally and antagonizing Murdoch. He was sacked after a year and replaced by Charles Douglas-Home, nephew of the former prime minister, Old Etonian, and keen foxhunter.

Like one or two other apparent chips off the old block who rose in the eighties, Douglas-Home was not what he seemed. The paper started to run more sports stories and to give greater coverage to crime, but the greatest change was in the leader columns. Previous editors had committed the paper to what Barrington-Ward called in the 1940s 'getting the best out of government'. It was an Olympian, conservative, slightly paternalist attitude, which might have been found in the upper reaches of the mandarinate and university common rooms as well.

Douglas-Home ditched the last of the Black Friars and surrounded himself with true-believing figures from the New Right. Murdoch was an uncritical admirer of Margaret Thatcher, and soon the paper's attitude to the government had become more-or-less supine. It was an abandonment of the High Ground which caused irreversible damage to the paper. With the death of Charles Douglas-Home in 1985, at the age of only forty-eight, *The Times* acquired yet another new editor, the fourth in five years. It was not a rate of turnover to give the impression of stability, and Wilson himself was to last only five years.

Charles Wilson was decidely not of Establishment stock. A squat Glaswegian with the build, and some of the fit, flattened looks, of a welter-weight boxer, his father had been a miner and virtual founder-member of the ILP. He had arrived at *The Times* after a career in provincial journalism, editing the *Glasgow Herald* and the *Scottish Sunday Standard*. To outward appearances, either of the two men appointed to edit other papers the following year – Max Hastings at the *Daily Telegraph*, with his penchant for shooting weekends, or *The Independent*'s Andreas Whittam Smith, who looked as if he farmed half of Norfolk, appeared more obviously in the mould of *Times* editors. Wilson, sprightly, direct and short-fused, seemed more the caricature Scottish sports editor, lacking only a green eyeshade to bring the cameo to life.

Charles Wilson could scarcely have been a greater contrast with old-fashioned *Times* editors. In 1922 Lloyd George had seriously thought of resigning as Prime Minister to edit the paper, and the man who got the job the following year, Geoffrey Dawson (Eton, All Souls, the Colonial Office and Yorkshire grousemoors), was on such close terms with Stanley Baldwin that they would discuss together who should or should not be in the cabinet or sent to be Viceroy of India. That neither Hastings nor Whittam Smith – nor Wilson's successor, Simon Jenkins – falls into the same category is further reflection of the way in which the old élite has fragmented.

The editor of *The Times* is still forever having his ear bent by one aggrieved minister or diplomat or another, in the hope of a sympathetic line emerging in the leader columns, but the credibility of today's paper operates on a law of increasing returns: the further away from London, the more seriously it is taken. Overseas *The Times* is still considered *the* British paper, the voice of the ruling class, even until recently in some corners of Eastern Europe, the voice of the Foreign Office. At home, an editorial on, say, proposed changes to the National Health Service will undoubtedly be read by those who are actually planning the changes, simply because it gets included in the cuttings service circulated to ministers and permanent secretaries. But there is no evidence that *The Times* is taken more seriously than, say, *The Independent* or even the *Daily Telegraph*. Indeed, there were sophisticated lobbyists who argued in the eighties that the only leader-writer worth cultivating was Mr Ronald Spark of the *Sun*, on the grounds that his columns not only had by far the biggest readership, but that the paper's editorial column was one of the few actually read by Margaret Thatcher.

One of the political dramas to have been most directly influenced by a *Times* editorial in recent years came in 1982, after the Argentine Army had invaded the Falkland Islands. *The Times* called on the Foreign Secretary, Lord Carrington, to resign. An honourable man, he had privately reached the same decision already, but upon cabinet colleagues who were wavering, the editorial tolled a knell. 'Naturally, the tabloid press was more dramatic and indeed, in some cases worse. But they would have been easier to disregard,' thought the then Home Secretary, William Whitelaw.[11]

But it would be hard to find a cabinet minister among the younger generation who would attach such importance to the views of *The Times*, since it has become just one newspaper among many. One of them told me he worried much more about what the *Daily Telegraph* had to say because of its loyal readership among twinset Tories in the constituency parties. All round, as sales of the 'quality' papers have grown, so the influence of any one has declined. All of them seem less than wholehearted about their editorial columns, and one gets the sense that they survive more because they are part of the furniture than anything else. The more widely read columns are signed by people like Bernard Levin in *The Times*, Peter Jenkins and the reincarnated William Rees-Mogg in *The Independent*, and, the most highly regarded of them all, Hugo Young in the *Guardian*. The sheer diversity of voices (if not of political points of view) militates against the anonymous wisdom of the editorial columns.

But it is less the decline of the editorial than the overall change in character of *The Times* which makes older readers feel let down. The majority of those I interviewed while researching this book had once been *Times* readers, and almost all complained that it had become tendentious, garish and sloppy. Some are genuinely angry; the Duke of Devonshire comments, 'I'd like to shoot Mr Murdoch. I think he's a terrible influence on this country.'[12] Lord Shawcross, once appointed a director of *The Times* by his Sussex neighbour Lord Astor, finds it necessary now to read four broadsheets, where previously one would have sufficed. 'It's reporting far more of the stuff one had hitherto been accustomed to finding in the tabloids,' he says with distaste. Asked for an example, he lifts himself out his armchair and, with surprising speed and alacrity for a man in his late eighties, strides across to his desk. 'I mean look at this,' he said, as if pointing at a headless rat the cat had dropped on the carpet. WIFE'S ESCAPE KIT HELPED COCAINE BARON, or this, TAILED GUNMAN SHOT OFF-DUTY PC, or this, VICAR WHO KILLED WIFE SENTENCED. One would, to say the least, have been a little surprised to find that sort of thing when I was a director.'[13]

But this sort of story is the staple of other newspapers, and the reason *The Times* has become like any other paper is that it has adopted the techniques of other papers. Its claim to uniqueness was based upon its presumption of knowledge, its journalistic authority, its regular and extensive parliamentary and law reports, the obituaries, and the court circular. These secured a readership which made its letters column the natural forum in which the Establishment would talk to itself.

Parliamentary reports were cut back in the mid-eighties, but the paper retains a loyal readership in various nooks and crannies of the professional world. The law reports ensure it continues to drop through judges' and barristers' letter boxes. Among bishops and deans *The Times* still seems to hang on to something of a readership, a reflection upon the calibre of its Church correspondent, but the fact that it is no longer the only paper taken inevitably diminishes its influence. The announcements it carries about universities, military appointments and the Church give it squatter's rights in many a common room or mess. 'If one gave it up,' remarked Sir Michael Howard, when regius professor of Modern History at Oxford in 1986, 'it would be like resigning from a club to which all one's friends belong.'[14] It retains the sometimes grudging loyalty of what is left of 'society' and the royal family's fan club, and when there is talk of cutting the Court Circular there is a barrage of letters of complaint. Several aristocrats remarked that there was no other noticeboard like *The Times* births, engagements and deaths columns. 'The first reaction to a bereavement is still "Oh, Fred's dead. Must tell *The Times*"', was how one elderly peer put it.

No other forum has yet supplanted the letters page, which can still – very occasionally – give the feeling that not much in Britain has changed. Even though *The Independent* has captured much of the natural readership of *The Times*, its correspondence page has failed to make much of a dent in the volume of mail which pours into *The Times* at the rate of 70,000 or more letters a year. It continues to be able to operate its ban on letters from public relations officers or those which have appeared elsewhere, and still often has little difficulty finding twenty worth printing. But despite the speed of debate made possible by faxes, the arguments seem to lack urgency, and in recent years, increasing numbers who would once have been thought of as natural writers of letters to *The Times*, like Graham Greene, have begun to decamp to its competitors. These changes obviously do not bother the many thousands who take the paper for its bingo, 'Portfolio', but they alarm the old stalwarts. The push to increase circulation has inevitably resulted in a less differentiated readership.

The 'quality' newspapers of the fifties and sixties survived on tiny circulations by today's standards, which enabled them to operate on the basis both of shared knowledge about the world and shared assumptions. The presumptions of *The Times*' leader-writers were even shared by the *Guardian*. When David Marquand joined the paper in Manchester as a twenty-five-year-old leader-writer in 1959, he was fresh from a glittering university career. The editorials made few concessions. 'You operated on the assumption that the readers knew the news already,' he recalls. 'You were writing for a very élite audience. It wasn't that you were writing down to people: you assumed that they were as well-educated as you were.'[15]

At that time the combined circulation of the *Guardian* and *The Times* was about 426,000. Another million or so read the *Daily Telegraph*, making a total readership for the quality press of one and a half million.[16] By 1988, total sales of broadsheet newspapers had increased by over one million, to 2,600,000.[17] This much larger market simply does not share the terms of reference of the much smaller society who made up the natural readership of *The Times* of

Dawson or even Haley, The new, larger, educated class is more fragmented, more eclectic, and politically diffuse.

The editor of *The Independent*, Andreas Whittam Smith, is perpetually being told that his paper has become the new forum of the Establishment. It is an empty compliment, but it reflects the paper's attempt to steal some of *The Times*' clothes. Readership surveys show *The Times* and *The Independent* with roughly equal proportions of readers in the upper social groups, although the most startling characteristic of the readership of *The Independent* is its youth; half are aged thirty-four or less, almost one quarter are twenty-five or younger.[19] Whether, like an old *Times* tribe, they will come to regard it as a club from which they cannot resign, is a matter of time.

If any newspaper can claim to be the Top People's paper today, it is the *Financial Times*. It certainly has the richest, and therefore in one sense most powerful, readership. (Less than two out of ten of the readers of *The Times* belong to the higher managerial, administrative or professional class, the same proportion as are skilled or unskilled manual workers, while four out of ten of the readers, the largest single group, are intermediate managers.[20]) The *Financial Times* has more foreign correspondents than any other paper, and its voice is the more authoritative for being raised relatively infrequently.

In early 1990, *The Times* got yet another new editor. This time, the paper reverted to earlier moulds. Simon Jenkins combined a distinguished career as a columnist with a decade of service among the Great and Good, on things like the Historic Monuments Commission. Although he professed himself happy with much of the paper as it was, his task at *The Times* was the restoration of an historic monument too.

Certain changes were evident at once – the closing down of some softer features, the publication of a new style book to try to restore coherence to the paper's prose, more restrained headlines and, most importantly, a new independence of mind in the editorial columns. Although, he didn't write them himself, Charles Wilson had allowed the leader columns to continue with the slavish loyalty to Margaret Thatcher introduced under Charles Douglas-Home. Simon Jenkins, whose last job had been as a columnist on the *Sunday Times*, made a point of writing leader columns himself. The paper began to take a more independent, although by no means radical, line. The changes suggested that Mr Murdoch had now decided he wanted to recapture some of the paper's traditional readership.

It is a doomed venture. He may restore some of the paper's

authority, but *The Times* cannot regain its unique position. Nor does it deserve to. When it was the Establishment gazette it had the power to make – or break – people, as it demonstrated at the time of the Abdication. But its power corrupted, and the abuse of its authority during the Appeasement years ('I did my utmost, night after night, to keep out of the paper anything that might hurt their [the Nazis'] susceptibilities,' Dawson confessed) should serve as a warning of the dangers of a single newspaper having the ear of anyone who matters.

The educated class in Britain is now vastly greater than at the time when *The Times* could claim to be the house journal of the nation's rulers. As the better educated sector has grown, it has fragmented. That *The Times* failed to recognize that fragmentation was its misfortune. That it failed to cater for it was inevitable.

There was an inevitability about the loss of the privileged position of *The Times* which makes it something of a paradigm. There is no Establishment Gazette because the old Establishment, to which it was directed, no longer exists.

By the time that the columnists and satirists were attacking it in the 1950s its condition was already critical. The Establishment was the last remnant of the tension between authoritarian and democratic systems of government, and forces had been released in the rest of society which made the retention of power by such a small clique intolerable. In its original form, the worlds of 'society' and power had been coterminous. In the governing class which succeeded the old Establishment, the higher professions took on the mantle which the aristocracy had once worn. In this new form, the Establishment has proved remarkably durable.

The Labour party – consistently more radical in opposition than in government – managed to rub along with the professional Establishment because each tacitly recognized an effective separation of powers. In the event, it was Harold Wilson's defeat of Lord Home which paved the way for the most successful assault upon the new élite, for it committed the Tories to embracing a new generation of politicians in whom ambition replaced breeding.

That process led in time to the election of Margaret Thatcher as party leader, and her government administered the sharpest shock to the postwar coalition of vested interests that it had ever experienced. All attempts to smother her in the enfolding wisdom of the great institutions proved weaker than Mrs Thatcher's own vision of herself as an

outsider battling for what she believed in. Perhaps it was partly
because of her sex that she lacked that sixth sense under which the
male-dominated Establishment prescribed the limits of change. Certainly, she was not a gentleman and she did not respect the gentlemen's
agreements upon which the postwar balance of power rested. No
recent government has attempted such overtly political manipulation
of the public appointments system, and, seized of the rightness of her
cause, no-one had less need of the accumulated wisdom of the Great
and Good.

I set out to answer a simple question, Who runs Britain? The
experience of the eighties suggests that the only plausible answer is
the Prime Minister. Scarcely any of the great institutions remained
untouched by Thatcherism in its various manifestations, and when
even museums and opera houses are talking the language of the
marketplace, there can be no doubting the depth of its influence. The
gradual emasculation of the cabinet and its transformation from a
collection of equals into a series of isolated satrapies, the simple fact of
the Prime Minister's longevity and her sheer public prominence, all
increased the concentration of power in 10 Downing Street.

The accretion of authority within Downing Street was less the
consequence of any fundamental shift in the essential style of British
government – the creation of a 'presidential' role – than the expression
of the particular relationship between Margaret Thatcher and her
party. When the Thatcher era is over, the balance of power will shift
again, and the collegiate spirit in both major parties remains strong
enough for the dominant role of Downing Street to be reduced.

But in the eighties, as the influence of Downing Street grew, so the
standing of parliament diminished. The influence of the individual
MP is directly related to the Whips' need of his vote: the series of
thumping Tory majorities inevitably decreed that alternative points of
view were scarcely considered. The increased size of the payroll vote
meant that at any division in the House of Commons, processions of
ambitious young Conservative MPs would line up meekly to be
whipped through the Government lobby, their only ambition the hope
of preferment at the next ministerial reshuffle. Dissent was largely
confined to those whom infirmity, insouciance or incompetence
rendered unsuitable for further ministerial office. Hardly surprising,
then, that politicians seem to be held in even lower esteem now than
twenty years ago, with opinion polls showing them to be more
distrusted even than estate agents and insurance salesmen.

The extent of the impact of radical Toryism upon the pillars of the
Establishment is all the more remarkable in the light of the repeated
failure of Labour governments to dent them. It has been the repeated
complaint of one socialist minister after another that the creation of a
truly egalitarian society was obstructed by the machinations of powerful vested interest groups from the City to the civil service. The
Labour party was largely irrelevant in any serious consideration of the
parameters of power in the eighties, largely by reason of its own
unelectability. The bad taste in the mouth left by the Winter of
Discontent, the party's own preoccupation with its internal affairs,
and what seemed a sea-change in public sentiment left it generally out
in the cold. Similarly, the trade unions, which would once have been
automatically included in any audit of power in Britain, suffered one
reverse after another. Membership seeped away as traditional industries declined. Legislation on industrial action stripped them of much
of their might. The great confrontations of the eighties – the battle of
Wapping and the miners' strike – proved the superiority of the power
of the state and the entrepreneur over the might of organized labour.
So unpopular were they that even the Labour party, which was
created by the trade unions, was committed to reducing their influence
within the party.

The dominance of Margaret Thatcher did at least prove that the
days of the magic circle of well-connected chaps in the Conservative
party were gone for good. Those few aristocrats who survive in
political life do so by virtue of their talents rather than any family connections.

Those who enjoyed access to Downing Street during the Thatcher
years were maverick, entrepreneurial figures who had made it on their
own terms, and usually didn't give a fig about convention. What they
had in common was a business-like view of the world. They did not,
however, share a common background or education, and they did not
belong to a social network which extended into other areas of life
beyond a relatively small business-political nexus. There is no denying
that they constituted a temporary élite of sorts. But they were prickly
individualists, and they failed to achieve the durable cohesion of the
Great and Good. There is no denying their influence, but they failed
to become a new Establishment themselves.

The finance houses like to boast that nowadays every position, from
humblest messenger to a seat on the board, is open to talent, regardless
of background. It is less true than the propaganda proclaims, but it

reflects the style of the times. The contemporary heroes are entrepreneurs who dragged themselves up by their bootstraps, and who are proud to proclaim the fact. Does it follow that the incubus of the class system is dead?

The three great headstreams of the class system, the monarchy, the House of Lords and the public schools are all in excellent health. A class system might survive without the royal family. What is beyond doubt is that the special position of the royal family cannot survive without gradations of class. This is not to say that theirs is an easy job, nor that an elected presidency would necessarily be any more congenial. But their pre-eminent position owes nothing to endeavour and everything to an accident of birth. Despite the warnings about the dangers of letting daylight in upon magic, republicanism has failed to become a coherent political force and the younger members of the royal family, notably Prince Charles and Princess Anne, have developed a style for the House of Windsor – compassionate, concerned and slightly wry – which has given an institution teetering on the brink of irrelevance a quite unexpected vigour. They may not have meant to, but in doing so they have kept alive the source of that characteristically British phenomenon, the distinction between achievement and acceptance.

The aristocracy counts for less, of course. But its privileges – the connections with royalty, the seats in the House of Lords and the rest – are as intact now as they were sixty years ago. Only the most inbred nincompoop could have failed to use the opportunities of the so-called 'Enterprise Culture' to restore the family fortunes and add to ancestral wealth. After decades of swingeing death duties, you could hardly blame them if in the process they jettisoned many of their old social responsibilities. But it makes protestations about their endangerment and their historical duties ring pretty hollow.

The attempts which have been made to broaden the base of this privileged group, by the creation of life-peers, rather than watering down class distinctions, have actually injected new life into the whole business. The possibility of elevation to the House of Lords not only makes the swashbuckling takeover king look fondly on the social apparatus which once kept him down, it also tends to confer increased respectability upon those who happen to be there because they chose the right parents.

The prosperity of the independent schools is vivid testimony to an underlying lack of faith in state education. The peeling paintwork, demoralized teachers and concerned parents in so many areas are the greatest single obstacle to the achievement of a society in which advancement depends solely upon talent. The independent sector, by contrast, goes from strength to strength. The public schools' promise is less to provide an entry-ticket to that fabled upper-class network so beloved of picaresque novelists, than to improve the chances of passing public examinations and going on to one of the better universities. So each year the fee-paying schools continue to turn out young men and women equipped with the examination results to ensure that they will go on to command the same places in Whitehall, the City and the nation which the long list of names on the school roll of honour occupied before them.

That the schools are divisive is common ground, although it is less and less easy to tell their products from those who emerge from the state sector. The better independent schools have absorbed the criticism of one historian after another that they are prejudiced against industry and at least go through the motions of acquainting their pupils with business. More uncomfortable is the evidence of many public school headmasters that much of that distinctive morality which the schools proclaimed as their glory has been discarded along with the old prejudices. They compete aggressively to sell their services, the schools live and die by the quality of their exam results, and they have an uphill struggle, which many scarcely attempt any longer, in promoting the old public school virtues. The idea that duty is owed in return for privilege is deeply unfashionable.

The schools no more than reflect the spirit of the times. The sheer, naked selfishness which has been unleashed is a revolting thing to behold. 'There is no such thing as society,' Margaret Thatcher had once declared, and the juxtaposition of egocentric greed and public squalor gave flesh to her words.

'Ah, but what we've created is a new respect for business,' comes the reply. 'And you must agree that prejudice against business was one of the main reasons for Britain's awful economic performance over the last century.' But this too is eyewash. The children of the professional classes no more want to be businesspeople now than they did twenty years ago, as the figures from Cambridge University confirm. Like generations before them, they want to join that vast, parasitic 'respectable society' of professions of one kind or another.

What we have is not so much respect for business as reverence for money. Victorian industrialists bought great estates with the profits from their cotton mills and steel foundries, because possession of land conferred social standing. With the estates went a social position and social obligations. The modern entrepreneur who makes his fortune from selling time-shares on the Costa Brava may still hanker after a country pile. But he doesn't think he takes on any of the old baggage too.

Mere money, once a vulgar commodity, worthwhile only for what it could achieve, is now considered a good thing in itself. 'Blessed are the selfish' is the new beatitude. While demanding loyalty from their staff, the new-wave companies offer them little in return. Family business empires are increasingly swallowed up by massive multinational empires run by rootless men whose first and only responsibility is to anonymous institutional shareholders. And just as increasing numbers of individuals in the City are prepared to switch from firm to firm in pursuit of the next golden handshake, so the firms themselves are ready to accept and reject new customers in a similar fashion, and the loyalty of the whole of the Square Mile is less to a sovereign government or nation and more to some supranational priesthood of moneymen.

Small wonder that the idea of public service has come to count for so little. Teachers, to whom we give the delicate and awesome responsibility of nurturing the minds of the next generation, are looked down upon by their charges because they earn so little. If wealth generators are to be the heroes of the hour, then public servants, by definition wealth consumers, are its villains.

The public service still manages to attract talented young people, but the contrast with some earlier generations is in their motivation. Where many of their predecessors were drawn to the administration from a high moral purpose, their contemporary counterparts go into it solely for intellectual challenge or the thrill of being close to power.

The civil service seems out of joint with the times because it still prides itself upon being the preserve of the generalist. Generalism was the terrain of the professional Establishment. The expansion of the universities undermined the élite by creating a hugely enlarged educated class with a diversity of backgrounds and viewpoints and setting free unstoppable demotic forces in a youth culture accountable only to its own peers.

But while the number of people with university education is larger, they are products of a system which encourages them to specialize at an increasingly early age. Between them, the schools and universities turn out better and better qualified people in narrower and narrower fields. If *The Times* is a less sophisticated paper than it was forty years ago it is partly because its readers know less of the world.

The idea of 'the civilized man', familiar with the arts, politics and science, means less and less. It was from that confluence that the Establishment drew whatever moral strength it possessed. It was all right to make money, but those who did so had responsibilities as well, towards the poor, the sick and refugees from oppression. The Church of England was the fount of many of these values, but the message it preaches has little or no relevance to the new mood of the times.

Countries, like families, schools or companies, take their tone from the top. For most of the post-war period, Britain was run by a more-or-less paternalist alliance of old money and members of the higher professions. Their values had been handed down, only slightly modified, from the Victorians. It would be wrongheaded to character-ize them as being motivated by philanthropy: they did what they did because they were fortunate or talented enough to be granted access to a particularly privileged élite.

But the sense of duty which motivated them percolated through the rest of society. Royal commissions might be the preserve of the few. But many could become school governors or work for charity. The sense of civic obligation was similar. In the age of the personal achiever, such ideas become unfashionable. There were plenty of reasons to dislike the old Establishment, but it had virtues as well as vices.

In his original article in the *Spectator*, Henry Fairlie had remarked upon the attempts of well-connected people to shield Melinda Maclean from the attentions of an intrusive press. But few episodes were more damaging to the old élite than the behaviour of Maclean, Burgess and Philby, men nurtured by the British ruling class who then set out to destroy it. The further the spy scandal was uncovered, the longer the roll-call of 'the right sort of people' to be exposed. With the unmasking of Sir Anthony Blunt, the list reached into the royal household. Since then, one outwardly unimpeachable name after another has been floated in the press as a potential 'Fifth Man' working for the victory of world communism. Like all the greatest acts of betrayal, this conspiracy of well-bred traitors had the effect of making even those whose loyalty was undimmed question what they stood for.

Unsure of its own integrity and set upon from without, the profes-sional Establishment is bloody and bowed. No coherent new élite has yet supplanted it, but neither has a true meritocracy been forged. In a

society with no written constitution, the Greater Athenaeum did hav
the merit of providing some sort of moral framework. In the effort to
create a new élite – an attempt which has had strictly limited success
so far – many of the values of the Greater Athenaeum were scorned.
The tension between the old and the new orders revealed how much
British public life depended upon gentlemen's agreements: there were
some things gentlemen just didn't do. The erosion of those values has
strengthened the case for statutory edifices to protect basic freedoms,
like a Bill of Rights.

In delineating the parameters of the possible, the Establishment
defined what it was to be British. It was at times a stifling, enervating
prescription, but as the nation dithered through the postwar years it
kept alive a sense of national identity. Britain's indecision over her
role in the postwar world, the uncertainties over her relations with
Europe, the United States and the Commonwealth, revealed the
paralysing tendency of the Establishment to cling to the past. Any
analysis of the miserable economic performance of Britain since the
war must also lay most of the blame on the prejudices and incompetence of the men in leather armchairs in St James's. They are the true
authors of the nation's malaise. But the consequences of that misfortune were at first less destructive than they might have been
because at its highest levels, Britain retained a reasonably coherent
vision of the sort of society the United Kingdom was.

As to what it means to be British in the nineties, there is now
mostly confusion, No-one who travelled abroad could fail to be aware
of the enormous impact Margaret Thatcher has had upon the
international stage. But a nation is more than one of its leaders. Faced
with the challenge of a rapidly uniting Europe, the United Kingdom
was unsure of what it wished to preserve, beyond a few totems. The
middle classes were already leading a largely European way of life
anyway, much of the rest of the population a mid-Atlantic lifestyle.
The division between the pasta classes and the hamburger classes can
be exaggerated, but it reveals a deep uncertainty.

The country needs a new vision, a new sense of what it means to be
British. And a new role. But to whom can the nation look?

Notes

Publication details of all titles cited in the notes are given in the bibliography.

Introduction

1. *Perfect Gents*, Alan Bennett, programme notes, *Simple Spies*.
2. How much Mishcon was acting off his own bat and how much on representations from the Palace is unknown. Certainly on earlier occasions the royal household had not been abashed about trying to censor plays which might offend. See Crossman Diaries, vol.2, p.442.
3. Peter Hennessy: 'The Most Elevated and Distinguished Casualties of the Thatcher Years', in the *Listener*, 7 February 1985.
4. Coleridge: 'On the Constitution of Church and State', chap. V, in *Collected Works* (ed. John Colmer, 1976), p.44.
5. Stirling, 'the phantom major' who founded the Special Air Service, set up GB75 in 1974, to seize control of power stations and sewage works in the event of a general strike. General Walker's organization, Unison, later renamed Civil Assistance, aimed to enrol three million members for similar duties.
6. This account comes from Ziegler, *Mountbatten*, p.659, and Cudlipp, *Walking on the Water*.
7. Although even Taylor may have been unconsciously picking up on a usage already minted by Ford Madox Ford. Ford used the term to refer to the comfortable, enclosed and philistine world of London society, against which he railed ineffectually. Waiting to be demobilized after the First World War, he had discovered there were eighteen categories in the priority list for return to civilian life. The first contained 'Administrators, bankers, manufacturers and working coal-miners, etc.' The eighteenth and last was headed 'totally unproductive', and listed 'travelling showmen, circus performers, all writers not regularly employed on newspapers, tramps, pedlars, all painters not employed as house, factory, industrial carriage or sign painters; all musicians, all unemployable men.' There are numerous references in his books to the anti-intellectual climate he saw pervading British society. In the *Transatlantic Review* of June 1924 he laid into the class he saw taking control:

   > Their power grows daily – and their numbers. Their occupations call for no gifts but industry, and that industry can be pursued slowly, at regular hours, without strain and without the need of any skill that is not easily attainable . . . And once fairly established and possessed of an awakened class conscious-ness, such a body tends to become a very formidable realm within such a realm as chooses to allow of such an establishment.

   (Quoted in Goldring, *The Nineteen Twenties*, p.225.) Ford eventually found the whole place so uncongenial that he left, first for Paris and then for the United States.
8. A.J.P. Taylor: *New Statesman*, 8 August 1953, vol.46, pp.236-7.
9. Ibid.
10. Henry Fairlie: 'Political Commentary' in the *Spectator*, 23 September 1955.

11. Lord Bonham-Carter, interview.

12. Sir Hartley Shawcross, House of Commons, 2 April 1946.

13. *Observer*, 1 October 1961.

14. Ibid.

15. *The Times*, 6 October 1961.

16. Brian Masters: *The Swinging Sixties*, p.57.

17. Susan Atkins.

18. Henry Fairlie, 'The BBC', in *The Establishment*, ed. Hugh Thomas, p.202.

19. Ibid., p.203. By now, even A.J.P. Taylor regretted the word:

> The very word, so plummy, so ponderous, so respectable, tempts us to acknowledge the moral superiority of 'the Establishment'. It conjures up benign, upholstered figures, calm, steady, reliable. They would never pass a dud cheque or cheat at cards. Not intellectually dazzling, perhaps, but patient, understanding and tolerant – above all tolerant . . . We ought to have revived Cobbett's name: THE THING. That suggests much better the complacency, the incompetence and the selfishness which lie behind the façade.

(*The Twentieth Century*, October 1957, vol.162, pp.293–7.)

20. 'The thing we really hated was Butskellism. We identified the Whigs as the real enemies in British history, because they always smoothed over everything.' *Financial Times*, 16 July 1988.

21. Professor David Marquand, interview.

22. 'The Crumbling of the Establishment' in the *Financial Times*, 16 July 1988.

23. Anthony Sampson: *The Anatomy of Britain*, p.624.

24. Peter Hennessy: *Whitehall*, p.76.

25. 'Friends in High Places' in *The Independent*, 21 October 1989.

CHAPTER ONE

Lords, Squires and Pipsqueaks

1. James Lees-Milne: *Ancestral Voices*, p.171.

2. James Lees-Milne: *Caves of Ice*, p.172.

3. James Lees-Milne: 'Landed Property and Proprietors' in *Burke's Landed Gentry*, p.xviii.

4. David Cecil: *The Young Melbourne*, p.5.

5. John Scott: *The Upper Classes: Property and Privilege in Britain*, p.100.

6. Lord Derby: 'Ireland and the Land Act', in *Nineteenth Century*, October 1881, p.474.

7. Marion Shoard: *This Land is Our Land*, p.97.

8. John Scott, op. cit., p.91.

9. F.M.L. Thompson: *English Landed Society in the Nineteenth Century*, p.302.

10. Heather Clemenson: *English Country Houses and Landed Estates*, p.111.

11. Doreen Massey & Alejandrina Catalano: *Capital and Land*, p.69.

12. C.F.G. Masterman: *England After the War*, p.31.

13. *The Times*, 19 May 1919.

14. Evelyn Waugh: *Brideshead Revisited*, p.1.

15. Robert Hewison: *The Heritage Industry*, p.54.

16. Lord Ferrers, interview.

17. Evelyn Waugh, op. cit., p.8.

18. Hugh Montgomery-Massingberd: *The Great British Families*, p.12.

19. Heather Clemenson: op. cit., pp.118–28.

20. John Martin Robinson: *The Latest Country Houses*, p.27.

21. Lord Kinross: 'The Dukes of England', *Life*, 15 November 1943.

22. Obituary, *Daily Telegraph*, 11 October 1988. Desperate to repair the family fortunes, the Duke was involved in a succession of financial scandals, remarking later, 'my involvement in business has brought me nothing but problems.'
23. Duke of Portland: *Men, Women and Things*, p.187.
24. Duke of Devonshire, interview.
25. Duke of Westminster, interview.
26. *Daily Telegraph*, 24 May 1986.
27. Brian Masters: *The Dukes*, p.164.
28. Thirty-nine million attended live arts performances, against forty-eight million visiting historic houses, according to *Facts About the Arts* (1986 ed.), quoted in Hewison, op. cit., p.27.
29. In 1987, the Museums Association discovered that of the 1,750 institutions which replied to their questionnaire, half had been founded since 1971. 'You can't project that rate of growth much further before the whole country becomes one big open-air museum, and you just join it as you get off [the plane] at Heathrow,' the Director of the Science Museum told Robert Hewison. Hewison, op. cit., p.24.
30. William Thackeray: *The Book of Snobs*, p.34.
31. Interview.
32. Nicholas Ridley, speech 22 November 1988.
33. G.R. Judd: 'Capital Taxation and the Farmer', in *Estates Gazette*, 5 April 1975, p.35.
34. Roy Strong: *The Destruction of the English Country House, 1875-1975*, p.7.
35. Robert Hewison, op. cit., p.68.
36. Evelyn Waugh: 'An Open Letter to the Hon. Mrs Peter Rodd (Nancy Mitford) on a Very Serious Subject', reprinted in *Noblesse Oblige*, p.80.
37. There are 193 packs of foxhounds in England and Wales, and a further eleven in Scotland. Comparable figures for 1936 are 185 (and ten in Scotland) and for 1906, 167 (plus eleven). Figures from the Master of Foxhounds Association.
38. Quoted in Masters, op. cit., p.21.
39. Lord Camoys, interview.
40. Lord March, interview.
41. *Municipal Yearbooks*, 1960, 1990.
42. Lord Harewood, interview.
43. Max Hastings, interview.
44. Hugh Montgomery-Massingberd, quoted in the *Spectator*, 22 October 1988, p.10.
45. 'The order of nobility is of great use, too, not only in what it creates, but in what it prevents. It prevents the rule of wealth – the religion of gold. This is the obvious and natural idol of the Anglo-Saxon. He is always trying to make money.' William Bagehot, *The English Constitution*.

CHAPTER TWO

The Fount of Honour

1. Malcolm Muggeridge: 'Royal Soap Opera', in the *New Statesman*, 22 October 1955, p.499.
2. John Osborne: 'And They Call it Cricket', in *Encounter*, October 1957, p.25.
3. *The English and National Review*, August 1957.
4. *News Chronicle*, 5 August 1957.
5. Lord Altrincham: 'The Rumpus – And After', in *The English and National Review*, September 1957. See also Henry Fairlie: An Anatomy of Hysteria, in the *Spectator*, 8 November 1957.
6. The phrase comes from *The Myth of Monarchy*, published in 1989. Other attacks were penned by Tom Nairn (*The Enchanted Glass*) and Christopher Hitchens (*The Monarchy: A Critique of Britain's Favourite Fetish*).
7. Angela Lambert: *1939, The Last Season of Peace*.

8. Quoted in Martin: *The Crown and the Establishment*, p.55.
9. House of Commons Debate, 26 February 1975, *Hansard* vol.887, cols 610–12. Also quoted in Harris: *The Making of Neil Kinnock*, p.87.
10. Harris, op. cit., p.225.
11. The circumstances of Lord Home's invitation to the Palace to form a government remain a matter of debate. Alastair Horne's authorized biography of Macmillan describes the scene in which the Queen went to Macmillan's bedside and asked for his advice as to his successor. Macmillan read from a memorandum he had written, nominating Home, and 'The Queen agreed with his recommendation.' (Horne, *Macmillan*, vol.II, p.566.) Did she do so because personally and politically the fourteenth Earl was a congenial choice? In the *New Statesman* of 24 January 1964, Paul Johnson argued that the Queen was not bound to accept Macmillan's advice, and that she had acted precipitately in inviting Home to form a government before lunch on the day in question. In his biography of Butler, the unsuccessful candidate, Anthony Howard comments that:

> The question may legitimately be asked why, if a sick 69-year-old outgoing Prime Minister felt so certain of the constitutional correctness of the advice he was proffering, it needed to be implemented with quite such precipitate haste: equally properly, a question arises as to the uncritical alacrity with which the Palace fell in with both the nature and timing of Macmillan's scheme.

(Howard, *RAB*, p.319.)
12. Quoted in Hennessy: *Whitehall*, p.349.
13. Figures taken from the Court Circular and compiled by Tim O'Donovan, published in *The Times*, 3 January 1990.
14. Anthony Sampson: *The Changing Anatomy of Britain*, p.14.
15. The relationship had begun when Callaghan was Foreign Secretary. In early 1976 he had been unsure about whether to follow up a mission to the rebel Rhodesian Prime Minister, Ian Smith. Meeting the Queen at a dinner thrown by the Italian ambassador in London, he asked her advice. The following day he received a letter from her private secretary, expressing the Queen's enthusiasm for further contacts. (Callaghan: *Time and Chance*, p.380, and interview with Lord Callaghan.)
16. For further details on the early military responsibilities of the lord lieutenancy, see the monograph *The County Lieutenancy in the United Kingdom*, by C. Neville Packett, MBE.
17. Michael De-la-Noy: *The Honours System*, p.66.
18. John Walker: *The Queen Has Been Pleased*, p.192.
19. *The Times*, 24 August 1973.
20. John Walker, op. cit., p.4.
21. *The Times*, editorial, 27 May 1976.
22. Kenneth Rose: *King George V*, p.248.

CHAPTER THREE

Etonians and Estonians

1. Julian Critchley: *Westminster Blues*, pp.29–30.
2. Anthony King: 'The Rise of the Career Politician in Britain – and its Consequences', *British Journal of Political Science*, July 1981, p.259.
3. The percentage from the professions was the same in both parliaments (forty-two per cent), while the number from miscellaneous other occupations – journalists, political organizations, etc. – had dropped from twenty-three per cent to twenty per cent. Figures from the David Butler *British General Election* series.
4. King, op. cit., p.278.

5. Francis Fulford: 'An Eclipse of Rural Tory MPs' in the *Field*, December 1988.
6. Quoted in 'The New Tories', *New Society*, 2 February 1984.
7. Montgomery-Massingberd: 'Top and Bottom of the Tory Class', in the *Spectator*, 3 May 1986.
8. Anthony Sampson: *The Anatomy of Britain*, p.89.
9. 'What Happened', in the *Spectator*, 17 January 1964.
10. Alastair Horne: *Macmillan*, vol.I, p.461.
11. Connolly: *Enemies of Promise*, p.228.
12. Professor Sammy Finer, interview.
13. Tom Arnold MP, interview.
14. Martin Burch and Michael Moran: 'The Changing Political Elite', in *Parliamentary Affairs*, vol.38, no.1, Winter 1985, p.1. I am also indebted to Byron Criddle, of Aberdeen University, for assistance with research on MPs' backgrounds.
15. Quoted in Wiener: *English Culture and the Decline of the Industrial Spirit 1850–1980*, p.110.
16. Interview.
17. Interview.
18. Sir Keith Joseph, speech, 5 September 1974.
19. Sir John Hoskyns, interview.
20. Ibid.
21. Earl Ferrers, interview.
22. Andrew Adonis: 'No Longer Tory Leader's Poodle – But Hardly A Tiger', in the *Financial Times*, 12 May 1988.
23. Lord Hailsham: 'Elective Dictatorship', the 1976 Richard Dimbleby Lecture, in the *Listener*, 21 October 1976.
24. Quoted in Massereene and Ferrard: *The Lords*, p.155.
25. Duke of Westminster, interview.
26. Figure from *The Independent*, 9 August 1989, p.4.
27. Massereene and Ferrard, op. cit., p. 18.
28. Quoted in the *Field*, 12 April 1986.
29. Ibid.
30. *Analysis*, BBC Radio 4, 'The Other Opposition', 5 November 1987.
31. Lord Carrington, interview.
32. Jessica Mitford, *Hons and Rebels*, p.21.
33. Baroness Seear, quoted in 'Distinguished Women of Today' in *Debrett's Distinguished People of Today*, p.37.

CHAPTER FOUR

Let Us Now Praise Famous Men

1. Baron Rothschild: *Meditations of a Broomstick*, p.170.
2. Quoted in Hennessy: *The Great and the Good*, p.68. I am indebted to this excellent monograph for much of the background information in this and following paragraphs on the Public Appointments Unit.
3. Figures from Cabinet Office, January 1990.
4. In April 1989, there were 49,565 appointments to a total of 1954 public bodies, including national health authorities, nationalized industries, etc.
5. Lord Benson, interview.
6. Lord Shawcross, interview.
7. The Committee was never called into being, and the issue was effectively shelved by being passed to a Cabinet sub-committee under Lord Kilmuir, the Lord Chancellor. See Hennessy, *Whitehall* p.548.
8. Lord Shawcross, interview.

9. Professor Sir Richard Southwood, interview.
10. Lord Annan, interview.
11. Lord Shawcross, interview.
12. A.P. Herbert: 'Sad Fate of a Royal Commission' in *Mild and Bitter*.
13. *Falkland Islands Review* para. 339, p.90.
14. 'Franks "a bucket of whitewash" says scornful Callaghan', in the *Guardian*, 27 January 1983.
15. 'The Wealth of Nations', quoted in Lewis and Maude, *Professional People*, p.14.
16. Quoted in Lewis and Maude, op. cit., p.26.
17. R.H. Tawney: *The Acquisitive Society*, p.110.
18. Professor A.M. Carr Saunders: *The Professions*, p.497.
19. Frank Rutter, quoted in 'The Edwardians and After', in *Christie's International Magazine*, October/November 1988.
20. A steady filtering process was at work. Just over half (fifty-four per cent) of law students came from professional or managerial families. But by the time of admission to Middle Temple or Gray's Inn, the proportion had risen to three quarters (seventy-six and seventy-seven per cent), *Royal Commission on the Legal Services* (Cmnd 7648, 1979), vol.2, p.46.
21. *The Times*, 18 April 1989.
22. R.H. Tawney, op. cit., p.108.
23. Henry Fairlie: 'The BBC', in *The Establishment*, ed. Thomas, pp.203-4.
24. H.H. Wilson: *Pressure Group*, p.214.
25. Cabinet Office papers, Public Record Office, 128/27. CC(54)53, 26 July 1954, item 6.
26. Kenneth Clark: *The Other Half*, p.138.
27. Quoted in Shaw: *The Arts and The People*, p.80.
28. Quoted in Curran: *Power Without Responsibility*, p.134.
29. Tony Benn: *Out of the Wilderness*, p.215.
30. Henry Fairlie: 'The BBC', op. cit., p.191.
31. Ibid., p.204.
32. 'Serving Thatcher's children', in the *Financial Times*, 20 July 1988.
33. Melvyn Bragg, interview.
34. Quoted in Briggs: *Governing the BBC*, p.157.
35. Requests to the 10 Downing Street Press Office for a full list of appointments, or even a total, elicited only the otiose sentence, 'The wide range of appointments include Higher Preferment in the Church of England, Lord Lieutenants of counties, Trustees of national museums and galleries, judicial appointments, scholastic appointments, membership of Royal Commissions, etc.' All of which is scarcely revelatory. Letter, 16 February 1989.
36. Professor A.M. Honoré, interview.
37. Lord Rees-Mogg, interview.
38. The quotation is from his weekly column in *The Independent*, quoted in 'Sage in Suede Shoes', in the *Sunday Correspondent*, 29 October 1989.
39. Lord Rees-Mogg, interview.
40. Lord Bonham-Carter, interview.
41. 'It is high time a return is made to finding people of the highest standing as Governors of the BBC, not just people who are "one of us".' Milne, *DG*, p.83.
42. Crossman Diaries, vol.II, p.445.
43. Op. cit., p.443.
44. 'Questions of Procedure for Ministers', quoted in Hennessy, *The Great and the Good*, p.14.
45. Barbara Castle: *The Castle Diaries 1974-76*, p.541.
46. Peter Jay, interview.
47. Patrick Cosgrave: *Thatcher: The First Term*, p.169.

48. Tim Bell, interview.
49. Sir John Hoskyns, interview.
50. Tim Bell, interview.
51. Peter Morgan, speech to Institute of Directors, 27 February 1990.
52. Professor Sammy Finer, interview.
53. Lord Flowers, interview.
54. John Lloyd: 'The Crumbling of the Establishment', in the *Financial Times*, 16 July 1988.
55. Lord Dainton, interview.
56. Seventy-nine per cent were men, fifty-six per cent had been privately educated, forty-nine per cent were at Oxbridge. See 'The "One of Us" Board Game', in the *Guardian*, 15 January 1990.

CHAPTER FIVE

The Eunuch's Consolation

1. Gladstone: letter to Lord John Russell, January 1854, quoted in 'Civil Service reform 1853-5', in *History*, June 1942, p.63.
2. Lord Sherfield, interview.
3. C.R. Attlee: *As it Happened*, p.149.
4. James Prior: *A Balance of Power*, p.90.
5. Sir Derek Mitchell, interview.
6. Quoted in Harold Perkin: *The Rise of Professional Society*, p.264.
7. Peter Kellner and Lord Crowther-Hunt: *The Civil Servants*, p.193.
8. Kevin Theakston and Geoffrey Fry: 'Britain's Administrative Elite', p.132.
9. Thomas Balogh: 'The Apotheosis of the Dilettante', in *The Establishment* (ed. Hugh Thomas), p.111.
10. Ibid., p.84.
11. Fulton Committee Report, Cmmnd 3638, p.104.
12. Hugo Young and Anne Sloman: *The Thatcher Phenomenon*, p.24.
13. Anne Mueller, 'The New Civil Service', in *Reforms at Work in the Civil Service*, Cabinet Office, January 1987.
14. Peter Hennessy: 'Scrutinies Bring Savings, but Bigger Prizes Await', in *The Independent*, 21 December 1987.
15. Richard Crossman: *The Diaries of a Cabinet Minister*, 5 October 1965.
16. Quoted in Hennessy: 'Thatcher Sows the Seeds of a Civil Service Revolution', in *The Independent*, 26 October 1988.
17. 'I am not at all satisfied with the quality of the very top chaps and it is becoming increasingly clear to me that a Civil Service department cannot generate the impetus necessary to make a growth industry grow and expand at the necessary rate. The attitudes are too rigid, the wage structure is too tightly under Treasury control and the political supervision of prices and practices makes the job impossible.' Tony Benn: *Out of the Wilderness, Diaries 1963-1967*, 18 December 1964, p.197.
18. Private conversation.
19. Private conversation.
20. Private conversation.
21. Interview.
22. In 1990, the number of cars at the French embassy in London was an official secret 'for security reasons', while the number of official vehicles at the British embassy in Paris had risen to fourteen.
23. Sir Kenneth Berrill, interview.
24. Baroness Blackstone, interview.

25. Sir Kenneth Berrill, interview.
26. *The Guardian*, 25 April 1977.
27. Quoted in Blackstone and Plowden: *Inside the Think Tank*, p.167.
28. Private information.
29. John Bright, speech in Glasgow, 21 December 1858 (reported in *The Times* 23 December 1858). Austen Henry Layard, an MP who scrutinized the Foreign Office List in June 1855, discovered that the heads of twenty-eight British overseas missions included seven lords, nine honourables, two baronets, and three 'gentlemen of noble family', against a mere seven 'gentlemen'. The dominance of the upper class extended throughout the service, from secretaries of legations to attachés, leading him to conclude that 'honest, able, hard-working men give themselves up to despair . . . there is nothing but favouritism in diplomacy.' (Quoted in Valerie Cromwell, *Aspects of Government in Nineteenth Century Britain*, p.49.)
30. Figure taken from *The Ruling Few*, by Sir David Kelly. The title of this book is characteristic of a certain cast of mind among senior British diplomats – another memoir, by Sir Ivone Kirkpatrick, was titled *The Inner Circle*. Kelly, who spent a lifetime in diplomatic service, felt himself something of an outsider because, unlike most of the other recruits, he had been at St Paul's rather than Eton.
31. PRO FO 366/780, 14 June 1918. Quoted in Moorhouse, *The Diplomats*, p.53.
32. PRO FO 366/781, 20 January 1939, quoted in Hennessy, *Whitehall*, p.79-80.
33. Quoted in Geoffrey Moorhouse: *The Diplomats*, p.175.
34. Quoted in Hennessy: *Whitehall*, p.114.
35. 'Political Commentary', in the *Spectator*, 23 September 1955.
36. John Sparrow, letter to the editor, the *Spectator*, 30 September 1955.
37. Moorhouse, op. cit., p.59.
38. Six out of nineteen. See Theakston and Fry, op. cit., p.133.
39. Figures from parliamentary answers to Robert Wareing MP, quoted in *The Independent*, 3 August 1988. Younger Foreign Office staff stress that they are trying to broaden the base of the organization, but their most worrying problem is that it looks a less appealing career to an intelligent young graduate who could equally easily – and more profitably – spend his life working overseas for a multinational company or a bank. In the five years between 1985 and 1989, applications for the Administrative grade fell by half and there was a similar drop in applications for entry to the Executive grade.
40. David Owen, interview.
41. Paul Gore-Booth: *With Great Truth and Respect*, p.424.
42. Private interview.
43. Interview.
44. Nicholas Henderson: *The Private Office*, p.121.
45. David Owen, interview.
46. In 1969, the FCO employed 8,040 UK-based staff. By 1974, the figure had fallen to 7,819. In 1979 there were 7,268 in this category, a total which had fallen to 6,545 by 1989. Locally engaged staff had also fallen, from 8,724 in 1969 to 7,000 twenty years later. The number of countries covered had grown from 136 in 1968, to 165 by 1988.
47. The Federal Republic employs 4,900 recruited in Germany and a further 2,300 engaged abroad. With this number they manage to run 203 missions – five fewer than the UK.

CHAPTER SIX

Floreat Etona

1. Eric Anderson: 'Education is the Great Equalizer', in *The Independent*, 28 January 1989.

2. The RAF is the most broadly-based of the services, with nine out of its fourteen senior officers coming from state schools. The Royal Navy has six public school alumni among its top fourteen.

3. Thirty-one were graduates of Oxford or Cambridge.

4. All figures relate to early 1990.

5. *Sunday Times*, 8 April 1990.

6. Dr John Rae, interview.

7. Quoted in Darwin: *The English Public Schools*, p.107.

8. Clarendon Commission report, *Parliamentary papers 1864,20*, vol.1, p.56.

9. Thomas Hughes: *Tom Brown's Schooldays*, p.80.

10. Quoted in Warner: *English Public Schools*, p.25.

11. Paul Johnson: 'The Education of an Establishment', in *The World of the Public Schools*, London, Weidenfeld & Nicolson, 1979. According to Johnson, Wellington disliked Eton, refusing to make a contribution to its rebuilding fund. His famous remark, perhaps the best-known aphorism on English education, originated in comments about the garden of his lodging-house, which were repeated in gossip, translated into French, and then re-emerged in English.

12. Noël Coward: 'The Stately Homes of England'.

13. Quoted in *The World of the Public Schools*, p.36.

14. Quoted in David Watt, 'The Fate of the Public Schools', *Encounter*, May 1964.

15. Anthony Lejeune: 'The Gentleman's Estate', in *Burke's Landed Gentry* (1972 ed.).

16. Quoted in Warner, op. cit., p.40.

17. George Orwell, 'Boys' Weeklies', in *Horizon*, March 1940.

18. In 1977, there were 4,761,223 children in maintained secondary schools and 229,144 at independent schools. In 1987, 3,582,180 attended maintained schools, and 276,318 were at independent schools. *Source* Department of Education and Science.

19. Lord Annan, interview.

20. Roy Hattersley, quoted in *The Public School Revolution*, p.13.

21. A number of pupils benefit from the Assisted Places Scheme developed by the Thatcher government.

22. *The Times*, 6 July 1989.

23. Figures from Harrow School and Winchester College and *Choosing Your Independent School*, Independent Schools Information Service, 1987. In 1985/86, out of 140 Wykehamist school leavers, 114 went on to university. In 1986/87, ninety-three out of 129 leavers did likewise, fifty-one of them to Oxford and Cambridge.

24. Quoted in Paul Johnson, op. cit.

25. Lord Charteris, interview.

26. Dr Eric Anderson, interview.

27. Lord Charteris, interview.

28. *Choosing Your Independent School*, p.7.

29. Richard Bull, interview. Further information about the school comes from other interviews with staff and pupils at Rugby.

30. Quoted in Bence-Jones and Montgomery-Massingberd: *The British Aristocracy*, p.14.

31. G. de S. Barrow: *The Life of General Sir Charles Carmichael Monro*, p.242.

32. Michael Mavor, letter to *The Times*, 16 October 1989.

33. Dr John Rae, interview.

34. David Newsome, unpublished address to the 27 Club, 11 May 1987.

35. Dr John Rae 'Tom Brown's Porsche Days', in *The Times*, 31 July 1987.

CHAPTER SEVEN

Money by Degrees

1. Professor Ralf Dahrendorf, interview.
2. Lord Dainton, interview.
3. Robert McCrum, interview.
4. Based upon figures in D. and G. Butler, *British Political Facts 1900–1985*, p.83.
5. *The British General Election of 1987*, p.202.
6. Quoted in Hennessy: *Whitehall*, p.145.
7. Bill Weinstein, quoted in the *Sunday Telegraph*, 4 March 1984.
8. Ms Currie had been treasurer of the Oxford Union when William Waldegrave was president. Douglas Hogg had been president before him. See Abdela: *Women With 'X' Appeal*, p.11.
9. A.L. Rowse: *All Souls and Appeasement*, p.2.
10. A.L. Rowse, *The English Past*, p.5.
11. *Spectator*, 7 October 1955.
12. Douglas Jay: *Change and Fortune*, p.39. Lord Jay also believes that the All Souls group called themselves 'the Establishment', a claim repeated in recent books. Other dons at the time dispute the recollection, which A.L. Rowse describes as 'absurd'.
13. Lord Jay, interview.
14. Private information.
15. Private conversation.
16. Private conversation.
17. Quoted in 'Mrs Thatcher's Kindergarten', in the *Spectator*, 23 April 1988, p.9.
18. Interview.
19. Tim Bell, interview.
20. Professor Sir Richard Southwood, interview.
21. Professor Ralf Dahrendorf, interview.
22. Hugo Young: 'Why the dons show they've learnt the new politics', in the *Guardian*, 4 February 1985.
23. Interview.
24. J.H. Newman: The Idea of a University, in *The Idea of a Liberal Education*, pp. 101-2.
25. J.H. Newman: *My Campaign in Ireland*, p.315.
26. J.H. Newman: The Idea of a University, op. cit., p.105.
27. Lord Flowers, interview.
28. 'There will be a role for the state there, yes. In other words we want charity, real charity for those who genuinely can't afford to go.' *Times Higher Education Supplement*, 14 October 1988.
29. Hennessy: op. cit., p.660.
30. David Walker: 'How cosy links with halls of academe are breaking,' in *The Times*, 16 May 1988.
31. Figures from Cambridge University Careers Service annual reports.
32. Bill Kirkman, interview.
33. Pearson and Pike: *The Graduate Labour Market in the 1990s*, Institute of Manpower Studies, Sussex University, 1989.
34. Professor Sir Richard Southwood, interview.
35. *University Academic and Related Staff Recruitment and Retention Survey 1987/8*, Committee of Vice Chancellors and Principals, p.1.
36. Professor Ralf Dahrendorf, interview.
37. Professor Norman Cantor, New York University, quoted in *Newsweek*, 19 June 1989, p.61.
38. Bernard Williams, the *Observer*, 18 January 1987.

39. *The Revolutionary Historian*, in *The Times*, 13 May 1989, p.31.

40. Professor Norman Stone, interview.

41. In six of the eight years between 1980 and 1987, academic staff leaving Britain were outnumbered by others arriving. Letter from Robert Jackson MP to the *Daily Telegraph*, 8 June 1989. The other two years in question were 1981, when 203 academics left Britain and 183 came; and 1982 when 214 left and 118 arrived.

42. Kenneth Baker: 'Higher Education: The Next 25 Years', reprinted in *The Times Higher Education Supplement*, 13 January 1989, p.7.

CHAPTER EIGHT

God Save The Church of England

1. I am indebted to Peter Hennessy for drawing this toast to my attention. It appears in Lord Radcliffe's *Not in Feather Beds*, p.175, and in his own *The Great and the Good*, p.6.

2. Coleridge: 'On the Constitution of Church and State', in *Selected Poetry and Prose* (ed. Stephen Potter), p.467.

3. Figures from Lewis and Maude: *Professional People* and Church House.

4. Church Commissioners' Annual Report, 1989.

5. C.F. Alexander: 'All Things Bright and Beautiful'.

6. See, for example, 'Drift from the churches; secondary school pupils' attitudes to Christianity', in *British Journal of Religious Education*, vol.11, 1989.

7. Interview.

8. *Faith in the City* (popular version), p.3.

9. Clifford Longley: 'More than a creed of greed?', in *The Times*, 11 April 1988.

10. This last claim comes from Charles Moore et al.: *The Church in Crisis*, p.28.

11. Ibid., p.28.

12. Dr Hugh Montefiore, quoted in the *Observer*, 13 December 1987.

13. The phrase was coined by John Gummer, a Conservative MP and member of the General Synod.

14. Butler and Rose: *The British General Election of 1959*, quoted in Hugo Young: *One of Us*, p.422.

15. 'The Social and Educational Backgrounds of Anglican Bishops', in *British Journal of Sociology*, vol.20, no.3, 1969, p.298.

16. Sixty-three per cent of Suffragan Bishops attended public schools, seventy-three per cent had Oxbridge degrees. I am indebted to Dr Grace Davie of Exeter University for these figures.

17. Figures from the Advisory Council for the Church's Ministry, the General Synod of the Church of England.

18. Graham Turner: 'The Gospel According to Marx', in the *Sunday Telegraph*, 6 November 1988.

19. *Crockford's Clerical Directory 1987/8*, p.68.

20. Dr John Habgood: *Church and Nation in a Secular Age*, p.93.

21. Dr John Habgood, interview.

22. *Hansard*, Fifth Series, xiii. 1205 (12 February 1913).

23. *Britain 1989: An Official Handbook*, p.216.

24. Dr John Habgood, interview.

CHAPTER NINE

Stand Uneasy

1. In 1939 there was one soldier for every 120 members of the population. In 1989 the figure was one in 175. Figures based upon most recent previous censuses (1931 and 1981).

2. In 1960, there were 347 officers on county councils. In 1990 there were thirty-five. Source: *Municipal Yearbooks*, 1960, 1990.
3. Quoted in Correlli Barnett: *Britain and Her Army*, p.123.
4. Clode: *The Military Forces of the Crown: Their Administration and Government*, vol.2, p.62.
5. Quoted in Hugh Thomas: *The Story of Sandhurst*, 1961, p.20.
6. Ibid., p.108.
7. John Scott: *The Upper Classes: Property and Privilege in Britain*, p.108.
8. In an average year between 1878 and 1899, five cadets were the sons of the aristocracy, eighteen were the sons of clergymen, twenty-one were the sons of imperial civil servants, nine the sons of doctors, fifteen came from naval families, and 161 were the sons of officers. (Thomas, op. cit., p.151.)
9. J.F.C. Fuller, letter in *Encounter*, June 1959.
10. Ibid.
11. Correspondence with Sandhurst, 24 May 1989.
12. Simon Raven, 'Perish by the Sword', in *Encounter*, vol.XII, May 1959.
13. Ibid.
14. General Simon Cooper, letter.
15. Norman Dixon: *On the Psychology of Military Incompetence*, p.232.
16. Michael Yardley: 'Daddy's Army', in the *Sunday Telegraph* magazine, 25 October 1987.
17. Interview.
18. General Sir John Hackett, paper to Royal United Services Institute, 23 November 1960, quoted in Sampson: *The Anatomy of Britain*, p.260.
19. Forty-seven per cent in the army, 29.5 per cent in the navy and thirty-five per cent in the air force. Figures from correspondence with Ministry of Defence.
20. Denis Healey: *The Time of My Life*, p.267.
21. Sir James Glover, interview.
22. Twenty-six schools were represented altogether. Fifteen of the would-be officers hoped to go to university before taking their commissions. Ministry of Defence figures.
23. Hills Road Sixth Form College.
24. Charterhouse, Cranleigh, Downside, Malvern, Milton Abbey and Stowe had three candidates apiece; Radley, Rugby and Uppingham two each. Fourteen were in higher education, with Edinburgh and Dublin universities and Cirencester Agricultural College having two apiece. Ministry of Defence figures.
25. Lord Carrington: *Reflect on Things Past*, p.24.
26. Colonel Trevor Morris, interview.
27. Air Marshal Sir Michael Beetham, interview, 7 April 1989.
28. Interview.
29. Gallup Poll, *Sunday Telegraph*, 14 August 1988.
30. Sir Frank Cooper, in *Science and Mythology in the Making of Defence Policy*.
31. Air Marshal Sir Michael Beetham, interview.
32. Paul Kennedy: *The Rise and Fall of the Great Powers*, p.482.
33. Sir Ewen Broadbent: *The Military and Government*, p.87.
34. Sir Frank Cooper, interview.

CHAPTER TEN

The Unexpected Return Of Samuel Smiles

1. Sir Hector Laing, interview.
2. Samuel Smiles: *Self Help*, p.35.

NOTES

348

3. W.L. George: Labour and Housing at Port Sunlight, quoted in *Sunlighters*, p.13.
4. Charles Wilson: *History of Unilever*, pp.146-7
5. Angus Watson, quoted in Wilson, p.149.
6. Ibid., p.150.
7. R.A. Butler: *The Art of the Possible*, p.19.
8. Quoted in D.C. Coleman: 'Gentlemen and Players', p.100.
9. Quoted in Goldsmith and Ritchie: *The New Elite*, p.100.
10. Op. cit., p.100.
11. In *The Conservative Enemy*, Crosland extolled the virtues of the managers who went for growth while subject to 'a sense of social responsibility' and a desire for 'good public and labour relations'. Op. cit., p.88.
12. Among ministers were Lord Chandos at AEI, Lord Monckton at Midland Bank, Lord Amory at the Hudson's Bay Company. Civil servants included Lord Plowden at Tube Investments, Sir Maurice Bridgeman at BP, Sir Leslie Rowan at Vickers.
13. According to a *Sunday Times* poll, 5 November 1989.
14. 'Lord of the Fleas', in the *Guardian*, 20 January 1987.
15. 'Who's Afraid of the Tiger?' in *The Times*, 10 September 1987.
16. *Financial Weekly*, 15 December 1988.
17. Owen Green, from a profile in *Financial Weekly*, 15 December 1988.
18. Stephen O'Brien, interview.
19. Tim Bell, interview.
20. Sam Whitbread, interview.
21. Allen Sheppard, interview.
22. *The Economist*, 16 July 1870, quoted in Clemenson, *English Country Houses and Landed Estates*, p.93.
23. 'Where The Collector Entertained the Prince', in the *Daily Telegraph*, 24 November 1989.

CHAPTER ELEVEN

Bowler Hats and White Socks

1. Walter Bagehot: *Lombard Street*, p.260.
2. T. Lupton and C.S. Wilson: The Social Background and Connections of Top Decision Makers.
3. Gavin Laird, interview.
4. Paul Ferris: *The City*, p.11.
5. Hugh Massingham: 'Our Man In Threadneedle Street', in *Queen*, 6 February 1962.
6. The full list reads 1. Abbey National 2. Standard Chartered 3. TSB Group 4. S.G. Warburg 5. Kleinwort Benson 6. Morgan Grenfell 7. Bank of England 8. Union Discount Company 9. Grindlays Bank 10. Hambros 11. Gerrard and National Holdings 12. Yorkshire Bank 13. N.M. Rothschild 14. Scandinavian Bank Group 15. Schroders 16. Orion Royal Bank 17. Barings 18. Saudi International Bank 19. Banque Nationale de Paris 20. Cater Allen Holdings. Source: *Times 1,000, 1989-90.*
7. Cary Reich: 'The Confessions of Siegmund Warburg', in *Institutional Investor*, March 1980.
8. Lord Cairns, interview.
9. 'New Blood for Rich Rothschild Vein', in *Financial Times*, 17 October 1988.
10. 'A Banker Who Sells Cigars, Insurance and Houses', in the *Financial Times*, 25 June 1988.
11. *Report of the Fraud Trials Committee* (The Roskill Committee), London, HMSO, 1986, p.1.
12. Sir Kenneth Berrill, interview.

13. *Financial Times* leader, 25 February 1988.
14. Lord Shawcross, interview.
15. Lord Benson, interview.

CHAPTER TWELVE

The Arts Tsars

 1. Edward Bond: '"The Romans" and the Establishment's figleaf', in the *Guardian*, 3 November 1980.
 2. Robert Hutchison: *The Politics of the Arts Council*, p.33. At the time of writing, both the chairman of the Arts Council, Peter Palumbo, and the Labour spokesman on the arts, Mark Fisher, were Old Etonians.
 3. Kenneth Clark: *The Other Half*, p.129.
 4. Michael Frayn in Sissons and French (eds): *The Age of Austerity*, p.56.
 5. Richard Eyre, interview.
 6. David Hare, on *Desert Island Discs*, 26 February 1989.
 7. Bryan Appleyard: *The Culture Club*, p.28.
 8. David Hare, on *Desert Island Discs*.
 9. Ibid.
10. Richard Eyre, interview.
11. Sir Claus Moser, interview.
12. Rodney Miles: *Opera*, March 1989, p.269.
13. In 1990, the Royal Opera House received £15,231,000 from the Arts Council. Comparable figures for the National Theatre were £8,940,000, and for the Royal Shakespeare Company £6,045,000.
14. Robert Hutchison: op. cit., p.28.
15. They are Andrew Edwards (main board), John Wiggins (development board), Michael Johnson (ballet board) and Michael Scholar (opera board).
16. Sir Roy Shaw, interview.
17. Sir John Pope-Hennessy: 'The Fall of a Great Museum', in the *New York Review of Books*, 27 April 1989.
18. Both quoted in Hugo Young: *One of Us*, p.411.
19. Sir Roy Shaw: *The Arts and The People*, p.42.
20. Sir Roy Shaw, interview.
21. *The Times*, 17 October 1988.
22. Lord Goodman, interview.
23. Ibid.
24. Richard Hoggart, interview in *The Late Show* (BBC2), 22 March 1989.
25. Nick Serota, interview.
26. Sir Richard Southwood, interview.
27. Sir Roy Strong, interview in *The Late Show* (BBC2), 22 March 1989.
28. Sir John Pope-Hennessy: op. cit.
29. Richard Eyre, interview.
30. Sir Roy Shaw, interview.
31. Lord Goodman, interview.
32. *Business Sponsorship of the Arts – A Tax Guide*, Association for Business Sponsorship of the Arts, 1985, p.9.
33. Allen Sheppard, interview.
34. Quoted in Shaw: op. cit., p.62.
35. Mark Fisher, Labour Arts spokesman, interview.
36. Max Stafford-Clark, interview.
37. Interview.
38. Interview.
39. Lord Harewood, interview.

CHAPTER THIRTEEN

Bring on the Comfortable Men

1. Quoted in Cockerell: *Live from Number 10*, p.53.
2. Lord Butler: *The Art of the Possible*, Penguin ed. 1973, pp. 158-9.
3. The only area of British life where old-fashioned clubs continue to exert direct authority is in a few sports. Of all of them, the Jockey Club, responsible for sixty racecourses, nearly eight thousand jockeys, trainers and stable staff and thirteen thousand horses, is the one to have survived the twentieth century most unscathed. It was the place which invented the blackball system and it remains a tight, self-perpetuating oligarchy, which reckons it has adjusted well enough by ensuring that only half of the hundred or so members are titled.

   The governing hierarchy remains distinctly upper-crust. In the summer of 1989 the Duke of Devonshire's heir, the Marquess of Hartington (Eton and Oxford), succeeded Lord Fairhaven (Eton and the Royal Horse Guards), as Senior Steward. The deputy Senior Steward, Lord Chelsea, another Etonian, represented the third generation of Cadogans to be a member of the Club. A fourth Etonian, the beef magnate Lord Vestey, was head of the disciplinary committee. A fifth Etonian, Major Michael Wyatt, previously of the 17/21st Lancers, was the steward responsible for race planning. The two remaining stewards broke the educational mould, though hardly the pedigree. They were a baronet, Sir John Barlow (Winchester and Cambridge), former high sheriff of Cheshire, and Colonel Andrew Parker Bowles, commander of the Household Cavalry and Silver Stick in Waiting to the Queen.

   To be fair to the Jockey Club, British racing is less corrupt than in many countries, a state of affairs for which it can take some of the credit. But there are limits to the capacities of amateurs, even if day-to-day responsibility is delegated to the professionals in Weatherbys. When off-course betting was legalized in 1961, the club ducked out of involvement, partly, according to racing insiders, because several of the senior figures in the club were in hock to bookmakers at the time. The consequence is that the British racing industry receives less than one quarter of the betting percentage levied in France, or one sixth of the United States figure. It is a high price to pay for the sensitivities of a few aristocrats.
4. Boswell, *Life of Johnson*, p.767.
5. The Other Club, founded by Churchill and F.E. Smith when they couldn't get elected to the Club, is a more explicitly political affair. Limited to fifty members, of whom half may be MP's, it meets about ten times a year at 8.15 p.m. on Thursdays in the Pinafore Room at the Savoy Hotel. The first member to arrive orders a bottle of champagne, and further bottles are added by each arriving member. Churchill insisted that dinner began with Essence de Pot-Au-Feu, a thick meat and vegetable soup, although now menus are more varied. By the end of the meal, few are in any mood to listen to serious speeches, which anyway are banned. The constitution is solemnly read. 'The names of the Executive Committee shall remain wrapped in impenetrable mystery,' reads rule ten. Rule twelve states that, 'Nothing in the intercourse of the Club shall interfere with the rancour or asperity of party politics,' and although past non-political members have included figures as diverse as Arnold Bennett, P.G. Wodehouse, John Buchan, Laurence Olivier and General Montgomery, it is the parliamentary membership which makes the place interesting. Partly because it was founded by a Liberal and a Conservative, the Other Club continues to have a cross-party flavour to it, and includes among its members prominent Labour figures like John Smith, while James Callaghan was an active member for several years. Callaghan maintains that 'absolutely no significance at all' can be attached to membership of the Other Club, which may be true in the sense that no business is transacted there. But, like The Club, it has

been an important forum in the past, and could be so again. It was at Other Club dinners that Churchill expounded his anti-Chamberlain views on Appeasement, and in so doing discovered another institution to balance the calls to toe the party line. Duff Cooper and Lord Cranbourne, whose resignations shifted opinion against Chamberlain, had both been swung against Appeasement after trying to hold their own in argument with Churchill over dinner on 29 September 1938.

6. Figures from the Hansard Society report, *Women at the Top*, to which I am indebted for some other statistics in the following paragraphs.
7. *Powder in the Boardroom*, Ashridge Management College, 1989.
8. P.D. James, Jane Glover and Shahwar Sadeque.
9. Quoted in Leapman: *Barefaced Cheek*, p.187.
10. Peter Jay, interview.
11. Whitelaw: *The Whitelaw Memoirs*, p.204.
12. Duke of Devonshire, interview.
13. Lord Shawcross, interview.
14. *Listener*, 18/25 December 1986.
15. David Marquand, interview.
16. Source: Audit Bureau of Circulation.
17. Individual sales were as follows: *Times*, 446,000; *Guardian*, 459,000; *Independent*, 378,000; *Daily Telegraph*, 1,134,000; *Financial Times*, 204,000. Source: ABC.
18. Source: National Readership Survey, April 1988–March 1989 and interview, Andreas Whittam Smith.
19. Source: National Readership Survey, January–December 1988.

Select Bibliography

The following books are referred to in the text, or provided important background information.

ABDELA, LESLEY: *Women With 'X' Appeal*, London, Optima, 1989.

ABDY, JANE AND CHARLOTTE GERE: *The Souls*, London, Sidgwick & Jackson, 1984.

ADDISON, PAUL: *Now the War is Over*, London, BBC, 1985.

ANDREW, CHRISTOPHER: *Secret Service*, London, Heinemann, 1985.

ANNAN, NOEL: 'The Intellectual Aristocracy', in *Studies in Social History*, London, Longman, 1955.

APPLEYARD, BRYAN: *The Culture Club*, London, Faber & Faber, 1984.

APPLEYARD, BRYAN: *The Pleasures of Peace*, London, Faber & Faber, 1989.

ARCHBISHOP OF CANTERBURY'S COMMISSION ON URBAN PRIORITY AREAS: *Faith in the City*, London, Church House, 1985.

ARNOLD, MATTHEW: *Culture and Anarchy*, London, John Murray, 1920.

ATTLEE, C.R.: *As it Happened*, London, Odhams, 1954.

BAGEHOT, WALTER: *The English Constitution*, London, Chapman & Hall, 1867.

BAGEHOT, WALTER: *Lombard Street*, London, Kegan Paul, 1888.

BARNETT, CORRELLI: *Britain and Her Army 1509-1970*, London, Allen Lane, 1970.

BARNETT, CORRELLI: *The Collapse of British Power*, London, Eyre & Methuen, 1972.

BARNETT, CORRELLI: *The Audit of War*, London, Macmillan, 1986.

BARROW, GEORGE DE S.: *The Life of General Sir Charles Carmichael Monro*, London, Hutchinson, 1931.

BAYNES, LT.-COL. J.C.M.: *The Soldier in Society*, London, Eyre & Methuen, 1972.

BECKETT, J.V.: *The Aristocracy in England 1660-1914*, Oxford, Blackwell, 1986.

BELOFF, MAX AND GILLIAN PEELE: *The Government of the United Kingdom*, London, Weidenfeld & Nicolson, 1980.

BENCE-JONES, MARK AND HUGH MONTGOMERY-MASSINGBERD: *The British Aristocracy*, London, Constable, 1979.

BENN, TONY: *Arguments for Socialism*, London, Penguin, 1980.

BENN, TONY: *Out of the Wilderness, Diaries 1963-1967*, London, Hutchinson, 1987.

BENN, TONY: *Office Without Power, Diaries 1968-1972*, London, Hutchinson, 1988.

BERLINS, MARCEL AND CLARE DYER: *The Law Machine*, London, Penguin, 1986.

BERRY, RITCHIE AND WALTER GOLDSMITH: *The New Elite*, London, Penguin, 1988.

BLACKSTONE, TESSA AND WILLIAM PLOWDEN: *Inside the Think Tank*, London, Heinemann, 1988.

BLAKE, ROBERT: *The Conservative Party From Peel to Thatcher*, London, Methuen, 1985.

BOSWELL, JAMES: *The Life of Samuel Johnson*, Oxford, OUP, 1953.

BOURDIEU, PIERRE: *La Noblesse de l'Etat: Grandes Ecoles et Esprit de Corps*, Paris, Editions de Minuit, 1989.

BOWER, TOM: *Maxwell the Outsider*, London, Aurum Press, 1988.

BRIGGS, ASA: *The History of Broadcasting* vol. iv. Oxford, Oxford University Press, 1979.

BRIGGS, ASA: *Governing the BBC*, London, BBC, 1979.

BRIGGS, ASA: *The BBC – The First 50 Years*, Oxford, Oxford University Press, 1985.

BRITTAIN, VERA: *Women at Oxford*, London, George Harrap, 1960.

BROADBENT, SIR EWEN: *The Military and Government*, London, Macmillan, 1988.

BRUCE, RICHARD: *The Entrepreneurs*, Bedford, Libertarian Books, 1976.

BRUCE-GARDYNE, JOCK: *Ministers And Mandarins*, London, Sidgwick & Jackson, 1986.

BURCH, MARTIN AND MICHAEL MORAN: 'The Changing British Political Elite, 1945-1983', in *Parliamentary Affairs*, vol 38, no. 1, Winter 1985.

BUTLER, DAVID AND ROSE, CHARLES: *The British General Election of 1959*, London, Macmillan, 1960.

BUTLER, DAVID AND GARETH: *British Political Facts 1900-1985*, London, Macmillan, 1986.

BUTLER, DAVID, AND DENNIS KAVANAGH: *The British General Election of 1987*, London, Macmillan, 1988.

BUTLER, R.A.: *The Art of the Possible*, London, Hamish Hamilton, 1971.

CALLAGHAN, *Time and Chance*, London, Collins, 1987.

CARR SAUNDERS, PROFESSOR A.M.: *The Professions*, Oxford, Clarendon Press, 1933.

CARRINGTON, LORD: *Reflect on Things Past*, London, Collins, 1988.

CARTWRIGHT, J.: *Royal Commissions and Departmental Committees in Britain*, London, Hodder & Stoughton, 1975.

CARVER, FIELD MARSHAL LORD: *Twentieth Century Warriors*, London, Weidenfeld & Nicolson, 1988.

CASTLE, BARBARA: *The Castle Diaries*, London, Weidenfeld & Nicolson, 1980.

CECIL, DAVID: *The Young Melbourne*, London, Constable, 1939.

CENTRAL OFFICE OF INFORMATION: *Britain 1989: An Official Handbook*, London, HMSO, 1989.

CHIPPINDALE, PETER AND CHRIS HORRIE: *Disaster! The Rise and Fall of News on Sunday*, London, Sphere, 1988.

CHURCH OF ENGLAND CENTRAL BOARD OF FINANCE: *Church and State*, London, CIO, 1970.

CLARK, KENNETH: *The Other Half: A Self-Portrait*, London, John Murray, 1977.

CLARKE, WILLIAM M.: *How The City of London Works*, London, Waterlow, 1986.

CLEMENSON, HEATHER A.: *English Country Houses and Landed Estates*, London, Croom Helm, 1982.

CLODE, CHARLES M.: *The Military Forces of the Crown*, London, John Murray, 1869.

COCKERELL, MICHAEL: *Live From Number 10*, London, Faber & Faber, 1988.

COCKERELL, M. AND OTHERS: *Sources Close to the Prime Minister*, London, Macmillan, 1984.

COCKETT, RICHARD: *Twilight of the Truth*, London, Weidenfeld & Nicolson, 1989.

COLEMAN, D.C.: *Courtaulds: An Economic and Social History*, Oxford, Clarendon Press, 1969.

COLEMAN, D.C.: 'Gentlemen and Players', in *Economic History Review*, vol. XXVI, 1973.

COLERIDGE, SAMUEL: *On the Constitution of Church and State*, London, Chance & Co., 1830.

COLERIDGE, SAMUEL: *Selected Poetry and Prose* (ed. Stephen Potter), London, Nonesuch Press, 1933.

CONNOLLY, CYRIL: *Enemies of Promise*, London, G. Routledge & Sons, 1938.

COOTE, COLIN: *The Other Club*, London, Sidgwick & Jackson, 1971.

COPEMAN, G.H.: *Leaders of British Industry*, London, Gee & Company, 1955.

COSGRAVE, PATRICK: *Carrington: A Life and a Policy*, London, J.M.Dent, 1985.

COSGRAVE, PATRICK: *Thatcher: The First Term*, London, Bodley Head, 1985.

COURTNEY, NICHOLAS: *In Society*, London, Pavilion, 1986.

CRITCHLEY, JULIAN: *Westminster Blues*, London, Elm Tree Books, 1985.

CROMWELL, VALERIE AND OTHERS: *Aspects of Government in Nineteenth Century Britain*, Dublin, Irish University Press, 1978.

CROSLAND, ANTHONY: *The Conservative Enemy*, London, Jonathan Cape, 1962.

CROSSMAN, RICHARD: *The Diaries of a Cabinet Minister* (3 vols), London, Hamish Hamilton, 1979.

CUDLIPP, HUGH: *Walking on the Water*, London, Bodley Head, 1976.

CURRAN, JAMES AND JEAN SEATON: *Power Without Responsibility*, London, Methuen, 1985.

DANZIGER, DANNY: *Eton Voices*, London, Viking, 1988.

DARWIN, BERNARD: *The English Public Schools*, London, Longman, 1929.

DELAMONT, SARA: *Knowledgeable Women*, London, Routledge, 1989.

DE-LA-NOY, MICHAEL: *The Honours System*, London, Alison and Busby, 1985.

DENNING, THE RT. HON. LORD: *What Next in the Law*, London, Butterworth, 1982.

DENNIS, NIGEL: *Cards of Identity*, London, Weidenfeld & Nicolson, 1955.

DINER, HELEN: *Emperors, Angels and Eunuchs*, London, Chatto & Windus, 1938.

DIXON, NORMAN: *On The Psychology of Military Incompetence*, London, Jonathan Cape, 1976.

DUGGAN, MARGARET: *Runcie: The Making of an Archbishop*, London, Hodder & Stoughton, 1983.

DUNCAN, ANDREW: *The Reality of Monarchy*, London, Heinemann, 1970.

ENGEL, A.J.: *From Clergyman to Don*, Oxford, Clarendon Press, 1983.

EVANS, HAROLD: *Good Times, Bad Times*, London, Weidenfeld & Nicolson, 1983.

FAY, STEPHEN: *Portrait of an Old Lady*, London, Viking, 1987.

FERRIS, PAUL: *The City*, London, Gollancz, 1960.

FERRIS, PAUL: *Gentlemen of Fortune*, London, Weidenfeld & Nicolson, 1984.

FIDLER, JOHN: *The British Business Elite*, London, Routledge & Kegan Paul, 1981.

FOOT, MICHAEL: *Aneurin Bevan*, vol. II, London, Davis Poynter, 1973.

FRANKS, LORD: *Falkland Islands Review*, Privy Council Report, London, Cmmnd 8787, HMSO, 1983.

FRASER, GEORGE MACDONALD (ED.): *The World of the Public Schools*, London, Weidenfeld & Nicolson, 1977.

GILBERT, MARTIN AND RICHARD GOTT: *The Appeasers*, London, Weidenfeld & Nicolson, 1963.

GOLBY, J.M. AND PURDUE, A.W.: *The Monarchy and The British People*, London, Batsford, 1988.

GOLDRING, DOUGLAS: *The Nineteen Twenties*, London, Nicolson & Watson, 1944.

GOLDSMITH, WALTER AND BERRY RITCHIE: *The New Elite: Britain's Top Chief Executives*, London, Weidenfeld & Nicolson, 1987.

GORE BOOTH, PAUL: *With Great Truth and Respect*, London, Constable, 1974.

GOW, MICHAEL: *Trooping The Colour*, London, Souvenir Press, 1988.

GREEN, JONATHON: *Days in the Life*, London, Heinemann, 1988.

GREEN, SHIRLEY: *Who Owns London?*, London, Weidenfeld & Nicolson, 1986.

GREENHALGH, JOHN AND ELIZABETH RUSSELL: *Building in Love*, London, St Mary's Bourne Street, 1990.

GRIFFITH, J.A.G.: *The Politics of the Judiciary* (3rd ed.), London, Fontana, 1985.

GUTTSMAN, W.L.: *The English Ruling Class*, London, Weidenfeld & Nicolson, 1969.

HABGOOD, JOHN: *Church and Nation in a Secular Age*, London, Darton, Longman & Todd, 1983.

HACKETT, GEN. SIR JOHN: *The Profession of Arms*, London, Sidgwick & Jackson, 1983.

HAILSHAM, LORD: *The Door Wherein I Went*, London, Collins, 1986.

HAINES, JOE: *The Politics of Power*, London, Jonathan Cape, 1977.

HAMILTON, WILLIE: *My Queen and I*, London, Quartet, 1975.

HANSARD SOCIETY: *Report of the Hansard Society Commission on Women at the Top*, London, 1990.

HARRINGTON, C.H.: *Plumer of Messines*, London, John Murray, 1935.

HARRIS, KENNETH: *Thatcher*, London, Weidenfeld & Nicolson, 1988.

HARRIS, ROBERT: *Gotcha!: The Media, The Government and The Falklands Crisis*, London, Faber & Faber, 1983.

HARRIS, ROBERT: *The Making of Neil Kinnock*, London, Faber & Faber, 1984.

HARVEY, JAMES AND KATHERINE HOOD: *The British State*, London, Lawrence & Wishart, 1958.

HEALD, TIM: *Networks*, London, Hodder & Stoughton, 1983.

HEALEY, DENIS: *The Time of My Life*, London, Michael Joseph, 1989.

HENDERSON, NICHOLAS: *The Private Office*, London, Weidenfeld & Nicolson, 1984.

HENNESSY, PETER: *Cabinet*, Oxford, Blackwell, 1986.

HENNESSY, PETER: *The Great and the Good*, London, Policy Studies Institute, 1986.

HENNESSY, PETER: *Whitehall*, London, Secker & Warburg, 1989.

HENNESSY, PETER AND ANTHONY SELDON (EDS): *Ruling Performance*, Oxford, Basil Blackwell, 1987.

HERBERT, A.P.: *Mild and Bitter*, London, Methuen, 1936.

HEREN, LOUIS: *Alas, Alas for England*, London, Hamish Hamilton, 1981.

HEREN, LOUIS: *The Power of the Press?*, London, Orbis, 1985.

HEREN, LOUIS: *Memories of Times Past*, London, Hamish Hamilton, 1988.

HEWISON, ROBERT: *The Heritage Industry*, London, Methuen, 1987.

HEWISON, ROBERT: *In Anger – British Culture in the Cold War 1945-60*, London, Weidenfeld & Nicolson, 1981.

HITCHINS, CHRISTOPHER: *The Monarchy*, London, Chatto & Windus, 1990.

HILTON, ANTHONY: *City Within a State*, London, I.B. Tauris, 1987.

HOLLINGSWORTH, MARK: *The Press and Political Dissent*, London, Pluto Press, 1986.

HORNE, ALISTAIR: *Macmillan* (2 vols), London, Macmillan, 1988 & 1989.

HOWARD, ANTHONY: *RAB: The Life of R.A. Butler*, London, Jonathan Cape, 1987.

HOWARD, PHILIP: *The British Monarchy in the Twentieth Century*, London, Hamish Hamilton, 1977.

HUGHES, THOMAS: *Tom Brown's Schooldays*, London, Macmillan, 1857.

HUTCHISON, ROBERT: *The Politics of the Arts Council*, London, Sinclair Browne, 1982.

ISAACS, JEREMY: *Storm Over Four*, London, Weidenfeld & Nicolson, 1989.

JAY, DOUGLAS: *Change and Fortune*, London, Hutchinson, 1980.

JENKINS, SIMON AND ANNE SLOMAN: *With Respect, Ambassador*, London, BBC, 1985.

JOHNSON, FRANKLYN A.: *Defence By Ministry*, London, Duckworth, 1980.

JOHNSON, PAUL: *The Offshore Islanders*, London, Weidenfeld & Nicolson, 1972.

JOHNSON, PAUL: 'The Education of an Establishment' in *The World of the Public Schools* (ed. George Fraser), London, Weidenfeld & Nicolson, 1977.

JONES, RAY: *The Nineteenth Century Foreign Office, an Administrative History*, London, Weidenfeld & Nicolson, 1971.

JONES, ROBERT AND OLIVER MARRIOTT: *Anatomy of a Merger*, London, Jonathan Cape, 1970.

KELLNER, PETER AND LORD CROWTHER-HUNT: *The Civil Servants*, London, Macdonald, 1980.

KELLY, DAVID: *The Ruling Few*, London, Hollis & Carter, 1952.

KENNEDY, PAUL: *The Realities Behind Diplomacy: Background Influences on British External Policy 1865-1980*, London, Allen & Unwin, 1981.

KENNEDY, PAUL: *The Rise and Fall of the Great Powers*, New York, Random House, 1987.

KOSS, STEPHEN: *The Rise and Fall of the Political Press in Britain*, London, Hamish Hamilton, 1984.

LACEY, ROBERT: *Majesty*, London, Hutchinson, 1977.

LACEY, ROBERT: *Aristocrats*, London, Hutchinson, 1983.

LAMBERT, ANGELA: *1939: The Last Season of Peace*, London, Weidenfeld & Nicolson, 1989.

LEAPMAN, MICHAEL: *Barefaced Cheek: The Apotheosis of Rupert Murdoch*, London, Hodder & Stoughton, 1983.

LEAPMAN, MICHAEL: *The Last Days of the Beeb*, London, Allen & Unwin, 1986.

LEE, SIMON: *Judging Judges*, London, Faber & Faber, 1988.

LEES-MILNE, JAMES: *Ancestral Voices*, London, Chatto & Windus, 1975.

LEES-MILNE, JAMES: *Caves of Ice*, London, Chatto & Windus, 1983.

356

SELECT BIBLIOGRAPHY

LEWIS, ROY AND ANGUS MAUDE: *The English Middle Classes*, London, Phoenix House, 1949.

LEWIS, ROY AND ANGUS MAUDE: *Professional People*, London, Phoenix House, 1952.

LONGFORD, LORD: *A History of the House of Lords*, London, Collins, 1988.

LUPTON, T. AND C.S. WILSON: 'The Social Background and Connections of Top Decision Makers', in *The Manchester School*, vol. 27, January 1959.

MACDONALD, IVERACH: *The History of The Times*, vol. V, London, Times Books, 1984.

MACGREGOR, IAN: *The Enemies Within*, London, Collins, 1986.

MACKENZIE, NORMAN AND JEANNE: *The First Fabians*, London, Weidenfeld & Nicolson, 1977.

MACMILLAN, HAROLD: *At the End of the Day*, London, Macmillan, 1973.

MARGACH, JAMES: *The Abuse of Power*, London, W.H. Allen, 1978.

MARTIN, KINGSLEY: *The Crown and the Establishment*, London, Hutchinson, 1962.

MASSEREENE AND FERRARD, THE VISCOUNT: *The Lords*, London, Leslie Frewin, 1973.

MASSEY, DOREEN AND CATALANO, ALEJANDRINA: *Landownership by Capital in Great Britain*, London, Edward Arnold, 1978.

MASTERMAN, CHARLES F.G.: *England After the War: A Study*, London, Hodder & Stoughton, 1922.

MASTERS, BRIAN: *The Dukes*, London, Blond & Briggs, 1977.

MASTERS, BRIAN: *The Swinging Sixties*, London, Constable, 1985.

MEDHURST, KENNETH AND GEORGE MOYSER: *The Church of England and Politics*, in *Parliamentary Affairs*, vol. 42, no. 2, April 1989.

MILLER, C.A.: *Anecdotes of the Literary Club*, New York, Exposition Press, 1948.

MILNE, ALASDAIR: *DG – The Memoirs of a British Broadcaster*, London, Hodder & Stoughton, 1988.

MITFORD, JESSICA: *Hons and Rebels*, London, Victor Gollancz, 1960.

MITFORD, NANCY (ED.): *Noblesse Oblige*, London, Hamish Hamilton, 1956.

MOND, ALFRED: *Industry and Politics*, London, Macmillan, 1927.

MONTGOMERY-MASSINGBERD, HUGH: *The Great British Families*, London, Debrett, 1988.

MOORE, CHARLES, GAVIN STAMP AND A.N. WILSON: *The Church in Crisis*, London, Hodder & Stoughton, 1986.

MOORHOUSE, GEOFFREY: *The Diplomats*, London, Jonathan Cape, 1977.

MORGAN, D.H.J.: 'The Social and Educational Background of Anglican Bishops', in *British Journal of Sociology*, vol. 20, no. 3, 1969.

MORRELL, DAVID: *Indictment – Power and Politics in the Construction Industry*, London, Faber & Faber, 1987.

Municipal Yearbook, London, Municipal Journal Ltd., annual.

NAIRN, TOM: *The Enchanted Glass*, London, Century Hutchinson, 1988.

NEWMAN, JOHN HENRY: *My Campaign in Ireland*, Aberdeen, A. King & Co., 1896.

NEWMAN, JOHN HENRY: 'The Idea of a University', in *The Idea of a Liberal Education*, ed. Henry Tristram, London, Harrap, 1953.

NICHOLSON, MAX: *The System*, London, Hodder and Stoughton, 1967.

NICOLSON, HAROLD: *Diaries and Letters* (3 vols), London, Collins, 1966.

NORMAN, E.R.: *Church and Society in England 1770-1970*, Oxford, Oxford University Press, 1976.

ODDIE, WILLIAM: *The Crockford's File*, London, Hamish Hamilton, 1989.

PACKETT, C. NEVILLE: *The County Lieutenancy in the United Kingdom (1547-1975)*, Bradford, published by author, 1975.

PAGET, SIR JULIAN: *The Story of the Guards*, London, Osprey Publishing, 1976.

PANNICK, DAVID: *Judges*, Oxford, Oxford University Press, 1987.

PERKIN, HAROLD: *The Rise of Professional Society: England Since 1880*, London, Routledge, 1989.

PERROTT, ROY: *The Aristocrats*, London, Weidenfeld & Nicolson, 1968.

PHILLIPS, ANNE (ED.): *A Newnham Anthology*, Cambridge, Cambridge University Press, 1979.

PICK, JOHN: *Managing the Arts?* London, Rhinegold Publishing, 1986.

PLUMB, J.H. (ED.): *Studies in English Social History*, London, Longman, 1955.

PLUMB, J.H.: *The Growth of Political Stability in England 1675–1725*, London, Macmillan, 1967.

PONTING, CLIVE: *Whitehall, Tragedy and Farce*, London, Hamish Hamilton, 1986.

PORTLAND, DUKE OF: *Men, Women and Things*, London, Faber & Faber, 1937.

PRIOR, JAMES: *A Balance of Power*, London, Hamish Hamilton, 1986.

RADCLIFFE, LORD: *Not in Feather Beds*, London, Hamish Hamilton, 1968.

RAE, JOHN: *The Public School Revolution*, London, Faber & Faber, 1981.

RAVEN, SIMON: *The English Gentleman*, London, Anthony Blond, 1961.

READER, WILLIAM J.: *ICI*, Oxford, Oxford University Press, 1970–75.

REID, MARGARET: *All Change in the City*, London, Macmillan, 1988.

RENTOUL, JOHN: *The Rich Get Richer*, London, Unwin, 1987.

ROBINSON, JEFFREY: *The Risk-Takers*, London, Allen & Unwin, 1985.

ROBINSON, JOHN MARTIN: *The Latest Country Houses*, London, Bodley Head, 1984.

ROBINSON, JOHN MARTIN: *The English Country Estate*, London, Hutchinson, 1988.

ROGERS, BARBARA: *Men Only*, London, Pandora, 1988.

ROSE, KENNETH: *The Later Cecils*, London, Weidenfeld & Nicolson, 1975.

ROSE, KENNETH: *King George V*, London, Weidenfeld & Nicolson, 1983.

ROSE, KENNETH: *Kings, Queens and Courtiers*, London, Weidenfeld & Nicolson, 1985.

ROTHSCHILD, BARON: *Meditations of a Broomstick*, London, Collins, 1977.

ROTHSCHILD, BARON: *Random Variables*, London, Collins, 1984.

ROWSE, A.L.: *The English Past*, London, Macmillan, 1951.

ROWSE, A.L.: *All Souls and Appeasement*, London, Macmillan, 1961.

SAMPSON, ANTHONY: *The Anatomy of Britain*, London, Hodder & Stoughton, 1962.

SAMPSON, ANTHONY: *Macmillan: A Study in Ambiguity*, London, Hodder & Stoughton, 1967.

SAMPSON, ANTHONY: *The Changing Anatomy of Britain*, London, Hodder & Stoughton, 1982.

SCOTT, JOHN: *The Upper Classes: Property and Privilege in Britain*, London, Macmillan, 1982.

SEDGEMORE, BRIAN: *The Secret Constitution*, London, Hodder & Stoughton, 1980.

SELLERS, SUE: *Sunlighters*, London, Unilever PLC, 1988.

SHAW, ROY: *The Arts and The People*, London, Jonathan Cape, 1987.

SHELL, DONALD: *The House of Lords*, Oxford, Philip Allan, 1988.

SHEPHERD, ROBERT: *A Class Divided: Appeasement and the Road to Munich*, London, Macmillan, 1988.

SHEPPERD, ALAN: *Sandhurst*, London, Country Life Books, 1980.

SHOARD, MARION: *This Land is Our Land*, London, Paladin, 1987.

SILK, PAUL: *How Parliament Works*, London, Longman, 1987.

SISSONS, M. AND P. FRENCH (EDS): *The Age of Austerity*, London, Hodder & Stoughton, 1963.

SKIDELSKY, ROBERT (ED.): *Thatcherism*, London, Chatto & Windus, 1988.

SLOMAN, ALBERT: *A University in the Making*, London, BBC, 1964.

SMILES, SAMUEL: *Self Help*, London, John Murray, 1859.

STANHOPE, HENRY: *The Soldiers*, London, Hamish Hamilton, 1979.

STANWORTH, PHILIP AND ANTHONY GIDDENS: *Elites and Power in British Society*, Cambridge, Cambridge University Press, 1974.

STEINER, ZARA: *The Foreign Office and Foreign Policy, 1898–1914*, Cambridge, Cambridge University Press, 1969.

STONE, LAWRENCE AND JEANNE C. FAWTIER STONE: *An Open Elite? England 1540–1880*, Oxford, Oxford University Press, 1986.

STRONG, ROY: *The Destruction of the English Country House, 1875–1975*, London, Thames & Hudson, 1974.

SUTHERLAND, DOUGLAS: *The Landowners*, London, Muller, 1988.

TAWNEY, R.H.: *The Acquisitive Society*, London, Longman, 1921.

TAYLOR, A.J.P.: *Englishmen and Others*, London, Hamish Hamilton, 1957.

THACKERAY, WILLIAM: *The Book of Snobs*, New York, D. Appleton & Co., 1852.

THEAKSTON, KEVIN AND GEOFFREY FRY: 'Britain's Administrative Elite: Permanent Secretaries 1900–1986', in *Public Administration*, vol. 67, no. 2, Summer 1989.

THOMAS, HUGH (ED.): *The Establishment*, London, Anthony Blond, 1959.

THOMAS, HUGH: *The Story of Sandhurst*, London, Hutchinson, 1961.

THOMPSON, F.M.L.: *English Landed Society in the Nineteenth Century*, London, Routledge & Kegan Paul, 1963.

THOMPSON, F.M.L.: *The Rise of Respectable Society*, London, Fontana, 1988.

THOMSON, ROY: *After I was Sixty*, London, Hamish Hamilton, 1975.

TOWLER, ROBERT AND A.P.M. COXON: *The Fate of the Anglican Clergy*, London, Macmillan, 1970.

TUGENDHAT, CHRISTOPHER AND WILLIAM WALLACE: *Options for British Foreign Policy in the 1990s*, London, Routledge, 1988.

TURNER, E.S.: *Gallant Gentlemen: A Portrait of the British Officer 1600–1965*, London, Michael Joseph, 1965.

TURNER, FRANK M.: *The Greek Heritage in Victorian Britain*, New Haven, Yale University Press, 1981.

TYLER, RODNEY: *Campaign! The Selling of the Prime Minister*, London, Grafton, 1987.

URRY, JOHN AND JOHN WAKEFORD: *Power in Britain*, London, Heinemann, 1973.

VARIOUS AUTHORS: *The World of the Public Schools*, London, Weidenfeld & Nicolson, 1977.

WALKER, JOHN: *The Queen Has Been Pleased*, London, Secker & Warburg, 1986.

WALKLAND, S.A. AND MICHAEL RYLE: *The Commons Today*, London, Fontana, 1981.

WARNER, REX: *English Public Schools*, London, Collins, 1945.

WASS, DOUGLAS: *Government and the Governed*, London, Routledge & Kegan Paul, 1984.

WATT, DAVID: *The Inquiring Eye*, London, Penguin, 1988.

WAUGH, EVELYN: *Brideshead Revisited*, London, Chapman & Hall, 1945.

WELSBY, PAUL A.: *A History of the Church of England 1945–80*, Oxford, Oxford University Press, 1984.

WELSBY, PAUL: *How the Church of England Works*, London, CIO Publishing, 1985.

WEST, NIGEL: *The Friends*, London, Weidenfeld & Nicolson, 1988.

WHEELER-BENNETT, SIR JOHN: *King George VI: His Life and Reign*, London, Macmillan, 1958.

WHITELAW, WILLIAM: *The Whitelaw Memoirs*, London, Aurum, 1989.

WIENER, MARTIN J.: *English Culture and the Decline of the Industrial Spirit 1850–1980*, Cambridge, Cambridge University Press, 1981.

WILKINSON, RUPERT: *The Prefects*, Oxford, Oxford University Press, 1964.

WILLIAMS, BERNARD AND OTHERS: *Politics, Ethics and Public Service*, London, Royal Institute of Public Administration, 1985.

WILSON, CHARLES: *History of Unilever*, London, Cassell, 1954.

WILSON, EDGAR: *The Myth of British Monarchy*, London, Journeyman Press, 1989.

WILSON, HAROLD: *The Governance of Britain*, London, Weidenfeld & Nicolson, 1976.

WILSON, H.H.: *Pressure Group: The Campaign for Commercial Television*, London, Secker & Warburg, 1961.

WINCHESTER, SIMON: *Their Noble Lordships*, London, Faber & Faber, 1978.

WINDSOR, DAVID B.: *The Quaker Enterprise*, London, Frederick Muller, 1980.

WOODS, OLIVER AND JAMES BISHOP: *The Story of The Times*, London, Michael Joseph, 1983.

WRENCH, JOHN EVELYN: *Geoffrey Dawson and Our Times*, London, Hutchinson, 1955.

WRIGHT, PETER: *Spycatcher*, New York, Viking Penguin, 1987.

YOUNG, HUGO: *One of Us*, London, Macmillan, 1989.

YOUNG, HUGO AND ANNE SLOMAN: *No, Minister: An Inquiry into the Civil Service*, London, BBC, 1982.

YOUNG, HUGO and ANNE SLOMAN: *The Thatcher Phenomenon*, London, BBC, 1986.

ZIEGLER, PHILIP: *Mountbatten*, London, Collins, 1985.

ZIMAN, J. AND J. ROSE: *Camford Observed*, London, Gollancz, 1984.

Index

Oxford and Cambridge Club, 312, 313
Oxford Union, 177
Oxford University, 20, 126, 134, 173–96
passim, 250, 270, 271, 280; affair of Mrs
Thatcher's honorary degree, 184–6; All
Souls College, 13n, 117, 178–81; Balliol
College, 42, 118, 131, 134, 176, 177;
Bodleian Library, 190; Christ Church, 12,
134, 191, 288; St Anthony's College, 173;
St Benet's Hall, 18; St Hugh's College,
174; St John's College, 173; Somerville
College, 185; Trinity College, 300

Packer, Kerry, 255
Palliser, Sir Michael, 280
Palmer, Colonel Gordon, 65
Palmerston, Viscount, 142–3, 145
Palumbo, Peter, 304
Parkinson, Cecil, 80, 84, 123
Pattinson, Derek, 206–7
Pearson, Weetman, 264
Peat Marwick McLintock, 193
Penshurst (Kent), 43
Per Cent Club, 261
Perrin, Alain D., 245
'Peterhouse Mafia', 182
Philby, Kim, 334
Philip, Prince, Duke of Edinburgh, 26, 56,
58, 59, 290
Pickering, Sir Edward, 322
Pile, Sir William, 137
Pilkington, Alastair, 256
Pilkington, Anthony, 256
Pilkington Brothers, 255–7, 258
Piper, David, 291
Pirie, Madsen, 182
Pliatzky, Sir Leo, 163
Plowden, Lord, 83, 143
Plowden, Dr William, 140
Policy Unit, Downing Street, 125, 182, 281
Poole, Sir Ernest, 289–90
Poole, Oliver, 78
Pope-Hennessy, Sir John, 302
Popular Television Association, 111
Port Sunlight, 247–8, 249, 261
Poulson, John, 311
Powderham Castle, Devon, 33
Powell, Anthony, 69, 191
Powell, Charles, 123
Powell, Enoch, 6, 12, 79, 95
Pratt's Club, 312
Press Council, 101, 181
Press secretary, Queen's, 53, 54
Prince's Business Trust, 259
Prior, Jane, 318
Prior, Jim, 70, 132–3, 257
Privy Council/Councillors, 53, 57–8, 63,
104, 135
Project Fullemploy, 257
Public Appointments Unit, 100–1

public schools, viii, ix–x, 18, 67, 78, 79,
80, 84, 85, 92, 109, 122, 131, 134, 148,
149, 156–72, 175, 213, 214, 231, 315,
331–2; army officers from, 223, 224–5,
226, 232
Pym, Francis (Lord), 71, 238, 315

Queen's Counsels (QCs), 109
Quinton, Lord, 315

Race Relations Board, chairman of, 11,
121
Radcliffe, Lord (Cyril), 102, 104
Radley (public school), 169
Rae, Dr John, 157, 171
Ramphal, Sir Shridath, 191
Ramsey, Michael, Archbishop of
Canterbury, 214
Raven, Simon, 226–7
Rayne, Lord (Max), 2–3, 4, 300
Rayner, Sir Derek, 70, 123, 137
Redesdale, second Lord, 96
Redwood, John, 79–80, 179, 281
Reece, Gordon, 72, 124
Rees, Merlyn, 104
Rees-Mogg, William (Lord), 118–20, 129,
184, 299, 305, 313, 320, 324
Reform Club, 310
Reilly, Sir D'Arcy, 179
Reith, Lord, 111, 114, 116
Reith Lectures (1963), 188
Reynolds, Sir Joshua, 20, 40, 314
Rhodesian UDI (1965), 234
Richardson, Gordon, 271
Richardson, Michael, 281
Richmond, tenth Duke of, 41, 42, 43, 45
Ricks, Professor Christopher, 194
Riddell, Sir John, 55, 267
Ridley, Nicholas, 37, 42, 77, 80
Ridley, third Viscount, 77
Ridley, fourth Viscount, 37, 52
Rifkind, Malcolm, 84
Rittner, Luke, 305
Robbins, Lord, 187, 188, 189
Robinson, John Martin, 26
Rockingham Castle (Northants.), 35, 36, 38
Rogers, Richard, 299
Roman Catholics, 202, 204, 216, 218
Roskill Committee (1985), 282
Roth, Andrew, 76, 94
Rothschild, Evelyn de, 280
Rothschild family, 268, 276
Rothschild, Lord (Jacob), 100, 102, 125,
254–5, 304
Rothschild, N. M., merchant bank, 275, 278,
280–1
Rousham, 20
Rowse, A. L., 179, 180
Royal Academy of Arts, 106, 304
Royal Air Force (RAF), 241, 344n